STUDY GUIDE for use with

Third Canadian Edition

MICROECONOMICS

COLANDER
RICHTER
ROCKERBIE

Prepared by
Oliver Franke
Athabasca University

David C. Colander
Middlebury College

Douglas Copeland
Johnson County Community College

Jenifer Gamber

McGraw-Hill Ryerson

Toronto Montréal New York Burr Ridge Bangkok Bogotá Caracas Lisbon London
Madrid Mexico City Milan New Delhi Seoul Singapore Sydney Taipei

Study Guide for use with
Microeconomics
Third Canadian Edition

ISBN: 0-07-095103-9

1 2 3 4 5 6 7 8 9 10 CP 0 9 8 7

Printed and bound in the Canada

Statistics Canada information is used with the permission of the Minister of Industry, as Minister responsible for Statistics Canada. Information on the availability of the wide range of data from Statistics Canada can be obtained from Statistics Canada's Regional Offices, its World Wide Web site at <http://www.statcan.ca>, and its toll-free access number 1-800-263-1136.

Care has been taken to trace ownership of copyright material contained in this text; however, the publisher will welcome any information that enables them to rectify any reference or credit for subsequent editions.

Publisher: Lynn Fisher
Developmental Editor: Maria Chu
Economics Editor: Ron Doleman
Senior Marketing Manager: Kelly Smyth
Sales Manager: Megan Farrell
Supervising Editor: Jaime Smith
Senior Production Coordinator: Madeleine Harrington
Page Layout: First Image Design
Cover Design: Dianna Little
Cover Image: © Glen Allison/Getty Images
Printer: Canadian Printco, Ltd.

Contents

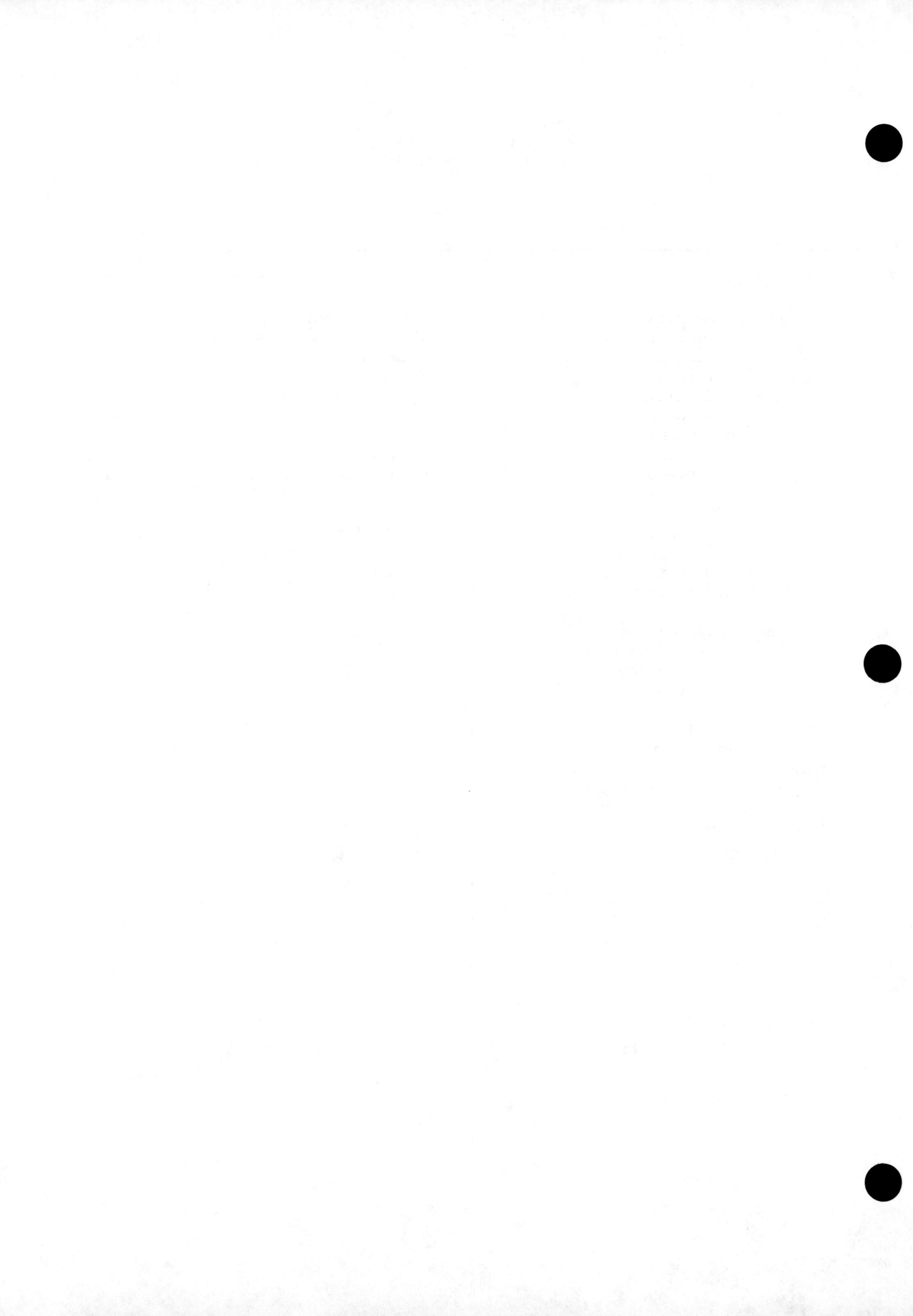

Preface

We wrote this study guide to help you do well in your economics courses. Even using a great book like the Colander textbook, we know that studying is not all fun. The reality is: most studying is hard work and a study guide won't change that. Your textbook and classroom lectures will give you the foundation for doing well. So the first advice we will give you is:

1. Read the textbook.
2. Attend class.

We cannot emphasize that enough. Working through the study guide will not replace the text or lectures; this study guide is designed to help you focus in on the most important theories, concepts and definitions so that you can retain the knowledge gained from the textbook and classroom by practicing the tools of economics. It is not an alternative to the textbook and class; it is **in addition to them**.

Having said that, we should point out that buying this study guide isn't enough. You have to use it. Really, if it sits on your desk, or even under your pillow, it won't do you any good. Osmosis only works with plants. This study guide should be well worn by the end of the semester — dog-eared pages, scribbles beneath questions, areas underlined and highlighted, some pages even torn out. It should look used.

WHAT CAN YOU EXPECT FROM THIS BOOK?

This study guide concentrates on the terminology and models presented in your textbook. It does not expand upon the material, but rather reinforces it. The study guide primarily serves to give you a good foundation to understanding principles of economics. Your professor has chosen this study guide for you, suggesting that your economics exams are going to focus on this kind of foundational understanding. You should be sure of this: if your professor is going to give you mainly essay exams, or complex questions about applying the foundations (like the more difficult end-of-chapter questions in your textbook), this study guide will not be enough to ace that exam.

To get an idea of what your exams will be like, ask your professor to take a look at these questions and tell the class whether they are representative of the type of questions that will be on the exam. And if they will differ, how. This study guide also has several practice exams in order to test your understanding of the material.

HOW SHOULD YOU USE THIS STUDY GUIDE?

As we stated above, this book works best if you have attended class and read the textbook. Ideally, you were awake during class and took notes, you have read the textbook chapters more than once, and have worked through some of the questions at the end of the chapter. (So, we're optimists.)

Just in case the material in the textbook isn't fresh in your mind, before turning to this study guide, it is a good idea to refresh your memory about the material in the textbook. To do so:

1. Read through the margin comments in the textbook; they highlight the main concepts in each chapter.
2. Turn to the last few pages of the chapter and reread the chapter summary.
3. Look through the key terms, making sure they are familiar. (O.K., we're not only optimists, we're wild optimists.)

Even if you do not do the above, working though the questions in the study guide will assist you in determining whether you really do know the material in the textbook chapters.

STRUCTURE OF THE STUDY GUIDE

This study guide has two main components: (1) a chapter-by-chapter review and (2) pretests based upon groups of chapters.

Chapter-by-chapter review

Each chapter has eight elements:

1. A chapter at a glance: A brief exposition and discussion of the learning objectives for the chapter.
2. A test of matching the terms to their definitions.
3. Multiple choice questions.
4. Short-answer questions keyed to the learning objectives.
5. Problems and applications.
6. A brain teaser.
7. Potential essay questions.
8. Answers to all questions..

Each chapter presents the sections in the order that we believe they can be most beneficial to you. Here is how we suggest you use them:

Chapter at a Glance: These should jog your memory about the textbook and the classroom lectures. If you don't remember ever seeing the material before, you should go back and reread the textbook chapter. The numbers in parentheses following each learning objective refer to the page in the textbook that covers that objective. Remember, reading a chapter when you are thinking about a fantasy date is almost the same as not having read the chapter at all.

Match the Terms and Concepts to Their Definitions: Since the definitions are listed, you should get most of these right. The best way to match these is to read the definition first, and then find the term on the left that it defines. If you are not sure of the matching term, circle that definition and move on to the next one. At the end, return to the remaining definitions and look at the remaining terms to complete the matches. After completing this part, check your answers with those in the back of the chapter and figure our what percent you got right. If that percent is below the grade you want to get on your exam, try to see why you missed the ones you did and review those terms and concepts in the textbook.

Multiple Choice Questions: The next exercise in each chapter is the multiple choice test. It serves to test the breadth of your knowledge of the textbook material. Multiple choice questions are not the final arbiters of your understanding. They are, instead, a way of determining whether you have read the textbook and generally understood the material.

Give the answer that most closely corresponds to the answer presented in your textbook. If you can answer these questions you should be ready for the multiple choice part of your exam.

Work through all the questions before grading yourself. Looking up the answer before you try to answer the questions is a poor way to study. For a multiple choice exam, the percent you answer correctly will be a good predictor of how well you will do on the test.

You can foul up on multiple choice questions in two ways—you can know too little and you can know too much. The answer to knowing too little is obvious: Study more—that is, read the chapters more carefully (and maybe more often). The answer to knowing too much is more complicated. Our suggestions for students who know too much is not to ask themselves "What is the answer?" but instead to ask "What is the answer the person writing the question wants?" Since, with these multiple choice questions, the writer of many of the questions is the textbook author, ask yourself: "What answer would the textbook author want me to give?" Answering the questions in this way will stop you from going too deeply into them and trying to see nuances that aren't supposed to be there.

For the most part, questions in this study guide are meant to be straightforward. There may be deeper levels at which other answers could be relevant, but searching for those deeper answers will generally get you in trouble and not be worth the cost.

If you are having difficulty answering a multiple choice question, make your best guess. Once you are familiar with the material, even if you don't know the answer to a question, you can generally make a reasonable guess. What point do you think the writer of the question wanted to make with the question? Figuring out that point and then thinking of incorrect answers may be a way for you to eliminate wrong answers and then choose among the remaining options.

Notice that the answers at the end of the chapter are not just the lettered answers. We have provided an explanation for each answer — why the right one is right and why some of the other choices are wrong. If you miss a question, read that rationale carefully. If you are not convinced, or do not follow the reasoning, go to the page in the textbook referred to in the answer and reread the material. If you are still not convinced, see the caveat on the next page.

Short-Answer Questions: The short-answer questions will tell you if you are familiar with the learning objectives. Try to answer each within the space below each question. Don't just read the questions and assume you can write an answer. Actually writing an answer will reveal your weaknesses. If you can answer them all perfectly, great. But, quite honestly, we don't expect you to be able to answer them all perfectly. We only expect you to be able to sketch out an answer.

Of course, some other questions are important to know. For example, if there is a question about the economic decision rule and you don't remember that it excludes past costs and benefits, you need more studying. So the rule is: Know the central ideas of the chapter and be less concerned about the specific presentation of those central ideas.

After you have sketched out all your answers, check them with those at the end of the chapter and review those that you didn't get right. Since each question is based upon a specific learning objective in the text, for those you didn't get right, you may want to return to the textbook to review the material covering that learning objective.

Problems and Applications: Now it's time to take on any problems in the chapter. These problems are generally more difficult than the short-answer questions. These problems focus on numerical and graphical aspects of the chapter.

Working through problems is perhaps one of the best ways to practice your understanding of economic principles. Even if you are expecting a multiple choice exam, working through these problems will give you a good handle on using the concepts in each chapter.

If you expect a multiple choice exam with no problems, you can work through these fairly quickly, making sure you understand the concepts being tested. If you will have a test with problems and exercises, make sure you can answer each of these questions accurately.

Work out the answers to all the problems in the space provided before checking them against the answers in the back of the chapter. Where our answers differ from yours, check to find out why. The answers refer to specific pages in the textbook so you can review the textbook again too.

Most of the problems are objective and have only one answer. A few are interpretative and have many answers. Some questions can be answered in different ways than provided. If you cannot reconcile your answer with those in the answer section, check with your professor. Once you are at this stage — worrying about different interpretations — you're ahead of most students and, most likely, prepared for the exam.

A Brain Teaser: This section consists of one problem that is generally one step up in the level of difficulty from the "Problems and Applications" exercises or is a critical thought question. It is designed to provide a challenge to those few students who have studied the way we have suggested.

Potential Essay Questions: These questions provide yet another opportunity to test your understanding of what you have learned. Answering these questions will be especially helpful if you expect these types of questions on the exams. We have only sketched the beginning to an answer to these. This beginning should give you a good sense of the direction to go in your answer, but be aware that on exam a more complete answer will be required.

Questions on Appendices: In the chapters, we have included a number of questions on the textbook appendices. To separate these questions from the others, the letter A and/or B precedes the question number. They are for students who have been assigned the appendices. If you have not been assigned them (and you have not read them on your own out of your great interest in economics), you can skip these.

Answers to All Questions: The answers to all questions appear at the end of each chapter. They begin on a new page so that you can tear out the answers and more easily check your answers against ours. It cannot be emphasized enough that the best way to study is to answer the questions yourself first, and then check out the answers. Just looking at the questions and the answers may tell you what the answers are but will not give you the chance to see where your knowledge of the material is weak.

Pretests

Most class exams cover more than one chapter. To prepare you for such an exam, multiple choice pretests are provided for groups of chapters. These pretests consist of 25-40 multiple choice questions from the selected group of chapters. These questions are identical to earlier questions so if you have done the work, you should do well on these. It is suggested that you complete the entire exam before grading yourself.

We also suggest taking these under test conditions. Specifically,

Use a set time period to complete the exam.
Sit at a hard chair at a desk with good lighting.

Each answer will tell you the chapter on which the qEach answer will tell you the chapter on which the question is based, so if you did not cover one of the chapters in the text for your class, don't worry if you get that question wrong. If you get a number of questions wrong from the chapters your class has covered, worry.

There is another way to use these pretests which we hesitate to mention, but we're realists so we will. That way is to forget doing the chapter-by-chapter work and simply take the pretests. Go back and review the material you get wrong.

However you use the pretests, if it turns out that you consistently miss questions from the same chapter, return to your notes from the lecture and reread your textbook chapters.

A FINAL WORD OF ADVICE

That's about it. If you use it, this study guide can help you do better on the exam by giving you the opportunity to use the terms and models of economics. However, we reiterate one last time: The best way to do well in a class is to attend every class and read every chapter in the textbook as well as work through the chapters in this study guide. Start early and work consistently. Do not do all your studying the night before the exam.

Oliver Franke
David Colander
Douglas Copeland
Jenifer Gamber

ECONOMICS AND ECONOMIC REASONING

CHAPTER AT A GLANCE

Chapter 1 introduces students to the discipline called economics – the study of how individuals, firms, and governments make optimal choices from among a set of alternatives when facing scarce resources. Human beings coordinate their wants and desires, given the decision-making mechanisms, social customs, and political realities of society.

Central to the study of economics is making choices. Everyday, we are faced with deciding what to do among the alternatives present. An optimal choice requires that some sort of criteria be derived to determine when a choice is the best choice for the decision maker. Economic analysis utilizes a variety of criteria depending upon the nature of the decisionmaker. This could be in terms of maximizing satisfaction for a consumer, maximizing profit for firms, or maximizing some sort of social welfare for governments. In making choices, there are two defining principles – the fact that our society has limited resources and that every one in society has unlimited wants and desires. The dilemma becomes how to as efficiently as possible utilize our scarce resources in order to satisfy as many wants and desires as possible. In any decision making process, choices have to be made and there is a cost to us for making one choice over another. In economics, this cost is called opportunity cost.

Understanding economics allows us to become more aware of our surroundings and to more fully understand why certain things happen, and why people and firms react in certain ways. We will see that the behaviour of various groups or economic entities in our economy will be influenced by many factors – economic, political, legal, social, and historical. Economics has a role to play in sociology, history, and politics, just as sociology, history, and politics have roles to play in economics.

The discipline of economics is based on theories and principles, many of which are only generalizations – only true under certain circumstances. This is due to the fact that the real world is a very complex place and economics attempts to simplify our society in order to better understand all of the intricate workings of our economy. Yet, our society is so complicated and people and firms all react differently that theories can only explain a portion of the behaviour. Despite the economic generalizations being simplified and abstract representations of the real world, they can based on actual data and facts. Even with this shortcoming, economic theories, models and principles are very important to understanding the workings of the economy, to solve specific economic problems and to achieve specific economic goals.

Economic theory is divided in two broad categories – microeconomics and macroeconomics. Microeconomic theory considers economic reasoning and behaviour of individuals and firms. Macroeconomics studies the economy as a whole and considers broad economic aggregates such as inflation, unemployment, business cycles, and economic growth.

This review is based upon the learning objectives that open the chapter.

1a. Economics is the study of how individuals, firms, and governments make optimal choices from among a set of alternatives when facing scarce resources. (4)

1b. An optimal choice requires that some sort of criteria be used to determine when a choice is the best choice for the decisionmaker. Economics assumes that decisionmakers face scarce resources when making their choices. (5)

2. If the marginal benefits of doing something exceed the marginal costs, do it. If the marginal costs of doing something exceed the marginal benefits, don't do it. This is known as the economic decision rule. (6)

You really need to think in terms of the marginal, or "extra" benefits (MB) and marginal, or "extra" costs (MC) of a course of action.

Economic decision rule:

If MB>MC ⇒ Do more of it because "it's worth it."

If MB<MC ⇒ Do less of it because "it's not worth it."

NOTE: The symbol " ⇒ " means "implies" or "logically follows."

3. Opportunity cost is the basis of cost/benefit economic reasoning; it is the benefit forgone, or the cost of the next-best alternative to the activity you've chosen. In economic reasoning, that cost is less than the benefit of what you've chosen. (7)

Opportunity cost ⇒ "What must be given up in order to get something else." Opportunity costs are often "hidden." You need to take into consideration all costs when making a decision.

4. Economic reality is controlled by economic forces, social forces and political forces: (8-10)

What happens in a society can be seen as the reaction and interaction of these 3 forces.

- Economic forces (the invisible hand);
  These are the market forces of demand, supply, and prices, etc.
- Social and cultural forces;
  Social forces can prevent economic forces from becoming market forces.
- Political and legal forces.
  Political and legal forces affect decisions too.

5. 3 important definitions: (11-12)

- An economic model is a set of simple assumptions about how decisionmakers behave that simplifies the real world so that decisions can be explained using economics.
- Economic principles form the key assumptions in economics that are common to all economic models.
- The invisible hand is a market economy, through the price mechanism, will allocate resources efficiently.

6. Microeconomics considers economic reasoning from the viewpoint of individuals and builds up to the analysis of the whole economy; macroeconomics considers economic reasoning from the aggregate, or whole, and builds down into components. (13)

Microeconomics (micro) is concerned with some particular segment of the economy.

Macroeconomics (macro) is concerned with the entire economy.

7a. *Positive economics* is the study of what is, and how the economy works. (15)

Deals with "what is" (objective analysis).

7b. *Normative economics* is the study of what the goals of the economy should be. (15)

Deals with "what ought to be" (subjective analysis).

7c. The *science of economics* is the application of the knowledge learned in positive economics to the achievement of the goals determined in normative economics. (15)

The art of economics is sometimes referred to as "policy economics."

"Good" policy tries to be objective. It tries to weigh all the benefits and costs associated with all policy options and chooses that option in which the benefits outweigh the costs to the greatest degree.

See also, Appendix A: "The Language of Graphs"

In Appendix A, remember 2 types of relationships:

- *Direct (Positive) Relationship: expressed as an upward sloping curve.*

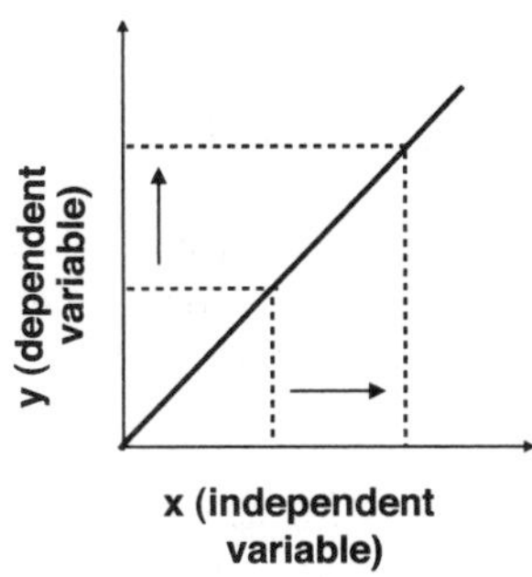

Note: as x increases, y increases; as x decreases, y decreases.

- *Inverse (Negative) Relationship: expressed as a downward sloping curve.*

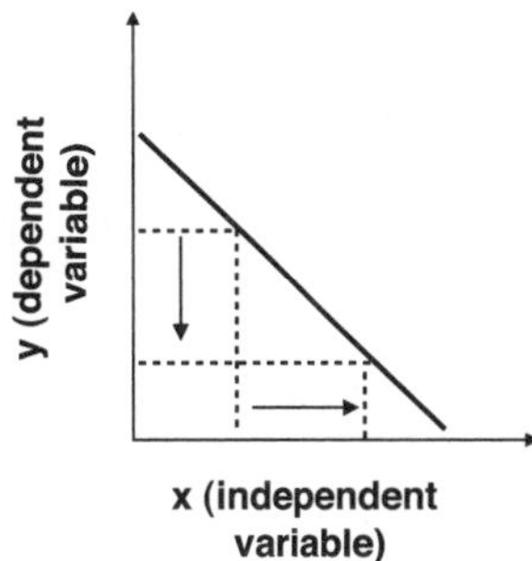

Note: as x increases, y decreases; as x decreases, y increases.

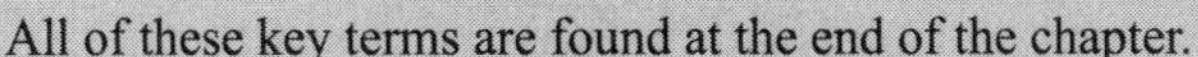

MATCHING THE TERMS

Match the terms to their definitions

All of these key terms are found at the end of the chapter.

___ **1.** economic decision rule
___ **2.** economic forces
___ **3.** economic model
___ **4.** economic policies
___ **5.** economic principle
___ **6.** economics
___ **7.** efficiency
___ **8.** invisible hand
___ **9.** macroeconomics
___ **10.** marginal benefit
___ **11.** marginal cost
___ **12.** market force
___ **13.** microeconomics
___ **14.** normative economics
___ **15.** opportunity cost
___ **16.** positive economics
___ **17.** scarcity
___ **18.** science of economics
___ **19.** sunk costs

a. Additional benefit above what you've already derived.
b. Additional cost above what you've already incurred.
c. If benefits exceed costs, do it. If costs exceed benefits, don't.
d. The study of individual choice, and how that choice is influenced by economic forces.
e. Necessary reactions to scarcity.
f. The benefit forgone, or the cost, of the best alternative to the activity you've chosen.
g. The study of what is, and how the economy works.
h. The study of the economy as a whole, which includes inflation, unemployment, business cycles, and growth.
i. The study of how individuals, firms, and governments make optimal choices.
j. Goods available are too few to satisfy individuals' desires.
k. The application of the knowledge learned in positive economics to the achievement of the goals determined in normative economics.
l. An economic force that is given relatively free rein by society to work through the market.
m. The price mechanism.
n. A framework that places the generalized insights of theory in a more specific contextual setting.
o. A commonly-held economic insight stated as a law or general assumption.
p. Achieving a goal as cheaply as possible.
q. Actions taken by government to influence economic events.
r. Study of what the goals of the economy should be.
s. Costs that have already been incurred and cannot be recovered.

MULTIPLE CHOICE

Circle the one best answer for each of the following questions:

1. Economic reasoning
   a. provides a framework with which to approach questions.
   b. provides correct answers to just about every question.
   c. is only used by economists.
   d. should only be applied to economic business matters.

2. Scarcity could be reduced if
   a. individuals work less and want fewer consumption goods.
   b. individuals work more and want fewer consumption goods.
   c. world population grows and world production remains the same.
   d. innovation comes to a halt.

3. In the textbook, the authors focus on optimal choices rather than scarcity as the central point of the definition of economics because
   a. economics is not really about scarcity.
   b. scarcity involves coercion, and the author doesn't like coercion.
   c. choices have to be made to efficiently allocate scarce resources.
   d. the concept "scarcity" does not fit within the institutional structure of the economy.

4. In the Canadian economy, who is in charge of organizing and coordinating overall economic activities?
   a. Government.
   b. Corporations.
   c. No one.
   d. Consumers.

5. You bought stock A for $10 and stock B for $50. The price of each is currently $20. Assuming no tax issues, which should you sell if you need money?
   a. Stock A.
   b. Stock B.
   c. It doesn't matter which.
   d. You should sell an equal amount of both.

6. In deciding whether to go to lectures in the middle of the semester, you should
   a. include tuition as part of the cost of that decision.
   b. not include tuition as part of the cost of that decision.
   c. include a portion of tuition as part of the cost of that decision.
   d. only include tuition if you paid it rather than your parents.

7. In making economic decisions, you should consider
   a. marginal costs and marginal benefits.
   b. marginal costs and average benefits.
   c. average costs and average benefits.
   d. total costs and total benefits, including past costs and benefits.

8. In arriving at a decision, a good economist would say that
   a. one should consider only total costs and total benefits.
   b. one should consider only marginal costs and marginal benefits.
   c. after one has considered marginal costs and benefits, one should integrate the social and moral implications and reconsider those costs and benefits.
   d. after considering the marginal costs and benefits, one should make the decision on social and moral grounds.

9. In making decisions, economists primarily use
   a. monetary costs.
   b. opportunity costs.
   c. benefit costs.
   d. dollar costs.

10. The opportunity cost of reading Chapter 1 of the text
    a. is about 1/20 of the price you paid for the book because the chapter is about one twentieth of the price of the book.
    b. zero since you have already paid for the book
    c. has nothing to do with the price you paid for the book.
    d. is 1/20 the price of the book plus 1/20 the price of the tuition.

11. Rationing devices that our society uses include
a. the invisible hand only.
b. the invisible hand and social forces only.
c. the invisible hand and political forces only.
d. the invisible hand, the social forces, and political forces.

12. If at Female College there are significantly more females than males (and there are not a significant number of gays) economic forces
a. will be pushing for females to pay on dates.
b. will be pushing for males to pay on dates.
c. will be pushing for neither to pay on dates.
d. are irrelevant to this issue. Everyone knows that the males always should pay.

13. Individuals are prohibited from practicing medicine without a license. This is an example of
a. the invisible hand.
b. social forces.
c. political forces.
d. market forces.

14. Which of the following is most likely an example of a microeconomic topic?
a. The effect of a flood in B.C. on the price of bottled water.
b. How a government policy will affect inflation.
c. The relationship between unemployment and inflation.
d. Why an economy goes into a recession.

15. Which of the following is an example of a macroeconomic topic?
a. The effect of a frost on the Florida orange crop.
b. Wages of cross-country truckers.
c. How the unemployment and inflation rates are related.
d. How income is distributed in Canada.

16. The statement, "The distribution of income should be left to the market," is
a. a positive statement.
b. a normative statement.
c. an science-of economics statement
d. an objective statement.

17. "Given certain conditions, the market achieves efficient results" is an example of a
a. positive statement.
b. normative statement.
c. art-of-economics statement.
d. subjective statement.

A1. In the graph below, the point A represents
a. a price of 1 and a quantity of 2.
b. a price of 2 and a quantity of 2.
c. a price of 2 and a quantity of 1.
d. a price of 1 and a quantity of 1.

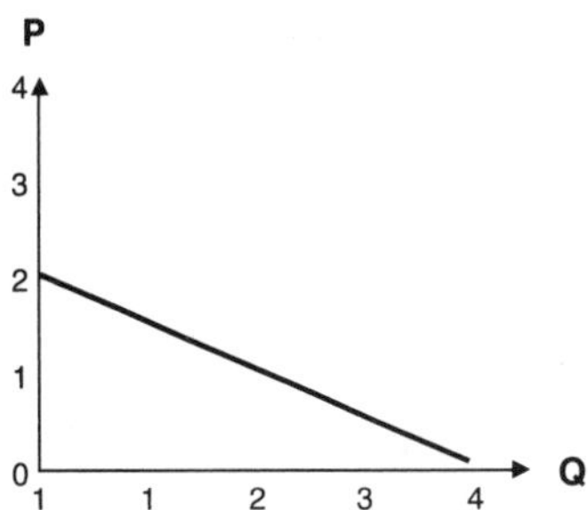

A2. The slope of the line in the graph below is
a. 1/2.
b. 2.
c. minus 1/2.
d. minus 2.

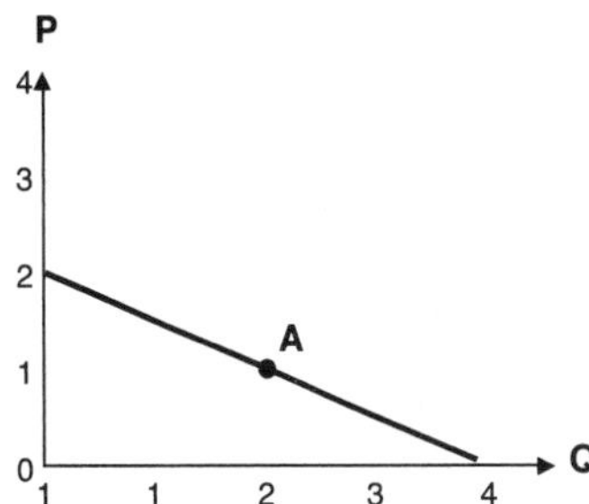

A3. At the maximum and minimum points of a nonlinear curve, the value of the slope is equal to
a. 1.
b. zero.
c. minus 1.
d. indeterminate.

A4. Which of the four lines in the graphs below has the larger slope?

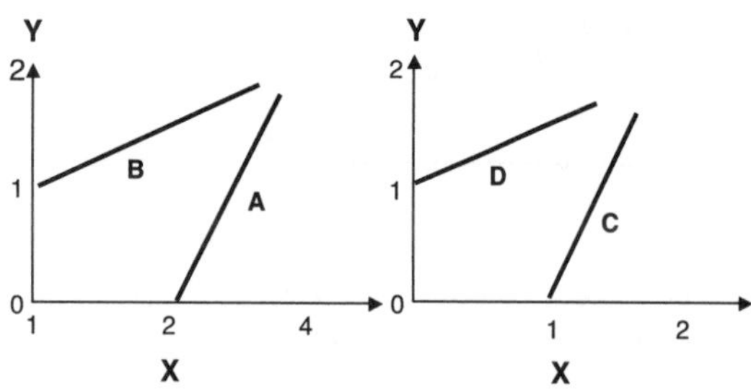

a. A.
b. B.
c. C.
d. A and C.

SHORT-ANSWER QUESTIONS

1. What is economics?

2. State the economic decision rule.

3. Define opportunity cost.

4. What is the importance of opportunity cost to economic reasoning?

5. What is scarcity? What are two elements that comprise scarcity? How do they affect relative scarcity?

6. What is an economic force? What are the forces that can keep an economic force from becoming a market force?

7. How does microeconomics differ from macroeconomics? Give an example of a macroeconomic issue and a microeconomic issue.

8. Define positive economics, normative economics, and the science of economics. How do they relate to one another?

PROBLEMS AND APPLICATIONS

1. State as best you can:

   a. The opportunity cost of going out on a date tonight with the date you made last Wednesday.

   b. The opportunity cost of breaking the date for tonight you made last Wednesday.

   c. The opportunity cost of working through this study guide.

   d. The opportunity cost of buying this study guide.

2. Assume you have purchased a $15,000 car. The salesperson has offered you a maintenance contract covering all major repairs for the next 3 years, with some exclusions, for $750.

   a. What is the opportunity cost of purchasing that maintenance contract?

   b. What information would you need to make a decision based on the economic decision rule?

   c. Based upon that information how would you make your decision?

3. State what happens to scarcity for each good in the following situations:

   a. New storage technology allows college dining services to keep peaches from rotting for a longer time. (Good: peaches).

   b. More students desire to live in single-sex dormitories. No new single-sex dormitories are established. (Good: single-sex dormitory rooms).

4. State for each of the following whether it is an example of political forces, social forces or economic forces at work:

   a. Warm weather arrives and more people take Sunday afternoon drives. As a result, the price of gasoline rises.

   b. In some states, liquor cannot be sold before noon on Sunday.

c. Minors cannot purchase cigarettes.

d. Many parents will send money to their children in college without the expectation of being repaid.

A BRAIN TEASER

1. Suppose you are a producer of handcrafted picture frames. The going market price for your frames is $250 a piece. No matter how many frames you sell your revenue per unit (equal to the selling price per unit) is constant at $250 per frame. However, your per unit costs of producing each additional picture frame are not constant. Suppose the following table summarizes your costs of producing picture frames. Use benefit/cost analysis to determine the most economical (profit maximizing) number of frames to produce given the price per unit and the cost schedule shown below. What are your total profits per week?

# of frames	Price	Total Cost
0	$250	$0
1	$250	$25
2	$250	$75
3	$250	$150
4	$250	$300
5	$250	$560

POTENTIAL ESSAY QUESTIONS

You may also see essay questions similar to the "Problems & Applications" and "Brain Teasers" exercises.

1. Respond to the following statement: "Theories are of no use to me because they are not very practical. All I need is the facts because they speak for themselves."

2. Canada is one of the wealthiest nations on earth, yet our fundamental economic problem is scarcity. How can this be?

3. Does economics help teach us how to approach problems, or does it give us a set of answers to problems?

4. Can we say that what is true for the part (micro) is necessarily true for the whole (macro)?

ANSWERS

MATCHING

1-c; 2-e; 3-n; 4-q; 5-o; 6-i; 7-p; 8-m; 9-h; 10-a; 11-b; 12-l; 13-d; 14-r; 15-f; 16-g; 17-j; 18-k; 19-s.

ANSWERS

MULTIPLE CHOICE

1. a As discussed on page 6, the textbook authors clearly believe that economic reasoning applies to just about everything. This eliminates c and d. They also carefully points out that it is not the only reasoning that can be used; hence b does not fit. So the correct answer must be a.

2. b On page 8 of the textbook, the author states that the problem of scarcity depends upon our wants and our means of fulfilling those wants. An implication of this is that scarcity could be reduced if individuals worked more and wanted less.

3. c On page 4 of the textbook, the authors emphasize the human action as being the reason for focusing on coordination. They explicitly point out that scarcity is important, but that the concept of coordination is broader.

4. c As discussed on page 9, the invisible hand of the market coordinates the activities and is a composite of many individuals rather than just any one individual. If you were tempted to say b, corporations, your instincts are right, but the "overall" eliminated that as a possible answer.

5. c As is discussed on page 6 of the book, in making economic decisions you consider that only costs from this point on are relevant; historical costs have no relevance. Since the prices of the stocks are currently the same, it doesn't matter which you sell.

6. b As discussed on page 6, in economic decisions, you only look at costs from this point on; sunk costs are sunk costs, so tuition can be forgotten. Economic decisions focus on forward-looking marginal costs and marginal benefits.

7. a The economic decision rule is "If benefits exceed costs, do it." As is discussed on page 6 of the text, however, the relevant benefits and relevant costs to be considered are marginal (additional) costs and marginal benefits. The answer d is definitely ruled out by the qualifying phrase referring to past benefits and costs. Thus, only a is correct.

8. c As the textbook points out on pages 6 and 7, economists use a framework of costs and benefits initially, but then later they add the social and moral implications to their conclusions. Adding these can change the estimates of costs and benefits, and in doing so can change the result of economic analysis, so there is an integration between the two. (This was a hard question which required careful reading of the text to answer correctly.)

9. b As discussed on page 7 of the text, opportunity costs include measures of nonmonetary costs. The other answers either do not include all the costs that an economist would consider, or are simply two words put together. The opportunity costs include the benefit forgone by undertaking an activity.

10. c As discussed on pages 7 and 8, the correct answer is that it has nothing to do with the price you paid since that is already paid, so a and d are wrong. The opportunity cost is not zero, however, since there are costs of reading the book. The primary opportunity cost of reading the book is the value of the time you're spending on it which is determined by what you could otherwise be doing with that time.

11. d As discussed on page 9 of the text, all of these are rationing devices. The invisible hand works through the market and thus is focused on in economics. However, the others also play a role in determining what people want, either through legal means or through social control.

12. a As discussed on pages 9 and 10 of the text, if there are significantly more of one gender than another, dates with that group must be rationed out among the other group. Economic forces will be pushing for the group in excess quantity supplied (in this case women) to pay. Economic forces may be pushing in that direction even though historical forces may push us in the opposite direction. Thus, even if males pay because of social forces, economic forces will be pushing for females to pay.

13. c Laws are legal forces.

14. a As discussed on pages 13 and 14, macroeconomics is concerned with inflation, unemployment, business cycles and growth. Microeconomics is the study of individuals and individual markets.

15. c As discussed on pages 13 and 14, macroeconomics is concerned with inflation, unemployment, business cycles and growth. Microeconomics is the study of individuals. The distribution of income is a microeconomic topic because it is concerned with the distribution of income among individuals.

16. b As discussed on pages 15 and 16, this could be either a normative or an science-of-economics statement, depending on whether there is an implicit "given the way the real-world economy operates to best achieve the growth rate you desire." Since these qualifiers are not there, "normative" is the preferable answer.

17. a As discussed on page 15 this is a positive statement. It is a statement about *what is,* not about what should be.

A1. a As discussed in Appendix A, page 22 and 23, a point represents the corresponding numbers on the horizontal and vertical number lines.

A2. c As discussed on pages 22 to 23 of Appendix A, the slope of a line is defined as rise over run. Since the rise is -2 and the run is 4, the slope of the above line is minus 1/2.

A3. b As discussed on page 23 of Appendix A, at the maximum and minimum points of a curve the slope is zero.

A4. c As discussed in Appendix A, page 22, the slope is defined as rise over run. Line C has the largest rise for a given run so c is the answer. Even though, visually, line A seems to have the same slope as line C, it has a different coordinate system. Line A has a slope of 1 whereas line B has a slope of 1/4. Always be careful about checking coordinate systems when visually interpreting a graph.

ANSWERS

SHORT-ANSWER QUESTIONS

1. Economics is the study of how individuals, firms, and government make optimal choices from among a set of alternatives when facing scarce resources. (4)

2. If the marginal benefits of doing something exceed the marginal costs, do it. If the marginal costs of doing something exceed the marginal benefits, don't do it. (6)

3. Opportunity cost is the benefit forgone by undertaking an activity. It is the benefit forgone of the next best alternative to the activity you have chosen. Otherwise stated, it is what must be given up in order to obtain something else. (7)

4. Opportunity cost is the basis of cost/benefit economic reasoning. In economic reasoning, opportunity cost is less than the benefit of what you have chosen. (7)

5. Scarcity occurs when there are not enough goods available to satisfy individuals' desires. (8)

6. An economic force is the necessary reaction to scarcity. All scarce goods must be rationed in some way. If an economic force is allowed to work through the market, that economic force becomes a market force. The invisible hand is the price mechanism, the rise and fall of prices that guides our actions in a market. Social and political forces can keep economic forces from becoming market forces. (8-9)

7. Microeconomic theory considers economic reasoning from the viewpoint of individuals and builds up while macroeconomics considers economic reasoning from the aggregate and builds down. Microeconomics studies things like household buying decisions such as how much of one's income to save and how much to consume. Macroeconomics studies things like the unemployment rate, inflation and growth. (13-14)

8. Positive economics is the study of what is and how the economy works. Normative economics is the study of what the goals of the economy should be. The science of economics is the application of the knowledge learned in positive economics to the achievement of the goals one has determined in normative economics. (15)

ANSWERS

PROBLEMS AND APPLICATIONS

1. **a.** The opportunity cost of going out on a date tonight that I made last Wednesday is the benefit forgone of the best alternative. If my best alternative was to study for an economics exam, it would be the increase in my exam grade that I would have gotten had I studied. Many answers are possible. (7-8)
   b. The opportunity cost of breaking the date for tonight that I made last Wednesday is the benefit forgone of going out on that date. It would be all the fun I would have had on that date. Other answers are possible. (7-8)
   c. The opportunity cost of working through this study guide is the benefit forgone of the next-best alternative to studying. It could be the increase in the grade I would have received by studying for another exam, or the money I could have earned if I were working at the library. Many answers are possible. (7-8)
   d. The opportunity cost of buying this study guide is the benefit forgone of spending that money on the next-best alternative. Perhaps it is the enjoyment forgone of eating two pizzas. Other answers are possible. (7-8)

2. **a.** The opportunity cost of purchasing the maintenance contract is the benefit I could receive by spending that $750 on something else like new tires. (7-8)
   b. I would need to know the benefit of the maintenance contract to assess whether the cost of $750 is worthwhile. (7-8)
   c. For me, the benefit of the maintenance contract is the expected cost of future repairs that would be covered and the peace of mind of knowing that future repairs are covered by the contract. The cost is the opportunity cost of using the $750 in another way. If the benefit exceeds the cost, do it. If the cost exceeds the benefit, do not do it. (7-8)

3. **a.** Scarcity will fall because fewer peaches will rot. (8)
   b. Scarcity of single-sex dorm rooms will rise since the number of students desiring single-sex dorm rooms has risen, but the number available has not. (8)

4. **a.** This is an example of an economic force. (9)
   b. This is an example of legal forces. Some U.S. states have laws, called blue laws, against selling liquor on Sundays altogether or selling it before noon. (9)
   c. This is an example of a legal force. This is a federal law. (9)
   d. This is an example of a social force. (9)

ANSWERS

A BRAIN TEASER

1. The most economical (profit-maximizing) quantity of frames to produce is 4 frames. This is because the marginal benefit of producing frames (the revenue per unit–equal to the price per unit of $250)–exceeds the marginal (extra) cost of producing frames through the first 4 frames produced. The 5th frame should not be produced because the marginal benefit (the price received) is less than the marginal (extra) cost of production. You would be adding more to your costs than to your revenues and thereby reducing your profits. Your profit would total $700 per week.

(Q)	Price (P) Marginal Benefit	Total Cost (TC)	Marginal Cost	Total Revenue (TR=PQ)	Profit (TR–TC)
0	$250	$0	—	$0	$0
1	$250	$25	$25	$250	$225
2	$250	$75	$50	$500	$425
3	$250	$150	$75	$750	$600
4	$250	$300	$150	$1000	$700
5	$250	$560	$260	$1250	$690

ANSWERS

POTENTIAL ESSAY QUESTIONS

The following are annotated answers. They indicate the general idea behind the answer.

1. Theories are practical because they are generalizations based on real world observations or facts. They enable us to predict and to explain real-world economic behavior. Because they are generalizations, they enable us to avoid unnecessary details or facts. The drawback, however, is that because they are generalizations, at times, there will be exceptions to the prediction we would generally expect to observe.

   Facts, on the other hand, do not always speak for themselves. One can often be overwhelmed by a large set of data or facts. Not until one systematically arranges, interprets and generalizes upon facts, tying them together, and distilling out a theory (general statement) related to those facts, do they take on any real meaning. In short, theory and facts are inseparable in the scientific process because theory gives meaning to facts and facts check the validity of theory.

2. Canada is still faced with scarcity because we are unable to have as much as we would like to have. Our resources (as vast as they are) are still scarce relative to the amount of goods and services we would like to have (indeed, our wants appear to be unlimited).

3. Economics is a methodology, or an approach to how we think about the world. It does not come to us equipped with a whole set of solutions to complex real-world problems. However, it may help shed some light on the complexities of real world issues helping us to find solutions.

4. No, not necessarily. For example, if one farmer has a "bumper-crop" year, an unusually large harvest, he will be better off. But, if all farmers experience the same thing, then the increased supply of the crop made available in the market will drive its price down and all farmers will be worse off.

THE ECONOMIC ORGANIZATION OF SOCIETY

2

CHAPTER AT A GLANCE

Chapter 2 highlights the importance of economics in our society, to explain how our scarce resources are allocated and coordinated on order to solve problems facing any economy. These central problems are 1.) What, and how much, to produce, 2.) how to produce it, and 3.) for whom to produce it. How these economic problems are dealt with depends on the type of economic system that has been adopted by each society.

Two of the most important economic systems are market economy and command economy. A market economy is an economic system based on private property and the market. It gives private property rights to individuals, and relies on market forces to coordinate economic activity. A command economy is an economic system that places the ownership of private property in the hands of the state and coordinates all production planning with a central authority.

This chapter also develops a sample model to explain how an economy can get the most out of its scarce resources and satisfy as many wants and desires as possible. The production possibilities curve is useful in illustrating many important economic concepts such as opportunity cost, scarcity, choice, and the principle of increasing marginal opportunity cost.

The last part of the chapter introduces students to the concept of international trade in an attempt to further the discussion of what an economy needs to do in order to efficiently use its scarce resources and given technology. Key concepts such as specialization, comparative advantage, absolute advantage, and the division of labour will be introduced.

This review is based upon the learning objectives that open the chapter.

1. A market economy is an economic system based on private property and the market. It gives private property rights to individuals, and relies on market forces to coordinate economic activity. (26-27)

A market economy ("market-oriented economy") is characterized by:
(I) mainly private ownership of resources
(II) market system solves the What? How? and For whom? problems.

A market economy's solutions to the central economic problems:
- *What to produce: what businesses believe people want, and what is profitable.*
- *How to produce: businesses decide how to produce efficiently, guided by their desire to make a profit.*
- *For whom to produce: distribution according to individuals' ability and/or inherited wealth.*

2a. A command economy is an economic system that places the ownership of private property in the hands of the state and coordinates all production planning with a central authority. (27)

A command economy ("government-controlled economy") is characterized by:
(I) government control over resources
(II) government solves the What? How? and For whom? problems.

Communism seeks to abolish all private property, aside from some consumer goods, and assigns all ownership of property to the state.

Communism's solutions to the three problems:
- *What to produce: what central planners believe is socially beneficial.*
- *How to produce: central planners decide, based on what they think is good for the country.*
- *For whom to produce: central planners distribute goods based on what they determine are individuals' needs.*

2b. A mixed economy is a blend of a market economy and a command economy, that is, both private markets and the government play important roles in the economy. (28)

3a. Remember this graph:

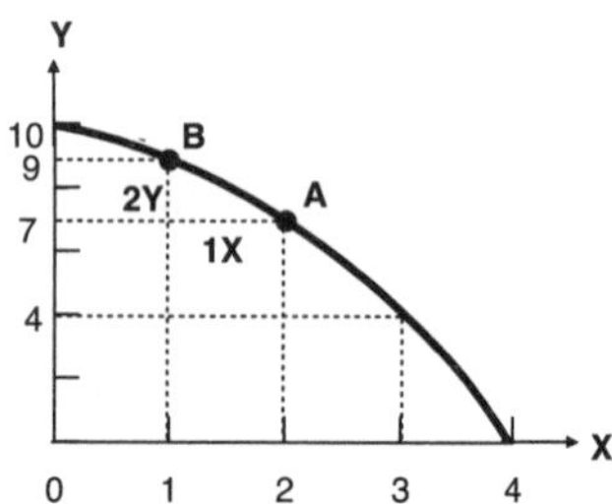

<u>Production Possibilities Curve</u>
Shows the trade-off (or opportunity cost) between two things.

The slope tells you the opportunity cost of good X in terms of good Y. In this particular graph, you have to give up 2 Y to get 1 X when you move from the combination of goods at point B to those at point A. (32-33)

3b. The principle of increasing marginal opportunity cost states that opportunity costs increase the more you concentrate on the activity. In order to get more of something, one must give up ever-increasing quantities of something else. (33)

The following production possibility curve and table demonstrate the principle of increasing marginal opportunity cost.

<u>Production Possibility Curve</u>

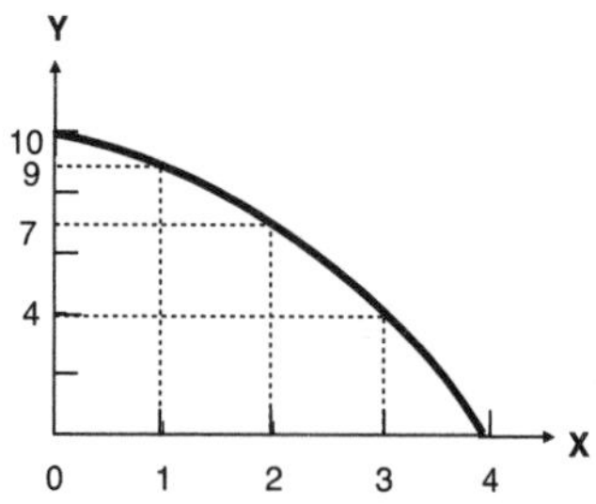

<u>Production Possibility Table</u>

Opportunity cost of X

X	Y	(amount of Y which must be foregone)
0	10	
		1
1	9	
		2
2	7	
		3
3	4	
		4
4	0	

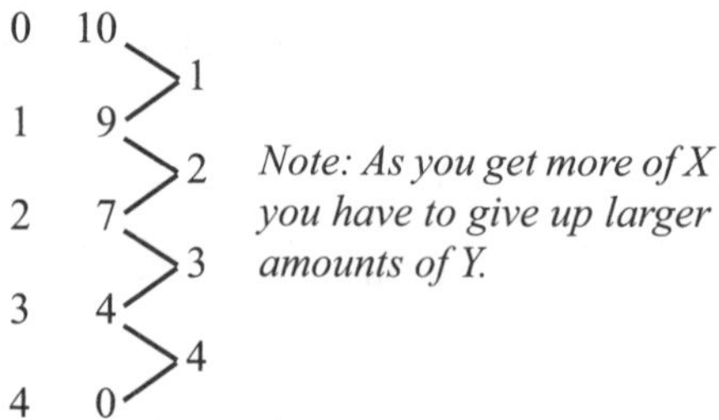

Note: As you get more of X you have to give up larger amounts of Y.

3c. Because decisions are contextual, what the production possibility curve for a particular decision looks like depends upon the existing institutions, and the analysis can be applied only in that institutional and historical context. (36-37)

The production possibility curve is an engine of analysis to make contextual choices, not a definitive tool to decide what one should do in all cases.

4. When individuals trade, using their comparative advantages, their combined production possibility curve shifts out. (37-39)

Specialization and trade based on comparative advantage is mutually beneficial to all involved.

Markets and trading make people better off.

To find the curve that shows the combined production possibilities for two people (assuming constant opportunity cost), do the following: (1) Find the amount of good A that can be produced if both produce good A. This is the A-axis intercept. (2) Find the amount of good B that can be produced if both produce good B. This is the B-axis intercept. (3) Determine the amount of each good A and B that can be produced if each person specializes and takes advantage of his or her comparative advantage. (4) Connect these three points and you've got it. As long as one person has a comparative advantage in one good, this curve will be bowed out.

See also, Appendix A: "The History of Economic Systems."

A1. Capitalism and socialism haven't existed forever. (45-46)
- *In the eighth century, feudalism—an economic system based upon tradition—dominated.*
- *In the fifteenth century, feudalism gave way to mercantilism—an economic system in which government doles out the right to undertake certain economic activities.*
- *In the eighteenth century, mercantilism gave way to capitalism*

MATCHING THE TERMS

Match the terms to their definitions

All of these key terms are found at the end of the chapter.

___ **1.** absolute advantage
___ **2.** allocative efficiency
___ **3.** communism
___ **4.** comparative advantage
___ **5.** decision tree
___ **6.** efficiency
___ **7.** inefficiency
___ **8.** input
___ **9.** market economy
___ **10.** NIMBY
___ **11.** output
___ **12.** principle of increasing marginal opportunity cost
___ **13.** private property rights
___ **14.** production possibility curve
___ **15.** production possibility table
___ **16.** productive efficiency
___ **17.** socialism

a. Control a private individual or firm has over an asset or a right.
b. Getting less output from inputs which, if devoted to some other activity, would produce more output.
c. The result of an activity.
d. Economic system that seeks to maximize the welfare of its citizens.
e. Determines what output will be produced.
f. Represents Not In My Back Yard; a phrase used by people who may approve of a project, but don't want it to be near them.
g. Achieving a goal using as few inputs as possible.
h. The advantage that attaches to a resource when that resource is better suited to the production of one good than to the production of another good.
i. In order to get more of something, one must give up ever-increasing quantities of something else.
j. A curve measuring the maximum combination of outputs that can be obtained from a given number of inputs.
k. Achieving as much output as possible from a given amount of inputs or resources.
l. An economic system based on private property and the market in which, in principle, individuals decide how, what, and for whom to produce.
m. Table that lists the maximum combination of outputs that can be obtained from a given number of inputs for given resources and technology.
n. Visual description of sequential choices demonstrating that the cost of reversing your path rises the further one is along the path.
o. What you put into a production process to achieve an output.
p. A country produces a good that it can produce more of with the same amount of resource inputs.
q. Seeks to abolish all private property, aside from some consumer goods, and assign all ownership of property to the state.
r. An economic system based on private property and the market.

MULTIPLE CHOICE

1. For a market to exist, you have to have
   a. public property rights.
   b. private property rights.
   c. a combination of public and private property rights.
   d. coordination rights.

2. In a market economy, individuals are encouraged to follow
   a. their own interests.
   b. their need to maximize profits.
   c. their own self-interest
   d. the wishes of the government.

3. In theory, a command economy is an economic system
   a. that places the ownership of private property in the hands of the state.
   b. is a blend of a market economy and socialism. ownership of the means of production.
   c. based on private property.
   d. based on markets.

4. A mixed economy is an economic system:
   a. that tries to organize society in the same ways as most families organize, striving to see that individuals get what they need.
   b. based on central planning and government ownership of the means of production.
   c. based on private property rights.
   d. based on markets.

5. In a market economy, the "what to produce" decision is made by
   a. consumers.
   b. the market.
   c. government.
   d. firms.

6. In a command economy, the "what to produce" decision is supposed to be made by
   a. what people want.
   b. what firms believe people want and will make a profit for firms.
   c. what government believes people want and what will make a profit for government.
   d. what central authorities want or what they believe is socially beneficial.

7. The Canadian economy today can best be described as
   a. socialist.
   b. pure capitalist.
   c. welfare capitalist.
   d. state socialist.

8. If the opportunity cost of good X in terms of good Y is 2Y, so you'll have to give up 2Y to get one X, the production possibility curve would look like
   a. a.
   b. b.
   c. c.
   d. a, b and c.

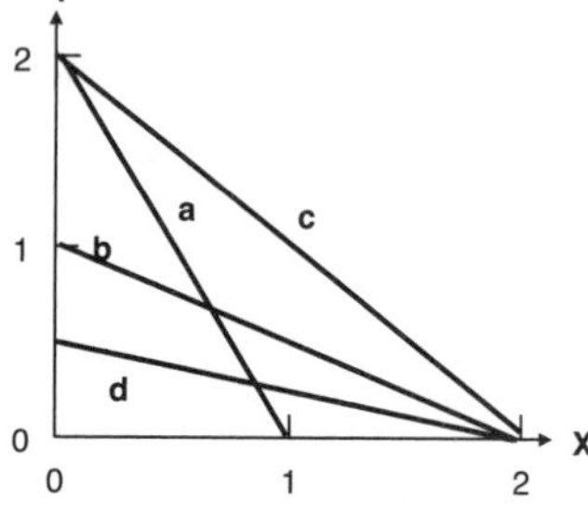

9. If the opportunity cost of good X in terms of good Y is 2Y, so you'll have to give up 2Y to get one X, the production possibility curve would look like
   a. a.
   b. b.
   c. c.
   d. d.

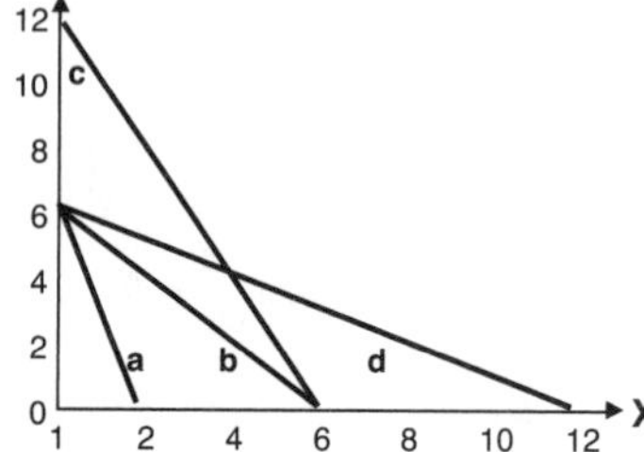

10. If the opportunity cost of good X in terms of good Y is 2Y, so you'll have to give up 2Y to get one X, the production possibility curve would look like
   a. a.
   b. b.
   c. c.
   d. a, b and c

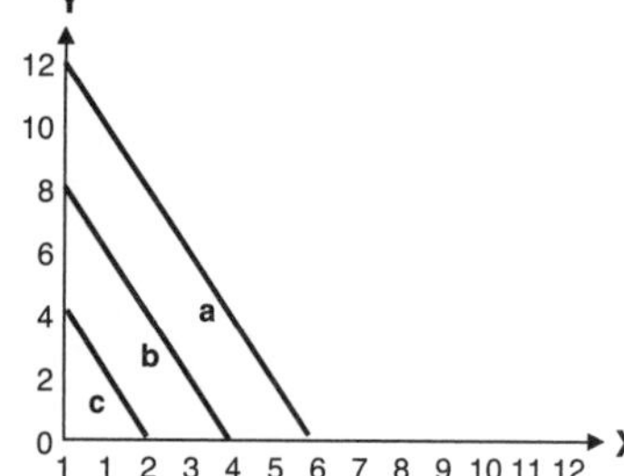

11. If the opportunity cost is constant for all combinations, the production possibility frontier will look like
   a. a.
   b. b.
   c. c.
   d. d.

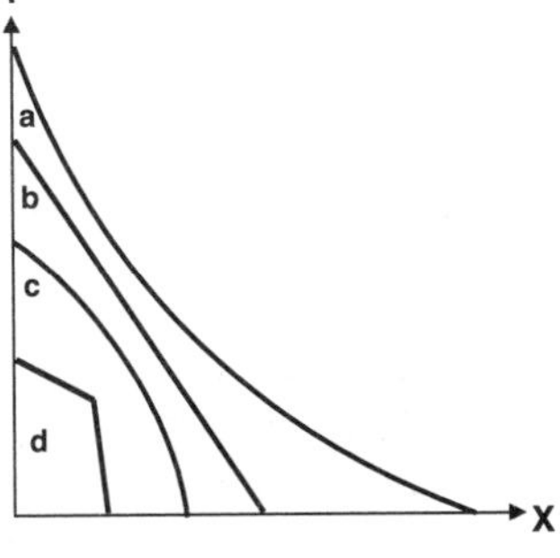

12. If the principle of increasing marginal opportunity cost applies at all points, the production possibility curve looks like
   a. a.
   b. b.
   c. c.
   d. d.

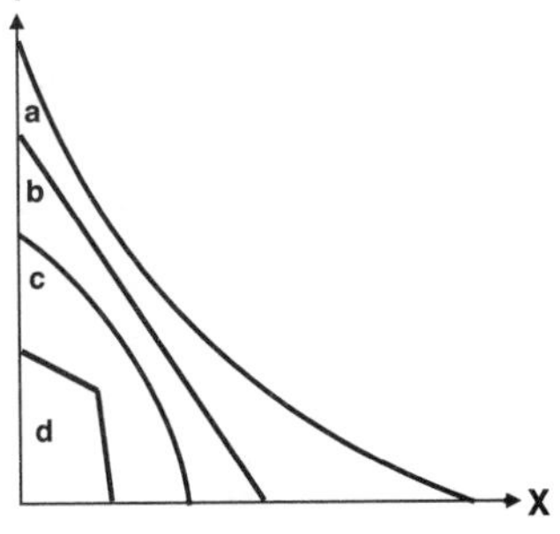

13. Given the accompanying production possibility curve, when you're moving from point C to B the opportunity cost of butter in terms of guns is
   a. 1/3.
   b. 1.
   c. 2.
   d. 3/2.

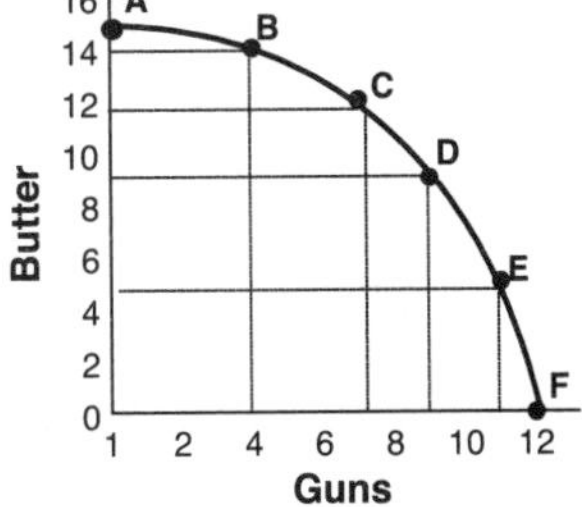

14. In the graph for question 14, in the range of points between A and B there is
   a. a high opportunity cost of guns in terms of butter.
   b. a low opportunity cost of guns in terms of butter.
   c. no opportunity cost of guns in terms of butter.
   d. a high monetary cost of guns in terms of butter.

15. In the accompanying production possibility diagram, point A would be

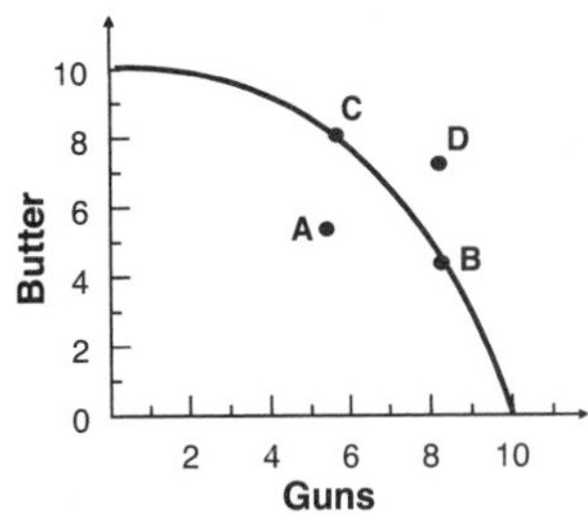

   a. an efficient point.
   b. a super-efficient point.
   c. an inefficient point.
   d. a non-attainable point.

16. A law about the growth of efficiency of computers states that computer chip technology doubles the efficiency of computers each year. If that holds true, which of the four arrows would demonstrate the appropriate shifting of the production possibility curve?

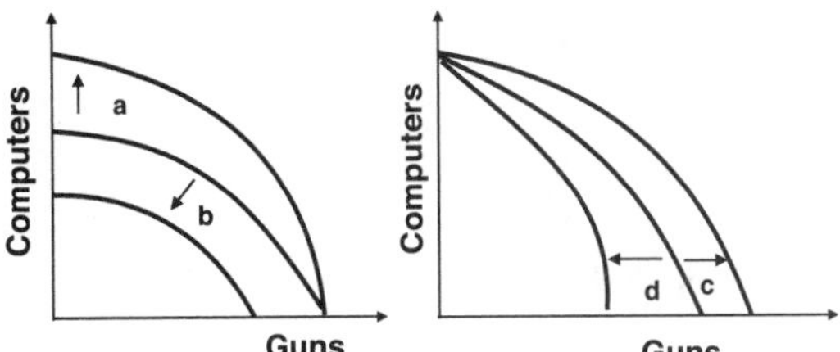

   a. a.
   b. b.
   c. c.
   d. d.

17. Say that methods of production are tied to particular income distributions, so that choosing one method will help some people but hurt others. Say also that method A produces significantly more total output than method B. In this case
   a. method A is more efficient than method B.
   b. method B is more efficient than method A.
   c. if method A produces more and gives more to the poor people, method A is more efficient.
   d. one can't say whether A or B is more efficient.

18. Productive efficiency
  - a. relates to what output will be produced and who will get it.
  - b. uses the most effective means to yield the maximum profits.
  - c. is achieving as much output as possible from a given amount of inputs or resources.
  - d. relates to the invisible hand.

19. If Canada and Japan have production possibility curves as shown in the diagram below, at what point would they most likely be after trade?
  - a. A
  - b. B
  - c. C
  - d. D

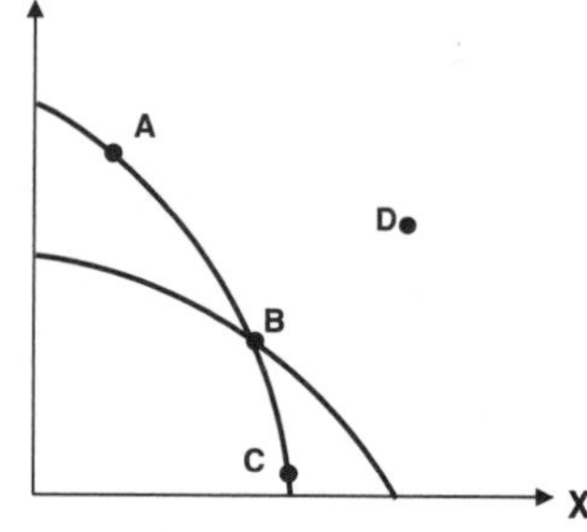

A1. In feudalism, the most important force was
  - a. the price mechanism.
  - b. cultural force.
  - c. legal force.
  - d. anarchy.

A2. In mercantilism, the guiding force is
  - a. the price mechanism.
  - b. legal force.
  - c. cultural force.
  - d. anarchy.

A3. Mercantilism evolved into capitalism because
  - a. government investments did not pan out.
  - b. the Industrial Revolution undermined the craft guilds' mercantilist method of production.
  - c. the guilds wanted more freedom.
  - d. serfs wanted more freedom.

A4. Marx saw the strongest tension between
  - a. rich capitalists and poor capitalists.
  - b. capitalists and government.
  - c. capitalists and the proletariat.
  - d. government and the proletariat.

A5. State socialism is an economic system in which
  - a. business sees to it that people work for their own good until they can be relied upon to do that on their own.
  - b. business sees to it that people work for the common good until they can be relied upon to do that on their own.
  - c. government sees to it that people work for their own good until they can be relied upon to do so on their own.
  - d. government sees to it that people work for the common good until they can be relied upon to do so on their own.

SHORT-ANSWER QUESTIONS

1. What is a market economy? How does it solve the three central economic problems?

2. What is a command economy? In practice, how has it solved the three central economic problems?

3. Name the economic systems that have evolved from the eighth century to today in the order that they occurred.

4. How can markets coordinate economic decisions without the active involvement of government?

5. Design a grade production possibility curve of studying economics and English, and show how it demonstrates the concept of opportunity cost.

6. State the principle of increasing marginal opportunity cost.

7. What would the production possibility curve look like if opportunity cost were constant?

8. What happens to the production possibility curve with trade? Why does trade make individuals better off?

9. Why is the production possibility curve more useful in discussing small changes than in discussing changes in entire economic systems?

A1. Why did feudalism evolve into mercantilism?

A2. Why did mercantilism evolve into capitalism?

A3. Explain what is meant by the statement that capitalism has evolved into welfare capitalism.

PROBLEMS AND APPLICATIONS

1. Suppose a restaurant has the following production possibility table:

Resources devoted to pizza in % of total	Output of pizza in pies per week	Resources devoted to spaghetti in % of total	Output of spaghetti in bowls per week
100	50	0	0
80	40	20	10
60	30	40	17
40	20	60	22
20	10	80	25
0	0	100	27

a. Plot the restaurant's production possibility curve. Put output of pizza in pies on the horizontal axis.

b. What happens to the marginal opportunity cost as the output of bowls of spaghetti increases?

c. What would happen to the production possibility curve if the restaurant found a way to toss and cook pizzas faster?

d. What would happen to the production possibility curve if the restaurant bought new stoves and ovens that cooked both pizzas and spaghetti faster?

2. Suppose Ecoland has the following production possibilities table:

% resources devoted to production of guns	Number of guns	% resources devoted to production of butter	Pounds of butter
100	50	0	0
80	40	20	5
60	30	40	10
40	20	60	15
20	10	80	20
0	0	100	25

a. Plot the production possibility curve for the production of guns and butter. Put the number of guns on the horizontal axis.

b. What is the per unit opportunity cost of increasing the production of guns from 20 to 30? From 40 to 50?

c. What happens to the opportunity cost of producing guns as the production of guns increases?

d. What is the per unit opportunity cost of increasing the production of butter from 10 to 15? From 20 to 25?

e. What happens to the opportunity cost of producing butter as the production of butter increases?

f. Given this production possibility curve, is producing 26 guns and 13 pounds of butter possible?

g. Is producing 34 guns and 7 pounds of butter possible? Is it efficient?

3. Using the following production possibility tables and using production possibility curves, show how the United States and Japan would be better off specializing in the production of either food or machinery and then trading rather than producing both food and machinery themselves and not trading.

United States Production per year		Japan Production per year	
Tons food	**1000 units machinery**	**Tons food**	**1000 units machinery**
10	0	12.5	0
8	5	10	1
6	10	7.5	2
4	15	5	3
2	20	2.5	4
0	25	0	5

4. Assume that France can produce wine at 25 francs per bottle and can produce butter at 5 francs per pound. Assume that Italy can produce wine at 16,000 lire per bottle and butter at 10,000 lire per pound.

a. In terms of pounds of butter, what is the opportunity cost of producing wine in each country?

b. Who has the comparative advantage in producing butter?

c. Which country should most likely specialize in wine and which should specialized in butter?

A BRAIN TEASER

1. Consider the production possibilities for an entire nation. Within any national economy, there are only two general kinds of products that can be produced–consumer products and capital products. Consumer products (e.g. food, clothes, medical services, etc ...) satisfy our wants directly when we use them and while we consume them. Capital products (e.g. machines, and other plant and equipment) satisfy our wants indirectly and in the future because they increase our productivity and help us produce even more products over time. Answer the following questions based on the production possibilities of consumer and capital products for a national economy shown in the graph below.

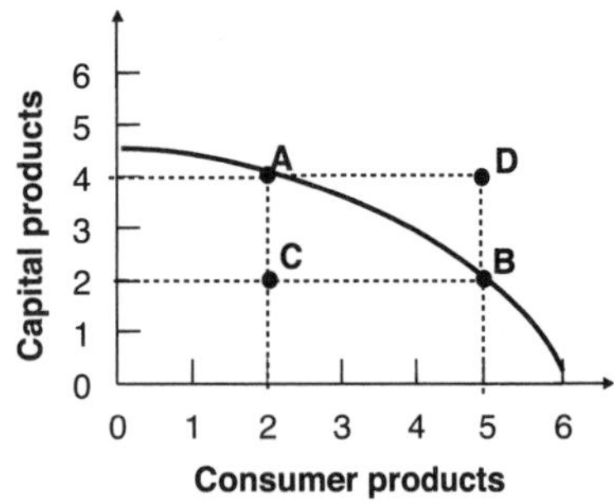

a. Between the production possibilities A and B, which would provide the greatest amount of current satisfaction? Why?

b. What is the opportunity cost of moving from point B to A?

c. Consider the choice of currently producing a relatively large amount of consumer products shown at point B (which means, given limited resources, relatively few capital products can be produced), compared to producing a relatively large amount of capital products now, shown at point A (which means relatively few consumer products can be produced). Which of these two points (or combinations of consumer and capital goods production) do you think will increase the production possibilities (shift the curve to the right) the most over time giving rise to the greatest rate of economic growth? Why? *(Hint: Whenever workers have more capital, like factories and machinery to work with, then they become more productive.)*

POTENTIAL ESSAY QUESTIONS

You may also see essay questions similar to the "Problems & Applications" and "Brain Teasers" exercises.

1. There has always been much political debate between "conservatives" and "liberals" in this country, as well as in other countries, over what constitutes the "appropriate" role for government to play in correcting for the problems of a market-oriented, capitalist economy.

   a. Is this controversy ever likely to go away? Why or why not?

   b. Could greater reliance upon positive economic analysis of "what is" as opposed to normative economic analysis of "what ought to be" help reduce some of this controversy?

2. Contrast capitalism's and socialism's solutions to the three economic problems.

3. What is a decision tree? What is its significance?

ANSWERS

MATCHING

1-p; 2-e; 3-q; 4-h; 5-n; 6-g; 7-b; 8-o; 9-r; 10-f; 11-c; 12-i; 13-a; 14-j; 15-m.;16-k;17-d.

ANSWERS

MULTIPLE CHOICE

1. b As discussed on page 27 and 28, markets require private property rights because these give people the framework within which they can trade and markets rely on trading. Markets also require government, but government and public property rights are not the same thing, which rules out a and c. And d is a throwaway answer.

2. c As discussed on pages 27, c represents a major characteristic of a market economy.

3. a As discussed on page 27, a is the correct answer. Answer b simply cannot exist, while c and d are characteristics of a market economy.

4. b As discussed on page 28, b is the correct answer. Answer a is a characteristic of the command economy, while c and d are characteristics of a market economy.

5. b In a market economy, firms decide what to produce based on what they think will sell. (26-27)

6. d As discussed on page 27, central authorities decide what to produce based upon what they believe society needs. We should point out that this is *ideally*; in practice, central authorities may not be concerned with society. Thus c is a possible answer, but the term "profit" makes it unacceptable. Central planners would not get profit—they might get rich, but it wouldn't be through profits.

7. c As discussed on pages 28 and 46, since in Canada the market is allowed to operate, but the government intervenes in determining distribution, Canada is best described as welfare capitalist.

8. a As discussed on pages 32-35, the production possibility curve tells how much of one good you must give up to get more of the other good; here you must give up 2Y to get one X, making a the correct answer.

9. c As discussed on pages 32-35, the production possibility curve tells how much of one good you must give up to get more of another good. Opportunity cost is a ratio; it determines the slope, not the position, of the ppc curve. Thus, the correct answer is c because the 12 to 6 trade-off reduces to a 2 to 1 trade-off.

10. d As discussed on pages 32-35, the production possibility curve tells how much of one good you must give up to get more of the other good. Opportunity cost is a ratio; it determines the slope, not the position, of the ppc curve. Since all have the same correct slope, all three are correct, so d is the right answer.

11. b As discussed on pages 30 and 31, if the opportunity costs are constant, the ppc is a straight line, so b must be the answer.

12. c As discussed on page 33, with increasing marginal opportunity costs, as you produce more and more of a good, you will have to give up more and more of the other good to do so. This means that the slope of the ppc must be bowed outward, so c is the correct answer. (See Figure 2-2, page 32 for an in-depth discussion.)

13. d As discussed on pages 30-32, the slope of the ppc measures the trade-off of one good for the other. Since moving from point c to b means giving up 3 guns for 2 pounds of butter, the correct answer is 3/2 or d.

14. b As discussed on pages 31-32, the flatter the slope, the higher the opportunity cost of the good measured on the vertical axis; alternatively, the flatter the slope the lower the opportunity cost of that good measured on the horizontal axis. In the AB range the slope is flat so guns have a low opportunity cost in terms of butter; one need give up only one pound of butter to get four guns.

15. c As discussed on page 34 (See Figure 2-3), point A is an inefficient point.

16. a As discussed on page 34 (See Figure 2-3), technological change that improves the efficiency of producing a good shifts the ppc out in that good, but not in the other good. So a is the correct answer.

17. d The answer is "You can't say," as discussed on pages 34-37. The term "efficiency" involve *using the most effective means to yield the maximum benefits*. Without specifying one's goal, one cannot say what method is more efficient. The concept efficiency generally presumes that the goal includes preferring more to less, so if any method is more productive, it will be method A. But because there are distributional effects that involve making additional judgments, the correct answer is d. Some students may have been tempted to choose c because their goals involve more equity, but that is their particular judgment, and not all people may agree. Thus c would be incorrect, leaving d as the correct answer.

18. c As discussed on page 33, productive efficiency deals with producing the most output for a given amount of scarce resources and a given level of technology. Answer a relates to allocative efficiency, while b is just wrong. Productive efficiency does not deal with profits.

19. d As discussed in Figure 2-6 on page 39, with trade, both countries can attain a point outside each production possibility curve. The only point not already attainable is D.

A1. b As discussed on page 41, in feudalism tradition reigned.

A2. b As discussed on page 42, in mercantilism government directed the economy.

A3. b See page 46.

A4. c See pages 49-50. To the degree that government was controlled by capitalists, d would be a correct answer, but it is not as good an answer as c, which represents the primary conflict. Remember, you are choosing the answer that best reflects the discussion in the text.

A5. d See page 51.

ANSWERS

SHORT-ANSWER QUESTIONS

1. A market economy is an economic system based on private property and the market. It gives private property rights to individuals, and relies on market forces to coordinate economic activity. In a market economy, businesses produce what they believe people want and think they can make a profit supplying. Businesses decide how to produce, guided by their desire to make a profit. Goods are distributed according to individuals' ability and/or inherited wealth. (26-27)

2. A command economy is an economic system that places the ownership of private property in the hands of the state and coordinates all production planning with a central authority. The central authorities decide what is to be produced, how much is produced, who is to produce it, and how it is to be distributed. (27)

3. Economic systems have evolved from feudalism (from the 8th to the 15th centuries) to mercantilism (from the mid-15th to the 18th centuries) to capitalism (from the 18th century to today). Economic systems are constantly evolving. (45-46)

4. The invisible hand — the price mechanism — guides the actions of suppliers and consumers to the general good. That is, competition directs individuals pursuing profit to do what society needs to have done. Markets coordinate economic decisions by turning self-interest into social good. (26-27)

5. The production possibility curve shows the highest combination of grades you can get with 20 hours of studying economics and English. The grade received in economics is on the vertical axis and the grade received in English is on the horizontal axis. The graph tells us the opportunity cost of spending any combination of 20 hours on economics and English. For example, the opportunity cost of increasing your grade in economics by 6 points is decreasing your English grade by 4 points (2/3 grade point reduction in English for one grade point improvement in Economics). (29-33)

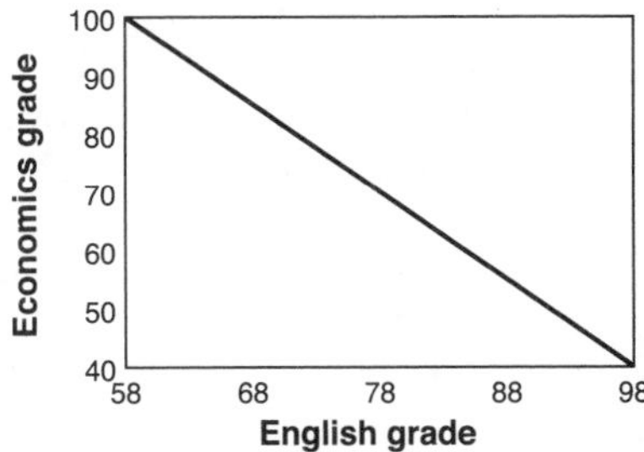

6. The principle of increasing marginal opportunity cost states that in order to get more of something, one must give up ever-increasing quantities of something else. (33)

7. Such a production possibility curve would be a straight line connecting the maximum number of units that could be produced of each product if all inputs were devoted to one or the other good. (31-32)

8. By comparing individual production possibility curves, one can determine those activities in which each has a comparative advantage. By concentrating on those activities for which one has a comparative advantage and trading those goods for goods for which others have a comparative advantage, individuals can end up with a combination of goods not attainable without trade. The production possibility curve shifts out with trade. (28-39)

9. The production possibility curve is best used when discussing small changes because the relationships between costs and production can be assumed to remain constant. Changes in economic systems can change the relationships that affect costs in everyday decisions and in production. The text's example of how changing from socialism to capitalism would affect the production possibility curve is a good example of how an analysis using just the production possibility curve can mask the probability that beneficial results of major structural changes may take many years. (36-37)

A1. Feudalism evolved into mercantilism as the development of money allowed trade to grow, undermining the traditional base of feudalism. Politics rather than social forces came to control the central economic decisions. (45-48)

A2. Mercantilism evolved into capitalism because the Industrial Revolution shifted the economic power base away from craftsmen toward industrialists and toward an understanding that markets could coordinate the economy without the active involvement of the government. (48-49)

A3. Capitalism has evolved into welfare capitalism. That is, the human abuses marked by early capitalist developments led to a criticism of the market economic system. Political forces have changed government's role in the market, making government a key player in determining distribution and in making the what, how, and for whom decisions. This characterizes the Canadian economy today. (46)

ANSWERS

PROBLEMS AND APPLICATIONS

1. a. The restaurant's production possibility curve is shown below. (29-32)

b. The number of pizza pies that must be given up to make an additional bowl of spaghetti increases as the number of bowls of spaghetti produced increases. (32-33)

c. If the restaurant found a way to toss and cook pizzas faster, the production possibility curve would rotate out along the pizza axis as shown below. (34)

d. The production possibility curve would shift out to the right as shown in the figure below. (34)

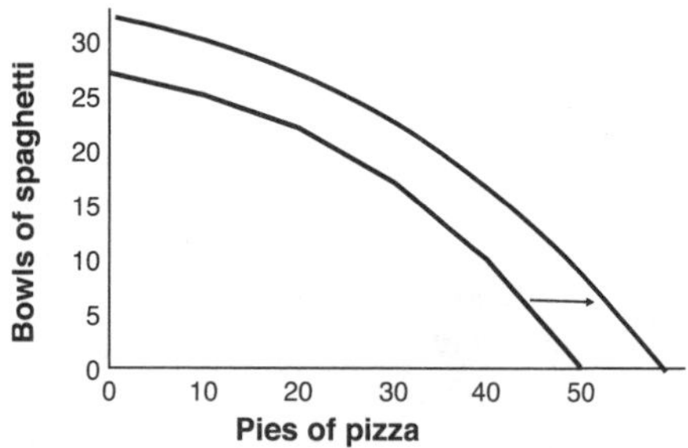

2. a. The production possibility curve is a straight line as shown below. (29-35)

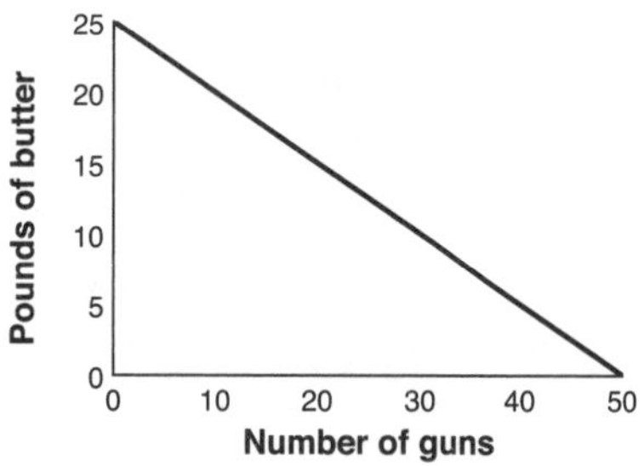

b. The opportunity cost of increasing the production of guns from 20 to 30 is 0.5 pounds of butter per gun. The opportunity cost of increasing the production of guns from 40 to 50 is also 0.5 pounds of butter per gun. (29-32)

c. The opportunity cost of producing guns stays the same as the production of guns increases. (29-32)

d. The opportunity cost of increasing the production of butter from 10 to 15 is 2 guns per pound of butter. The opportunity cost of increasing the production of butter from 20 to 25 is 2 guns per pound of butter. (29-32)

e. The opportunity cost of producing butter stays the same as the production of butter increases. (29-32)

f. Producing 26 guns and 13 pounds of butter is not attainable given this production possibility curve. We can produce 20 guns and 15 pounds of butter. To produce six more guns, Ecoland must give up 3 pounds of butter. Ecoland can produce only 26 guns and 12 pounds of butter. (29-32)

g. Ecoland can produce 34 guns and 7 pounds of butter. To see this, begin at 30 guns and 10 pounds of butter. To produce 4 more guns, 2 pounds of butter must be given up. Ecoland can produce 34 guns and 8 pounds of butter, which is more than 34 guns and 7 pounds of butter. This is an inefficient point of production. (29-32)

3. The production possibility of producing food and machinery for both Japan and the United States is shown in the graph below. The combined production possibility curve with trade is also shown. Clearly, trade shifts the production possibility curve out, showing that the two countries are better off with trade. The United States has a comparative advantage in the production of machinery. It must give up only 0.4 tons of food for each additional thousand units of machinery produced. Japan must give up 2.5 tons of food for each additional thousand units of machinery produced. A specific example is if Japan produced 12.5 tons of food and no machines while the United States produced 0 tons of food and 25 thousand units of machinery, Japan could offer the United States 2 tons of food for 3 thousand units of machinery. The United States would be at point A and Japan would be at point B. Each would be able to attain a level of production not attainable before. (29-32)

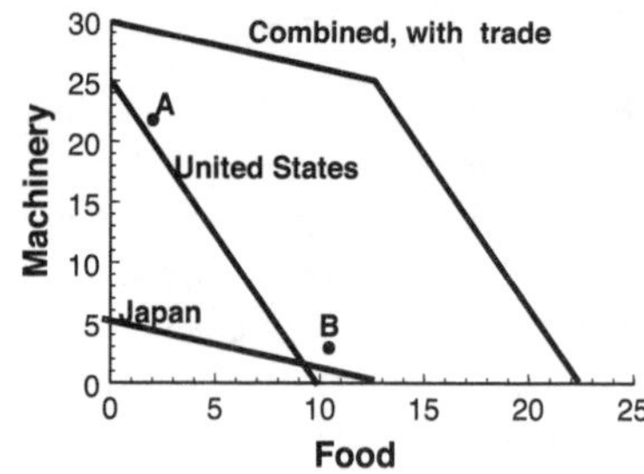

4. a. In France, the opportunity cost of producing wine is 5 pounds of butter. In Italy, the opportunity cost of producing wine is 1.6 pounds of butter. Calculate this by finding how much butter must be forgone for each bottle of wine in each country. (29-32)
   b. France has the comparative advantage in producing butter because it can produce butter for a lower opportunity cost. (29-32)
   c. Italy should specialize in producing wine and France should specialize in producing butter assuming one can produce only wine and the other must produce only butter. This is concluded from the principle of comparative advantage. (29-32)

ANSWERS

A BRAIN TEASER

1. a. Production possibility B. Why? Because consumer products provide for *current* satisfaction, and at B we are getting a relatively larger amount of consumer products.
   b. 3 units of consumer products.
   c. Point A. Producing a relatively larger amount of capital products now means workers will have more plant and equipment to work with in the future. This will increase worker's productivity and the nation's production possibilities over time. Producing more capital is an ingredient for economic growth (greater production possibilities).

ANSWERS

POTENTIAL ESSAY QUESTIONS

The following are annotated answers. They indicate the general idea behind the answer.

1. a. Although there is no debate over the existence of market failures, there is much debate over the extent to which they exist. Controversy often begins with equally reasonable and well intentioned people assessing the extent of the problem differently. (For example, consider the controversy surrounding the extent of ozone damage.) If a consensus is reached, then the same equally reasonable, equally well intentioned people will likely measure the benefits and costs associated with government involvement differently. This gives rise to debate concerning the appropriate extent of government involvement.
   b. There will likely always be some degree of inefficiency in measuring the benefits and the costs associated with any problem and of any government involvement. However, greater reliance upon positive economic analysis, because it is "objective" and deals with "what is," should help everyone to avoid emotion and to see more clearly the extent of any problem. Moreover, it should help everyone to more clearly assess the benefits and costs associated with government action, or inaction, in a particular case. This is because positive economics helps us to predict or anticipate consequences. As was stated in the first chapter, "the art of economics is the application of the knowledge learned in positive economics to the achievement of the goals determined in normative economics. In the art of economics, it is difficult to be objective but it is important to try." People can argue until they are blue in the face about "what ought to be" the appropriate role for government. But that emotionally held belief, when enacted as policy, usually has little to do with the resulting real-world consequences. Too often, dismal consequences were predicted using positive economic analysis, but were ignored. This applies with equal weight to many "conservative" and "liberal" positions alike. We have experienced a rich history of real-world cases to show that sometimes government can help while at other times it only makes matters worse. That which is effective, however, may not be "politically correct" at the time.

2. Both economic systems have to answer the three central economic problems. (1) What to produce? In capitalism, firms produce what they believe people want and will make a profit. In socialism, in practice central planners decide what was produced. (2) How to produce? In capitalism firms decide how to produce efficiently, guided by their desire to make a profit. In socialism, central planners decide how to produce. (3) For whom to produce? In capitalism, distribution is decided according to ability and inherited wealth. In socialism, distribution is according to individuals' needs (as determined by central planners).

3. A decision tree is a visual description of sequential choices. It points out that decisions are made in context. See page 36.

THE CANADIAN ECONOMY IN A GLOBAL SETTING

3

CHAPTER AT A GLANCE

Chapter 3 outlines how business, households and governments interact in a market economy. There are two broad categories that make up a market economy. The factor market, where households have the freedom to choose to supply the resources that they own, namely labour, and where firms employ those resources and pay households for that right. The goods market is where the firms produce goods and services demanded by households, which households purchase with the income earned in the factor market. The market economy brings firms and households together, which, with the forces of supply and demand, determine prices and allocate our scarce resources.

In essence, government has two key roles in our market economy. One is being a referee, setting rules that determine relations between business and households. This would include setting an appropriate legal system and regulations to guide behaviour. The other role is being an actor—collecting money in taxes and spending that money on their own projects such as education and defense.

The last part of the chapter discusses how economic entities such as households, business and government interact in the global economy. A large portion of goods purchased by households are produced by foreign countries. Firms are now competing internationally as well as within Canada and the role of government must include setting an environment conducive to freer trade. It is an accepted fact that engaging in international trade improves the economic well-being of our society. As result, economists have entered a variety of international trade agreements and organizations such as GATT, the WTO, the EU, and NAFTA.

This review is based upon the learning objectives that open the chapter.

1. Businesses, households and government interact in a market economy. (52)

For a bird's-eye view of the Canadian economy, see Figure 3-1 (sometimes called the "circular flow of income model"). Be able to draw and explain it.

Note: there are 3 basic economic institutions:

- *Businesses:*
  a. Supply goods in goods market
  b. Demand factors in factor market
  c. Pay taxes and receive benefits from government

- *Households:*
  a. Supply factors
  b. Demand goods
  c. Pay taxes and receive benefits from government

- *Government:*
  a. Demands goods
  b. Demands factors
  c. Collects taxes and provide services

2. The nature of business is changing with the emergence of the digital economy. E-commerce has grown enormously. Conducting business on the Internet removes the importance of geography and location for firms and reduces the costs of doing business. (55-56)

3. Households are groups of individuals living together and making joint decisions. They ultimately have great influence over government and business. Households' votes determines government policy, while decisions regarding the supply and labour and consumer preferences dictate what to produce. (56-57)

Note:

- *Do we control business and government, or do they control us?*
- *The distribution of income (rich vs. poor) determines the "for whom" question. If you're rich, you get more.*
- *Social forces affect what business and government do or don't do.*

4a. Two general roles of government are: (57-59)

- As an actor: Collects taxes and spends money.
- As referee: Sets the rules governing relations between households and businesses.

4b. For the government of Canada, the major sources of income are income taxes, consumption taxes, property taxes, and contributions to social insurance plans. The major sources of expenditures are social services, general purpose transfers, education and health care. (58)

5a. The importance of international trade to the Canadian economy is substantial. Exports as a share of GDP is 41.1%, one of the highest in the industrialized world. (60-61)

5b. The United States, the European Union and the Pacific Rim make up the largest percentage of total Canadian exports. (61)

See Figure 3-4 (a and b) on page 61 for Canadian exports and imports by region.

5c. Two ways in which *inter*national trade differs from *intra*national (domestic) trade are: (64-67)

- International trade involves potential barriers to trade; and

  Free and open international trade along the lines of comparative advantage is mutually beneficial to all economies involved.

- International trade involves multiple currencies.

  Foreign exchange markets exist to swap currencies.

6a. Three global trade organizations include: (67)

- The World Trade Organization (WTO),
- The General Agreement on Tariffs and Trade (GATT); and
- The North American Free Trade Agreement (NAFTA).

These are organizations that work toward lowering trade barriers among countries.

Economists generally like markets and favour trade being as free as possible.

6b. Four important international economic institutions are: (68)

- The UN
- The World Court
- The World Bank; and
- The IMF.

They are designed to enhance trade negotiations (to avoid trade wars).

Think internationally because we live in a global economy.

6c. In addition to formal institutions, there are informal meetings of various countries. (68)

- Group of Five
- Group of Ten

MATCHING THE TERMS

Match the terms to their definitions

All of these key terms are found at the end of the chapter.

___ **1.** balance of trade
___ **2.** business
___ **3.** consumer sovereignty
___ **4.** current account balance
___ **5.** entrepreneurship
___ **6.** European Union
___ **7.** exchange rate
___ **8.** exports
___ **9.** foreign exchange market
___ **10.** free trade associations
___ **11.** General Agreement on Tariffs and Trade (GATT)
___ **12.** global corporations
___ **13.** Group of Five
___ **14.** Group of Ten
___ **15.** households
___ **16.** IMF
___ **17.** imports
___ **18.** merchandise trade balance
___ **19.** nontariff barriers
___ **20.** NAFTA
___ **21.** profit
___ **22.** quotas
___ **23.** service balance
___ **24.** tariffs
___ **25.** trade deficit
___ **26.** trade surplus
___ **27.** transfer payments
___ **28.** World Bank
___ **29.** World Trade Organization (WTO)

a. A free trade association of 25 western European countries.
b. Principle that the consumer's wishes rule what's produced.
c. Corporations with substantial operations on both production and sales in more than one country.
d. Measures trade services.
e. The difference between exports and imports of goods.
f. Market in which one country's currency can be exchanged for another country's.
g. A U.S.-Canada-Mexico free trade zone that is phasing in reductions in tariffs.
h. The ability to organize and get something done.
i. Measures trade in goods and services and includes the interest payments made to foreigners for the use of their savings.
j. Limitations on how much of a good can be shipped into a country.
k. A multinational, international financial institution concerned primarily with monetary issues.
l. The result of a country's imports exceeding its exports.
m. A tax on an imported good.
n. The difference between the value of goods and services Canada exports and the value of goods and services it imports.
o. An organization committed to getting countries to agree not to impose new tariffs or other trade restrictions except under certain limited conditions.
p. The Group of Ten plus Canada, Italy, Belguim, the Netherlands and Switzerland.
q. Certificates of ownership in a company.
r. The rate at which one currency is traded for another.
s. What is left over from total revenues after all the appropriate costs have been subtracted.
t. The value of goods purchased abroad.
u. Japan, Germany, Britain, France and the United States.
v. Groups of countries that have reduced or eliminated trade barriers among themselves.
w. Name given to private producing units in our society.
x. When a country exports more than it imports.
y. An agreement among many subscribing countries on certain conditions of international trade.
z. The value of goods sold abroad.
z1. A multi-national, international financial institution that works with developing countries to secure low-interest loans.
z2. Group of individuals living together and making joint decisions.
z2. Indirect regulation restricting imports and exports.

MULTIPLE CHOICE

Circle the one best answer for each of the following questions:

1. In the factor market:
   a. businesses supply goods and services to households and government.
   b. government provides income support to households unable to supply factors of production to businesses.
   c. households supply labour and other factors of production to businesses.
   d. households purchase goods and services from businesses.

2. The ability to organize and get something done generally goes under the term
   a. the corporate approach.
   b. entrepreneurship.
   c. efficiency.
   d. consumer sovereignty.

3. Initial public offerings are a way for businesses to:
   a. finance expansion of an existing privately held business.
   b. finance expansion of an existing publicly-held business.
   c. increase sales by bringing in new customers.
   d. consolidate ownership of a company among a few stockholders.

4. The largest percentage of federal government expenditures is on:
   a. education
   b. health
   c. transportation and communication
   d. social services

5. The largest revenue source of provincial and local expenditures is on:
   a. income taxes
   b. general purpose transfers
   c. investment income
   d. sale of goods and services

6. All of the following are examples of government as referee *except*:
   a. setting limitations on when someone can be fired.
   b. collecting consumption taxes from workers' paychecks.
   c. setting minimum safety regulations for the workplace.
   d. disallowing two competitors to meet to fix prices of their products.

7. Debtor nations will
   a. run trade deficits.
   b. run trade surpluses.
   c. not necessarily run a trade surplus or a trade deficit.
   d. run foreign exchange sales.

8. If a country has a trade deficit, it is:
   a. consuming more than it is producing.
   b. borrowing from foreigners.
   c. selling financial assets.
   d. selling real assets.

9. In 2002 and 2003, Canada had a:
   a. services deficit.
   b. merchandise trade surplus.
   c. current account surplus.
   d. trade deficit.

10. An important way in which international trade differs from domestic trade is:
    a. international trade involves potential barriers to the flow of inputs and outputs.
    b. the use of different communication systems.
    c. the use of different transportation systems.
    d. that money is not used in international trade.

11. A quota is
    a. taxes on imports.
    b. indirect regulatory restrictions.
    c. limitations on how much a good can be shipped into a country.
    d. taxes on exports.

12. In a foreign exchange market:
    a. imports are exchanged for exports.
    b. exports are exchanged for imports.
    c. labour services, exports, imports and currencies are exchanged.
    d. one currency is exchanged for another.

13. The general plan of NAFTA is
   a. to adjust tariffs so that they are equal across products and countries.
   b. to replace tariffs with quotas.
   c. to move towards political integration among Canada, Mexico, and the United States.
   d. to remove tariffs on most goods traded in North America within 15 years of signing.

14. The EU is an economic free trade area
   a. but not a political organization.
   b. and a loose political organization.
   c. and a federation of individual countries.
   d. and a nation-state.

15. The Group of Five consists of
   a. Japan, Germany, Britain, France and the United States.
   b. Japan, Germany, Britain, France and Italy.
   c. Italy, Japan, Germany, Britain, and the United States
   d. Canada, Japan, Germany, the United States, and France.

16. The WTO is an organization mainly committed to
   a. increasing competitive quotas and tariffs among countries
   b. legalizing international trade by getting countries to refrain from imposing new tariffs or restrictions.
   c. creating independent trade zones throughout the world
   d. increasing security alliances around the world

17. If a country is found guilty in the World Court
   a. its leaders will be put in jail.
   b. it will be forced by the UN to pay a fine.
   c. it may or may not comply with the remedy decreed by the Court, depending on whether it chooses to comply or not.
   d. its dues to finance the World Court will be doubled.

SHORT-ANSWER QUESTIONS

1. Draw a diagram of the Canadian economy showing the three groups that comprise the Canadian economy. What is the role of each group in the economy?

2. Although businesses decide what to produce, who ultimately makes the decision what to produce?

3. Why is much of the economic decision-making done by business and government even though households have the ultimate power?

4. What are two general roles of government?

5. Which two countries are Canada's largest trading partners? With which two other areas does Canada primarily trade?

6. State two ways international trade differs from domestic trade.

7. Name 3 important free trade organizations and 4 important international economic policy organizations.

PROBLEMS AND APPLICATIONS

1. State whether the trade restriction is a quota, tariff, or nontariff barrier.
   a. The EU requires beef to be free of growth-inducing hormones in order to be traded in EU markets.

   b. Hong Kong has maintained rice import controls on quantity since 1955 in order to keep local rice importers in business and to secure a steady wartime food supply.

   c. To encourage domestic production of automobile parts, Japan limits the importation of automobile parts according to a rigid schedule of numbers.

   d. The United States charges French wineries 10% of the value of each case of French wine imported into the United States.

2. Complete the blanks in the table below.

Currency	USD equivalent	Currency per USD
British Pound	______	0.61
German Mark (DM)	______	1.90
Sri Lankan rupee	______	72.50
Japanese yen	0.0095	______
Eu euro	1.03	______

   a. How many Sri Lankan rupees buys one Japanese yen?

   b. How many USD (U.S. dollars) are needed to buy a German Porsche at a cost of 92,000 DM?

   c. How many British pound(s) buys one euro?

A BRAIN TEASER

1. a. What are the three general types of trade barriers which a nation's government might impose on foreign producers?

b. Assuming one of these trade barriers is going to be imposed, which one do you think might be most beneficial to the government imposing the trade barrier? Why?

POTENTIAL ESSAY QUESTIONS

You may also see essay questions similar to the "Problems & Applications" and "Brain Teasers" exercises.

1. Uglies is a brand of boxer shorts sold on the Internet. Their claim to fame is that each side of the shorts don't match. Their marketing ploy is boxer-short-of-the-month club. Suppose you were the one who came up with the idea for Uglies and wanted to start the business. What form of business would you select and why? (Thinking about where the funds to start the business will come from, who will make the shorts, and how the shorts will be sold will help you answer the question.)

2. Is it better to be a creditor nation or a debtor nation? Explain your answer.

3. Large trade deficits often inspire politicians to call for trade restrictions prohibiting imports. However, most economists oppose such restrictions because of the negative effects they may create. What are some of the problems associated with trade restrictions?

ANSWERS

MATCHING

1-n; 2-w; 3-b; 4-i; 5-h; 6-a; 7-r; 8-z; 9-f; 10-v; 11-y; 12-c; 13-u; 14-p; 15-z2; 16-k; 17-t; 18-e; 19-z3; 20-g; 21-s; 22-j; 23-d; 24-m; 25-l; 26-x; 27-q; 28-z1; 29-o.

ANSWERS

MULTIPLE CHOICE

1. c See page 52-53.
2. b See page 54.
3. a An initial public offering is when a company first offers some of its stock to the general public. See pages 55.
4. d See Figure 3-3b on page 58.
5. a See Figure 3-2a on page 57.
6. b Collecting consumption taxes is government as an actor. Government as referee refers to laws regulating interaction between households and businesses. See pages 57-58.
7. c A debtor nation may currently be running a surplus if it ran deficits in the past. See p. 63-64.
8. a If a country has a trade deficit, it is importing (consuming) more than it is exporting (producing). See page 63.
9. c See page 64.
10. a International trade involves potential barriers to trade. See page 64.
11. c See page 65.
12. d See page 67.
13. d See page 67.
14. b See page 67.
15. a See page 68 for the list of the Group of Five.

16. b See page 67.

17. c The World Court has no enforcement mechanism. See page 68.

ANSWERS

SHORT-ANSWER QUESTIONS

1. As seen in the diagram below, the three groups that comprise the Canadian economy are households, business, and government. Households supply factors of production to businesses; businesses produce goods and services and sell them to households and government. The government taxes businesses and households, buys goods and services from businesses and labour services from households, and provides goods and services to each of them. (52-53)

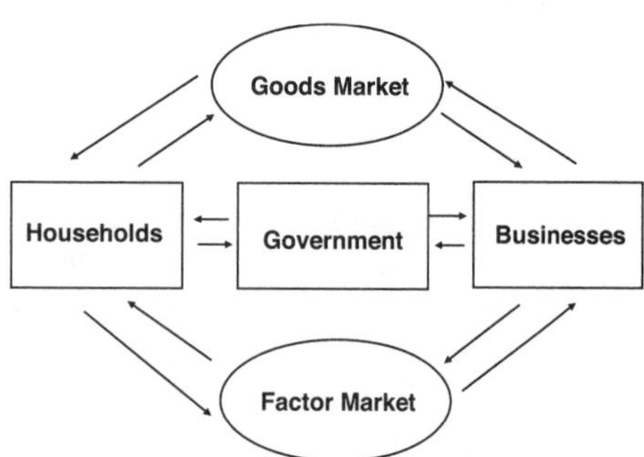

2. Although businesses decide what to produce, they are guided by consumer sovereignty. Businesses want to make a profit, so they will produce what they believe consumers will buy. That is not to say that businesses don't affect the desires of consumers through advertising. (54)

3. Business and government do much of the economic decision-making even though households retain the ultimate power. This is because in practice people have delegated much of that power to institutions and representatives – firms and the government – that are sometimes removed from the people. In the short run, households only indirectly control government and business. (56-57)

4. Two general roles of the government are as referee and actor. (56-57)
5. The United States, the European Union and the Pacific Rim make up the largest percentage of total Canadian exports. Canada also trades with the Pacific Rim. (61)

6. The two ways in which international trade differs from intranational trade are: (1) International trade involves potential barriers to trade; that is, producers' rights to sell can be limited by government-imposed quotas, tariffs, and nontariff barriers. (2) International trade involves multiple currencies that are traded in foreign exchange markets. (64-65)

7. Three important free trade organizations are the World Trade Organization (WTO), The North American Free Trade Association (NAFTA), and the General Agreement on Tariffs and Trade (GATT) the predecessor to the WTO. Four important international economic policy organizations are the United Nations (U.N.), World Bank, World Court, and the International Monetary Fund (IMF). (67-68)

ANSWERS

PROBLEMS AND APPLICATIONS

1. **a.** Nontariff barrier because this a regulation that has the final effect of reducing imports without a tax or numerical limitation. (64-65)
   b. Quota. It is a numerical restriction on the amount of rice entering the country. (64-65)
   c. Quota because it is a numerical restriction on imports. (64-65)
   d. Tariff because it is a tax on imports. (64-65)

2. The table is filled in below. (64-65)

Currency	USD equivalent	Currency per USD
British Pound	1.6393	0.61
German Mark (DM)	0.5263	1.90
Sri Lankan rupee	0.0138	72.50
Japanese yen	0.0095	105.26
Eu euro	1.03	0.97

a. 0.6888 rupees buys one Japanese yen. Calculate this by first finding the yen per dollar (105.26) and Sri Lankan rupees per dollar (72.50). To find rupees per yen, divide rupees per dollar by Japanese yen per dollar. (64-67)

b. $48,421.05 are needed to buy a German Porsche Carrera at a cost of 92,000 DM. To calculate this, find the German mark per U.S. dollar (1.90) and divide this into the cost of the Porsche in marks. (64-67)

c. 0.6289 pounds are needed to buy one Euro. Calculate this by finding the British pound per USD (0.61) and euro per dollar (0.97). To find British pounds per euro, divide British pounds per dollar euro per dollar. (64-67)

ANSWERS

A BRAIN TEASER

1. a. The three general types of trade barriers a nation's government might impose on foreign producers are tariffs, quotas, and nontariff barriers. (64-65)

b. Although all barriers will be costly for the host government to "police," only tariffs (a tax on an imported product) will raise revenues for the government. (64-65)

ANSWERS

POTENTIAL ESSAY QUESTIONS

The following are annotated answers. They indicate the general idea behind the answer.

1. The answer to this question will vary from person to person and will depend upon personal finances, how much risk one is able and willing to undertake, how much responsibility one wants to take on, and whether or not you want to share in any profits. Given limited financial resources, I'd find a partner I can trust who has the funds needed to launch a web site, hire a firm to carry out transactions and build inventory. With a partnership I can share the work and the risks of the venture. Since the liability associated with selling boxer shorts is not too great, unlimited liability with a partnership is not a problem. Not a corporation because establishing one is a legal hassle requiring even more money. Not a sole proprietorship because I don't have the funds to start the company on my own.

2. Whether it is better to be a creditor or debtor nation is debatable. A debtor nation is able to consume more that it produces. Countries can do this by living off foreign aid, past savings, or loans. The U.S. finances its deficits (as a debtor nation) by selling financial assets (such as stocks and bonds) and real assets (such as real estate and corporations) to foreigners. The problem with being a debtor nation is that country has to make interest payments on those bonds and has to pay profits to the foreigners who own the corporations. A creditor nation receives those interest payments and profits, but must consume less than it is producing.

3. Generally, there are two problems. First, trade restrictions reduce competition. Less competition means consumers have to pay higher prices than if the foreign competition were allowed. Second, trade restrictions often bring retaliation from other countries (they impose stricter trade restrictions as well). This reduces the amount domestic firms would otherwise be able to sell abroad.

SUPPLY AND DEMAND

CHAPTER AT A GLANCE

Chapter 4 introduces one of the more important tools of economic analysis—the model of supply and demand. The interaction of the forces of supply and demand determine market prices in a competitive market. This is the way wheat and crude oil prices are determined in our global economy. Of course, not all prices are determined by the forces of supply and demand, however, the model does provide great insight into the behaviour of consumers and producers in a wide variety of situations.

The chapter emphasizes the law of demand and supply and the various factors influencing how much of a particular good is demanded or supplied. Demand and supply can be represented in a number of different ways—algebraically, in tabular form, or by the use of graphs. Graphing demand and supply is a very important skill that students will have to master. It will provide important insight into what happens in a market economy when external influences affect demand and supply.

Mastery of the demand and supply model will also require an understanding of specific important concepts and terms such as "demand", "quantity demanded", "supply", and " quantity supplied".

Equilibrium market prices and quantity are determined by the intersection of the demand and supply curves. Changes in demand and supply causes shifts in the demand and supply curves, which will alter the level of equilibrium price and quantity. You should become comfortable in being able to determine the resulting change in equilibrium price and quantity resulting from changes in demand and supply.

This review is based upon the learning objectives that open the chapter.

1a. The law of demand states that the quantity of a good demanded is inversely related to a good's price. When price goes up, quantity demanded goes down. When price goes down, quantity demanded goes up. (73)

Law of Demand (Inverse Relationship):
arrows move in opposite directions $\uparrow P \Rightarrow \downarrow Q_d$
$\downarrow P \uparrow \Rightarrow Q_d$

Law of Demand expressed as a *<u>downward-sloping curve</u>:*

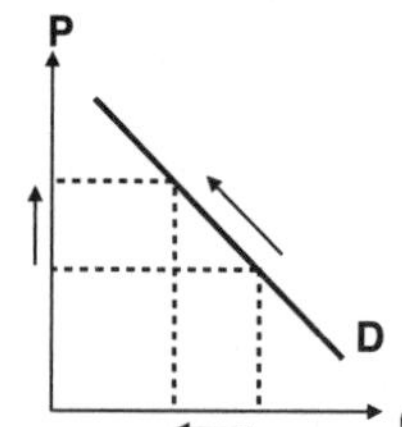

1b. Changes in quantity demanded are shown by movements along a demand curve. Shifts in demand are shown by a shift of the entire demand curve. (73-76) (Note: "Δ" means "change.")

Don't get this confused on the exam!

ΔQ_d is caused <u>only</u> by a Δ in the P of the good itself.

$\Delta P \Rightarrow Q_d \Rightarrow$ movement along a given D curve.

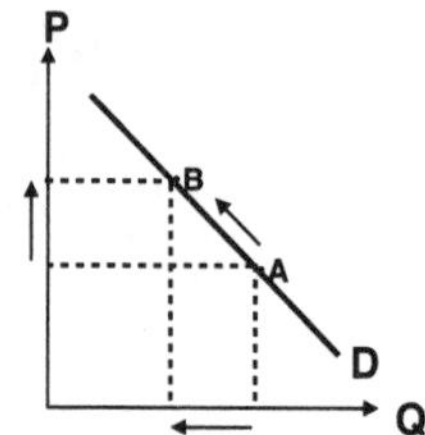

$\uparrow P \Rightarrow \downarrow Q_d$: movement along a curve (e.g. from point A to point B).
Δ is caused only by Δs in the shift factors of D (not a Δ in the P of the good itself!)
Δ <u>in shift factors of D</u> = ΔD <u>shift of a D curve</u>

Know what can cause an increase and decrease in demand:

↑*D* *Rightward Shift* ↓*D* *Leftward Shift*

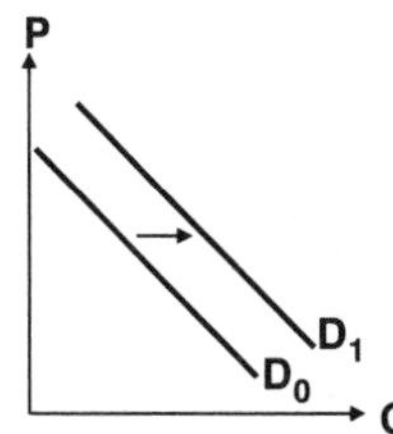

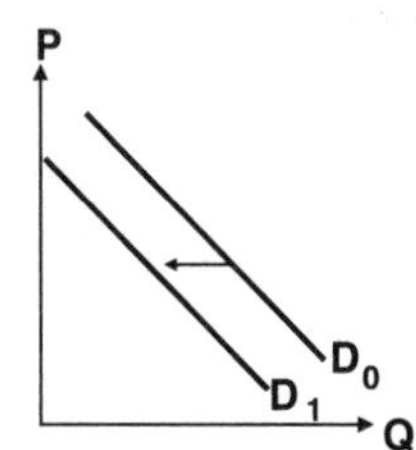

1c. To derive a demand curve from a demand table you plot each point on the demand table on a graph and connect the points. (76-77)

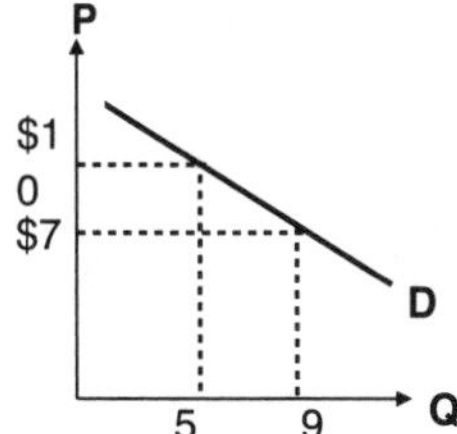

P	Q
$10	5
7	9

1d. Market demand curves are the horizontal sum of all individual demand curves. At each price, the quantities demanded related to the various individual demand curves are summed together. (77-78)

2a. The law of supply states that the quantity supplied of a good is directly related to the good's price. When price goes up, quantity supplied goes up. When price goes down, quantity supplied goes down. (80)

Law of Supply (Direct Relationship):
arrows move in same direction ↑*P* ↑Q_s ↓*P* ↓Q_s

Law of Supply expressed as an upward-sloping curve:

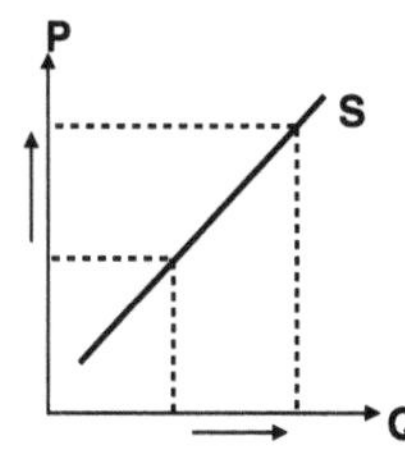

2b. Just as with demand, it is important to distinguish between a shift in supply (a shift of the entire supply curve) and a movement along a supply curve (a change in the quantity supplied due to a change in price). (80-83)

Don't get this confused on the exam!

ΔQ_s is caused only by a Δ in the P of the good itself.

ΔP ΔQ_s movement along a given S curve.

↑P ↑Qs: movement along a curve (e.g. from point A to point B).

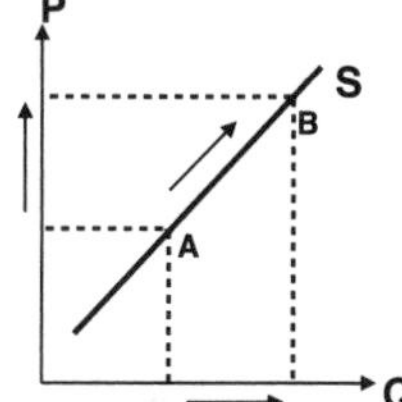

ΔS is caused only by Δs in the shift factors of S (not a Δ in the P of the good itself!)
Δ in shift factors of S ΔS shift of a S curve

Know what can cause an increase and decrease in supply:

↑*S* *Rightward Shift* ↓*S* *Leftward Shift*

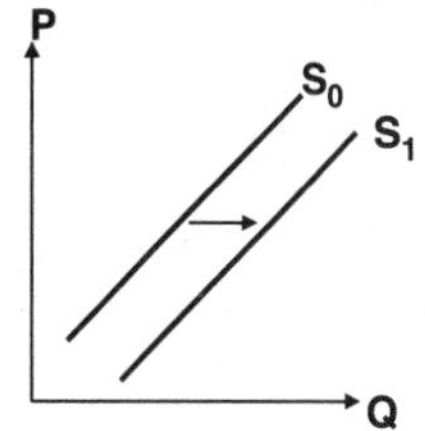

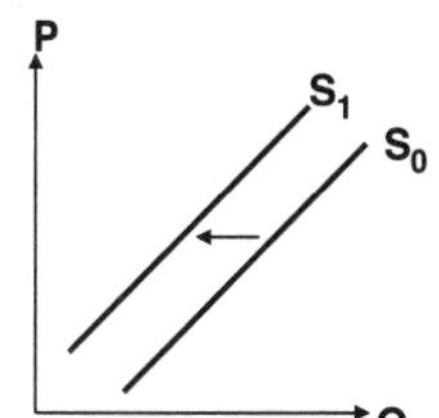

2c. To derive a supply curve from a supply table, plot each point on the supply table on a graph and connect the points. (83-84)

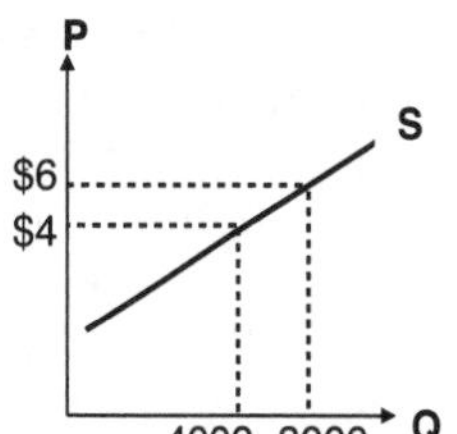

P	Q
$6	8000
$4	4000

2d. Market supply curves are the horizontal sum of all individual supply curves. At each price, the quantities supplied related to the various individual supply curves are summed together. (83-84)

3a. Demand and supply curves enable us to determine the equilibrium price and quantity. In addition, changes (shifts) in demand and supply curves enable us to predict the effect on the equilibrium price and quantity in a market. (87-89)

Anything other than price that affects demand or supply will shift the curves.

Know how a change in demand or supply affects the equilibrium price and quantity! Note:

$\uparrow D \Rightarrow \uparrow P;\ \uparrow Q$

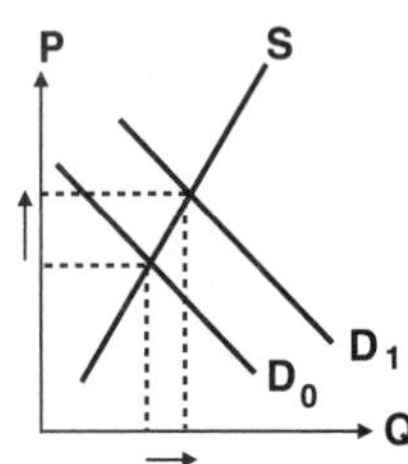

$\downarrow D \Rightarrow \downarrow P;\ \downarrow Q$

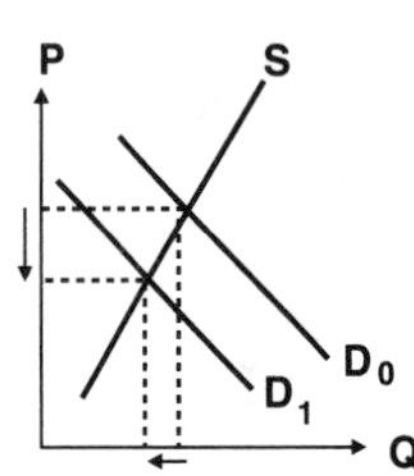

$\uparrow S \Rightarrow \downarrow P;\ \uparrow Q$

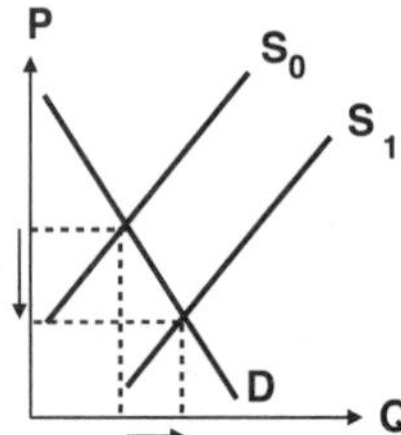

$\downarrow S \Rightarrow \uparrow P;\ \downarrow Q$

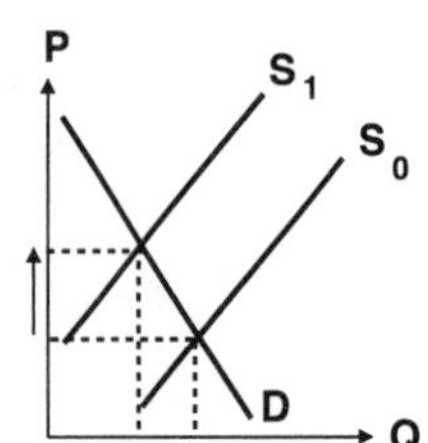

3b. Equilibrium is where quantity supplied equals quantity demanded: (84-87)

- If quantity demanded is greater than quantity supplied, prices tend to rise;
- If quantity supplied is greater than quantity demanded, prices tend to fall.
- Whenquantity demanded equals quantity supplied, prices have no tendency to change.

<u>*Know this!*</u>

If $Q_d > Q_s \Rightarrow$ Shortage $\Rightarrow$ *P* will $\uparrow$.
If $Q_s > Q_d \Rightarrow$ Surplus $\Rightarrow$ *P* will $\downarrow$.
If $Q_s = Q_d \Rightarrow$ Equilibrium $\Rightarrow$ no tendency for *P* to change (because there is neither a surplus nor a shortage).

<u>Shortage</u>	**<u>Surplus</u>**	**<u>Equilibrium</u>**
($Q_d > Q_s$)	($Q_s > Q_d$)	($Q_s = Q_d$)
P is below equilibrium	P is above equilibrium	

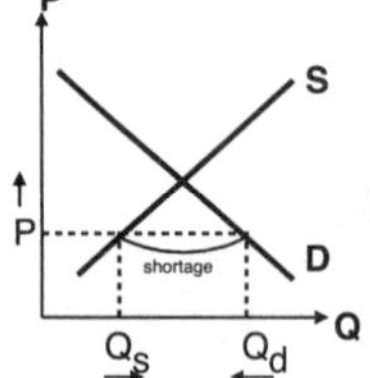

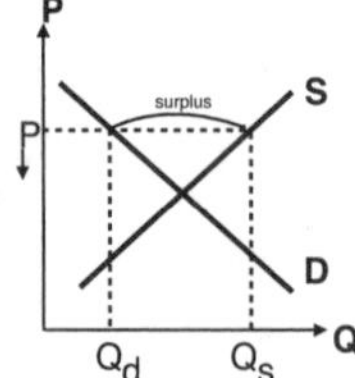

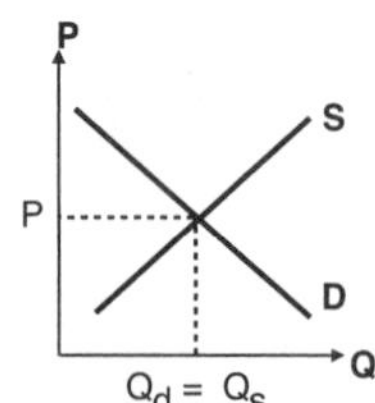

3c. Changes (shifts) in demand and supply are what cause changes in the price and the quantity traded in real-world markets. (87-93)

Shifts in both demand and supply can be tricky. But remember, simply locate the new point of intersection. When both curves shift, the effect on either price or quantity depends on the relative size of the shifts. Moreover, the effect on either price or quantity (one of them) will be certain, while the effect on the other will be uncertain. Note:

$\uparrow D$ and $\uparrow S \Rightarrow ?P;\ \uparrow Q$

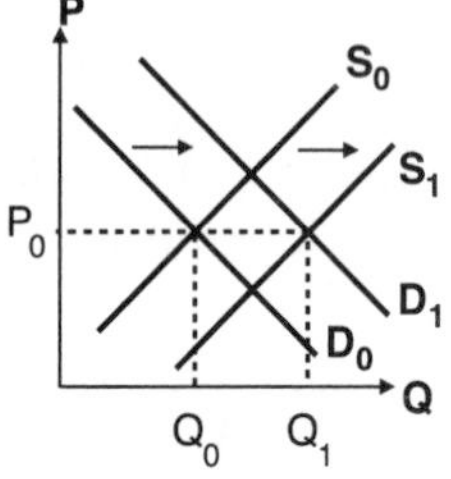

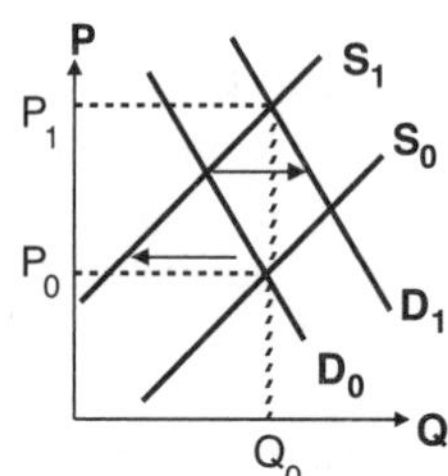

$\uparrow D$ and $\uparrow S \Rightarrow ?P;\ \uparrow Q$ *$\uparrow D$ and $\downarrow S \Rightarrow \uparrow P;\ ?Q$*

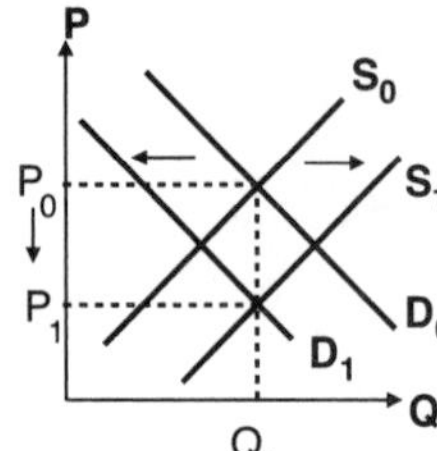

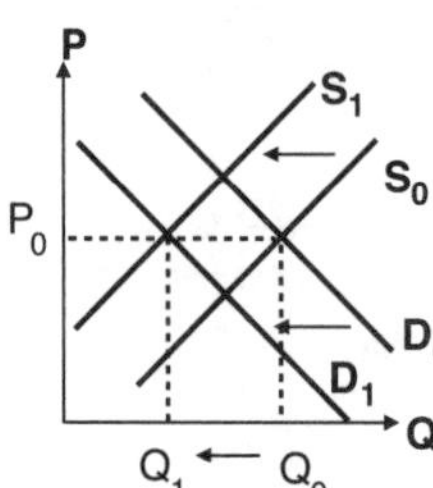

4a. The resulting changes in equilibrium price and quantity from shifts in the demand or supply curve are very important elements of the demand-supply model. Practice shifting the curves and ensure that you get the following results: (87-93)

$\uparrow D \Rightarrow \uparrow P \ \uparrow Q$
$\downarrow D \Rightarrow \downarrow P \ \downarrow Q$
$\uparrow S \Rightarrow \downarrow P \ \uparrow Q$
$\downarrow S \Rightarrow \uparrow P \ \downarrow Q$

4b. When Qd > Qs, prices tend to rise.
When Qd < Qs, prices tend to fall. (87-89)

See also, "Appendix A: Algebraic Representation of Supply, Demand, and Equilibrium."

MATCHING THE TERMS

Match the terms to their definitions

All of these key terms are found at the end of the chapter.

___ **1.** complements
___ **2.** demand
___ **3.** demand curve
___ **4.** equilibrium
___ **5.** equilibrium price
___ **6.** equilibrium quantity
___ **7.** excess demand
___ **8.** excess supply
___ **9.** inferior good
___ **10.** law of demand
___ **11.** law of supply
___ **12.** market demand curve
___ **13.** market supply curve
___ **14.** movement along a demand curve
___ **15.** movement along a supply curve
___ **16.** normal good
___ **17.** quantity demanded
___ **18.** quantity supplied
___ **19.** shift in demand
___ **20.** shift in supply
___ **21.** supply
___ **22.** supply curve

a. A specific amount that will be demanded per unit of time at a specific price, other things constant.
b. Curve that tells how much of a good will be bought at various prices.
c. The effect of a change in a nonprice factor on the supply curve.
d. Curve that tells how much of a good will be offered for sale at various prices.
e. The graphic representation of the effect of a change in price on the quantity supplied.
f. Quantity demanded rises as price falls, other things constant.
g. Quantity supplied rises as price rises, other things constant.
h. A schedule of quantities of a good that will be bought per unit of time at various prices, other things constant.
i. Quantity supplied is greater than quantity demanded.
j. A concept in which opposing dynamic forces cancel each other out.
k. The effect of a change in a nonprice factor on demand.
l. The price toward which the invisible hand (economic forces) drives the market.
m. The horizontal sum of all individual demand curves.
n. Amount bought and sold at the equilibrium price.
o. Quantity demanded is greater than quantity supplied.
p. The graphical representation of the effect of a change in price on the quantity demanded.
q. A specific amount that will be offered for sale per unit of time at a specific price.
r. A schedule of quantities a seller is willing to sell per unit of time at various prices, other things constant.
s. The demand for a good decreases as income increases.
t. Goods whose demand increases with an increase in income.
u. The horizontal sum of all individual supply curves.
v. An increase in the price of one good will reduce the quantity demanded of it and the good whose price remained fixed.

MULTIPLE CHOICE

Circle the one best answer for each of the following questions:

1. The law of demand states
   a. quantity demanded increases as price falls, other things constant.
   b. more of a good will be demanded the higher its price, other things constant.
   c. people always want more.
   d. you can't always get what you want at the price you want.

2. There are many more substitutes for good A than for good B.
   a. The demand curve for good B will likely shift out further.
   b. The demand curve for good B will likely be flatter.
   c. You can't say anything about the likely relative flatness of the demand curves.
   d. The demand curve for good A will likely be flatter.

3. If the weather gets very hot, what will most likely happen?
   a. The supply of air conditioners will increase.
   b. Quantity demanded of air conditioners will increase.
   c. Demand for air conditioners will increase.
   d. The quality demanded of air conditioners will increase.

4. If the price of air conditioners falls, there will be
   a. an increase in demand for air conditioners.
   b. an increase in the quantity demanded of air conditioners.
   c. an increase in the quantity supplied of air conditioners.
   d. a shift in the demand for air conditioners.

5. An increase in demand
   a. is reflected as a rightward (outward) shift of the demand curve.
   b. is caused by a decrease in price.
   c. means demanders are buying less at any price
   d. shifts the demand curve to the left (inward).

6. The demand curve will likely shift outward to the right if
   a. society's income falls.
   b. the price of a substitute good falls.
   c. the price of the good is expected to rise in the near future.
   d. the good goes out of style.

7. The difference between the quantity demanded and demand is
   a. the quantity demanded is associated with a whole set of prices, whereas demand is associated with a particular price.
   b. the quantity demanded is associated with a particular price, whereas demand is associated with a whole set of prices.
   c. the quantity demanded is the whole demand curve, whereas demand is a particular point along a demand curve.
   d. a change in the quantity demanded is reflected graphically as a shift of the demand curve, whereas a change in demand is reflected as movement along a given demand curve.

8. If there is a flood, what will most likely happen in the market for bottled water?
   a. Demand will increase.
   b. Demand will fall.
   c. Supply will increase.
   d. Supply will decrease.

9. The movement in the graph below from point A to point B represents

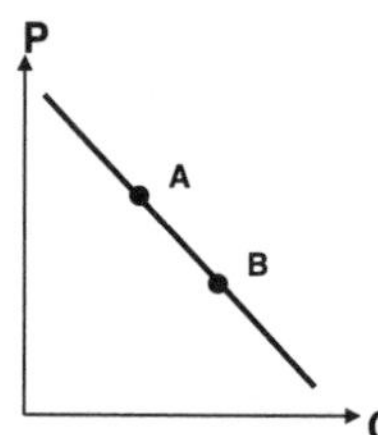

   a. an increase in demand.
   b. an increase in the quantity demanded.
   c. an increase in the quantity supplied.
   d. an increase in supply.

10. Using the standard axes, the demand curve associated with the following demand table is

Demand Table

P	Q
7	5
9	4
11	3

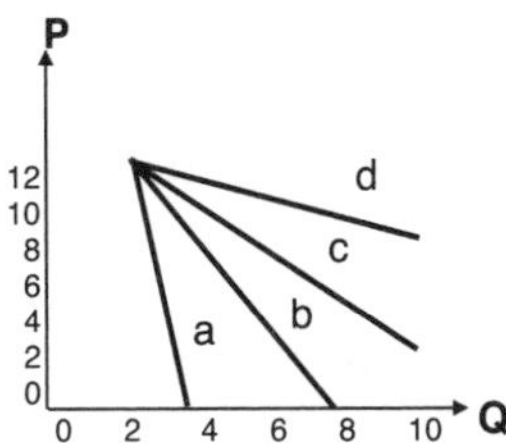

a. a
b. b
c. c
d. d

11. To derive a market demand curve from two individual demand curves
a. one adds the two demand curves horizontally.
b. one adds the two demand curves vertically.
c. one subtracts one demand curve from the other demand curve.
d. one adds the demand curves both horizontally and vertically.

12. The market demand curve will always
a. be unrelated to the individual demand curves and slope.
b. be steeper than the individual demand curves that make it up.
c. have the same slope as the individual demand curves that make it up.
d. be flatter than the individual demand curves that make it up.

13. The law of supply states that
a. quantity supplied increases as price increases, other things constant.
b. quantity supplied decreases as price increases, other things constant.
c. more of a good will be supplied the higher its price, other things changing proportionately.
d. less of a good will be supplied the higher its price, other things changing proportionately.

14. In the graph below, the arrow refers to

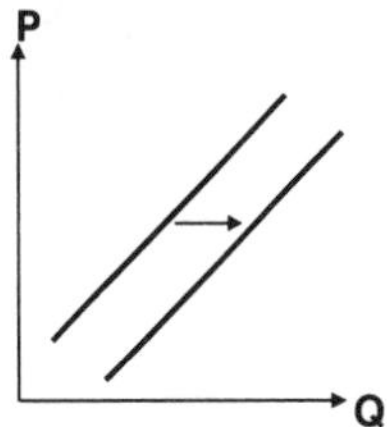

a. a shift in demand.
b. a shift in supply.
c. a change in the quantity demanded.
d. a change in the quantity supplied.

15. If there is an improvement in technology one would expect
a. a movement along the supply curve.
b. a shift upward (or to the left) of the supply curve.
c. a shift downward (or to the right) of the supply curve.
d. a movement down along the supply curve.

16. The market supply curve for the two individual supply curves S_1 and S_2 below would be

a. S_3.
b. S_4.
c. S_5.
d. S_6.

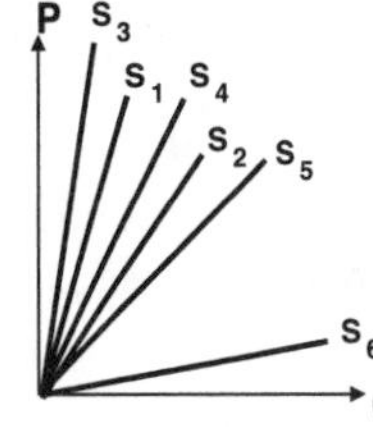

17. You're the supplier of a good and suddenly a number of your long-lost friends call you to buy your product. Your good is most likely
a. in excess supply.
b. in excess demand.
c. in equilibrium.
d. in both excess supply and demand.

18. At which point on the graph below will you expect the strongest downward pressure on prices?

a. a.
b. b.
c. c.
d. d.

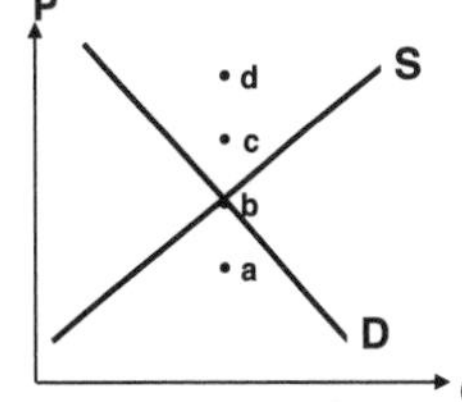

19. If at some price the quantity supplied exceeds the quantity demanded then:
a. a surplus (excess supply) exists and the price will fall over time as sellers competitively bid down the price.
b. a shortage (excess demand) exists and the price will rise over time as buyers competitively bid up the price.
c. the price is below equilibrium.
d. equilibrium will be reestablished as the demand curve shifts to the left.

20. If the price of a good
a. rises it is a response to a surplus (excess supply).
b. falls it is a response to a shortage (excess demand).
c. is below equilibrium then a shortage will be observed.
d. is below equilibrium then a surplus will be observed.

21. If the demand for a good increases you will expect
a. price to fall and quantity to rise.
b. price to rise and quantity to rise.
c. price to fall and quantity to fall.
d. price to rise and quantity to fall.

22. Compared to last year, fewer oranges are being purchased and the selling price has decreased. This could have been caused by
a. an increase in demand.
b. an increase in supply.
c. a decrease in demand.
d. a decrease in supply.

23. If demand and supply both increase, this will cause
a. an increase in the equilibrium quantity, but an uncertain effect on the equilibrium price.
b. an increase in the equilibrium price, but an uncertain effect on the equilibrium quantity.
c. an increase in the equilibrium price and quantity.
d. an decrease in the equilibrium price and quantity.

24. An increase in demand for a good will cause
a. excess demand (a shortage) before price changes.
b. movement down along the demand curve as price changes.
c. movement down along the supply curve as price changes.
d. a higher price and a smaller quantity traded in the market.

25. If a frost in Florida damages oranges, what will likely happen to the market for Florida oranges?
a. Demand will increase.
b. Demand will fall.
c. Supply will increase.
d. Supply will decrease.

26. Assume that the cost of shipping automobiles from Canada to Japan decreases. What will likely happen to the equilibrium price and quantity of cars made in Canada and sold in Japan?
a. The price will rise, and quantity will fall.
b. Both price and quantity will rise.
c. The price will fall, and quantity will rise.
d. The price will fall, what happens to quantity is not clear.

27. What will likely happen to the price and quantity of cricket bats in Trinidad as interest in cricket dwindles following the dismal performance of the national cricket team, while at the same time taxes are repealed on producing cricket bats?
a. The price will decrease, but what happens to quantity is not clear.
b. The price will decrease, and quantity will increase.
c. The price will increase, but what happens to quantity is not clear.
d. It is not clear what happens to either price or quantity.

28. If a frost hits the Florida orange orchards,
a. demand falls causing equilibrium price and quantity to fall.
b. demand rises causing equilibrium price and quantity to rise.
c. supply falls causing equilibrium price to rise and quantity to fall.
d. Supply rises causing equilibrium price to fall and quantity to rise.

SHORT-ANSWER QUESTIONS

1. What is the law of demand?

2. What does the law of supply say that most individuals would do if their wage increased? Explain the importance of substitution in this decision.

3. Demonstrate graphically a shift in demand.

4. Demonstrate graphically a movement along a demand curve.

5. Draw a demand curve from the following demand table.

Demand Table

P	P
50	1
40	2
30	3
20	4

6. State the law of supply.

7. Demonstrate graphically the effect on the supply of Red Hot Chili Pepper CDs of a new technology that reduces the cost of producing Red Hot Chili Pepper CDs.

8. Demonstrate graphically the effect of a rise in the price of Red Hot Chili Pepper CDs on the quantity supplied.

9. Draw a supply curve from the following supply table.

Supply Table

Q	P
20	1
30	2
40	3
50	4

10. What are three things to note about supply and demand which help to explain how they interact to bring about equilibrium in a market?

11. Given the graph below, at what price is there no pressure on price to change? Why?

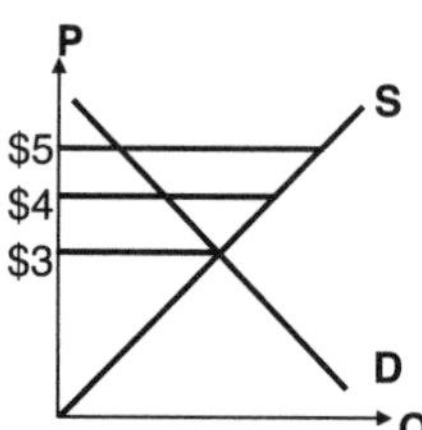

12. Demonstrate graphically what happens to the equilibrium price and quantity of M&Ms if they suddenly become more popular.

13. Demonstrate graphically what happens to the equilibrium price and quantity of oranges if a frost destroys 50 percent of the orange crop.

14. Demonstrate graphically what happens in the following situation: Income in Canada rose in the 1990s and more and more people began to buy luxury items such as caviar. However, about that same time, the dissolution of the Soviet Union threw suppliers of caviar from the Caspian Sea into a mire of bureaucracy, reducing their ability to export caviar. Market: Caviar sold in Canada.

PROBLEMS AND APPLICATIONS

1. Draw two linear curves on the same graph from the following table, one relating P with Q_1 and the other relating P with Q_2.

P	Q_1	Q_2
$30	60	100
35	70	90
40	80	80
45	90	70

a. Label the curve that is most likely a demand curve. Explain your choice.

b. Label the curve that is most likely a supply curve. Explain your choice.

c. What is equilibrium price and quantity? Choose points above and below that price and explain why each is not the equilibrium price.

2. Correct the following statements, if needed, so that the terms "demand," "quantity demanded," "supply," and "quantity supplied" are used correctly.

   a. As the price of pizza increases, consumers demand less pizza.

   b. Whenever the price of bicycles increases, the supply of bicycles increases.

   c. The price of electricity is cheaper in the northwestern part of the United States and therefore the demand for electricity is greater in the northwest.

   d. An increase in incomes of car buyers will increase the quantity demanded for cars.

   e. An increase in the quantity demanded of lobsters means consumers are willing and able to buy more lobsters at any original price.

   f. A decrease in the supply of frog legs means suppliers will provide fewer frog legs at any original price.

3. You are given the following individual demand tables for compact discs.

Price	Juan	Philippe	Ramone
$7	3	20	50
$10	2	10	40
$13	1	7	32
$16	0	5	26
$19	0	3	20
$22	0	0	14

   a. Determine the market demand table.

   b. Graph the individual and market demand curves.

   c. If the current market price is $13, what is the total market quantity demanded? What happens to total market quantity demanded if the price rises to $19 a disc?

   d. Say that a new popular 'N Sync compact disc hits the market which increases demand for compact discs by 25%. Show with a demand table what happens to the individual and market demand curves.

   Demonstrate graphically what happens to market demand.

4. The following table depicts the market supply and demand for oranges in the United States (in thousands of bushels).

Price	Quantity supplied	Quantity demanded
$15	7000	2000
$14	5500	3000
$13	4000	4000
$12	2500	5000
$11	1000	6000

a. Graph the market supply and demand for oranges.

b. What is the equilibrium price and quantity of oranges in the market? Why?

c. Suppose the price is $14. Would we observe a surplus (excess supply) or a shortage (excess demand)? If so, by how much? What could be expected to happen to the price over time? Why?

d. Suppose the price is $12. Would we observe a surplus or a shortage? If so, by how much? What could be expected to happen to the price over time? Why?

5. Draw a hypothetical demand and supply curve for cyber cafes — coffee houses with computers hooked up to the Internet with access to daily newspapers (among other things) at each table. Show how demand or supply is affected by the following:

a. A technological breakthrough lowers the cost of computers.

b. Consumers' income rises.

c. A per-hour fee is charged to coffee houses to use the Internet.

d. The price of newspapers in print rises.

e. Possible suppliers expect Cyber cafes to become more popular.

6. Use supply and demand curves to help you determine the impact that each of the following events has on the market for surfboards in Southern California.

a. Southern California experiences unusually high temperatures, sending an unusually large number of people to its beaches.

b. Large sharks are reported feeding near the beaches of Southern California.

c. Due to the large profits earned by surfboard producers there is a significant increase in the number of producers of surfboards.

d. There is a significant increase in the price of epoxy paint used to coat surfboards.

7. Use supply and demand curves to help you determine the impact that each of the following events has on the market for beef.

a. New genetic engineering technology enables ranchers to raise healthier, heavier cattle significantly reducing costs.

b. The CBS program "60 Minutes" reports on the unsanitary conditions in poultry processing plants that may increase the chances of consumers getting sick by eating chicken.

c. In addition to developing new genetic engineering technology, we have been mistaken in the past. Highly credible new research results report that abundant consumption of fatty red meats actually prolongs average life expectancy.

d. Consumers expect the price of beef to fall in the near future.

8. Suppose you are told that the price of Cadillacs has increased from last year as well as the number bought and sold. Is this an exception to the law of demand, or has there been a change in demand or supply that could account for this?

9. The following table depicts the market supply and demand for milk in the Canada.

a. Graph the market supply and demand for milk.

b. What is the equilibrium market price and quantity in the market?

Price in dollars per litre	Quantity of litres supplied in 1,000	Quantity of litres demanded in 1,000
$0.70	600	800
$0.90	620	720
$1.10	640	640
$1.30	660	560
$1.50	680	440

A1. The supply and demand equations for strawberries are given by $Qs = 10 + 5P$ and $Qd = 20 - 25P$ respectively, where P is price in dollars per litres, Qs is millions of litres of strawberries supplied, and Qd is millions of litres of strawberries demanded.

a. What is the equilibrium market price and quantity for strawberries in the market?

b. Suppose a new preservative is introduced that prevents more strawberries from rotting on their way from the farm to the store. As a result supply of strawberries increases by 20 million litres at every price. What effect does this have on market price and quantity sold?

c. Suppose it has been found that the spray used on cherry trees has ill effects on those who eat the cherries. As a result, the demand for strawberries increases by 10 million litres at every price. What effect does this have on market price for strawberries and quantity of strawberries sold?

A2. The supply and demand equations for roses are given by $Qs = -10 + 3P$ and $Qd = 20 - 2P$ respectively, where P is dollars per dozen roses and Q is dozens of roses in hundred thousands.

a. What is the equilibrium market price and quantity of roses sold?

b. Suppose the government decides to make it more affordable for individuals to be able to give roses to their significant others, and sets a price ceiling for roses at $4 a dozen. What is the likely result?

A BRAIN TEASER

1. The invention of a self-milking cow machine allows cows to milk themselves. Not only does this reduce the need for higher-cost human assistance in milking, but it also allows the cow to milk herself three times a day instead of two, leading to both a healthier cow and increased milk production.

   a. Show the effect of this innovation on the equilibrium quantity and price of milk.

   b. Show the likely effect on equilibrium price and quantity of apple juice (a substitute for milk).

POTENTIAL ESSAY QUESTIONS

You may also see essay questions similar to the "Problems & Applications" and "Brain Teaser" exercises.

1. Many university campuses sell parking permits to their students allowing them to park on campus in designated areas. Although most students complain about the relatively high cost of these parking permits, what annoys many students even more is that after having paid for their permits, vacant parking spaces in the designated lots are very difficult to find during much of the day. Many end up having to park off campus anyway, where permits are not required. Assuming the University is unable to build new parking facilities on campus due to insufficient funds, what recommendation might you make to remedy the problem of students with permits being unable to find places to park on campus?

2. Some products are considered to be "inferior" by most consumers. The key characteristic of inferior products is that the demand for these goods decreases as consumer incomes rise. List a few "inferior" goods.

3. Discuss how a change in demand or supply impacts a market equilibrium price and quantity.

ANSWERS

MATCHING

1-v; 2-h; 3-b; 4-j; 5-l; 6-n; 7-o; 8-i; 9-s; 10-f; 11-g; 12-m; 13-u; 14-p; 15-e; 16-t; 17-a; 18-q; 19-k; 20-c; 21-r; 22-a.

ANSWERS

MULTIPLE CHOICE

1. a As discussed on page 73, the correct answer is a. A possible answer is d, which is a restatement of the law of demand, but since the actual law was among the choices, and is more precise, a is the correct answer.

2. d An equal rise in price will cause individuals to switch to other goods more, the more substitutes there are. See page 73.

3. c As discussed on pages 74-76, it is important to distinguish between a change in the quantity demanded and a change in demand. Weather is a shift factor of demand, so demand, not quantity demanded, will increase. Supply will not increase; the quantity supplied will, however. Who knows what will happen to the quality demanded? We don't.

4. b As discussed on pages 74-76, when the price falls there is a movement along the demand curve which is expressed by saying the quantity demanded increased.

5. a As discussed on page 74, an increase in demand is expressed as an outward (or rightward) shift of the demand curve. It is caused by something else other than the price. It means people will buy more at any price or pay a higher price for a given quantity demanded.

6. c All of these are shift factors of demand. However, only c will increase demand and shift the demand curve to the right. See page 74.

7. b As is discussed on pages 74-76, especially page 75, b is the only correct response.

8. a A flood will likely bring about a significant increase in the demand for bottled water since a flood makes most other water undrinkable. A flood would be a shift factor of demand for bottled water. See pages 75-76.

9. b The curve slopes downward, so we can surmise that it is a demand curve; and the two points are on the demand curve, so the movement represents an increase in the quantity demanded, not an increase in demand. A shift in demand would be a shift of the entire curve. (See the figures on page 76 of the text.)

10. b This demand curve is the only demand curve that goes through all the points in the table. See page 77.

11. a As discussed in the text on page 77 (Figure 4-4), market demand curves are determined by adding individuals' demand curves horizontally.

12. d Since the market demand curve is arrived at by adding the individual demand curves horizontally, it will always be flatter. See page 77.

13. a As discussed on page 80, the law of supply is stated in a. The others either have the movement in the wrong direction or are not holding all other things constant.

14. b It is a shift in supply because the curve is upward sloping; and it's a shift of the entire curve, so it is not a movement along. See page 82 and Figure 4-6.

15. c As discussed on pages 81-82, technology is a shift factor of supply so it must be a shift of the supply curve. Since it is an improvement, it must be a shift rightward (or downward). (See also page 82, Figure 4-6)

16. c The market supply curve is determined by the horizontal addition of individual supply curves. See page 83, Figure 4-7.

17. b When there is excess demand, demanders start searching for new suppliers, as discussed on page 85.

18. d The greater the extent to which the quantity supplied exceeds the quantity demanded, the greater the pressure for the price to fall. See pages 85-86.

19. a As discussed on pages 85-86, this is a surplus (excess supply) when the price is above equilibrium. A surplus will motivate sellers to reduce price to rid themselves of their excess supplies. As the price falls, the quantity demand rises and the quantity supplied rises; demand and supply curves do *not* shift.

20. c As discussed on pages 85-87 whenever the price is below equilibrium, a shortage is observed, and the price rises.

21. b Since this statement says demand increases, it is the demand curve shifting. There is no change in the supply curve. Assuming an upward sloping supply curve, that means that price will rise and quantity will rise. See pages 87-88.

22. c Only a decrease in demand will result in a decrease in quantity and a decrease in price. See pages 87-88.

23. a An increase in demand has a tendency to increase price and increase the quantity. An increase in supply has a tendency to *decrease* the price and increase the quantity. So, on balance, we are certain of an increase in the equilibrium quantity, but we are uncertain about the impact on the price in the market. See page 92.

24. a An increase in demand causes the quantity demanded to exceed the quantity supplied creating excess demand (a shortage). This increases the price causing movement *up* along the demand and supply curves resulting in a *greater* quantity traded in the market. See pages 87-88.

25. d A frost will reduce the quantity of oranges available for sale at every price. Supply will decrease. See pages 87-88.

26. c The supply curve will shift out, market price will fall and the quantity will rise. See pages 87-88.

27. a Demand for cricket bats will fall, shifting the demand curve in, while the tax repeal will shift the supply curve out. Price will fall, and quantity may change depending on the relative shifts of the supply and demand curves.

28. c See P. 92

ANSWERS

SHORT-ANSWER QUESTIONS

1. The law of demand states that the quantity of a good demanded is inversely related to the good's price. When price goes up, quantity demanded goes down, other things constant. (73)

2. The law of supply states that quantity supplied rises as price rises; the quantity supplied falls as price falls. According to this law, most individuals would choose to supply a greater quantity of labour hours if their wage increased. That is, they will substitute work for leisure. (80)

3. A shift in demand is shown by a shift of the entire demand curve resulting from a change in a shift factor of demand as shown in the graph below. (76)

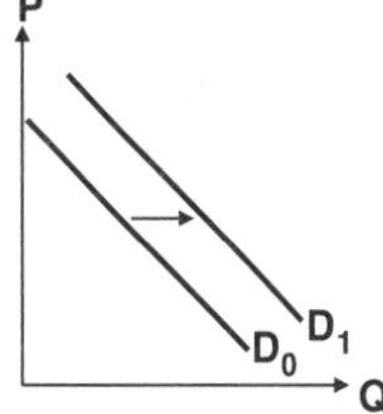

4. A movement along a demand curve is a change in quantity demanded resulting from a change in price as is shown in the graph below as a movement from *A* to *B*. (76)

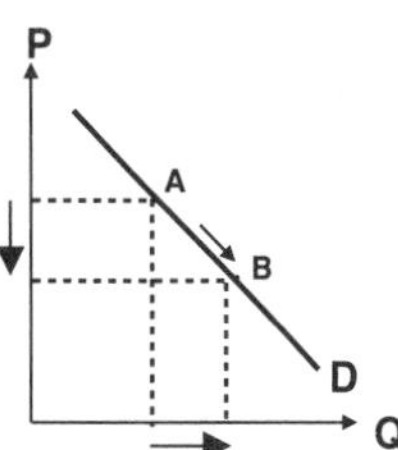

5. To derive a demand curve from a demand table, you plot each point on the demand table on a graph and connect the points. This is shown on the graph below. (76-77)

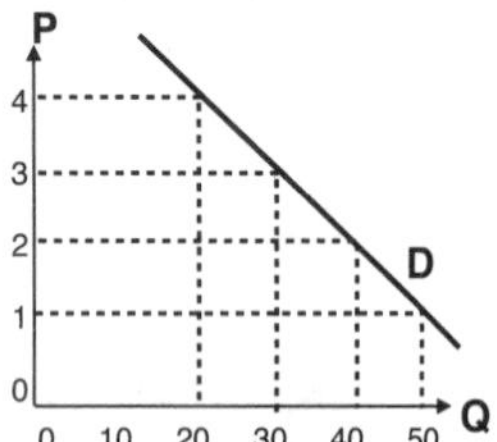

6. The law of supply states that the quantity supplied rises as price rises. Or alternatively: Quantity supplied falls as price falls. (80)

7. A new technology that reduces the cost of producing Red Hot Chili Pepper CDs will shift the entire supply curve to the right from S_0 to S_1, as shown in the graph below. (82)

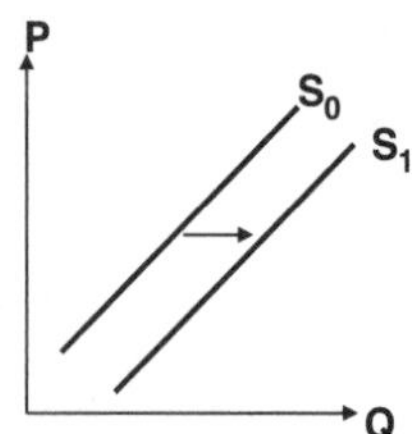

8. A rise in the price of Red Hot Chili Pepper CDs from P_0 to P_1 results in a movement up along a supply curve; quantity of Red Hot Chili Pepper CDs supplied will rise from Q_0 to Q_1 as shown in the graph below. (81-82)

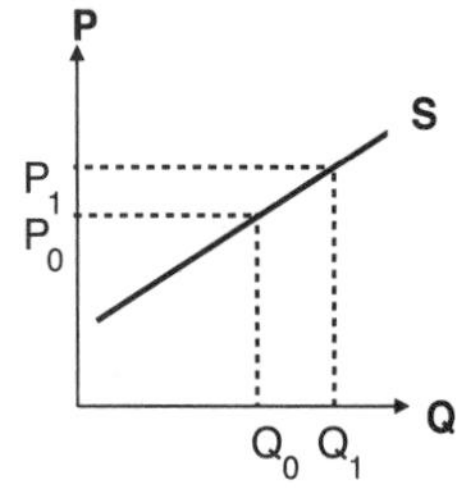

9. To derive a supply curve from a supply table, you plot each point on the supply table on a graph and connect the points. This is shown on the graph below. (84)

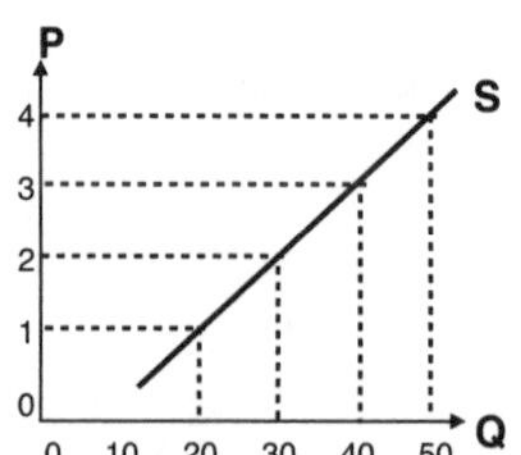

10. The first things to note is that when quantity demanded is greater than quantity supplied, prices tend to rise and when quantity supplied is greater than quantity demanded, prices tend to fall. Each case is demonstrated in the graph below. Price tends away from P_1 and P_2 and toward P_0.

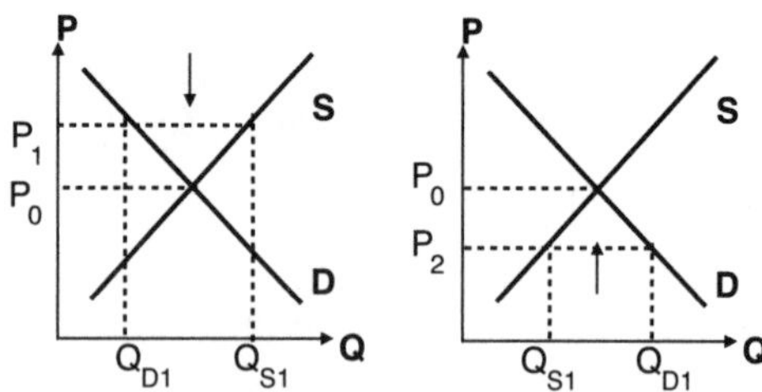

The second thing to note is that the larger the difference between quantity supplied and quantity demanded, the greater the pressure on prices to rise (if there is excess demand) or fall (if there is excess supply). This is demonstrated in the graph below. At P_2, the pressure for prices to fall toward P_0 is greater than the pressure at P_1 because excess supply is greater at P_2 compared to excess supply at P_1.

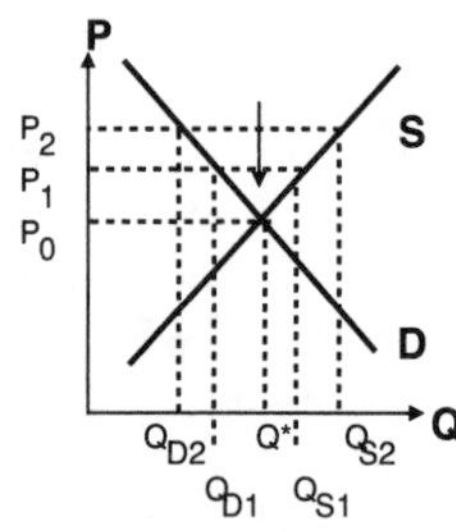

The third thing to note is that when quantity demanded equals quantity supplied, the market is in equilibrium. (85-87)

11. Because we are in equilibrium at $3 there is no pressure to change at this price. At the other prices, surpluses exist putting downward pressure on price. (96-97)

12. Increasing popularity of M&Ms means that at every price, more M&Ms are demanded. The demand curve shifts out to D1, and both equilibrium price and quantity rise to P1 and Q1 respectively. (87-88)

13. A frost damaging oranges means that at every price, suppliers are willing to supply fewer oranges. The supply curve shifts to the left to S1, and equilibrium price rises to P1, and quantity falls to Q1. (90-93)

14. The demand curve for Russian caviar shifts out; the supply shifts in; the price rises substantially. What happens to quantity depends upon the relative sizes of the shifts. (90)

ANSWERS

PROBLEMS AND APPLICATIONS

1. The linear curves are shown on the right. (77, 82)

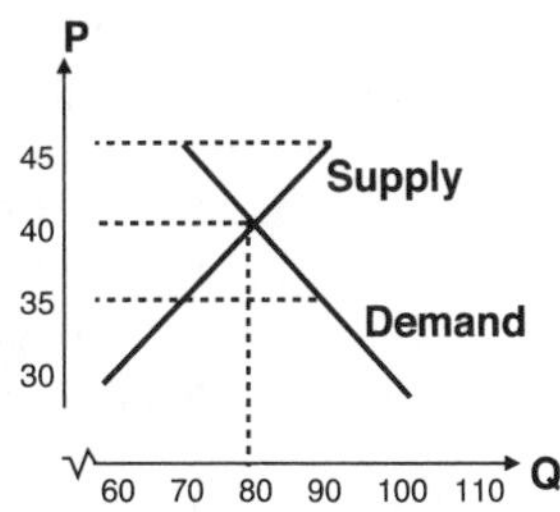

   a. As shown in the graph, the downward sloping curve is a demand curve. We deduce this from the law of demand: quantity demanded rises (falls) as the price decreases (increases). (74)

   b. As shown in the graph, the upward sloping curve is a supply curve. We deduce this from the law of supply: quantity supplied rises (falls) as the price rises (falls). (80-81)

   c. The equilibrium price and quantity are where the demand and supply curves intersect. This is at P = $40, Q = 80. At a price above $40, such as $45, quantity supplied exceeds quantity demanded and there is pressure for price to fall. At a price below $40, such as $35, quantity demanded exceeds quantity supplied and there is pressure for price to rise. (85-87)

2. **a.** As the price of pizza increases, the *quantity demanded* of pizza decreases. (74-76)

Note that a change in the price of an item will cause a change in the quantity demanded; not demand! A change in something else other than the price may cause a change in demand–such as a change in one of the shift factors of demand discussed in the textbook.

b. Whenever the price of bicycles increases, the *quantity supplied* also increases. (81-83)

Note that a change in the price will cause a change in the quantity supplied; not supply! A change in something else other than the price may cause a change in supply–such as a change in one of the shift factors of supply discussed in the textbook.

c. The price of electricity is cheaper in the northwestern part of the United States and therefore the *quantity demanded* of electricity is greater in the northwest. (74-76)

d. An increase in incomes of car buyers will increase the *demand* for cars. (74-76)

Notice that a change in a shift factor of demand, such as income, will change demand; not the quantity demanded!

e. An increase in the *demand* for lobsters means consumers are willing and able to buy more lobsters at any given price (whatever the current price is). (74-76)

In order for there to be an increase in the quantity demanded there would have to be a decrease in the price. Moreover, recall that an increase in demand is reflected as a rightward shift of the demand curve. Upon viewing a graph where the demand curve has shifted to the right you will see that more will be purchased at any given price.

f. This is a correct usage of the term "supply." Also note that a decrease in supply is reflected graphically as a leftward shift of the curve. Upon viewing a graph where the supply curve has shifted to the left you will see that less will be provided in the market at any given price. (81-83)

3. **a.** The market demand table is the summation of individual quantities demanded at each price as follows (77-79):

P	Q
$7	73
10	52
13	40
16	31
19	23
22	14

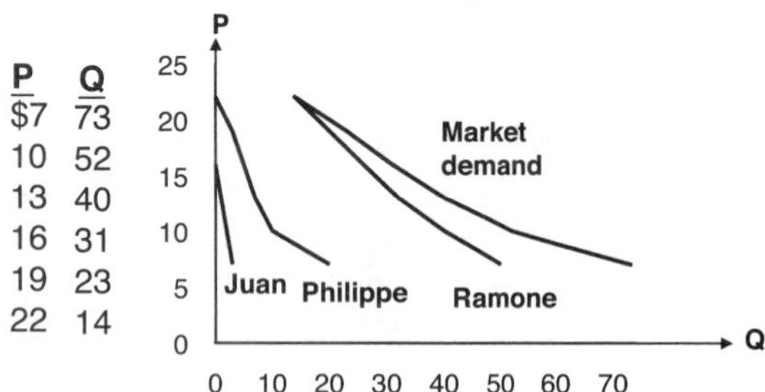

b. The individual and market demand curves are shown to the right of the demand table. (77-79)

c. At $13 a disc, total market quantity demanded is 40 discs. Total market quantity demanded falls to 23 when the price of discs rises to $19 per disc. (77-79)

d. Quantity demanded at each price rises by 25% for each individual and for the market as a whole. The new demand table is shown below. Graphically, both the individual and market demand curves shift to the right. The graph below shows the rightward shift in market demand. (77-79)

Price	Juan	Philippe	Ramone	Market
$7	3.75	25	62.50	91.25
$10	2.50	12.5	50	65
$13	1.25	8.75	40	50
$16	0	6.25	32.5	38.75
$19	0	3.75	20	28.75
$22	0	0	17.5	17.5

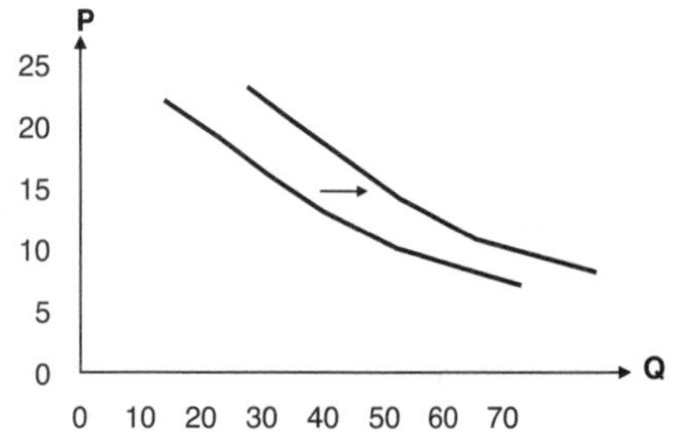

4. **a.** See the graph below. (77, 82)

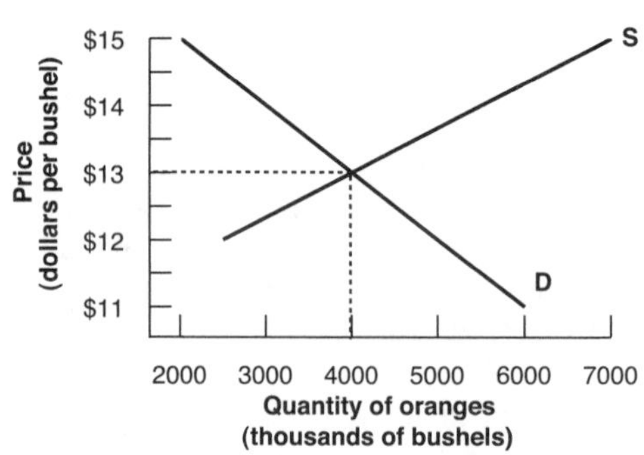

b. The equilibrium price is $13, the equilibrium quantity is 4000. This is an equilibrium because the quantity supplied equals the quantity demanded at this price. That is, there is neither a surplus (excess supply) nor a shortage (excess demand) and hence no tendency for the price to change. (85-87)

c. Because the quantity supplied exceeds the quantity demanded when the price is $14 per bushel, we would observe a surplus of 2,500 bushels (in thousands of bushels). We can expect the price of oranges per bushel to fall as sellers scramble to rid themselves of their excess supplies. (85-87)

d. Because the quantity demanded exceeds the quantity supplied at $12 per bushel, we would observe a shortage of 2,500 bushels (in thousands of bushels). We can expect the price of oranges per bushel to rise as some buyers competitively bid up the price just to get some oranges. (85-87)

5. A hypothetical market for cyber cafes shows an upward sloping supply curve, a downward sloping demand curve and an equilibrium price and quantity where the two curves intersect.

a. A technological breakthrough that lowers the cost of computers will shift the supply of cyber cafes to the right as shown in the graph below. (81-82)

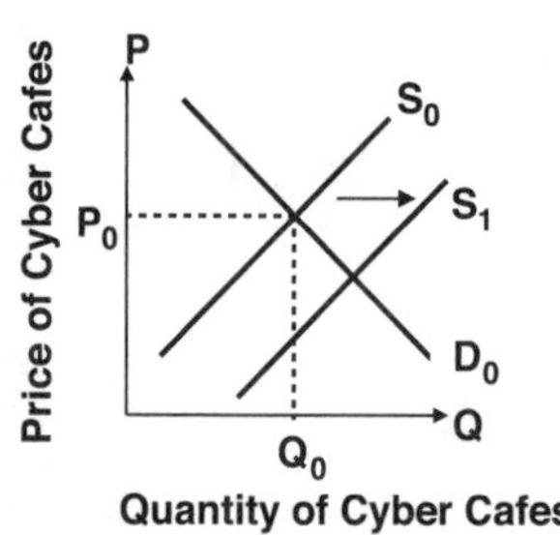

b. A rise in consumers' income will shift the demand for cyber cafes to the right as shown in the graph below. (75)

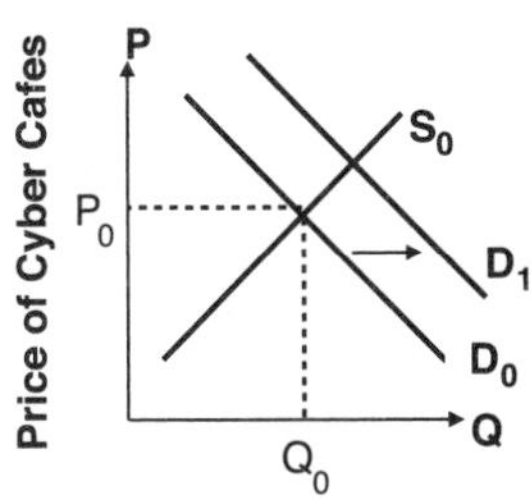

c. If a fee is charged to coffee houses to use the Internet, the supply of cyber cafes will shift to the left as shown below. (75)

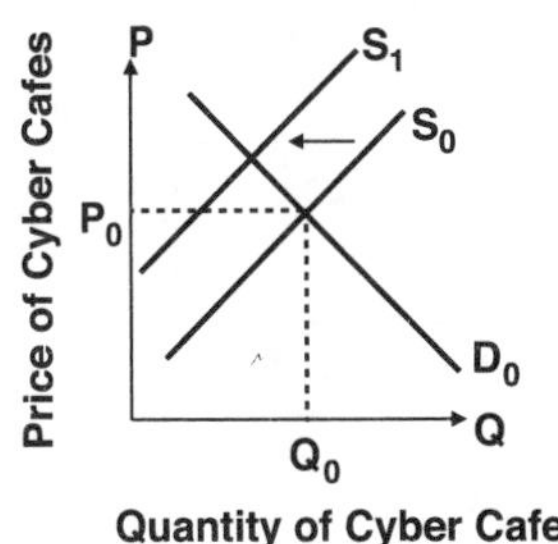

d. If the price of newspapers in print rises, the demand for cyber cafes will shift to the right as shown in the graph for answer (b). (75)

e. If possible suppliers expect cyber cafes to become more popular, the supply of cyber cafes will shift to the right as shown for answer (a). (81-82)

6 **a.** This will increase the demand for surfboards shifting the demand curve to the right. At the original price a temporary shortage would be observed putting upward pressure on price. We end up with a higher equilibrium price and a greater equilibrium quantity as illustrated in the graph below. (When dealing with a change in D or S curves, just remember to go from the initial point of intersection between the curves to the new point of intersection. The initial point of intersection will give you the initial equilibrium P and Q and the new point of intersection the new equilibrium P and Q. Then recall that if the price went up in the market, it was a response to a temporary shortage (excess demand). If the equilibrium price went down, then it was a response to a temporary surplus (excess supply). (87-93)

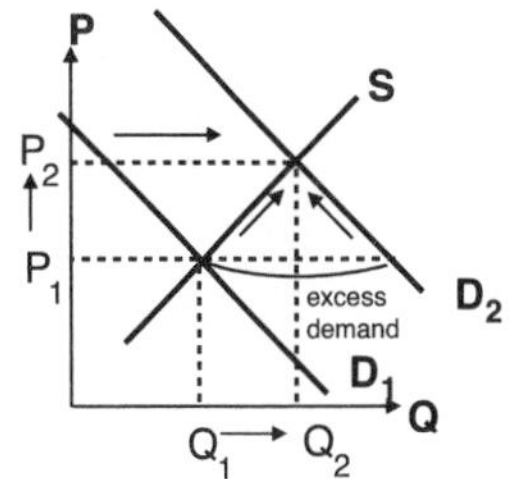

b. This would cause a decrease in the demand for surfboards shifting the demand curve to the left. At the original price a temporary surplus would be observed putting downward pressure on price. We end up with a lower equilibrium price and a lower equilibrium quantity as illustrated in the graph below. (87-93)

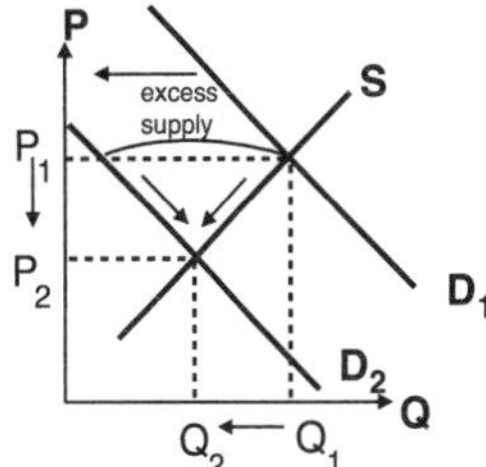

c. This would cause an increase in the supply of surfboards shifting the supply curve to the right. At the original price a temporary surplus would be observed putting downward pressure on price. We end up with a lower equilibrium price and a higher equilibrium quantity as illustrated in the graph below. (87-93)

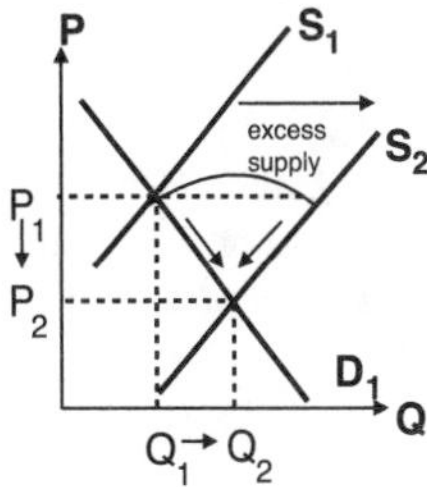

d. This would cause a decrease in the supply of surfboards shifting the supply curve to the left. At the original price a temporary shortage would be observed putting upward pressure on price. We end up with a higher equilibrium price and a lower equilibrium quantity as illustrated in the graph below. (87-93)

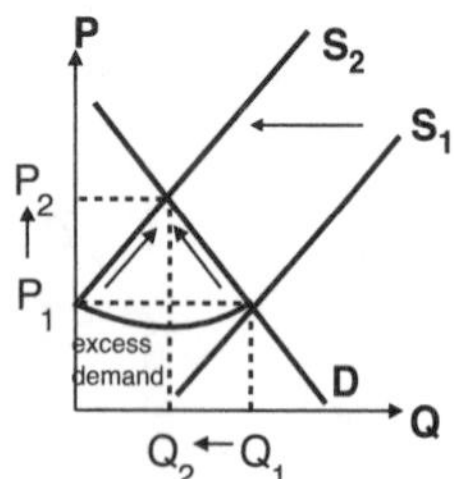

7. **a.** An increase in production technology will increase the supply of beef. The temporary surplus (excess supply) of beef at the original price will cause the market price to fall. Eventually we get a lower equilibrium price of beef and a greater amount bought and sold in the market. (87-93)

b. Chicken and beef are substitute goods–they can be used instead of each other. Therefore, this "60 Minutes" report will likely increase the demand for beef. The temporary shortage (excess demand) at the original price will cause the price to be competitively bid up. Eventually we observe a higher equilibrium price and a greater equilibrium quantity. (87-93)

c. The new development would increase the supply of beef while the reports of the health benefits of beef would increase the demand for beef. Quantity of beef sold would rise. The impact on equilibrium price depends upon the relative sizes of the shifts. (87-93)

d. Because people will postpone their purchases of beef until the price decreases this will reduce the demand for beef today. A decrease in demand is reflected as a leftward shift of the demand curve. The temporary excess supply (surplus) that is created at the original price puts downward pressure on the market price of beef. Eventually we get a lower equilibrium price and quantity. (87-93)

8. This is not an exception to the law of demand (there are very few exceptions). Instead, an increase in demand could account for a higher price and a greater amount bought and sold as is illustrated in the figure below. (87-93)

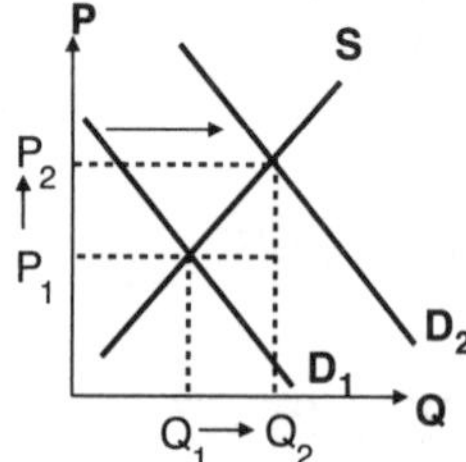

9. **a.** The market supply and demand for milk is graphed below.

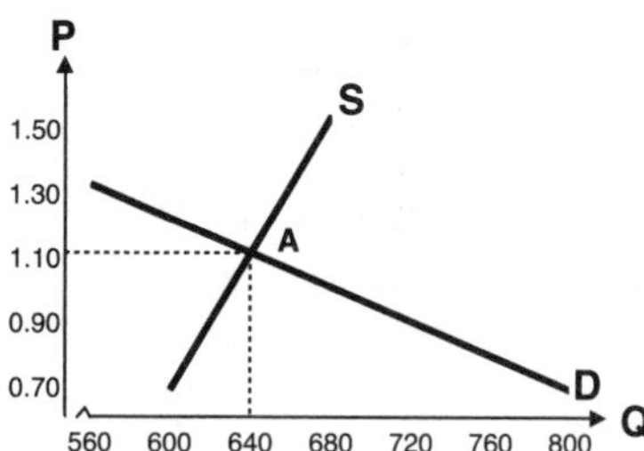

b. The equilibrium market price is $1.10 and equilibrium quantity in the market is 640 thousand gallons of milk. This is point A on the graph above. (87-93)

A1. a. Equating Qs to Qd and then solving for equilibrium price gives us $3 per quart. Substituting $3 into the demand and supply equations, we find that equilibrium quantity is 5 million quarts. (99-101)

b. Since supply increases by 20 million quarts, the new supply equation is $Qs = 10 + 5P$. Equating this with the demand equation, we find the new equilibrium price to be $1 per quart. Substituting into either the new supply equation or the demand equation we find that equilibrium quantity is 15 million quarts. (99-101)

c. With demand increasing, the new demand equation is $Qd = 30 - 5P$. Setting Qs equal to Qd and solving for price we find equilibrium price to be $4 per quart. Substituting this into either the new demand or the supply equation we find equilibrium quantity to be 10 million quarts. (99-101)

A2. a. Equating Qs and Qd, then solving gives equilibrium price $6 and quantity 8 hundred thousand dozen. (99-101)

b. If price ceiling is set at $4, Qs = 2, and Qd = 12; the resulting shortage is 10 hundred thousand dozen. (99-101)

ANSWERS

A BRAIN TEASER

1. a. This innovation will shift the supply curve to the right as shown in the graph on the left below. As a result, this creates excess supply and the equilibrium price falls while the equilibrium quantity rises. (81-82)

b. The market demand and supply for apple juice is shown below on the right. As a result of the fall in milk prices, the demand for apple juice shifts to the left. This creates excess supply of apple juice. The equilibrium price will fall. The equilibrium quantity will also fall. (87-93)

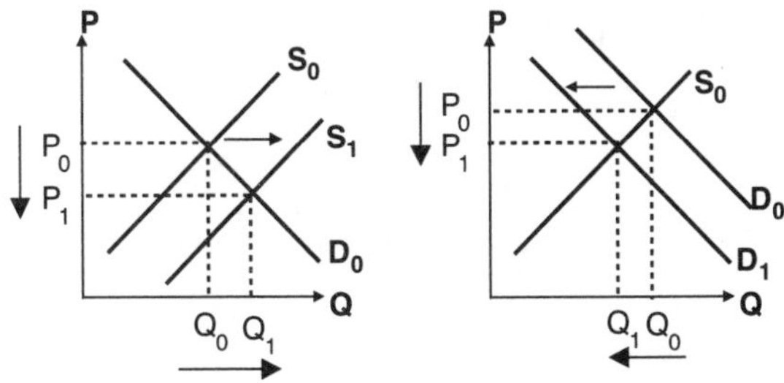

ANSWERS

POTENTIAL ESSAY QUESTIONS

The following are annotated answers. They indicate the general idea behind the answer.

1. The shortage of parking spaces implies that permit prices are below equilibrium. The price of a permit should be increased. At least with the purchase of a permit you could be reasonably certain that a space would be available.

2. Examples include lower grade liquor, wine, beer, "cheaper" grades of meat, and used clothes.

3. Suppose there is an increase in demand. The demand curve shifts out to the right, creating a temporary shortage (excess demand) at the original price. As a result, buyers competitively bid up the price. The quantity demanded falls (movement up along the demand curve toward the new point of intersection) and the quantity supplied rises (movement up along the supply curve toward the new point of intersection). Eventually, the price rises enough until the quantity demanded is once again equal to the quantity supplied. Because there is neither a shortage nor a surplus at this new point of intersection, the new market equilibrium price and quantity is obtained. The market equilibrium price and quantity will both increase as a result of an increase in demand. *You should be able to illustrate this graphically as well.*

DESCRIBING DEMAND AND SUPPLY: ELASTICITIES

CHAPTER AT A GLANCE

This chapter extends the discussion of demand and supply to introduce a concept that measures the magnitude by which consumers and producers alter their behavior as a result of a price change—the elasticity of demand and supply. The real-world applications of elasticities are vast and will extend our understanding of the behaviour of various economic entities.

Terms such as elastic, inelastic, unitary elastic, perfectly elastic and perfectly inelastic will be introduced. They represent the various extremes of responses that consumers and producers have to price changes. Elastic demand, for example, refers to consumers reacting significantly. If prices rise, consumers substantially reduce their consumption of this good. This behaviour is usually associated with luxury-type of goods—those that are not required for day-to-day living. Inelastic demand, on the other hand, refers to a small response to a price change and is usually associated with necessity-type of goods—goods that one would purchase regardless of the price, for example, prescription drugs, natural gas for heating homes and milk.

Elasticites are particularly important from a producer's point of view because, in order to increase revenues, a producer will have to know the elasticity of the good he/she is producing. Different elasticities yield different revenues when prices are altered. Other elasticities will also be introduced including income elasticity of demand and cross price elasticity of demand.

Be sure to know the different types of elasticities as well as how to calculate them.

This review is based upon the learning objectives that open the chapter.

1. Elasticity is defined as percentage change in quantity divided by percentage change in some variable that affects demand or supply (or quantity demanded or supplied). The most commonly used elasticity concept is price elasticity of demand. (104)

The price elasticity of demand measures the responsiveness of consumers to a price change. It equals the percentage change in quantity demanded divided by the percentage change in price.

2. To calculate elasticity over a range, economists use the mid-point formula. It avoids the end-point problem by using average prices and average quantities. (105-108)

This formula can be used to calculate the elasticity of demand and supply.

$$\textit{Elasticity} = \frac{\text{percentage change in quantity}}{\text{percentage change in price}}$$

$$\textit{Percentage change in quantity} = \frac{Q_2 - Q_1}{\frac{1}{2}(Q_1 + Q_2)}$$

$$\textit{Percentage change in price} = \frac{P_2 - P_1}{\frac{1}{2}(P_1 + P_2)}$$

3. Five elasticity terms are: elastic ($E > 1$); inelastic ($E < 1$); unit elastic ($E = 1$); perfectly elastic (E = infinity); and perfectly inelastic ($E = 0$). (110-111)

Consider the price elasticity of demand for a good.

- *An elastic demand for a good means buyers are relatively responsive to a price change (the percentage change in the quantity demanded is greater than the percentage change in the price).*
- *An inelastic demand for a good means buyers are relatively unresponsive to a price change (the percentage change in the quantity demanded is less than the percentage change in the price).*
- *When the demand for an item is unit elastic, buyers are neither relatively responsive nor unresponsive—(the percentage change in the quantity demanded equals the percentage change in the price).*
- *A perfectly elastic demand curve is a horizontal line.*
- *A perfectly inelastic demand curve is a vertical line, indicating there is no change in the quantity demanded given a change in the price.*

4. The more substitutes, the more elastic the demand and the more elastic the supply. (111-112)

The number of substitutes a good has is affected by several factors. Four of the most important determinants of substitutability that give rise to a greater elasticity of demand for a good are:

- *The larger the time interval considered, or the longer the run.*
- *The less the good is considered a necessity.*
- *The more narrowly (specifically) the good is defined. (This is because the more specifically the good is defined, the greater the number of substitutes.)*
- *The greater the expenditure is relative to one's income.*

5. With elastic demands a rise in price decreases total revenue. With inelastic demands a rise in price increases total revenue. (113-115)

Therefore, firms have a strong incentive to separate out people with a more inelastic demand and charge them a higher price.

6. Income elasticity of demand shows the responsiveness of demand to changes in income. Cross-price elasticity shows the responsiveness of demand to changes in prices of other goods. (116-120)

Income elasticity of demand equals the percentage change in quantity demanded divided by the percentage change in income.

Normal goods have income elasticities greater than zero while inferior goods have negative income elasticities. Moreover, luxuries have an income elasticity greater than 1 while necessities have an income elasticity less than 1 (but still positive).

Cross-price elasticity of demand equals the percentage change in quantity demanded divided by the percentage change in the price of another good. Substitutes have positive cross-price elasticities; complements have negative cross-price elasticities.

7. The price elasticity of supply measures the responsiveness of firms to a price change. It equals the percentage change in quantity supplied divided by the percentage change in price. (121-122)

- An inelastic supply means that the quantity supplied does not change much with a change in price.
- An elastic supply means that quantity supplied changes by a larger percentage than the percentage change in price.
- The most important factor influencing elasticity of supply is time – the greater the amount of time under consideration, the greater the elasticity of supply (this is because the greater the amount of time one has to react to a price change, the greater the ability of sellers to respond.)

8. Figure 5-8 reviews the effect of shifts in demand and supply with various elasticities. (122-123)

Knowledge of elasticity enables us to determine to what extent there will be a change in the equilibrium quantity and the equilibrium price given a change in demand and supply. For example, if demand is highly inelastic and supply shifts in to the left, the price rises significantly while the quantity hardly decreases at all.

MATCHING THE TERMS

Match the terms to their definitions

All of these key terms are found at the end of the chapter.

___ 1. complements
___ 2. cross-price elasticity of demand
___ 3. elastic
___ 4. income elasticity of demand
___ 5. income inelastic normal demand
___ 6. inelastic
___ 7. inferior goods
___ 8. law of demand
___ 9. normal goods
___ 10. perfectly elastic
___ 11. perfectly inelastic
___ 12. price elasticity of demand
___ 13. price elasticity of supply
___ 14. substitutes
___ 15. unit elastic

a. A measure of the percent change in the quantity demanded divided by the percent change in the price of that good.
b. Goods whose consumption decreases when income increases.
c. Goods that can be used in place of one another.
d. Goods that are used in conjunction with other goods.
e. Goods whose consumption increases with an increase in income.
f. Quantity responds enormously to changes in price. E_d = infinity.
g. The percent change in quantity is greater than the percentage change in price. $E_d > 1$.
h. The percent change in quantity is less than the percentage change in price. $E_d < 1$.
i. A good that has an income elasticity less than one.
j. The percentage change in quantity is equal to the percentage change in price. $E_d = 1$.
k. Quantity does not respond at all to changes in price. $E_d = 0$.
l. The percentage change in quantity demanded divided by percentage change in income.
m. The percentage change in quantity demanded divided by the percentage change in the price of a related good.
n. Quantity demanded is inversely related to price.
o. A good that has an income elasticity greater than one.
p. A measure of the percent change in the quantity supplied divided by the percent change in the price of that good.
q. When income rises, consumers respond by increasing their purchases less than proportionately.

MULTIPLE CHOICE

Circle the one best answer for each of the following questions:

1. The definition of price elasticity is
a. the change in quantity demanded over change in price.
b. the percentage change in quantity demanded divided by the percentage change in price.
c. the percentage change in price divided by the percentage change in quantity demanded.
d. change in price over the change in quantity demanded.

2. When the price of a good was raised from $10 to $11, the quantity demanded fell from 100 to 99. The price elasticity of demand is approximately
a. 0.1.
b. 1.
c. 10.
d. 100.

3. If a firm can sell 1,200 units at a price of $14 per unit and 2,000 units at a price of $10 per unit, we can conclude
a. the mid-point elasticity of demand for that good is 2.99.
b. that the demand for this good is inelastic.
c. that a price reduction would decrease the firm's total revenues.
d. there must be very few substitutes for this good.

4. As the manager of a hotel, you want to increase the number of occupancies by 12%. It has been determined that the price elasticity of demand for rooms in your hotel is 2. This information implies:
   a. the demand for rooms in your hotel is inelastic.
   b. if you lower your rates by 6% then you will increase the number of occupancies by 12%.
   c. if you were able to raise your rates your total revenue would rise.
   d. there must be few substitutes for your hotel services.

5. A rise in price has just increased total revenue. One would surmise that the demand for the firm's product is
   a. inelastic.
   b. elastic.
   c. unit elastic.
   d. none of the above.

6. As a manager, you have determined that the demand for your good is quite elastic. Therefore,
   a. increasing the price of your good will increase revenues.
   b. decreasing the price of your good will increase revenues.
   c. increasing the price of your good will have no impact on the quantity demanded.
   d. any change in your price will not impact revenues.

7. In reference to the graph below, which of the following is true?

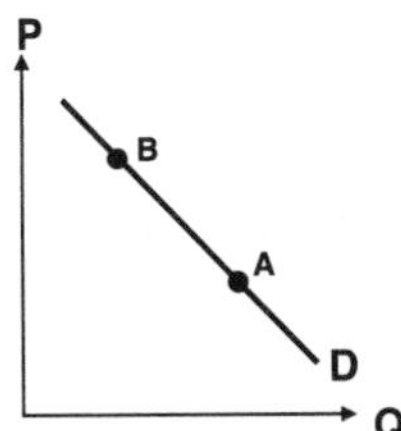

   a. Point B is more elastic than point A.
   b. Point A is more elastic than point B.
   c. Points A and B have equal elasticity.
   d. One cannot say anything about the elasticities without more information.

8. The elasticity of the curve below is

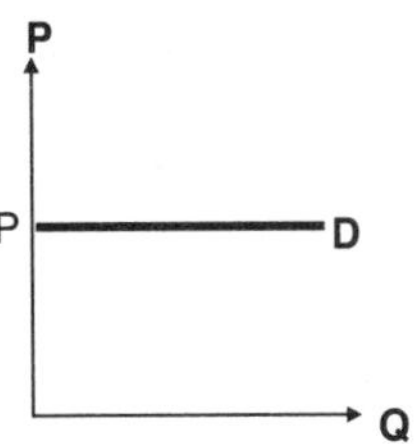

   a. perfectly elastic.
   b. perfectly inelastic.
   c. unit elastic.
   d. partially inelastic.

9. The more a good is a necessity
   a. the more elastic its demand curve.
   b. the more inelastic its demand curve.
   c. the more unit elastic its demand curve.
   d. the flatter the demand curve

10. The more specifically or narrowly a good is defined
   a. the more substitutes it has and therefore the more elastic its demand curve.
   b. the more substitutes it has and therefore the more inelastic its demand curve.
   c. the fewer substitutes it has and therefore the more inelastic its demand curve.
   d. the more unit elastic its demand curve.

11. In the long run, the elasticity of demand is generally
   a. more elastic than in the short run.
   b. less elastic than in the short run.
   c. of equal elasticity in the short run.
   d. unrelated to the elasticity in the short run.

12. When price changes from 4 to 5, output supplied changes from 50 to 60. The elasticity of supply is approximately
   a. .5.
   b. .8.
   c. 1.25.
   d. 7.25.

13. In the graph below, point A on the supply curve, S_1, is

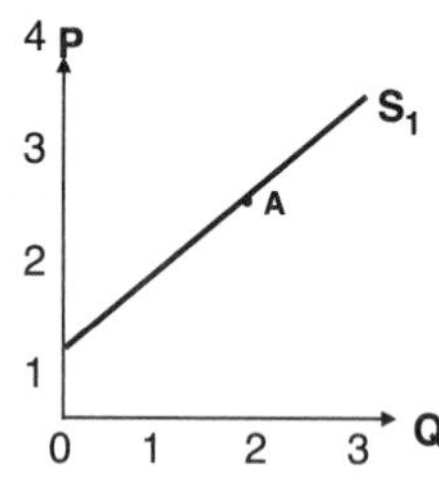

a. elastic.
b. inelastic.
c. unitary elastic.
d. unknown because one cannot say from the graph.

14. In the graph below, point A on the supply curve, S_1, is

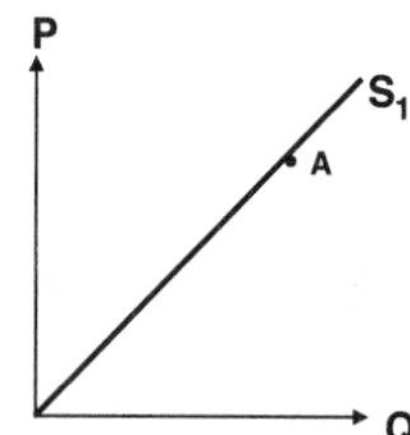

a. elastic.
b. inelastic.
c. unitary elastic.
d. unknown because one cannot say from the graph.

15. The supply curve in the graph below is

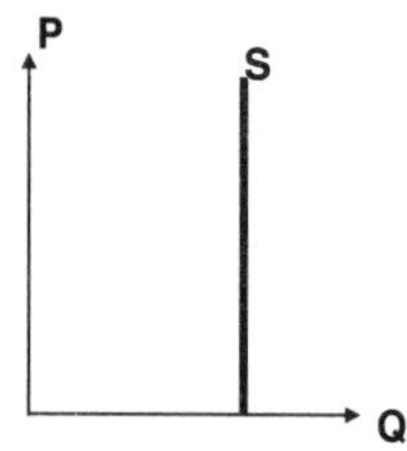

a. perfectly inelastic.
b. perfectly elastic.
c. unit elastic.
d. showing that its elasticity changes at various points.

16. A good whose consumption decreases when income increases is generally called
a. a normal good.
b. an inferior good.
c. a substitute good.
d. a complementary good.

17. Substitutes
a. are goods that are used in conjunction with each other.
b. have a negative income elasticity.
c. have a positive income elasticity.
d. have a positive cross-price elasticity.

18. Price discrimination is most likely to occur in markets
a. when all individuals have equal elasticities.
b. when some individuals have highly inelastic demands and some have highly elastic demands.
c. in which the elasticity of demand is 1.
d. in which the elasticity of demand is 0.

19. A significant price rise with virtually no change in quantity would most likely be caused by a
a. highly elastic demand and supply shifts to the right.
b. highly inelastic supply and a shift in demand to the right.
c. highly inelastic demand and supply shifts out.
d. highly elastic supply and demand shifts in.

20. A significant quantity rise with virtually no change in price would most likely be caused by a
a. highly elastic demand and supply shifts to the right.
b. highly inelastic supply and demand shifts to the right.
c. highly inelastic demand and supply shifts to the right.
d. highly elastic supply and demand shifts to the left.

21. A significant price decline with virtually no change in quantity would most likely be caused by a
   a. highly elastic demand and supply shifts to the right.
   b. highly inelastic supply and demand shifts to the right.
   c. highly inelastic demand and supply shifts out.
   d. highly elastic supply and demand shifts in.

22. A significant quantity decline with virtually no change in price would most likely be caused by a
   a. highly elastic demand and supply shifts to the right.
   b. highly inelastic supply and demand shifts to the left.
   c. highly inelastic demand and supply shifts to the right.
   d. highly elastic supply and demand shifts to the left.

SHORT-ANSWER QUESTIONS

1. Define the concepts *price elasticity of demand* and *price elasticity of supply.*

2. If the price of a good changes by 30 percent and quantity demanded for that same good remains unchanged, what is the price elasticity of demand for that good?

3. If price elasticity of supply is 4 and price changes by 10%, by what percent will quantity change?

4. Define the terms *elastic*, *inelastic* and *unit elastic* as applied to points on supply and demand curves.

5. What are the four main determinants of the price elasticity of demand?

6. What are the main determinants of the price elasticity of supply?

7. In each of the following cases, state what will be the effect of a rise in price on total revenue:

   a. Demand is inelastic.

b. Demand is elastic.

c. Demand is unitary elastic.

8. Define income elasticity of demand. How do the income elasticities of demand differ among normal goods, necessities and luxuries?

9. Define cross-price elasticity of demand.

10. What is a complementary good? What is a substitute good?

11. Explain how using the concept *elasticity* makes supply and demand analysis more useful.

PROBLEMS AND APPLICATIONS

1. Assume the price elasticity of demand for a good is 0.5 (after we take the absolute value—drop the negative sign). If there is a 10% decrease in the price, what would happen to the percentage change in the quantity demanded? What if the price was to rise by 15%?

2. Calculate the price elasticity for each of the following. State whether price elasticity of demand is elastic, unit elastic, or inelastic. Will revenue rise, decline, or stay the same with the given change in price?

a. The price of pens rises 5%; the quantity demanded falls 10%.

b. The price of a Boston Red Sox baseball game rises from $10 to $12 a game. The quantity of tickets sold falls from 160,000 tickets to 144,000.

c. The price of an economics textbook declines from $50 to $47.50. Quantity demanded rises from 1000 to 1075.

d. The price of water beds rises from $500 to $600. Quantity demanded falls from 100,000 to 80,000.

3. Suppose that in deciding what price to set for the video *Tarzan*, Disney decided to either charge $15.95 or $24.95. It estimated the demand to be quite elastic. What price did it most likely charge and why?

4. Calculate the price elasticity of the following products. State whether elasticity of supply is elastic, unit elastic, or inelastic.

   a. Cocoa Puffs: The price of a 14-oz. box of Cocoa Puffs rises 4 percent and the quantity supplied rises 15 percent.

   b. Japanese yen: The price of Japanese yen in terms of dollars rises from 100 yen per dollar to 110 yen per dollar. Its quantity supplied rises from 5,000,000 yen to 5,300,000 yen per year.

   c. Jansport backpacks: The price of Jansport backpacks falls from $30 a pack to $25 a pack. The quantity supplied falls from 150,000 to 125,000 per week.

5. Calculate the income elasticity of demand for the following goods. State whether each is a luxury, a necessity, or an inferior good.

   a. As average income per student rises from $10,000 to $12,000 a year, demand for ice cream cones increases from 30,000 cones to 37,500 cones per year.

   b. As income decreases from 120,000 to 100,000 French francs per year, demand for margarine increases from 50 to 60 pounds per year.

   c. As income decreases from $20,000 to $18,000 per year, demand for summer cottages in Vermont decreases from 80 to 75.

6. Determine the cross-price elasticity of demand for the following examples. Are they substitutes of complements? How do you know?

   a. The price of a pizza rises from $9 to $12, and the quantity demanded of Big Macs increases from 3 million to 4 million burgers per year.

   b. The price of hot dogs falls from $4 a pound to $2 a pound, and the quantity demanded of mustard increases from 15 tons to 20 tons per year.

7. What will likely happen to equilibrium price and quantity in the following cases?

   a. Demand is highly inelastic. The supply curve shifts out.

   b. Supply is highly inelastic. The demand curve shifts out.

   c. Supply is highly elastic. The demand curve shifts in.

A BRAIN TEASER

1. Farmers have a relatively inelastic demand for their crops. Suppose there is a bumper crop year (an unusually large harvest). Will farmers be happy or sad about the news there has been an unusually large amount of their crops produced this year? Why?

POTENTIAL ESSAY QUESTIONS

You may also see essay questions similar to the "Problems & Applications" and "Brain Teaser" exercises.

1. What can cause some products to exhibit an elastic demand while others have an inelastic demand?

2. Why are some businesses very interested in trying to determine which consumers have an elastic demand and which have an inelastic demand for the product being sold?

ANSWERS

MATCHING

1-d; 2-m; 3-g; 4-l; 5q; 6-h; 7-b; 8-n; 9-e; 10-f; 11-k; 12-a; 13-p; 14-c; 15j.

ANSWERS

MULTIPLE CHOICE

1. b See page 104.

2. a Substituting in the basic formula for elasticity gives .01/0.1 = 0.1. See page 105-106.

3. a Using the formula for the mid-point elasticity gives 2.99 (out of convention we always take the absolute value.) See pages 105-106.

4. b The price elasticity of demand of 2 means that for every 1% change in the price will occur a 2% change in the quantity demanded. To obtain a 12% increase in the quantity demanded means the price must fall by 6%. See the formula for elasticity on page 104.

5. a The revenue gain from the increase in price had to exceed the loss from the reduction in quantity, so the demand must be inelastic. See pages 113-115.

6. b When a good is price elastic then a price decrease will result in a proportionately larger increase in the quantity demanded and revenues rise. See pages 113-115.

7. a The elasticity changes along a straight line demand curve from highly elastic to highly inelastic. See page 110.

8. a A horizontal demand curve is perfectly elastic because the percentage change in quantity is infinite. See Figure 5-2 on page 109.

9. b Necessities tend to have few substitutes and the fewer the substitutes, the more inelastic the demand curve. See pages 111-112.

10. a The more specifically or narrowly a good is defined, the more substitutes it tends to have. See pages 111-112.

11. a The greater the time period under consideration, the greater the possibility for substitution. See pages 111-112.

12. b Elasticity of supply is the percent change in quantity divided by the percent change in price: 20% / 25% = 0.8. See page 121.

13. a You can either calculate the elasticity (percent change in quantity divided by the percent change in price) or you can use the trick in the Knowing The Tools Box (any straight line supply curve that intersects the vertical axis is elastic). See page 112.

14. c You can either calculate the elasticity (percentage change in quantity divided by the percent change in price) or you can use the trick in the Knowing the Tools Box (any straight line supply curve going through the origin will have unitary elasticity.) See page 112.

15. a For a vertical supply curve the percent change in quantity becomes zero, so the elasticity becomes zero, making it perfectly inelastic. (109)

16. b See the definition of an inferior good on page 117.

17. d When the price of a good increases and this increases the demand for its substitute, then the cross-price elasticity of demand is positive. See pages 118-119.

18. b Price discrimination requires separating out consumers by their elasticities and charging more to individuals who have inelastic demands. See page 114-116.

19. b Since price rose significantly while quantity remained virtually unchanged either demand or supply is inelastic. Since price rose, either demand shifted out or supply shifted in. See pages 122-123.

20. a Since quantity rose significantly while price remained unchanged either demand or supply is elastic. Since quantity rose, either demand shifted out or supply shifted out. See pages 122-123.

21. c Since price declined significantly while quantity remained unchanged either demand or supply is inelastic. Since price declined, either demand shifted in or supply shifted out. See pages 122-123.

22. d Since quantity declined significantly while price remained unchanged either demand or supply elastic. Since quantity declined, either demand shifted in or supply shifted in. See pages 122-123.

ANSWERS

SHORT-ANSWER QUESTIONS

1. *Price elasticity of demand* is the percentage change in quantity demanded divided by the percentage change in price. *Price elasticity of supply* is the percentage change in quantity supplied divided by the percentage change in price. (114; 121)

2. Price elasticity of demand is the percentage change in quantity demanded divided by the percentage change in price. Since the quantity demanded has not changed, the price elasticity of demand is zero. In other words, demand is perfectly inelastic. (111)

3. Price elasticity of supply is the percentage change in quantity supplied divided by the percentage change in price. Thus, if the elasticity of supply is 4 and price changes by 10%, quantity supplied will change by 40%. (121)

4. For elastic points, the percentage change in quantity is greater than the percentage change in price. For inelastic points the percentage change in quantity is less than the percentage change in price. For unit elastic points the percentage change in quantity is equal to the percentage change in price. (111)

5. The four main determinants of price elasticity of demand are (1) the time interval considered, (2) whether the good is a necessity or a luxury, (3) how specifically the good is defined, and (4) its percentage of one's total expenditures relative to one's income. The larger the time interval, the more elastic is demand. The less a good is a necessity, the more elastic is demand. The more specifically a good is defined, the more elastic is demand. The greater a percentage of one's expenditures, the more elastic. (111-112)

6. Price elasticity of supply essentially depends on the time period considered: the longer the time period, the more elastic the supply curve, because there are more options for change. Also, the easier it is to substitute a good, the more elastic the supply curve will be. (121-122)

7. **a.** If demand is inelastic the percent fall in quantity demanded will be less than the percent rise in price, so a rise in price will increase total revenue. (113-114)

b. If demand is elastic, the percent fall in quantity demanded will be greater than the percent rise in price, so a rise in price will reduce total revenue. (113-114)

c. If demand is unit elastic, the percent fall in quantity demanded will equal the percent rise in price, so a rise in price will not change total revenue. (113-114)

8. Income elasticity of demand is the percentage change in demand divided by the percentage change in income. Normal goods have positive income elasticities. Luxury goods have positive income elasticities greater than one, while necessities have positive income elasticities less than one. (116-118)

9. Cross-price elasticity of demand is the percentage change in quantity demanded of one good divided by the percentage change in the price of another good. (118-120)

10. A complementary good is a good whose consumption goes down when the price of the other good (for which it is a complement) goes up. Complements have negative cross-price elasticities. A substitute good is a good whose consumption goes up when the price of the other good (for which it is a substitute) goes up. Substitutes have positive cross-price elasticities. (119)

11. Knowledge of elasticity enables us to determine *to what extent* there will be a change in the equilibrium quantity and the equilibrium price given a change in demand and supply. (122-123)

ANSWERS

PROBLEMS AND APPLICATIONS

1. Given that the $E_d = 0.5$, and the price falls by 10% then the quantity demanded will rise by 5%. [The trick is to multiply the E_d coefficient (0.5), or number, by the percentage change in the price (10) to get the percentage change in the quantity demanded (5). But remember, the law of demand tells us that the quantity demanded moves in the opposite direction from the change in the price.] If the price was to rise by 15% then the quantity demanded would fall by 7.5% ($0.5 \times 15 = 7.5$). (104)

2. Price elasticity of demand is defined in your text as the percent change in quantity demanded divided by the percent change in price. Demand is elastic if the price elasticity is greater than one (always drop the negative sign—take the absolute value); a rise in price will lower total revenue. Demand is inelastic if the price elasticity is less than one; a rise in price will increase total revenue. Demand is unit elastic if the price elasticity is equal to one; a rise in price leaves total revenue unchanged. (For each of the following, we use the mid-point elasticity unless specifically noted.)
   - **a.** Price elasticity of demand is 10%/5% = 2. Since $2 > 1$, demand is elastic. Total revenue falls. (105-106, 115)
   - **b.** Price elasticity of demand is $|[(144{,}000 - 160{,}000)/152{,}000]/[(12-10)/11]| = 0.58$. Since $0.58 < 1$, demand is inelastic. Total revenue rises. (105-106, 114)
   - **c.** Price elasticity of demand is $|[(1075 - 1000)/1037.5]/[(47.5-50)/48.75]| = 1.41$. Since $1.41 > 1$, demand is elastic. Total revenue rises. (105-106, 114)
   - **d.** Price elasticity of demand is $|[(80{,}000 - 100{,}000)/90{,}000]/[(600-500)/550]| = 1.2$. Since $1.2 > 1$, demand is slightly elastic. Total revenue falls slightly. (105-106, 114)

3. It would charge the lower price, $15.95, because a lower price will increase total revenue when demand is elastic. (114)

4. **a.** Price elasticity of supply is 15%/4% = 3.75. Since $3.75 > 1$. Supply is elastic. (105-106)
   - **b.** Price elasticity of supply is $[(5{,}300{,}000 - 5{,}000{,}000)/5{,}150{,}000]/[(110-100)/105] = 0.61$. Since $0.61 < 1$, supply is inelastic. (105-106)
   - **c.** Price elasticity of supply is $[(150{,}000 - 125{,}000)/137{,}500]/[30-25/27.5] = 1$. Since $1 = 1$, supply is unit elastic. (105-106)

5. **a.** The income elasticity of demand is $[(37{,}500-30{,}000)/33{,}750]/[(12{,}000 - 10{,}000)/11{,}000] = 1.22$. Since $1.22 > 1$, ice cream cones are a luxury good. (116-118)
   - **b.** The income elasticity of demand is $[(60 - 50)/55]/[(100{,}000-120{,}000)/110{,}000] = -10$. Since $-1 < 0$, margarine is an inferior good. (116-118)
   - **c.** The income elasticity of demand is $[(75 - 80)/77.5]/[(18{,}000-20{,}000)/19{,}000] = 0.61$. Since $0 < 0.61 < 1$, summer cottages are a necessity. (116-118)

6. **a.** The cross-price elasticity of demand is $[(4{,}000{,}000-3{,}000{,}000)/3{,}500{,}000]/[(12 - 9)/10.5] = 1$. Since $1 > 0$, pizzas and Big Macs are substitutes. (118-120)
   - **b.** The cross-price elasticity of demand is $[(20 - 15)/17.5]/[(2-4)/3] = -0.43$. Since $-0.43 < 0$, hot dogs and mustard are complements. (118-120)

7. **a.** The price will fall considerably but quantity will not rise significantly, as shown in the graph (a) below. (122-123)

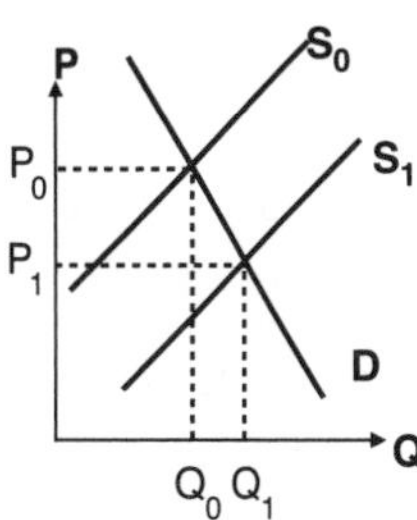

b. The price will rise considerably but quantity will not rise significantly, as shown in the graph (b) below. (122-123)

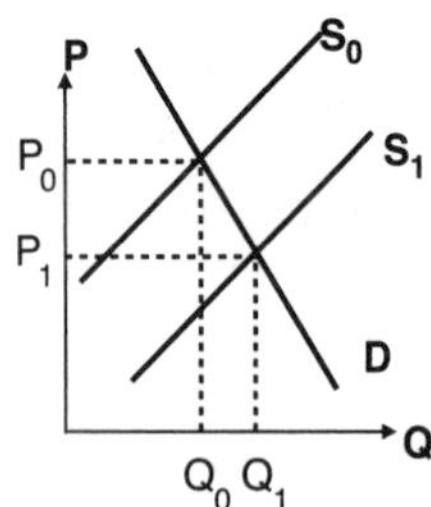

c. The quantity will fall considerably, but price will not fall significantly, as shown in the graph (c) below. (122-123)

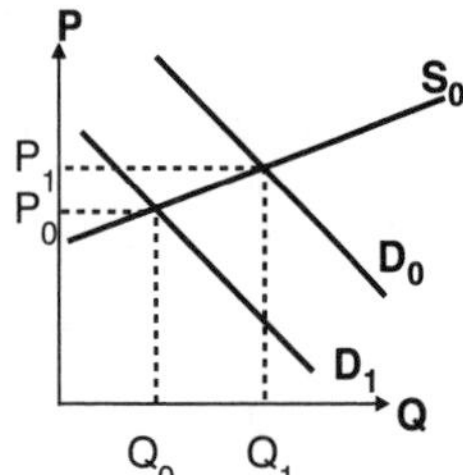

ANSWERS

A BRAIN TEASER

1. They will be sad. The bumper crop year will increase the supply of the crop and reduce the price significantly. A fall in the price given the inelastic demand will decrease total revenues—farmers' incomes. (122-123)

ANSWERS

POTENTIAL ESSAY QUESTIONS

The following are annotated answers. They indicate the general idea behind the answer.

1. As a general rule, the more substitutes a good has, the more elastic is its demand. The number of substitutes is, in turn, affected by the time interval under consideration, whether the good is considered a necessity or a luxury, the specificity with which the good is defined, and the importance of the good relative to one's income.

2. In order to maximize revenues firms will try to charge a higher price to those consumers that have a more inelastic demand (an increase in the price increases total revenue) and a lower price to those that have an elastic demand for the product.

USING DEMAND AND SUPPLY: TAXATION AND GOVERNMENT INTERVENTION

6

CHAPTER AT A GLANCE

This chapter expands on our discussion of elasticites from the previous chapter by introducing some important supply and demand applications, and, in particular, government intervention. Policy initiatives implemented by government are linked to specific goals that government is attempting to achieve or issues that it wishes to address. All are implemented within the context of the role that government plays within the economy. These roles are discussed in detail.

One of the most important applications of the elasticity concept pertains to the incidence of an excise tax, or who bares the burden of a government-imposed tax—consumers and/or producers. The burden of a tax will be determined by the elasticities of demand and supply. The impact of a tax on consumer and producer surpluses will also be explored.

If an economy is in equilibrium, external forces can come into play that alter demand and supply and bring the market back to equilibrium. But, there are many situations where the economy does not operate with market-determined prices. Government, at times, having their own agendas, may impose their will on the market economy to alter prices. This is done through the imposition of price floors (prices set above the equilibrium price) and price ceilings (prices set below the equilibrium prices).

Government intervention prevents the market from finding an equilibrium price and quantity and, therefore, creates distortions—price floors create surpluses and price ceilings create shortages.

This review is based upon the learning objectives that open the chapter.

1. There are six roles of government in a market economy: (128-132)

- Provide a stable set of institutions and rules.
  The government specifies "the rules of the game."

- Promote effective and workable competition.
  Know the different consequences associated with competition vs. monopoly power.

- Correct for externalities.
  Government attempts to restrict the production and consumption of negative externalities; while promoting the production and consumption of positive externalities.

- Ensure economic stability and growth.
  Government tries to ensure:
  Full employment
  Low inflation
  Economic growth (which increases the standard of living)

- Provide for public goods.
  Government provides public goods by collecting taxes from everyone to try to eliminate the free-rider problem.

- Adjust for undesired market results.
  Governments often attempt to redistribute income in a more "fair" manner through the use of taxes (and other methods). Know the difference between progressive, regressive, and proportional taxes. Government sometimes encourages merit (socially desirable) goods by subsidizing them, and discourages demerit (socially undesirable) goods or activities by taxing them. But, should government decide what is "good" or "bad" for us?

Government intervenes in the economy in an attempt to correct for "market failures." But just as the market can sometimes provide undesirable results, there is also government failure–government intervention that makes things worse.

2a. The cost of taxation to society includes the direct cost of the revenue paid to government, the loss of consumer and producer surplus caused by the tax, and the administrative costs of collecting the tax. (132-136)

Total cost to consumers and producers is more than the amount of the tax revenue. Refer to the graph below. Consumers pay rectangle B in tax revenue and also lose area C in consumer surplus. Producers pay area D in tax revenue and lose area E in producer surplus. The triangular area represented by areas C (lost consumer surplus) and E (lost producer surplus) represents a cost of taxation in excess of the revenue paid to government. It is lost consumer and producer surplus that is not gained by government. The loss of consumer and producer surplus from a tax is known as "deadweight loss." Graphically deadweight loss is shown by the "welfare loss triangle"—area C + E.

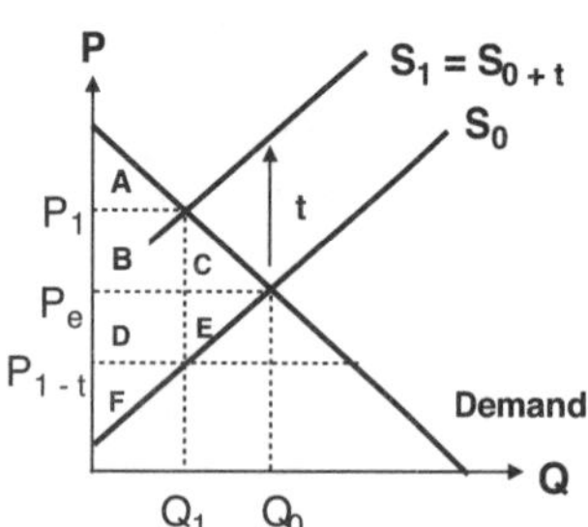

2b. The benefit principle of taxation states: individuals who receive the benefit of a good or service should pay the cost (opportunity cost) of the resources used to produce the good. In a market, that cost is represented by the price; for a pubic good, the cost is represented by the amount of the tax. (136-137)

The reasoning behind the benefit principle is that if you use it, you pay for it. For example, some people pay more gas taxes because they use the roads more.

2c. The ability-to-pay principle states: individuals who are most able to bear the burden of the tax should pay the tax. (137)

The reasoning behind the ability-to-pay principle is that the wealthy should pay more taxes because they can. There is much debate how a tax ought to be implemented if it is to be "fair."

3a. Tax burden is distributed by relative elasticities of supply and demand. (138-141)

The more inelastic one's relative supply and demand, the larger the burden of the tax one will bear.

The general rule about elasticities and tax burden is this: if demand is relatively more inelastic than supply, consumers will pay a higher percentage of the tax. If supply is relatively more inelastic than demand, suppliers will pay a higher share.

3b. A per unit tax levied on the supplier causes the costs of production to rise, resulting in the supply curve shifting to the left, thereby reducing quantity and raising the market price of the good or service. (138-140)

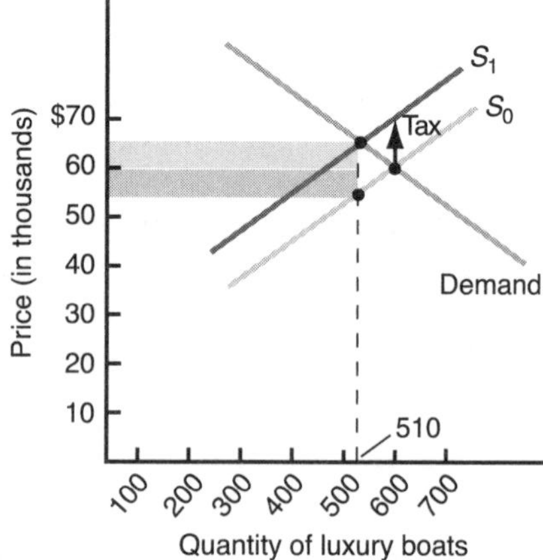

If demand is inelastic and supply is elastic, consumers bare a greater burden of the tax.

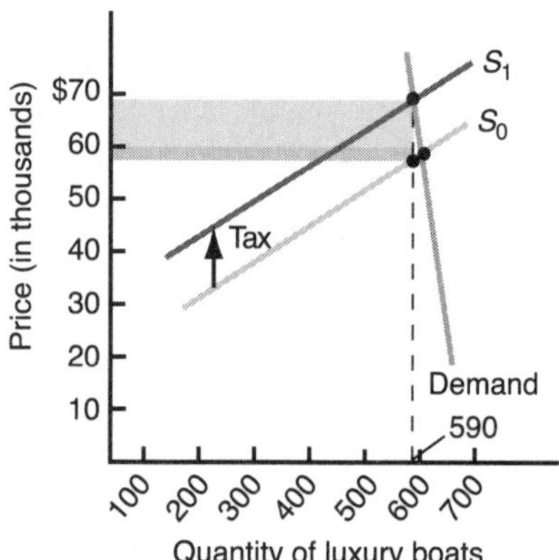

3c. The person who physically pays a tax is not necessarily the person who bears the burden of the tax. Who bears the burden of the tax (also know as tax incidence) depends upon who is best able to change their behavior in response to the tax, or who has the greater elasticity. (138-141)

4. Price ceilings cause shortages; price floors cause surpluses. (142-145)

A price ceiling is a legal price set by government below equilibrium. An example is rent controls. A price floor is a legal price set by government above equilibrium. An example is the minimum wage.

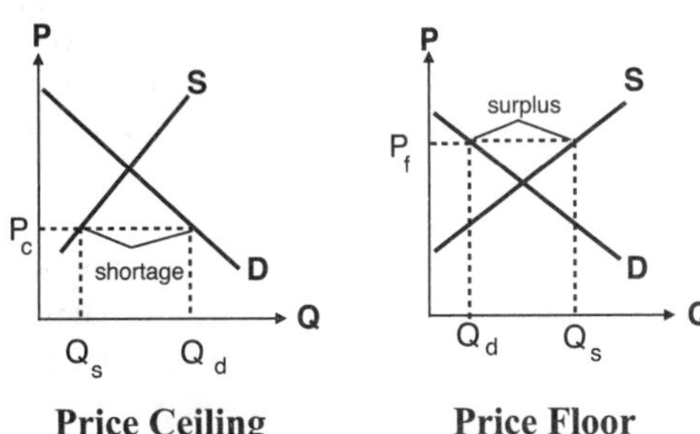

Price Ceiling **Price Floor**

5a. A price ceiling is in essence an implicit tax on producers and an implicit subsidy to consumers. (144-145)

Refer to the graph on the next page. With an effective price ceiling of P_1 the quantity supplied (and the amount consumed) falls from Q_e to Q_1. The welfare loss equals area C + E. This is the same effect as a tax. However, the loss of producer surplus, area D, is now transferred to consumers. It is as if government places a tax on suppliers and then gives that tax revenue to consumers when they consume the good.

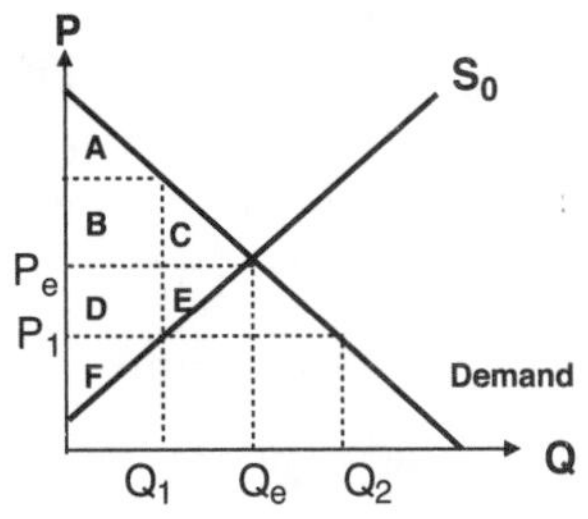

5b. Rent-seeking is an activity designed to transfer surplus from one group to another and expends valuable resources in unproductive re-distributive activities. If demand is inelastic, suppliers have an incentive to restrict supply to raise the price because this will raise their revenue. When the supply of a good is inelastic, consumers have an incentive to hold the price down. (145-146)

For example, the demand for food is inelastic. Farmers have an incentive to lobby government to restrict supply or to create a price floor because they will be better off.

On the other hand, when the supply of a good is inelastic like rental-occupied housing, and demand rises, rental rates will rise significantly and consumers will scream for rent controls. Government sometimes succumbs to political pressure for price controls (price floors and price ceilings). However, they create surpluses and shortages that only become more severe over time.

MATCHING THE TERMS

Match the terms to their definitions

All of these key-terms are found at the end of the chapter.

___ **1.** ability-to-pay principle
___ **2.** benefit principle
___ **3.** consumer surplus
___ **4.** deadweight loss
___ **5.** demerit goods or activities
___ **6.** externality
___ **7.** free rider
___ **8.** government failures
___ **9.** macroeconomic externalities
___ **10.** market failures
___ **11.** merit goods or activities
___ **12.** monopoly power
___ **13.** excise tax
___ **14.** price ceiling
___ **15.** price floor
___ **16.** private good
___ **17.** producer surplus
___ **18.** progressive tax
___ **19.** proportional tax
___ **20.** public choice economists
___ **21.** public goods
___ **22.** regressive tax
___ **23.** rent control
___ **24.** rent-seeking activities
___ **25.** tax incidence
___ **26.** welfare loss triangle

a. A tax that is levied on a specific good.
b. Economists who integrate an economic analysis of politics with their analysis of the economy.
c. The individuals who receive the benefit of the good or service should pay the tax necessary to supply that good.
d. A geometric representation of the welfare cost in terms of misallocated resources caused by a deviation from a market equilibrium.
e. The individuals who are most able to bear the burden of the tax should pay the tax.
f. The loss to society of consumer and producer surplus from a tax.
g. A government-imposed price above which price may not rise.
h. Activities designed to transfer surplus from one group to another.
i. A government-set price below which price may not fall.
j. Imposes a proportionally greater cost on lower income people.
k. The more income a person earns, the greater the amount of tax which is paid.
l. Difference between what consumers would be willing to pay and what they actually had to pay.
m. The difference between the price producers receive and the price at which they were willing to supply the product..
n. Who actually bears the tax burden.
o. The ability of individuals or firms currently in business to prevent other individuals or firms from entering the same kind of business.
p. The effect of a decision on a third party not taken into account by the decision maker.
q. The effect of an individual's decision that affects the levels of unemployment, inflation, or growth in an economy, or growth in an economy as a whole, but is not taken into account by the individual decision maker.
r. A good that, when consumed by one individual, cannot be consumed by another individual.
s. A good that, if supplied to one person, must be supplied to all simultaneously
t. A person who participates in something for free because others have paid for it.
u. A tax whose rates are constant at all income levels, no matter what a taxpayer's total income is.
v. Goods or activities that government believes are bad for people even though they choose to use the goods or engage in the activities.
w. Goods or activities that government believes are good for you even though you may not choose to engage in the activities or consume the goods.
x. Situations in which the market does not lead to a desired result.
y. Situations in which the government intervenes and makes things worse.
z. A price ceiling on rents set by government.

MULTIPLE CHOICE

Circle the one best answer for each of the following questions:

1. Assume equilibrium in the graph below. What area represents consumer surplus?
   a. A + B + C.
   b. D + C + E.
   c. E.
   d. E + F.

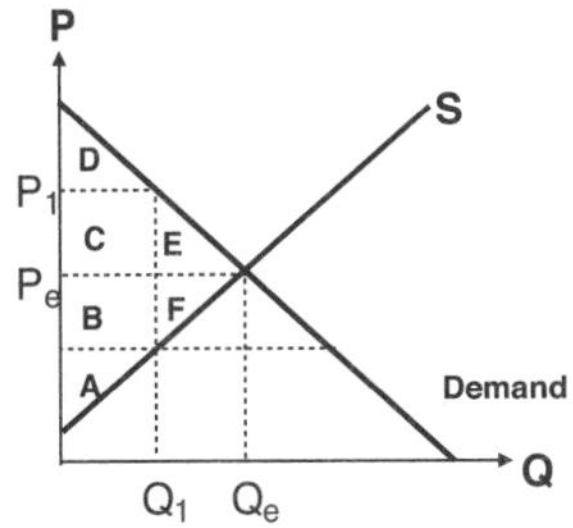

2. Refer to the graph for Question #1. Assume equilibrium. What area represents the welfare loss from a market charging a price P_1?
   a. B + C + E + F.
   b. C + B.
   c. B.
   d. E + F.

3. Refer to the graph below. If a per unit tax, t, is paid by sellers, which of the following is true?

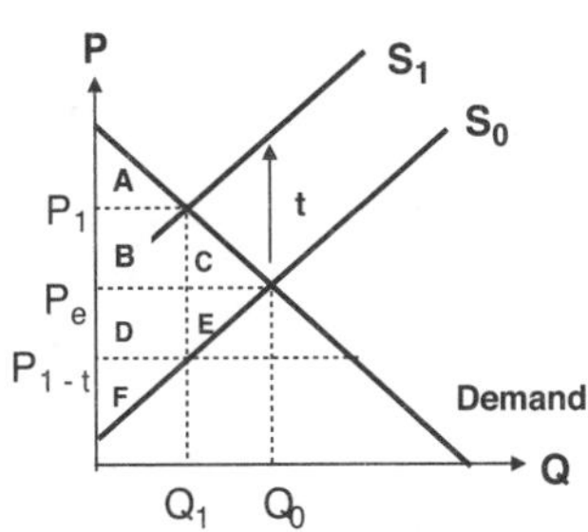

   a. Producer surplus is represented by areas A, B and C before the tax and A after the tax.
   b. Consumer surplus is represented by areas D, E and F before the tax and B after the tax.
   c. The tax, t, imposes a dead weight loss represented by the welfare loss triangle—areas C and E.
   d. Consumers lose surplus given by area E while producers lose surplus given by area C.

4. Refer to the graph in Question #3. If a per unit tax, t, is paid by sellers, which of the following is true?
   a. Tax revenue paid equals the tax, t, times the equilibrium quantity, Q1, or areas B and D.
   b. The total cost to consumers and producers is less than tax revenue to government.
   c. Producers pay area B in tax revenue and also lose area C in producer surplus.
   d. Consumers pay area D in tax revenue and lose area E in consumer surplus.

5. Deadweight loss is
   a. the loss of consumer surplus from a tax.
   b. the loss of producer surplus from a tax.
   c. the loss of consumer *and* producer surplus from a tax.
   d. the amount of tax revenues collected by government

6. The welfare loss triangle is a geometric representation of the
   a. welfare cost in terms of misallocated resources caused by a deviation from a market equilibrium.
   b. amount of tax paid by consumers and businesses.
   c. consumer surplus after a tax.
   d. producer surplus after a tax.

7. With regard to taxation, it is true that
   a. the benefit and ability-to-pay principles of taxation are easy to apply, in part, because they suggest the same taxes to raise revenue.
   b. if government, given its targeted revenue, wants to have as little effect on individual actions as possible, then it should tax goods with elastic demand or supply.
   c. if government wants to minimize the welfare loss, it should tax goods with inelastic demand and supply.
   d. if government wants to maximize the welfare loss, it should tax goods with inelastic supply and demand.

8. The burden of a tax is
   a. most heavily borne by those with the more inelastic demand or supply.
   b. most heavily borne by those with the more elastic demand or supply.
   c. usually equally split between buyers and sellers.
   d. usually passed on to consumers in the form of a higher price.

9. Refer to the graph below. If a tax is imposed on suppliers that shifts the supply curve from S_0 to S_1

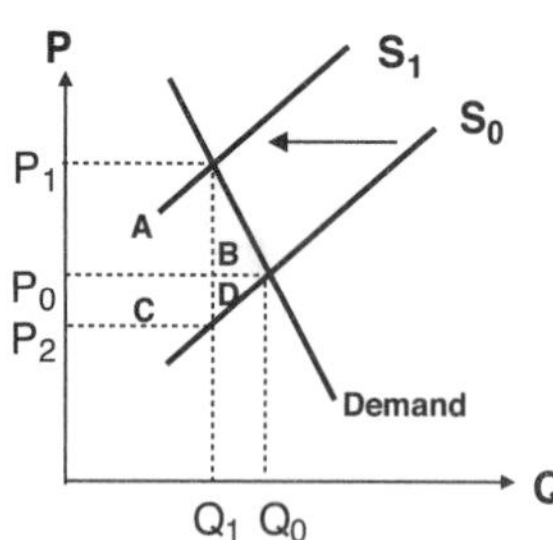

a. area A represents the burden paid by consumers.
b. area C + D represents the burden paid by con-sumers.
c. area B + D represents the burden on producers.
d. area C + D represents the burden on producers.

10. Refer to the graph in Question #9. If a tax is imposed on suppliers that shifts the supply curve from S_0 to S_1
a. the per unit tax is $P_1 - P_0$.
b. the tax revenue equals area A + B + C + D.
c. the portion of the per unit tax paid by consumers is $P_1 - P_0$.
d. the welfare loss equals A + C.

11. Employment Insurance premiums
a. levied by government more heavily on employees than employers, even though the burden of the tax is most heavily borne by employers.
b. most heavily borne by employers because the demand for labor tends to be more inelastic than supply.
c. most heavily borne by workers because the demand for labor tends to be more inelastic than the supply of labor.
d. most heavily borne by workers because the supply of labor tends to be more inelastic than the demand for labour.

12. A price ceiling is
a. a government-set minimum price.
b. a government-imposed limit on how high a price can be charged.
c. determines the market equilibrium price.
d. a mechanism to create surpluses.

13. An effective price ceiling
a. is a government-set price above market equilibrium price.
b. is in essence an implicit tax on producers and an implicit subsidy to consumers.
c. will create a surplus.
d. causes an increase in consumer and producer surplus.

14. If there is an effective price ceiling
a. the quantity demanded exceeds the quantity supplied.
b. the price is above equilibrium.
c. then a surplus is created.
d. the supply exceeds demand.

15. Effective rent controls
a. are examples of price floors.
b. cause the quantity demanded to exceed the quantity supplied of rental occupied housing.
c. create a greater amount of higher quality housing to be made available to renters.
d. create a surplus of rental occupied housing

16. An increase in the minimum wage can be expected to
a. cause unemployment for some workers.
b. cause a shortage of workers.
c. increase employment.
d. help businesses by reducing their costs of production.

17. Refer to the graph below. A price ceiling of P_1 will

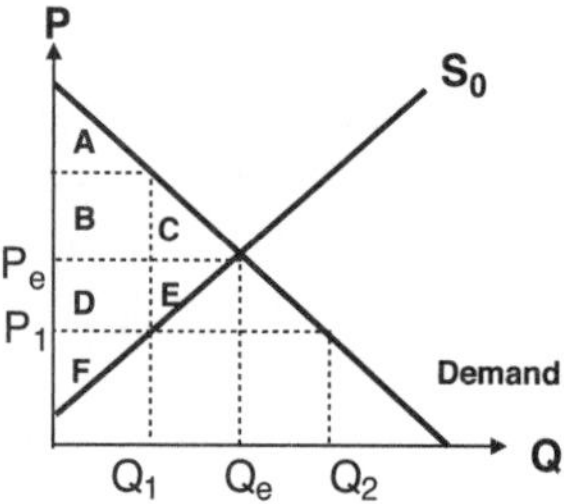

a. create a shortage of $Q_e - Q_1$.
b. transfer surplus D from producers to consumers .
c. create a dead weight loss equal to area A + B + C.
d. increase combined producer and consumer surplus by triangle C and E.

18. Rent-seeking activity is designed to
- **a.** produce additional revenue for government.
- **b.** transfer surplus from consumers to producers.
- **c.** transfer surplus from producers to consumers.
- **d.** transfer surplus from one group to another.

19. In which case will a price floor result in the greatest surplus?
- **a.** When both demand and supply are more inelastic—in the short run.
- **b.** When both demand and supply are more elastic—in the long run.
- **c.** When demand is elastic and supply is inelastic.
- **d.** When demand is inelastic and supply is elastic.

SHORT-ANSWER QUESTIONS

1. What are six roles of government?

2. What are the costs of taxation to society?

3. What are the benefits of taxation to society?

4. What is the benefit principle of taxation?

5. What is the ability-to-pay principle of taxation?

6. What is the general rule about who bears the relative burden of a tax?

7. What is the general rule about elasticities and tax burden?

8. What is a price ceiling? Demonstrate graphically the effect of a price ceiling on a market.

9. What is a price floor? Demonstrate graphically the effect of a price floor on a market.

10. Why are rent controls likely to worsen an existing shortage of housing?

11. What do price ceilings and price floors create? Shortages or surpluses?

12. For whom is a price ceiling an implicit tax? For whom is a price ceiling an implicit subsidy?

13. For whom is a price floor an implicit tax? For whom is a price floor an implicit subsidy?

14. What is an important similarity and an important difference between taxes and price controls (price ceilings and price floors)?

15. What is rent seeking?

16. How is rent seeking related to elasticity?

PROBLEMS AND APPLICATIONS

1. For each of the following, determine which role government is exercising.

   a. Government enforces legal and binding contracts.

   b. Government bans the use of a particular pesticide that has been determined to significantly increase the chances of those exposed to it getting cancer.

   c. Government deregulates an industry making it easier for entrepreneurs to enter into that business activity.

   d. Government raises tax rates on upper-income individuals because it has been politically determined that they are not paying their "fair" share.

   e. Government builds a new interstate highway system.

   f. Government increases the federal budget deficit because it is argued this will help to reduce unemployment and provide for greater rates of economic growth.

   g. Government subsidizes the "arts" (e.g. symphony orchestras).

2. Refer to the graph below when answering the following questions.

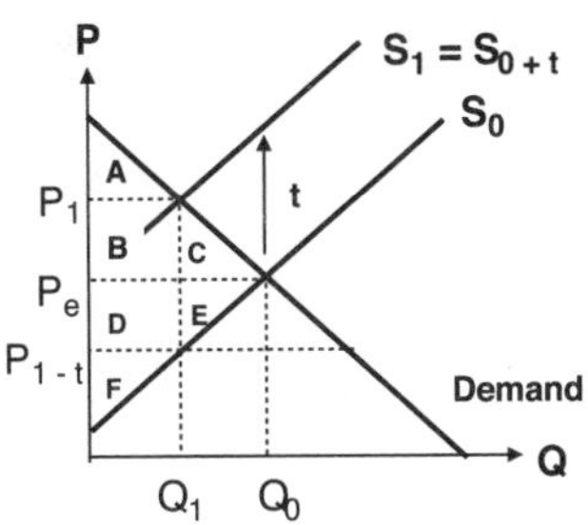

   a. Given supply curve S_0, what is the area representing consumer surplus at the market equilibrium price?

   b. Given supply curve S_0, what is the area representing producer surplus at the market equilibrium price?

   c. Now suppose a per unit tax, t, paid by the supplier shifts the supply curve up from S_0 to S_1. Equilibrium price rises from P_e to P_1 and equilibrium quantity falls from Q_0 to Q_1. What area represents consumer surplus after the tax?

   d. After the tax, what area represents what consumers pay in tax revenue to government?

   e. What area represents lost consumer surplus caused by the tax and that is not gained by government?

   f. What area represents producer surplus after the tax?

   g. After the tax, what area represents what producers pay in tax revenue to government?

   h. What area represents lost producer surplus caused by the tax and that is not gained by government?

   i. What area represents deadweight loss; that is, what is the welfare loss triangle?

3. For each of the following, determine whether the benefit principle or the ability-to-pay principle is being primarily relied on to raise revenues to provide for public goods and services.

   a. The gas tax.

   b. Camping site overnight fees.

   c. Tolls on highways and bridges.

   d. Income taxes.

   e. Property taxes.

   f. Employment Insurance Premiums.

4. The supply and demand for foreign cars in Bangladesh is shown in the graph below. Suppose the government imposes a tax on supply of 10,000 takas per car. The new equilibrium price and quantity is shown in the graph below.

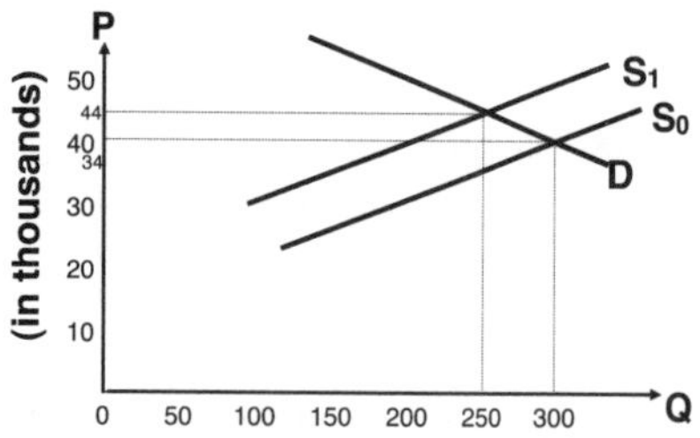

   a. What would be the tax paid by consumers? Suppliers? What price do suppliers with and without the tax receive?

   b. Demonstrate graphically the tax paid by each.

   c. From your answer to (b), what can you conclude about the relative elasticities of the supply and demand curves?

5. Suppose demand is inelastic and supply is elastic for a good. Do consumers or producers bear the biggest burden of a tax imposed on the good?

6. **a.** If government, given its targeted revenue from a tax, wants to have as large effect on individual actions as possible, then should it tax goods with an inelastic or elastic demand? Why?

   b. If government wants to raise revenues from a tax and minimize welfare loss, should it tax goods with *inelastic* demand or supply, or *elastic* demand or supply? Why?

7. Refer to the graph below when answering the following questions.

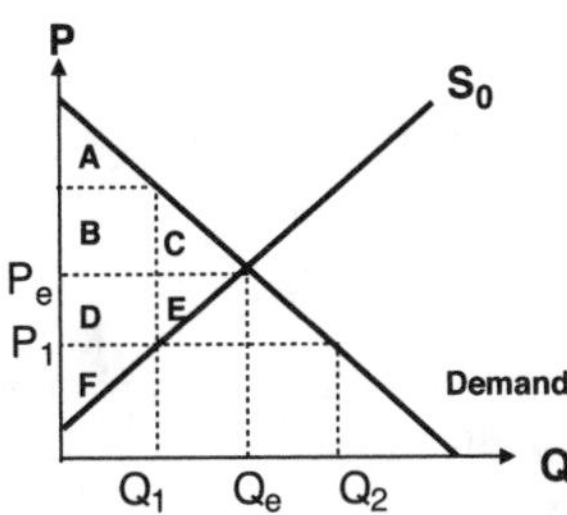

a. In market equilibrium, what area represents consumer surplus? Producer surplus?

b. Suppose government imposes a price ceiling of P_1. What happens to the quantity demanded and the quantity supplied?

c. What happens to consumer and producer surplus as a result of the price ceiling?

d. What is the welfare loss triangle as a result of the price ceiling?

e. How is a price ceiling equivalent to a tax on producers and a subsidy to consumers?

f. Suppose that instead of government imposing a price ceiling, it imposed a tax that reduced the quantity supplied to Q_1. What is an essential similarity between the two outcomes? What is an essential difference?

8. How could farmers lobbying government to restrict the supply of agricultural production or to pursue agricultural price supports be viewed as rent-seeking activity?

9. Why will shortages that result from price ceilings, and surpluses that result from price floors become more acute over time?

ANSWERS

A BRAIN TEASER

1. Who bears the larger burden of an excise tax on cigarettes: smokers or tobacco companies? If government increases the tax on cigarettes, what will happen to government's tax revenues?

ANSWERS

POTENTIAL ESSAY QUESTIONS

You may also see essay questions similar to the "Problems & Applications" and "Brain Teaser" exercises.

1. Discuss the six roles of government in the market economy. According to economic theory, to what extent should government intervene in our economy?

2. Discuss the relationship between elasticity and tax burden.

3. What are the basic similarities and differences between the effects of taxes and price controls?

ANSWERS

MATCHING

1-e; 2-c; 3-l; 4-f; 5-v; 6-p; 7-t; 8-y; 9-q; 10-x; 11-w; 12-o; 13-a; 14-g; 15-i; 16-r; 17-m; 18-k; 19-u; 20-b; 21-s; 22-j; 23-z; 24-h; 25-n; 26-d.

ANSWERS

MULTIPLE CHOICE

1. b Consumer surplus is the area under the demand curve above the equilibrium price. See the Knowing The Tools box on page 133 and the accompanying Figure, and text on pages 133-134.

2. d The loss to consumers is *E* and *C* (but C is gained by producers). The loss to producers is *F*. So the total loss is *E* + *F.* See pages 135-136 and Figure 6-2.

3. c The incorrect options have consumer and producer surplus confused. Deadweight loss is surplus lost by consumers and producers but not gained by anyone. It is a net loss to society from deviating from market equilibrium. See pages 135-136 and Figure 6-2.

4. a Tax revenue is the tax per unit times the units sold, area B + D. Option b should read "is *greater* than." Options c and d would be correct if we reversed the terms consumer and producer, as well as consumer surplus and producer surplus. See pages135-136 and Figure 6-2.

5. c See the definition of deadweight loss on page 136.

6. a The welfare loss triangle is the cost of taxation in *excess* of the revenue paid to government. It also represents the *loss* of consumer *and* producer surplus from a tax. See pages 135-136.

7. c The benefit and ability-to-pay principles of taxation are *not* easy to apply and *are* often in conflict. With regard to b, government should tax *inelastic* goods. See pages 136-137.

8. a Those with inelastic demand or supply are least able to change their behavior as a result of the tax and, therefore, bear a greater share of the tax. See pages 137-138.

9. d The burden of the tax paid by producers is areas C and D. The burden of the tax paid by consumers is the increase in the price times quantity purchased, area A, and lost consumer surplus, area B. Area B + D represents the welfare loss of the tax. See pages 138-139, especially Figure 6-3.

10. c The per unit tax is P_1–P_2. Of that, consumers pay $P_1 - P_0$ of the per unit tax. Tax revenues equal area A + C. The portion of the per unit tax paid by sellers is $P_0 - P_2$. The welfare loss equals area B + D. See pages 138-139, especially Figure 6-3.

11. d Government divides the taxes among employees and employers equally. However, since the supply of labor is relatively more inelastic, employees bear the greater burden of social security taxes. See pages 141-142.

12. b A price ceiling is imposed below the market equilibrium price. See pages 142-145.

13. b A price ceiling is a government-set price *below* equilibrium and creates a *shortage.* A price ceiling reduces consumer and producer surplus, but a portion of the lost producer surplus is transferred to consumers. A price ceiling creates welfare loss just like taxes do. See pages 144-145.

14. a As discussed on pages 142-145, the quantity demanded exceeds the quantity supplied. The price is below equilibrium, and a shortage is created. You don't use the terms supply and demand because that usage refers to the entire schedule (curve).

15. b Rent controls are price ceilings and therefore cause the quantity demanded to exceed the quantity supplied. Indeed, the quantity demanded rises while the quantity supplied falls creating a shortage. See pages 142-145 in the text.

16. a Because the minimum wage is a price floor it increases the quantity supplied and decreases the quantity demanded (decreasing employment) and creating a surplus of workers (causing some unemployment). The higher minimum wage would increase costs of production to businesses. See pages 142-145 in the textbook.

17. b A price ceiling creates a shortage equal to $Q_2 - Q_1$. It also creates a deadweight loss equal to are C + E and causes the combined producer and consumer surplus to *fall* by areas C and E (the welfare loss triangle). See pages 141-142, especially Figure 6-4.

18. d Rent-seeking activity is designed to transfer surplus form one group to another—whether it be from producers to consumers or the other way around. See page 146.

19. b When both parties have the greatest possibility of change, there will be the greatest surplus. This is in the long run when both demand and supply are more elastic. See pages 146-147.

ANSWERS

SHORT-ANSWER QUESTIONS

1. Six roles of government are (1) provide a stable set of institutions and rules, (2) promote effective and workable competition, (3) correct for externalities, (4) provide public goods, (5) ensure economic stability and growth, and (6) adjust for undesired market results. (128-132)

2. The cost of taxation to society includes (1) the direct cost of the revenue paid to government; (2) the loss of consumer and producer surplus caused by the tax; and (3) and the administrative costs of collecting the tax. (135-136)

3. The benefit of taxes to society are the goods and services that government provides (when fulfilling the six roles in a market economy as discussed in Chapter 5). (136)

4. The benefit principle follows the same principle as the market: *the individuals who receive the benefit of the good or service should pay the tax necessary to supply that good.* (136-137)

5. The ability-to-pay principle simply states: *the individuals who are most able to bear the burden of the tax should pay the tax.* (136)

6. The relative burden of a tax (also known as a tax incidence) follows the general rule: *The more inelastic one's relative supply and demand, the larger the burden of the tax one will bear.* (137-138)

7. The general rule about elasticities and tax burden is this: *if demand is relatively more inelastic that supply, consumers pay a higher percentage of the tax. If supply is relatively more inelastic than demand, suppliers pay a higher share.* (137-138)

8. A price ceiling is a government imposed limit on how high a price can be charged. An effective price ceiling below market equilibrium price will cause QD > QS (a shortage) as shown in the graph below. (142-145)

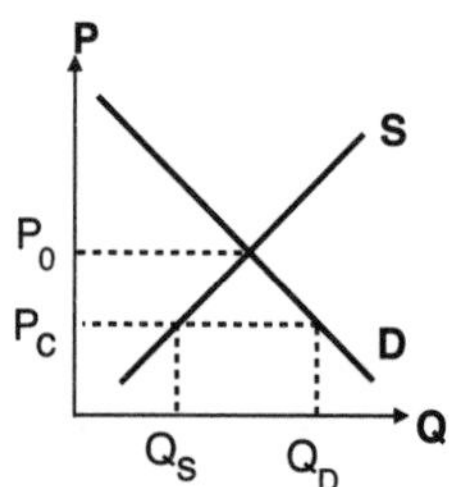

9. A price floor is a government imposed limit on how low a price can be charged. An effective price floor above market equilibrium price will cause QS > QD (a surplus) as shown in the graph below. (142-145)

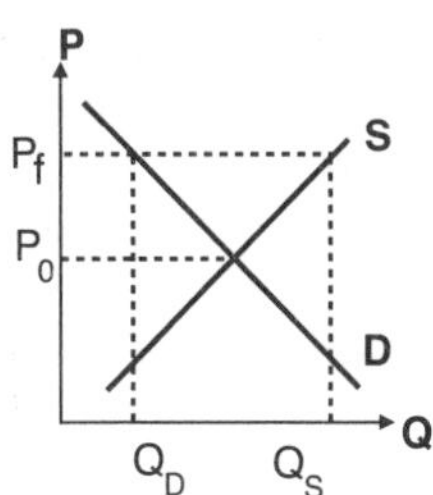

10. Rent controls are price ceilings and result in shortages in rental housing. As time passes and as the population rises, the demand for rental housing rises. On the supply side, other ventures become more lucrative relative to renting out housing. Owners have less incentive to repair existing buildings, let alone build new ones, reducing the supply of rental housing over time. The housing shortage increases. The shortage becomes more acute over time (142-145)

11. Price ceiling create shortages and price floors create surpluses. (142-145)

12. A price ceiling (a government-set price below market equilibrium price) is in essence an implicit tax on producers and an implicit subsidy to consumers. (144-145)

13. A price floor (a government-set price above market equilibrium price) is in essence an implicit tax on consumers and an implicit subsidy to producers. (145)

14. An important similarity between taxes and price controls (which include price ceilings and price floors) is that they all create a loss of consumer and producer surplus. That is, they all create a loss of producer and consumer surplus, shown graphically by a welfare loss triangle. An important difference between taxes and price controls is that price controls create surpluses (in the case of a price floor) and shortages (in the case of a price ceiling), while taxes do not create surpluses or shortages. (144)

15. Rent seeking is an activity designed to transfer surplus (consumer or producer surplus) from one group to another. (145-147)

16. The more inelastic demand, the greater the incentive suppliers have to drive the price up because this will increase their revenue and they will be better off. The more inelastic supply, the greater the incentive demanders have to lower the price because they will be better off. (145-147)

ANSWERS

PROBLEMS AND APPLICATIONS

1. a. Providing a stable set of institutions and rules. (128)
   b. Correcting for an externality (a negative externality in this case). (129)
   c. Promoting effective and workable competition. (129)
   d. Adjusting for undesired market results (an "unfair" distribution of income in this case). (131)
   e. Providing for public goods. (131)
   f. Ensuring economic stability and growth. (130)
   g. Adjusting for undesired market results (subsidizing a merit activity in this case). (131-132)

2. a. Area A + B + C represents consumer surplus at the market equilibrium price. (133-136, and Figure 6-2)
   b. Area D + E + F represents producer surplus at the market equilibrium price. (133-136, and Figure 6-2)
   c. Area A is consumer surplus after the tax. (133-136, and Figure 6-2)
   d. Area B is what consumers pay in tax revenues to government. This represents lost consumer surplus gained by government. (133-136, and Figure 6-2)
   e. Area C is lost consumer surplus not gained by government. (133-136, and Figure 6-2)
   f. Area F is producer surplus after the tax. (133-136, and Figure 6-2)
   g. Area D is what producers pay in tax revenues to government. This represents lost producer surplus gained by government. (133-136, and Figure 6-2)

h. Area E represents lost producer surplus not gained by government. (133-136, and Figure 6-2)

i. Area C + E is the deadweight loss from a tax. This area is the welfare loss triangle. (133-136, and Figure 6-2)

3. a. Benefit principle of taxation. Gas taxes raise revenues to provide roads to those who use them. (136-137)

b. Benefit principle of taxation. The fees raise revenues to provide public parks to those who use them. (136-137)

c. Benefit principle of taxation. The tolls raise revenues to provide roads to those who use them. (136-137)

d. Ability-to-pay principle. The income tax is a progressive tax (the percentage of taxes paid increases as income increases) because the wealthy can "afford" to pay more taxes. (136-137)

e. Ability-to-pay principle. The more property you own, the more you pay. (136-137)

f. Benefit principle of taxation. Although Employment Insurance premiums are used to pay benefits to those currently temporarily unemployed, the expectation is that if current employees ever become unemployed, a similar benefit would be paid to them from employment insurance premiums collected at that time. (136-137)

4. a. The consumers now have to pay 44,000 takas per car which is 4,000 takas more than before. Their tax burden is (4,000 × 250) = 1,000,000 takas. Suppliers now receive 34,000 takas (44,000−10,000) on each car they sell, which is 6,000 takas less per car than before the tax. Their tax burden is (6,000 250) = 1,500,000 takas. (135-140, especially Figure 6-3)

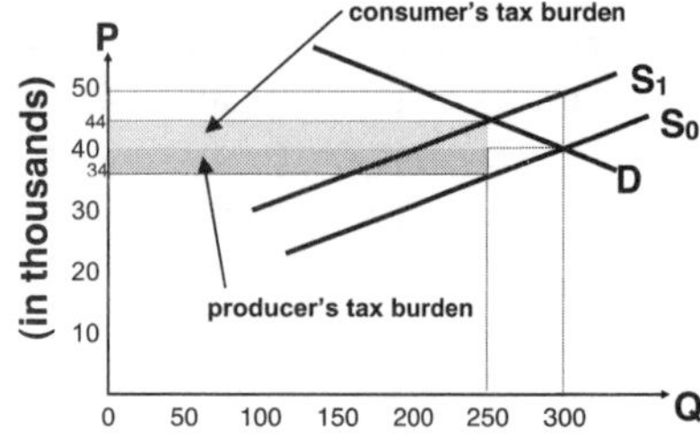

b. The graph above shows the relative taxes paid by consumers and producers. The upper shaded portion is consumers' tax burden. The lower shaded portion is suppliers' tax burden. (135-141, especially Figure 6-3)

c. Since the supplier's tax burden is greater, the supply curve is more inelastic than the demand curve. This is discussed in the textbook. (135-141, especially Figure 6-3)

5. Consumers pay the largest percentage of a tax when demand is inelastic and supply is elastic. (135-141)

6. a. Government should tax goods with *elastic* demand if it wishes to have as large effect on individual actions as possible. This is because an elastic demand means there are many substitutes buyers can turn to in response to the higher price as a result of the tax. Buyers will cut back on their consumption rather dramatically. (135-141)

b. Government should tax goods with *inelastic* demand or supply if it wishes to raise revenues and minimize welfare loss. Revenues to government will rise because an inelastic demand or supply means there are few substitutes or alternatives for buyers and sellers to turn to. Moreover, an inelastic demand or supply will minimize welfare loss because the welfare loss triangle will be smaller the steeper (the more inelastic) the demand or supply curves. (135-141, Figure 6-3, and the Applying The Tools box on page 140)

7. a. Market equilibrium is P_e and Q_e. Consumer surplus is area A + B + C. Producer surplus is area D + E + F. (135)

b. As a result of the price ceiling the quantity supplied falls from Q_e to Q_1 and the quantity demanded rises from Q_e to Q_2. This creates a shortage of $Q_2 - Q_1$. (142, especially Figure 6-5)

c. Consumer surplus becomes area A + B + D. Producer surplus becomes area F. (144-145)

d. The welfare loss triangle is area C + E. (144-145, especially Figure 6-6)

e. A price ceiling is equivalent to a tax on producers and a subsidy to consumers because area D is transferred from producers to consumers as a result of the price ceiling. (144-145, especially Figure 6-5)

f. The welfare loss would be the same (the welfare loss triangle would still be area C + E). However, an essential difference between the two is that a price ceiling creates a shortage while a tax would not. (144-145, especially Figure 6-5)

7. Because agricultural commodities have an inelastic demand, farmers have an incentive to get government to restrict supply or to create a price floor, thereby raising their revenue. This is rent seeking because farmers are attempting to shift some consumer surplus to themselves. (145-147)

8. Because in the long run, supply and demand tend to be more elastic than in the short run. (145-147)

ANSWERS

A BRAIN TEASER

1. Buyers will bear the biggest burden of the cigarette tax because the demand for cigarettes in inelastic (for those "hooked" on smoking there are few substitutes for cigarettes). If government increases the cigarette tax, this will increase the price by a greater percentage than the quantity demanded falls (because demand is inelastic). That is, few people stop smoking. Therefore, tax revenues to government rise. (138-141)

ANSWERS

POTENTIAL ESSAY QUESTIONS

The following are annotated answers. They indicate the general idea behind the answer.

1. Six roles of government are (1) provide a stable set of institutions and rules, (2) promote effective and workable competition, (3) correct for externalities, (4) provide public goods, (5) ensure economic stability and growth, and (6) adjust for undesired market results. Economic theory tells us that the government should intervene in our economy only if the benefits outweigh the costs. However, equally reasonable people are likely to weigh the benefits and costs of government involvement differently.

2. The general rule about elasticities and tax burden is this: if demand is relatively more inelastic than supply, consumers will pay a higher percentage of the tax. If supply is relatively more inelastic than demand, suppliers will pay a higher share.

3. Price controls and taxes are similar in that they both create welfare loss. They differ in that price controls create shortages (in the case of a price ceilings) and surpluses (in the case of a price floors), while taxes do not.

THE LOGIC OF INDIVIDUAL CHOICE: THE FOUNDATION OF SUPPLY AND DEMAND

CHAPTER AT A GLANCE

The law of demand was introduced in Chapter 4 and this chapter extends the discussion of the behaviour of consumer as to how they make their consumption decisions.

The first concept to be discussed is utility—the benefit or satisfaction a consumer gets from making a consumption decision. Other terms such as total utility, marginal utility and diminishing marginal utility are also discussed. In order to maximize utility, a consumer must allocate his/her income among products in order to ensure that the last dollar spent on each good or service provides the same level of marginal utility. This is called the utility maximizing rule or the principle of rational choice. A number of numerical examples are provided.

Topics such as indifference curves, which outline the combination of goods and services consumers prefer to purchase, and budget lines, which outline what the consumer can purchase given a specific level of income, are introduced in order to further the analysis of utility maximization. Subject to a budget constraint, or limited income, consumers will choose a specific combination of goods and services that yield the highest level of utility—that being where the budget line is tangent to a given indifference curve.

This review is based upon the learning objectives that open the chapter.

1a. Consumers makes individual choices based on individual differences. However, much of what people do reflects their rational self-interest. (154-155)

1b. Two things determine what people do: (154-155

1. The pleasure consumers derive from doing or consuming something.
2. The price of doing or consuming that something.

1c. The principle of diminishing marginal utility states that, at some point, the marginal utility received from each additional unit of a good begins to decrease with each additional unit consumed. (157)

Marginal means "extra."
Utility means "satisfaction."

2. The principle of rational choice tells us to spend our money on those goods that give us the most marginal utility per dollar. (157-158)

If $MU_x/P_x > MU_y/P_y$, choose to consume an additional unit of good *x*;

If $MU_x/P_x < MU_y/P_y$, choose to consume an additional unit of good *y;*

If $MU_x/P_x = MU_y/P_y$, you are maximizing utility; you cannot increase your utility by adjusting your choices.

$MU_x/P_x = MU_y/P_y$ means the extra satisfaction per last dollar spent on x equals that for y.

3. When the ratios of the marginal utility to the price of goods are equal, you're maximizing utility; that is the utility maximizing rule. (158)

The equality: $MU_x/P_x = MU_y/P_y$ *implies a combination of quantities of goods x and y consumed that will maximize your satisfaction given your budget, preferences, and the prices of x and y. No other combination of goods x and y will satisfy you as much.*

4. According to the principle of rational choice, if there is diminishing marginal utility and the price of a good goes up, we consume less of that good. Hence, the principle of rational choice leads to the law of demand. (161)

If $MU_x/P_x = MU_y/P_y$ *and then* P_x *increases, we get* $MU_x/P_x < MU_y/P_y$ *and we buy more of y and buy less of x.*

5. Consumer's decisions are made using simple conventions: (162)

1. Prices convey information.
2. Follow the leader.
3. Habit.
4. Custom

6a. An indifference curve shows the various combinations of goods which yield the same level of utility, or satisfaction. (164-165)

An indifference curve shows the various combinations of goods which yield the same level of utility, or satisfaction. (164-165)

The bowed nature of the indifference curve is due to the law of diminishing marginal rate of substitution. (165)

6b. The budget line shows the various combinations of goods an individual can afford (163-167)

Combining the indifference curve and the budget line yields the maximum utility derived given the consumer's income – at point D on the graph below.

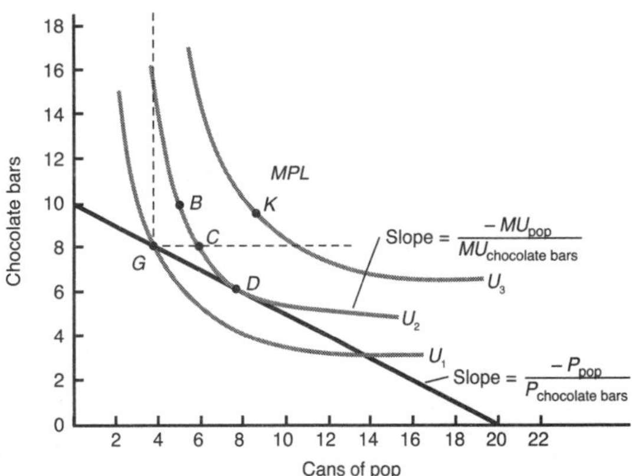

The law of demand tells us that less will be purchased at higher prices.

See also, Appendix A: "Describing Consumer Preferences Using Indifference Curves."

MATCHING THE TERMS

Match the terms to their definitions

All of these key terms are found at the end of the chapter.

___ 1. budget line
___ 2. diminishing marginal rated of substitution
___ 3. diminishing marginal utility
___ 4. income constraint
___ 5. indifference curve
___ 6. marginal rate of substitution
___ 7. marginal utility
___ 8. rational choice
___ 9. tangent
___ 10. total utility
___ 11. util
___ 12. utility
___ 13. utility-maximizing rule

a. The pleasure or satisfaction or happiness that one receives from consuming a good or service.
b. Consume that combination of goods where the ratios of their marginal utilities to the price of the two goods are equal.
c. A unit to measure utility.
d. Spend your money on those goods that give you the most marginal utility per dollar.
e. The satisfaction one gets from consuming one additional unit of a product above and beyond what one has consumed up until that point.
f. The total satisfaction one gets from consuming a product.
g. A curve that shows the various combinations of goods an individual can buy with a given income.
h. As you get more and more of a good, if some of that good is taken away, then the marginal addition of another good that you need to keep you on your indifference curve gets less and less.
i. The marginal utility that a person derives from consuming an additional unit of a good decreases with each additional unit consumed.
j. Illustrates a budget line.
k. A curve that shows the various combinations of goods which yield the same level of utility.
l. The rate at which one good must be added when the other is taken away in order to keep the individual indifferent between the two combinations.
m. Where the indifference curve and the budget line have the same slopes.

MULTIPLE CHOICE

Circle the one best answer for each of the following questions:

1. The principle of diminishing marginal utility says that at some point the marginal utility received from each additional unit of a good
a. remains constant with each additional good consumed.
b. increases with each additional unit consumed.
c. decreases with each additional unit consumed.
d. approaches infinity with each additional good consumed.

2. The utility of the first slice of pizza is 30 and the utility of the second slice of pizza is 20. From this we know
a. the marginal utility of the second slice of pizza is 50.
b. the total utility of the second slice of pizza is 50.
c. the marginal utility of the second slice of pizza is 20.
d. there is not information to compute the marginal utility.

3. With regard to utility, it is true that
   a. the total satisfaction one gets from one's consumption of a product is called marginal utility.
   b. if you buy one Big Mac that gives you marginal utility of 400 and a second one that gives you marginal utility of 250, total utility of eating two Big Macs is 650.
   c. according to the law of diminishing marginal utility the more we consume of something, the smaller the total satisfaction received from that good.
   d. when choosing between two goods, a rational consumer will choose that product that gives the greatest total utility per dollar.

4. The principle of rational choice specifically states that you choose how to spend additional income based on what gives you
   a. the most total utility per dollar.
   b. the most marginal utility per dollar.
   c. the most average utility per dollar.
   d. the least total utility per dollar.

5. The price of good A is $1; the price of good B is $2. The marginal utility you get from good A is 40; the marginal utility you get from good B is 60. You should
   a. consume more of good A and less of good B.
   b. consume more of good B and less of good A.
   c. keep consuming equal amounts of both goods.
   d. realize that you don't have enough information to answer the question.

6. The price of good A is $2; the price of good B is $2. The marginal utility you get from good A is 40; the marginal utility you get from good B is 60. You should
   a. consume more of good A and less of good B.
   b. consume more of good B and less of good A.
   c. keep consuming equal amounts of both goods.
   d. realize that you don't have enough information to answer the question.

7. The price of good A is $1; the price of good B is $2. The marginal utility you get from good A is 40; the marginal utility you get from good B is 80. You should
   a. consume more of good A and less of good B.
   b. consume more of good B and less of good A.
   c. keep consuming equal amounts of both goods.
   d. realize that you don't have enough information to answer the question.

8. Dennis is deciding where to spend his spring break. If he goes to Vail, Colorado, the trip will give him 10,000 units of utility (satisfaction) and will cost him $500. If, instead, he travels to Padre Island, Texas, the trip will give him 6000 units of pleasure and will cost him $400. Dennis should go to
   a. Vail because his total pleasure will be greater.
   b. Padre Island because it is cheaper.
   c. Vail because his pleasure per dollar spent will be greater.
   d. Padre Island because his pleasure per dollar spent will be greater.

9. Economists assume that consumers will choose to purchase and consume
   a. those goods that cost the least.
   b. those goods with the highest total utility.
   c. that combination of goods at which marginal utilities per dollar are equal.
   d. that combination of goods for which total utilities per dollar are equal.

10. The rational consumer will buy more of good X when
    a. $MU_X/P_X < MU_Y/P_Y$
    b. $MU_X/P_X > MU_Y/P_Y$
    c. $MU_X/P_X = MU_Y/P_Y$
    d. the price of good X increases

11. If $MU_X/P_X = MU_Y/P_Y$ and the price of Y decreases, then the rational consumer will
    a. continue consuming the same combination of X and Y.
    b. buy more of Y.
    c. buy more of X.
    d. buy less of X and Y.

12. If your marginal utility of additional income is 60 units of utility, your opportunity cost of working is $5.00 per hour, and you are currently working 10 hours per week at $6.00 per hour, how high a wage will you require to work another hour?
    a. 60 units of utility.
    b. $5.00.
    c. $6.00.
    d. Insufficient information has been given to answer this question.

13. The theory of bounded rationality suggests that
    a. all goods will be normal goods.
    b. all goods will be substitutes.
    c. many of our decisions are adjusted for our limitations.
    d. individual tastes will be bounded and hence there will be diminishing marginal utility.

14. Refer to the graph below. The budget line (or income constraint) reflects a relative price of chocolate (in terms of soda) of
    a. one-fourth.
    b. one-half.
    c. one.
    d. two.

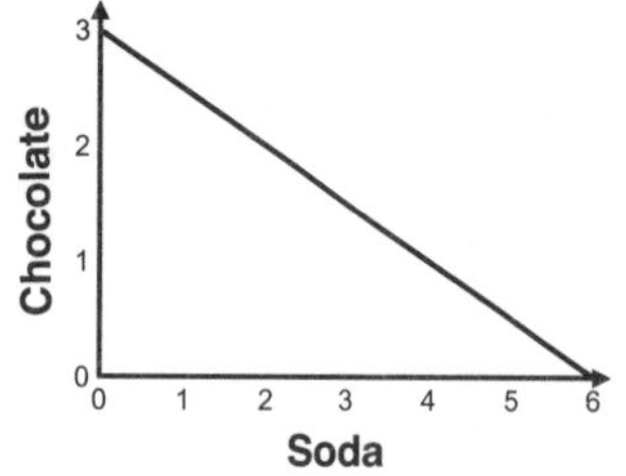

15. Refer to the graph below. If the price of chocolate falls, the income constraint will

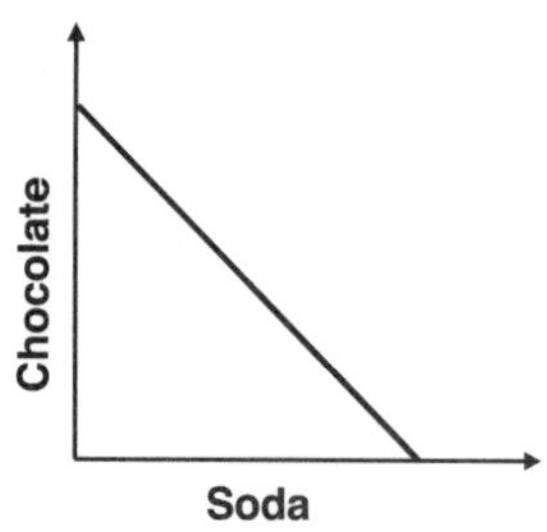

    a. rotate out and become flatter.
    b. rotate in but keep the same slope.
    c. rotate in and become steeper.
    d. rotate out and become steeper.

16. Refer to the graph below. The absolute value of the slope of the indifference curve represents

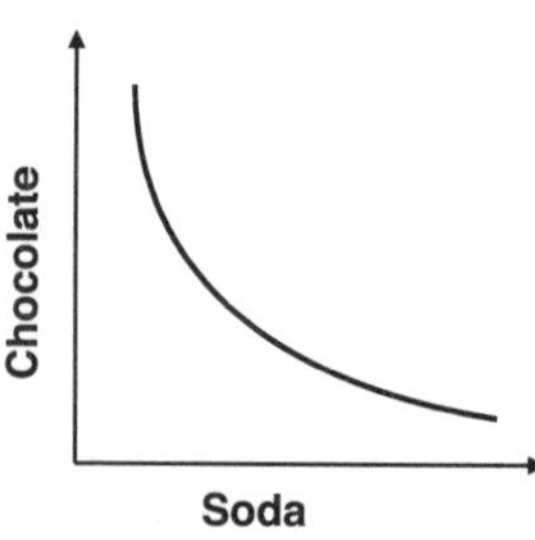

    a. the marginal utility of chocolate divided by the marginal utility of soda.
    b. the marginal utility of soda divided by the marginal utility of chocolate.
    c. the marginal utility of soda times the marginal utility of chocolate.
    d. the marginal utility of chocolate divided by price of chocolate.

17. Refer to the graph below. The equilibrium in the indifference curve model is at point
    a. A.
    b. B.
    c. C.
    d. D.

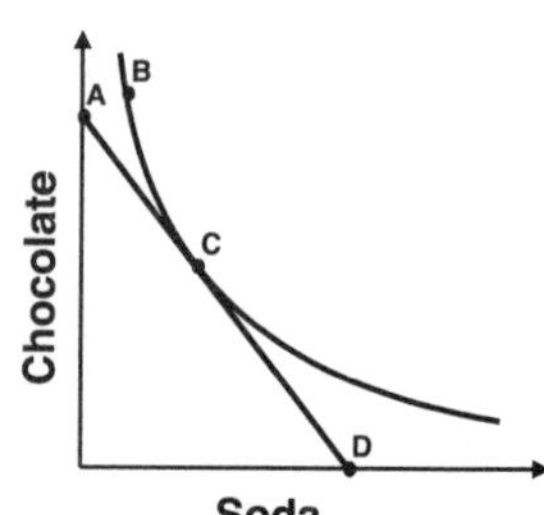

SHORT-ANSWER QUESTIONS

1. What is marginal utility?

2. Suppose you and your friend are studying hard for an economics exam. You have a craving for a double cheese pizza. You order a large one. Your mouth is watering as you sink your teeth into the first slice. Oh, the pleasure! You eagerly reach for the second slice. The additional pleasure that you get from this slice is less than the first. The third and fourth slice each give you even less pleasure. What principle does this describe? State the principle in general terms.

3. Suppose you had $5 to spend. You like going to see Michael Douglas movies a lot, but you like to see John Turturo movies even more. If these were your only choices to spend the $5 on, which movie would you go to see? Show how your choice follows the principle of rational choice.

4. What are the formulas that embody the principle of rational choice?

5. Explain why you're maximizing utility when the ratios of the marginal utility to the price of goods are equal.

6. Suppose you are maximizing utility by consuming two Big Macs at $2 apiece and three ice cream cones at $1 apiece. What happens to the number of Big Macs and ice cream cones consumed if the price of ice cream cones rises to $2 apiece? How does this change in consumption account for the law of demand?

PROBLEMS AND APPLICATIONS

1. a. Fill in the blanks for the following table that shows how marginal utility and total utility change as more and more chocolate chip cookies are consumed. (Marginal utility refers to the marginal utility of increasing to that row, e.g., the marginal utility of going from 0 to 1 is 20.)

Number of choc. chip cookies	Total utility	Marginal utility
1	—	20
2	37	—
3	51	—
4	—	11
5	—	8
6	—	5
7	77	—
8	—	–1

b. Graph the total utility curve of the table above on the axes below.

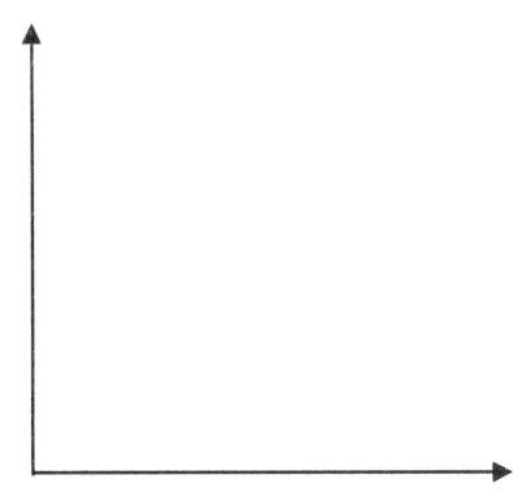

c. Graph the marginal utility curve on the axes as for b.

d. Is the principle of diminishing marginal utility operative in this case? Explain your answer.

e. At what point does the principle of diminishing marginal utility take effect? At what point does marginal utility become zero?

2. Using the principle of rational choice, choose the best option in each case:

a. A $2 slice of pizza giving you 80 units of utility and a $2 hero sandwich giving you 60 units of utility.

b. A $40,000 BMW giving you 200,000 units of utility and a $20,000 Toyota giving you 120,000 units of utility.

c. Taking an economics course that meets 3 times a week for ten weeks giving 900 units of utility or taking a history course that meets 2 times a week for ten weeks giving 800 units of utility. Both class periods last 50 minutes. There is no homework or studying.

d. Taking Tory out for a date to the Four Seasons restaurant in New York City at a cost of $120 which gives you 600 units of utility and taking Sam out at the corner pizza place at a cost of $15 which gives you 60 units of utility. (Tory is short for Victoria or Torrence and Sam is short for Samantha or Samuel — you choose which.)

3. Suppose you are taking courses from two different colleges, both on a part-time basis. One college offers only science courses. The other offers only humanities courses. Each class meets for the same amount of time and you have an unlimited number of hours you can devote to course work, but only $10,500 to devote to tuition. Science courses cost $1,500 a course and humanities courses cost $3,000 a course. You are taking the courses for enjoyment and you have estimated the utility from the consumption of these courses as presented in the following table:

Number of courses	Science Total utility	Humanities Total utility
0	0	0
1	4500	7500
2	7500	12,000
3	9750	15,750
4	11,250	18,750
5	11,750	21,000
6	12,000	22,500

a. How many science courses and how many humanities courses should you take (assuming you follow the principle of rational choice)?

b. Suppose the price of humanities courses falls to $1,000 a course, how would your answer to (a) change?

4. Suppose you have $10 to spend on pens and notebooks. Pens are 50 cents apiece and notebooks are $1 apiece. Draw the budget constraint putting pens on the vertical axis and notebooks on the horizontal axis.

a. What is the slope of the line?

b. What happens to the budget constraint if your income available to spend falls to $8? What is the slope of the new curve? Show this graphically on the graph for (a).

c. Given the new $8 budget constraint, now suppose the price of notebooks rises to $2 apiece. What happens to the budget constraint? Show this graphically using the same axes as in the graph for (a) and (b).

5. Suppose the following table depicts your indifference between combinations of pens and notebooks:

	Notebooks	Pens
A	12	6
B	8	7
C	6	8
D	5	10
E	4	14

a. Graph the indifference curve on the axes below, with pens on the vertical axis and notebooks on the horizontal axis.

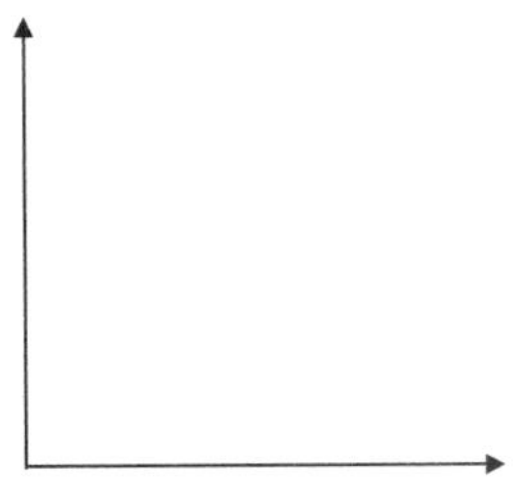

b. What is the marginal rate of substitution between combinations C and D?

c. Combine the indifference curve from question A2 with the $10 budget constraint from question A1 on the graph above. What is the combination of goods you will choose using the principle of rational choice?

ANSWERS

A BRAIN TEASER

1. The wedding industry is a $32 billion business. Weddings tend to be a onetime expense, with lavish expenditures on first marriages and smaller expenditures on later marriages. Would you expect the profit margins on wedding supplies to be higher or lower than for grocery stores? Why?

ANSWERS

POTENTIAL ESSAY QUESTIONS

You may also see essay questions similar to the "Problems & Applications" and "Brain Teaser" exercises.

1. Discuss the principle of diminishing marginal utility. How is this related to the principle of rational choice and the law of demand?

ANSWERS

MATCHING

1-g; 2-h; 3-i; 4-j; 5-k; 6-l; 7-e; 8-d; 9-m; 10-f; 11-c; 12-a; 13-b.

ANSWERS

MULTIPLE CHOICE

1. c The principle of diminishing marginal utility says that at some point, the additional satisfaction one gets from consuming additional units declines. See page 157.

2. c When we say that the utility of the second slice of pizza is 20, we mean we are getting an additional 20 units of utility, so the marginal utility of the second slice is 20. See page 157.

3. b Options a, c and d would be true statements if "total" was changed to "marginal." See pages 158-160, especially Table 7-1 on page 159.

4. b You are better off by choosing to spend an additional sum of money on the good that provides you the greatest marginal utility per dollar. See pages 158-159.

5. a Applying the rational choice rule, you divide the MU by the price. Increase consumption of the good that gives the greater marginal utility per dollar. Since 40/1 is greater than 60/2, then increase consumption of A and decrease consumption of B. See pages 158-160.

6. b Increase the consumption of that good that provides the greatest MU/P. Since 40/2 is less than 60/2 you consume more of good B. See pages 158-160.

7. c Increase the consumption of that good that provides the greatest MU/P. Since 40/1 equals 80/2 you consume equal amounts of both goods. See pages 158-160.

8. c The trip to Vail will give the greatest marginal utility per dollar spent. See pages 158-160.

9. c This is the rational choice. See pages 158-160.

10. b When $MU_X/P_X > MU_Y/P_Y$, the marginal utility for the money spent on good X exceeds that for good Y. You are getting more satisfaction for the last dollar spent on good X. Therefore, buy more of good X. See pages 159-160.

11. b A decrease in the price of Y will cause $MU_X/P_X < MU_Y/P_Y$. Therefore, one should buy more of good Y (and less of good X). See pages 159-160.

12. b Only the opportunity cost is needed to determine what would be required to get you to work another hour. See page 160.

13. c See the definition of bounded rationality in the text on page 162.

14. b Divide the intercept on the chocolate axis by the intercept on the soda axis to find the price of chocolate in terms of soda. One can buy either 3 chocolate bars or 6 sodas, or 1 bar for 2 sodas. See pages 162-165.

15. d A fall in the price of chocolate means that the same amount of soda will give more pieces of chocolate, so the income constraint rotates up from the intersection of the soda axis, hence becoming steeper. See pages 162-165.

16. b A movement down the curve represents the soda needed to compensate the individual—i. e., keep her utility constant—for giving up some chocolate. See pages 162-165.

17. c The equilibrium is where the indifference curve is tangent to the budget line. See pages 165-167.

ANSWERS

SHORT-ANSWER QUESTIONS

1. Marginal utility refers to the satisfaction one gets from the consumption of an incremental or additional unit of a product above and beyond what one has consumed up to that point. (155-156)

2. The fact that you enjoy each subsequent slice less and less follows the principle of diminishing marginal utility. It states that, at some point, the marginal utility received from each additional unit of a good begins to decrease with each additional unit consumed. (155-156)

3. You would choose to see the John Turturo movie because it would give more pleasure for the same amount of money. This decision follows the principle of rational choice which tells us to spend our money on those goods that give us the most marginal utility per dollar. (157-158)

4. The formulas that embody the principle of rational choice are:
If $MU_x/P_x > MU_y/P_y$, choose to consume an additional unit of good x;
If $MU_x/P_x < MU_y/P_y$, choose to consume an additional unit of good y;
If $MU_x/P_x = MU_y/P_y$, you're maximizing utility. (158; 160)

5. If the ratios of the marginal utility to the price of goods are equal, you cannot adjust your spending in any way to increase total utility. Changing your spending will result in additional utility for that good you increased. But that additional utility is less than the decrease in utility for that good that you have given up. Thus, the marginal utilities per dollar are no longer equal and total utility has fallen. Total utility is maximized where the ratios of the marginal utility to the price of goods are equal. (158-159)

6. If you were initially maximizing utility, it must be that $MU_{\text{Big Macs}}/\$2 = MU_{\text{i. c.}}/\$1$. If the price of ice cream cones rise, then you are no longer maximizing utility because $MU_{\text{Big Macs}}/\$2 > MU_{\text{i.c.}}/\$2$. To once again maximize utility, you would raise the marginal utility of ice cream cones and lower the marginal utility of Big Macs by choosing to consume more Big Macs and fewer ice cream cones. You would adjust your consumption to the point where the marginal utilities per dollar were once again equal. The price of ice cream cones *relative to Big Macs* rose and the quantity demanded fell; and the price of Big Macs *relative to ice creams* fell and the quantity demanded rose. This is the law of demand. (161)

ANSWERS

PROBLEMS AND APPLICATIONS

1. a. This question tests the concepts of marginal utility, total utility, and the principle of diminishing marginal utility. Marginal utility is the satisfaction one gets from the consumption of an *incremental* product. Total utility is the total satisfaction from all units consumed up to that point of consumption; it is the sum of all marginal utilities from consumption. (155-156)

Number of choc. chip cookies	Total utility	Marginal utility
1	20	20
2	37	17
3	51	14
4	62	11
5	70	8
6	75	5
7	77	2
8	76	–1

b. The total utility curve is shown below. It is bowed downward because the slope of the marginal utility curve is negative. (155-156; Figure 7-1)

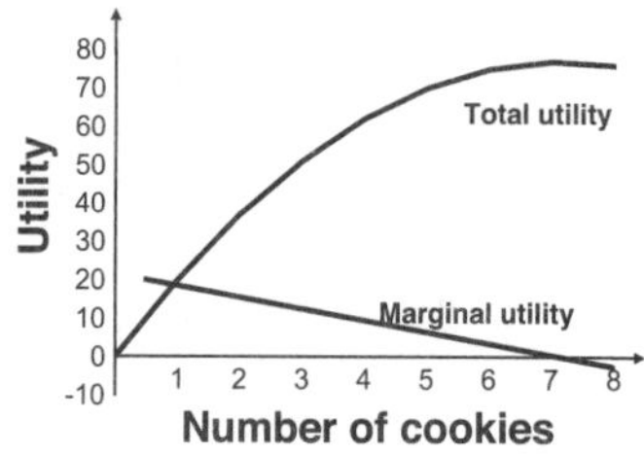

c. The marginal utility curve is shown on the previous page 1.b. Its slope is always negative because the marginal utility of each additional cookie is always declining. (155-156; Figure 7-1)
d. The principle of diminishing marginal utility is operative in this case. The principle of diminishing marginal utility as explained on pages 179-180 of your text states that as more of a good is consumed, beyond some point, the additional units of consumption will yield fewer units of utility than the previous units. This is shown in the table by the third column. Its values are always declining. (157)
e. The principle of diminishing marginal utility operates from the second cookie on. The second cookie gave less pleasure than the first cookie. This is true throughout, from 2 through 8. Marginal utility becomes zero between 7 and 8 cookies. The marginal utility of the 7th cookie is 2, but the marginal utility of the 8th is 1. (157)

2. The principle of rational choice, discussed on page 158, states: Spend your money on those goods that give you the most marginal utility (MU) per dollar. (158)
   a. Choose the $2 slice of pizza. Marginal utility per dollar of the slice of pizza is 80 units of utility/$2 = 40 units of utility per dollar. Marginal utility per dollar of a hero sandwich is 60/ $2 = 30 units of utility per dollar. 40>30. (158)
   b. Choose the $20,000 Toyota. Marginal utility per dollar for the Toyota is 120,000 units of utility/$20,000 = 6 units of utility per dollar. Marginal utility per dollar for the BMW is 200,000/ $40,000 = 5 units of utility per dollar. 6>5. (158)
   c. Choose the history course. Here the two alternatives have a cost in time, not money. The analysis is the same. Just calculate the marginal utility per minute and choose the one with the higher marginal utility per minute. Marginal utility per minute for the economics course is 900 units of utility/1500 minutes = 0.6 units of utility per minute. Marginal utility per minute for the history course is 800 units of utility/ 1000 minutes = 0.8 units of utility per minute. 0.8 > 0.6. (158)
   d. Take Tory out for a date to the Four Seasons. Marginal utility per dollar for taking Tory out is 600 units of utility/ $120 = 5 units of utility per dollar. Marginal utility per dollar for taking Sam out is 60 units of utility/ $15 = 4 units of utility per dollar. 5 > 4. (158)

3. This tests the principle of rational choice on page 158 which states that a rational individual will adjust consumption of all goods until the marginal utilities per dollar are equal.
   a. You should take 3 science courses and 2 humanities courses. To determine this, first you must calculate the marginal utilities and marginal utilities per dollar when you are spending all your money. We show the calculations to arrive at the answer in the table below. Following the principle of rational choice, select that combination where the marginal utilities per dollar are equal. Looking only at those combinations where you are spending all your money, this is at the combination of 3 science courses and 2 humanities courses. We figured this out by figuring out different combinations of courses beginning with 6 science courses, calculating how many humanities courses could be purchased with the remaining funds, and comparing marginal utilities per dollar. If the marginal utility per dollar of science courses is lower than that for humanities course, choose one less science course and repeat the calculation. Keep doing this until the marginal utilities per dollar are the same for both. (157-160)

SCIENCE COURSES

Number of Courses	Total utility	Marginal utility	MU per $
0	0	0	0
1	4500	4500	3
2	7500	3000	2
3	9750	2250	1.5
4	11250	1500	1
5	11750	500	0.33
6	12000	250	0.17

HUMANITIES COURSES

Number of Courses	Total utility	Marginal utility	MU per $
0	0	0	0
1	7500	7500	2.5
2	12000	4500	1.5
3	15750	3750	1.25
4	18750	3000	1
5	21000	2250	0.75
6	22500	1500	0.5

b. Now you should take 3 science courses and 6 humanities courses. First you must calculate the marginal utilities and marginal utilities per dollar. This is shown in the table below. Next, following the principle of rational choice, select that combination where the marginal utilities per dollar are equal and you cannot buy any more courses. This is at the combination of 3 science courses and 6 humanities courses. (157-160)

SCIENCE COURSES

Number of Courses	Total utility	Marginal utility	MU per $
0	0	0	0
1	4500	4500	3
2	7500	3000	2
3	9750	2250	1.5
4	11250	1500	1
5	11750	500	0.33
6	12000	250	0.17

HUMANITIES COURSES

Number of Courses	Total utility	Marginal utility	MU per $
0	0	0	0
1	7500	7500	7.5
2	12000	4500	4.5
3	15750	3750	3.25
4	18750	3000	3
5	21000	2250	2.25
6	22500	1500	1.5

4. The budget constraint is drawn below. It was constructed by first finding out the y-intercept —how many pens could be bought with the entire $10: 20 pens—and then finding out the x-intercept —how many notebooks could be bought with the entire $10: 10 notebooks. Connect these points to get the budget constraint. (162-167)

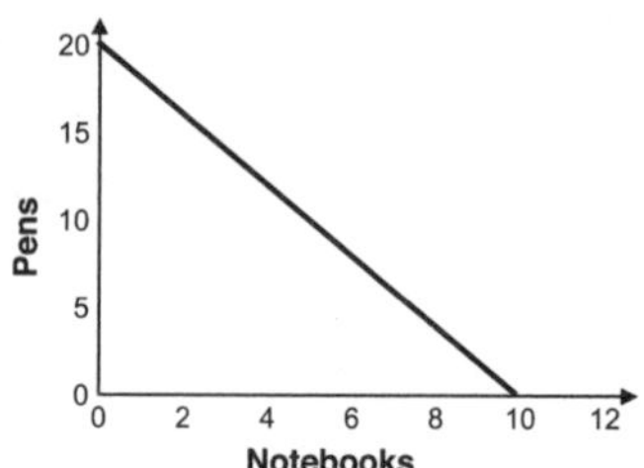

a. The slope the budget constraint is $P_{notebooks} / P_{pens}$ = $1/0.50 = 2. (194-195)

b. The budget constraint shifts in, intersecting the pen axis at 16 and notebook axis at 8. To find this, use the process described to find the initial budget constraint. Since relative prices did not change, the slope is still 2. This is shown below. (162-167)

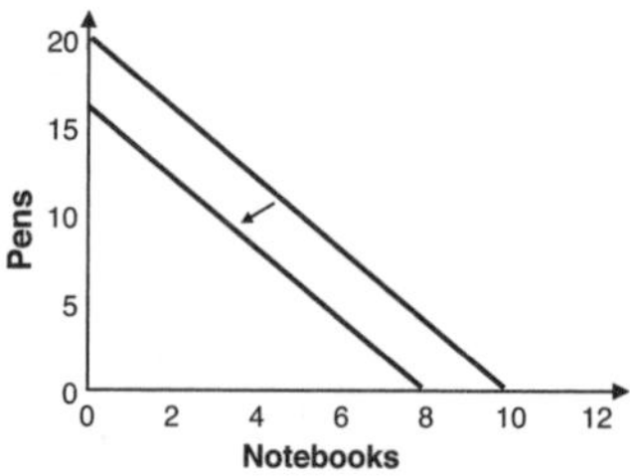

c. Since relative prices changed, the budget constraint rotates. To find the new budget constraint, find first how many notebooks can be bought at their new price: 4. The y-intercept remains at 16 since the price of pens did not change. The budget constraint rotates in along the notebook axis and intersects it at 4 notebooks. Since notebooks became more expensive, the slope became steeper. The slope of the line is $P_{notebooks} / P_{pens}$ = $2/0.50 = 4. This is shown in figure (C) below. (162-167)

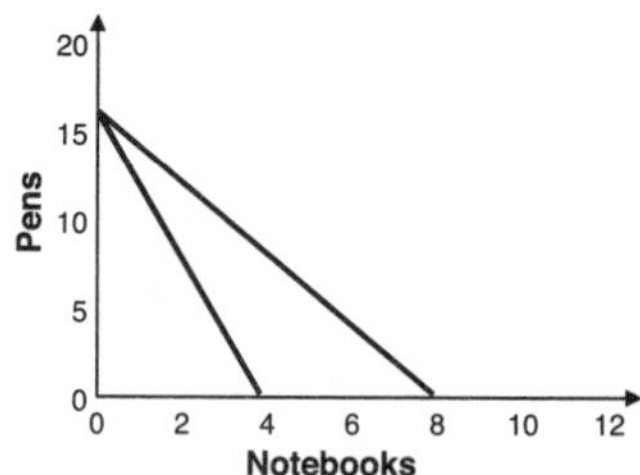

5. **a.** To graph the indifference curve, plot each set of points which give the same utility. This is done in graph (A) below. (162-167)

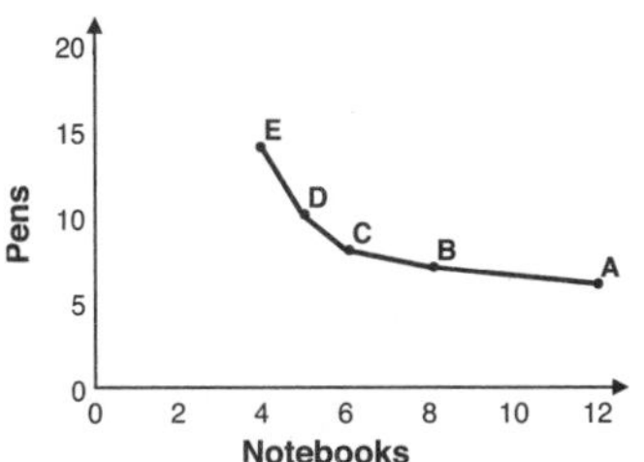

b. The marginal rate of substitution between the combinations C and D is equal to the slope between C and D, $MU_{notebooks} / MU_{pens}$ = 2. (162-167)

c. To find where you maximize utility given the budget constraint, find that point where the slope of the budget constraint equals the marginal rate of substitution between pens and notebooks. This is at points between C and D shown in the graph below. At points between C and D, the slope of budget constraint is equal to the marginal rate of substitution: $MU_{notebooks} / MU_{pens} = 2 = P_{notebooks} / P_{pens}$.
The budget constraint is tangent to the indifference curve at points between C and D. This implies that any other indifference curve that intersects the budget constraint line gives you less total utility than does the current indifference curve. A rational choice maximizes your own utility. Hence, you should choose combinations represented by points between C and D. (162-167)

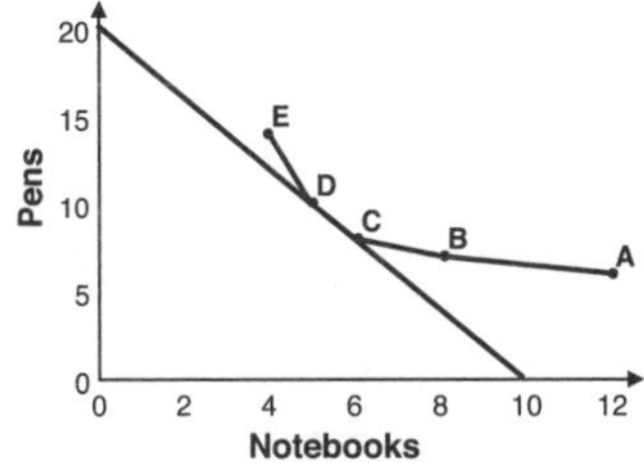

ANSWERS

A BRAIN TEASER

1. Higher, because the marginal utility on marriages is very high–especially for the first marriage. That is, people are willing to pay dearly for a memorable event. Moreover, there is a very inelastic demand (there are few "acceptable" substitutes) for the services and supplies provided for weddings. This, too, has a tendency to result in high prices. Moreover, there's more to life than a literal application of the rational choice model. We do crazy things just for the sake of doing crazy things. We follow rules of thumb–like we don't want to be seen as a "cheap skate" on our daughter's (or our future wife's) wedding day. All of these elements are not present for grocery store shopping. (178; 185-186)

ANSWERS

POTENTIAL ESSAY QUESTIONS

The following are annotated answers. They indicate the general idea behind the answer.

1. As we consume more of any good or service then the marginal utility declines. We consume that combination of goods and services for which the marginal utility in relation to the price is equal. If the price for good X falls then the marginal utility of good X is relation to its price is now greater than for other goods and services. We are simply getting more satisfaction for the money spent on the last unit of good X consumed. Therefore, we buy more of good X. So, as the price of good X falls we find it rational to buy more of good X. This is the law of demand.

PRODUCTION AND COST ANALYSIS I

8

CHAPTER AT A GLANCE

The next few chapters will concentrate on the theory of the firm and the behaviour of firms within specific industries or market structures. Before we can analyze the behaviour of firms, a framework for analysis is required.

This chapter introduces all of the costs of production that are incurred by a firm or an industry in the pursuit of profits. Once these costs are determined, they can be related to market price and profits or losses can be calculated.

The chapter begins by introducing two types of profits—an economic profit and an accounting profit. Economic profits includes explicit costs which are incurred during the day-to-day activities of running a firm and implicit costs which are opportunity costs of making the decision to enter into the business venture. Accounting profits are calculated using explicit costs only.

An important distinction is made between the short run and the long run—two time periods that a firm faces when making decisions. In the short run, costs are fixed and places a constraint on the firm's ability to adjust output. In the long run, all costs are variable and it is a period of time long enough to make any adjustments to all resources employed and output.

The short run cost structure for a typical firm is introduced. One must become familiar with all of the following costs—variable costs, fixed costs, total costs, average variable costs, average fixed costs, average total costs and marginal costs. It is important to be able to distinguish these costs, know how to calculate them and how to draw them graphically.

Understanding this chapter is essential for understanding the next few chapters. There are many terms and concepts introduced, so one will have to go over this chapter several times.

This review is based upon the learning objectives that open the chapter.

1a. A firm is an economic institution that transforms factors of production into goods and services. (177)

1b. A firm: (177)

a. organizes factors of production,
b. produces goods and services, and/or
c. sells produced goods and services.

1c. There are three types of firms: (177)

a. sole proprietor
b. partnership
c. corporation

Students should know the advantages and disadvantages of each type of firm. They are listed in Table 8-1 on page 177.

2. Accounting profit is revenue less explicit cost. Economists include revenue and both explicit and implicit costs in their determination of profit. (179)

Economic profit = revenue − (explicit and implicit cost).

Revenue equals total sales times price.

Implicit costs include the opportunity cost of time and capital provided by the owners of the firm. Accountants do not include these implicit costs in their calculations of profit.

3a. A long-run decision is a decision in which the firm can choose among all possible production techniques. A short-run decision is a decision in which the firm is constrained generally, by its current facility, in regard to what production decisions it can make. (180)

<u>Long run</u> ⇒ all inputs are variable ⇒ all costs are variable.

<u>Short run</u> ⇒ at least one input is fixed ⇒ some costs are fixed and some are variable (vary with the production level).

3b. The law of diminishing marginal productivity states that as more and more of a variable input is added to an existing fixed input, after some point, the additional output obtained from the additional input will fall. (182)

Sometimes called "flowerpot law." Its existence eventually causes costs of production to rise. <u>Study</u> all tables and figures in this chapter! Marginal product is the extra output that will result from an additional unit of an input.

Marginal productivity declines because of the law of diminishing marginal productivity. It is because of diminishing marginal productivity that costs of production eventually rise.

4. The most important categories of costs are shown in Table 8-1. Notice total costs, marginal costs, average fixed costs, average variable costs, and average total costs can be calculated given fixed costs and variable costs at each level of output. (183-184)

5a. Know how to calculate all 7 short-run cost figures! (FC, VC, TC, MC, AFC, AVC and ATC)(184-186)

$TC = FC + VC\ (= ATC \times Q)$
$VC = TC - FC\ (= AVC\ \ Q)$
$FC = TC - VC\ (= AFC\ \ Q)$
$MC = \Delta TC/\Delta Q\ (=\ TVC/\ Q)$
$ATC = TC/Q\ (= AFC + AVC)$
$AVC = VC/Q\ (= ATC\ \ AFC)$
$AFC = FC/Q\ (= ATC\ \ AVC)$

5b. The marginal cost curve goes through the minimum point of the average total cost curve and average variable cost curve; each of these curves is U-shaped. The average fixed cost curve slopes down continuously. (186)

See Figure 8-2b. Know why cost curves are shaped the way they are (because of increasing and diminishing marginal productivity)!

5c. When marginal cost exceeds average total cost, average total cost must be rising. When marginal cost is less than average total cost, average total cost must be falling. This relationship explains why marginal cost curves always intersect the average total cost curve at the minimum of the average total cost curve. (188-189)

If MC > ATC, then ATC is rising.
If MC = ATC, then ATC is at its low point.
If MC < ATC, then ATC is falling.

Study the "Review of Costs" box on page 189.

MATCHING THE TERMS

Match the terms to their definitions

All of these key terms are found at the end of the chapter.

___ **1.** accounting profit
___ **2.** average fixed cost
___ **3.** average product
___ **4.** average total cost
___ **5.** average variable cost
___ **6.** corporation
___ **7.** diminishing marginal productivity
___ **8.** economic profit
___ **9.** explicit cost
___ **10.** firm
___ **11.** fixed costs
___ **12.** implicit cost
___ **13.** limited liability
___ **14.** long-run decision
___ **15.** marginal cost
___ **16.** marginal product
___ **17.** partnership
___ **18.** production
___ **19.** production function
___ **20.** production table
___ **21.** profit
___ **22.** short-run decision
___ **23.** sole proprietorship
___ **24.** stock
___ **25.** total cost
___ **26.** total revenue
___ **27.** variable costs

a. A decision in which a firm chooses among all possible production techniques.
b. Additional output that will result from an additional worker, other inputs constant.
c. As more and more of a variable input is added to an existing fixed input, eventually, the additional output obtained from the additional input will fall.
d. Total revenue minus total cost.
e. Costs that do not change in the period of time under consideration, regardless of the firm's production level.
f. Equation that describes the relationships between inputs and outputs, telling the maximum amount of output that can be derived from a given number of inputs.
g. Firm is constrained by past choices in regard to what production decisions it can make.
h. Fixed cost divided by quantity produced.
i. Explicit payments to the factors of production plus the opportunity cost provided by the owners of the firm.
j. Variable cost divided by quantity produced.
k. Costs that change as output changes.
l. The cost of changing the level of output by one unit.
m. Total output divided by the quantity of the input.
n. Total cost divided by the quantity produced.
o. Revenue minus explicit and implicit costs.
p. Revenue minus explicit cost.
q. Costs that go into a firm's income statement.
r. An economic institution that transforms factors of production into goods and services.
s. The opportunity costs of the factors of production provided by the owners of the business.
t. Transformation of factors into goods and services.
u. A table showing the output resulting from various combinations of factors of production or inputs.
v. Total sales times price.
w. Businesses that have only one owner.
x. Businesses with two or more owners.
y. Businesses that are treated as a person and are legally owned by their stockholders.
z. Certificates of ownership in a company.
z1. The stockholder's liability to the amount that stockholder has invested in the company.

MULTIPLE CHOICE

Circle the one best answer for each of the following questions:

1. Economic profit
   a. equals revenues minus explicit and implicit costs.
   b. is the same as an accounting profit.
   c. will always be larger than an accounting profit.
   d. does not include the opportunity cost of the entrepreneur in the total revenue calculation.

2. The essential difference between the short run and the long run is that
   a. the short run pertains to a period of time less than one year; long run is longer than one year.
   b. in the short run, at least one input (factor of production) is fixed; in the long run, all inputs are variable.
   c. in the short run, some costs are fixed; in the long run, all costs are fixed.
   d. in the short run, all costs are variable; in the long run, all costs are fixed.

3. In a short-run decision
   a. a firm has more options than in the long run.
   b. a firm has fewer options than in the long run.
   c. a firm has the same number of options as in the long run.
   d. there is no relation between the number of options a firm has and whether it is a short-run decision or a long-run decision

4. If a firm can produce 560 units of output with 5 workers, 600 units of output with 6 workers then the
   a. marginal product of the 6th worker is 100 units.
   b. marginal product of the 6th worker is 40 units.
   c. average product of 6 workers is 70 units.
   d. average product of the 5 workers is 100 units.

5. Refer to the graph below. The range marked "A" shows

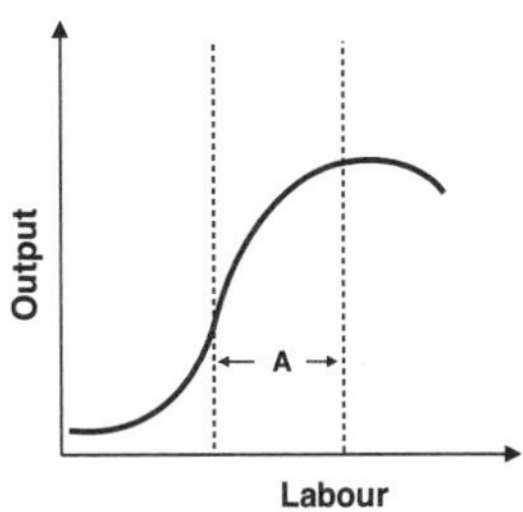

   a. increasing marginal productivity.
   b. diminishing marginal productivity.
   c. diminishing absolute productivity.
   d. diminishing absolute marginal productivity.

6. The law of diminishing marginal productivity
   a. states that as more and more of a variable input is added to an existing fixed input, after some point, the additional output obtained from the additional input will fall.
   b. states that as more and more of a variable input is added to an existing fixed input, after some point, the additional output obtained from the additional input will rise.
   c. explains why marginal costs of production fall as additional units of output are produced.
   d. explains why average productivity always rises.

7. When the law of law of diminishing marginal productivity is operating
   a. increasing returns to scale are realized.
   b. marginal productivity is falling and average productivity is rising.
   c. marginal productivity is falling and marginal costs are rising.
   d. marginal productivity is rising and marginal costs of are rising.

8. Five workers are producing a total of 28 units of output. A worker's marginal product
   a. is 5.
   b. is 28.
   c. is 28 divided by 5.
   d. cannot be determined from the information provided.

9. The firm is producing an output of 24 and has total costs of 260. Its marginal cost
   a. equals 10.83.
   b. equals 8.75
   c. equals 260.
   d. Cannot be determined form the information provided.

10. Fixed costs
   a. are costs that do not change with the output level.
   b. equal total costs plus variable costs.
   c. equal average fixed costs divided by the output level.
   d. rise at first then decline as output rises.

11. Concerning costs of production, it is true that
   a. if a firm shuts down for a month, its total costs for the month will equal its fixed costs for the month.
   b. average variable costs equal total variable costs multiplied by the output level.
   c. marginal costs equal the change in total costs divided by the change in variable costs.
   d. marginal cost equals average total cost multiplied by the output level.

12. A firm is producing 100 units of output at a total cost of $800. The firm's average variable cost is $5 per unit. The firm's
   a. marginal cost is $8.
   b. total variable cost is $300.
   c. average fixed cost is $3.
   d. average total cost is $500.

13. The only variable input used in the production of pickles in a small factory is labour. Currently 5 workers are employed; each works 40 hours per week and is paid $15 per hour. If fixed costs are $4000 per week and total output is 4000 jars of pickles per week, then
   a. average fixed cost is $16,000.
   b. total costs are $7000.
   c. total variable costs are $4,000.
   d. average total costs are $0.75.

14. A firm's total fixed costs are $100; total variable costs are $200; and average fixed costs are $20. The firm's total output
   a. is 1.
   b. is 5.
   c. is 10.
   d. cannot be determined from the information provided.

15. Refer to the graph below. The curves in the graph are

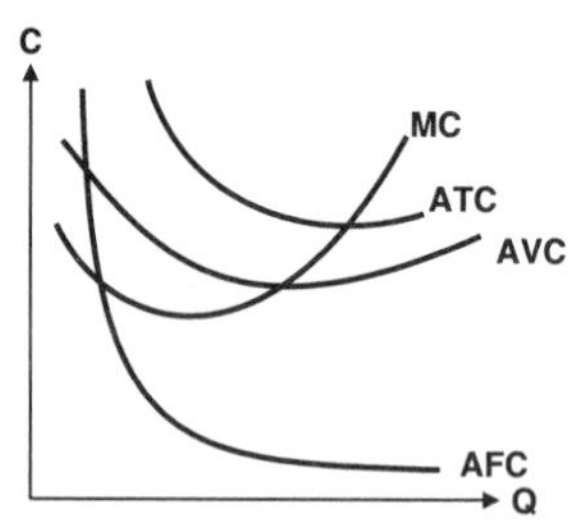

   a. correctly drawn.
   b. incorrectly drawn because the average total cost curve is above the average variable cost curve.
   c. incorrectly drawn because the marginal cost curve is positioned wrong.
   d. incorrectly drawn because marginal cost and average variable costs are confused.

16. Refer to the graph below. The curve represented is most likely

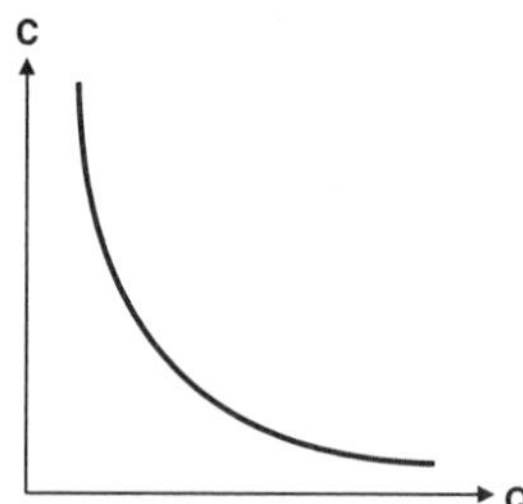

   a. an average total cost curve.
   b. an average variable cost curve.
   c. an average fixed cost curve.
   d. a total cost curve.

17. Concerning costs and cost curves for a firm, it is true that
   a. if a firm increases its output from 100 to 101 and total costs increase from $55 to $60 then marginal cost of producing the 101st unit of output is $115.
   b. if marginal cost exceeds average total cost then average total cost is falling.
   c. the vertical distance between the average total and average variable cost curves at any given output level equals average fixed cost at that output level.
   d. the marginal cost curve intersects the average variable and average total cost curves when they are sloping downward.

SHORT-ANSWER QUESTIONS

1. What is the difference between accounting and economic profit?

2. Suppose you are the president of a corporation who is designing a 2-year plan of operations and a 10-year plan of operations. How would those plans differ?

3. Suppose you are a novice gardener. You plant one seed in a flower pot and watch it grow into a stalk of wheat with plump wheat berries. The next year, you plant two seeds in that pot and harvest double the amount of wheat berries. You deduce that at this rate, you can provide the world's supply of wheat berries in your little pot. Why is this obviously not true? What principle is your answer based upon?

4. What is the algebraic relationship between total cost, total variable cost and total fixed cost? What is the algebraic relationship between average total cost, average variable cost and average fixed cost? What is marginal cost equal to?

5. What does the marginal cost curve measure?

6. What does the average variable cost curve measure?

7. What does the average fixed cost curve measure?

8. What does the average total cost curve measure?

9. How does the law of diminishing marginal productivity affect the shape of short-run cost curves?

10. Where does the marginal cost curve intersect the average total cost and average variable cost curves? Explain why the relationship between marginal cost and average cost is how you have described it.

11. Draw typical *AFC, AVC, ATC,* and *MC* curves on the same graph, making sure to maintain the relationships among them from question 10.

PROBLEMS AND APPLICATIONS

1. Suppose you and a friend are thinking about opening a fast food vending service at a nearby resort during your summer break. This will entail serving pizzas out of a vendor's truck. This is an alternative to working a factory job where you could each earn $7,000 over the summer break. A fully equipped truck could be leased for $9,000. Insurance and other miscellaneous operating expenses total $1,000. Given your projected sales revenues of $33,000, you anticipate your variable costs to total $8,000. Together, you and your friend have just enough money to cover all of the summer's fixed and variable costs of the business in the bank. If you pull that money out of the bank then you will have to collectively forgo $1,500 in interest income for the summer.

   a. What would be the accounting profit for your business?

   b. What would be the economic profit for your business?

2. Find *TC, AFC, AVC, ATC,* and *MC* for the following table. Also, graph the TC curve on one graph and graph AFC, AVC, ATC and MC on another graph.

Units	FC	VC	TC	MC	AFC	AVC	ATC
0	50	0					
1	50	90					
2	50	120					
3	50	165					
4	50	220					
5	50	290					

3. You are presented with the following table on average productivity. Labour is your only variable cost. The price of labour is $20 per hour, and the fixed cost is $50.

Labour	TP	MP	AP	TC	MC	AVC
1	2					
2	6					
3	15					
4	20					
5	23					
6	24					

a. Fill in the table above for marginal product (MP), average product (AP), total cost (TC), marginal cost (MC), and average variable costs (AVC).

b. Graph the average variable cost curve.

c. Show that the graph you drew in 2(b) is the approximate mirror image of the average productivity curve.

d. Graph the marginal cost and the marginal productivity curves. Show that they are approximate mirror images of each other.

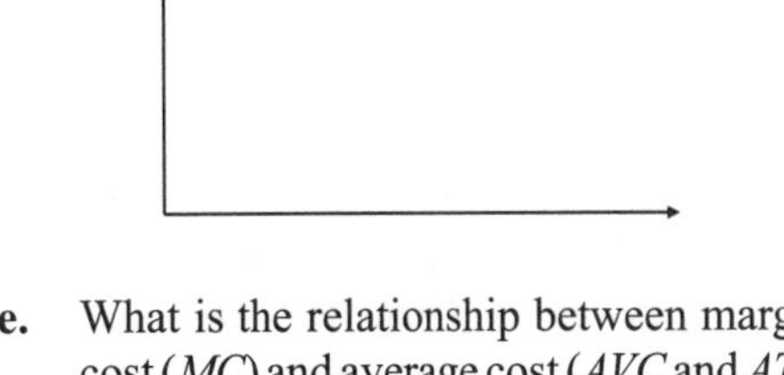

e. What is the relationship between marginal cost (*MC*) and average cost (*AVC* and *ATC*)? What is the relationship between marginal product (*MP*) and average product (*AP*)?

4. A firm has fixed cost of $50. Variable costs are as follows:

Units	VC
1	75
2	110
3	150
4	200
5	260
6	335

a. Graph *AFC*, *ATC*, *AVC*, and *MC* curves on the axes below the table (all on the same graph).

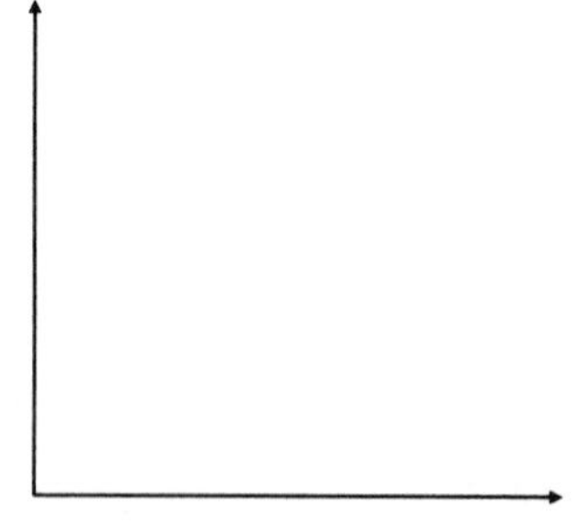

b. Explain the relationships between the *MC* curve and *ATC* and *AVC*. Between *ATC* and *AVC*.

c. Suppose fixed costs fall to $20, and graph new *AFC*, *ATC*, *AVC*, and *MC* curves.

d. Which curves shifted? Why?

5. A box of Wheaties cereal with a wholesale price of $1.60 has the following costs:

Labour:	0.15
Materials:	0.30
Sales cost:	0.30
Advertising:	0.15
Research and Development:	0.15
Rent on factory building and equipment:	0.15
Owner's profit:	0.40

a. Which are likely variable costs?

b. Which are likely fixed costs?

c. If output were to rise, what would likely happen to *ATC*?

A BRAIN TEASER

1. Refer to the cost curves for a firm shown below when answering the following questions. Assume the firm is currently producing 100 units of output.

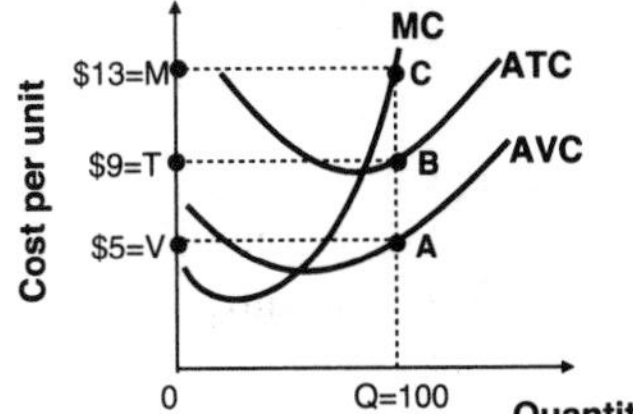

   a. What is the number representing the marginal cost of producing the 100th unit of output? What geometric line segment represents that number?

   b. What is ATC when output is 100? What geometric line segment represents that number?

   c. What is AVC when output is 100? What geometric line segment represents that number?

   d. What is AFC when output is 100? What geometric line segment represents that number?

   e. What is TC when output is 100? What geometric *area* represents that number?

   f. What is VC when output is 100? What geometric *area* represents that number?

   g. What is FC when output is 100? What geometric *area* represents that number?

   h. Why does the vertical distance between the AVC and ATC curves decrease as output expands?

POTENTIAL ESSAY QUESTIONS

You may also see essay questions similar to the "Problems & Applications" and "Brain Teaser" exercises.

1. Describe the relationship between the law of diminishing marginal productivity and costs of production in the short run.

2. Distinguish the various kinds of cost curves and describe the relationship between them.

ANSWERS

MATCHING

1-p; 2-h; 3-m; 4-n; 5-j; 6-y; 7-c; 8-o; 9-q; 10-r; 11-e; 12-s; 13-z1; 14-a; 15-l; 16-c; 17-x; 18-t; 19-f; 20-u; 21-d; 22-g; 23-w; 24-z; 25-i; 26-v; 27-k.

ANSWERS

MULTIPLE CHOICE

1. a Economic profit is revenue minus explicit and implicit costs. Economists include opportunity costs in total cost. See pages 179.

2. b There is no set calendar time associated with the short run or the long run. In the short run, some costs are fixed; in the long run, all costs are variable costs—because nothing is fixed in the long run. See page 180.

3. b The longer the time period, the more numerous the options. See page 180.

4. b Marginal product is the change in total product divided by the change in the number of workers. That is 600 560 = 40. Average product is total product divided by the number of workers. Average product of 5 workers is 112 and the average product of 6 workers is 100. See pages 180-181, especially Figure 8-1.

5. b A bowed downward production function has marginal product decreasing as output increases. See Figure 8-1 on page 181.

6. a Because of diminishing marginal productivity, marginal costs of production rise as additional units are produced. In addition, diminishing marginal productivity causes average productivity to fall. See page 182.

7. c When marginal productivity is falling, more inputs are necessary to increase production by the same amount. Thus, marginal costs are rising. See page 182 and especially pages 186-187.

8. d To determine marginal product, you need to know the change in the product as you add a worker. See page 181.

9. d To determine marginal costs, one must know the change in costs associated with a change in quantity. See page 184.

10. a Fixed costs remain constant no matter what output is. Also, fixed costs equal total costs minus variable costs. Moreover, fixed costs also equal average fixed costs multiplied by the output level. See pages 183-184.

11. a Total costs equal fixed costs when a firm shuts down. This is because there are no variable costs when a firm shuts down. Average variable costs equal total variable costs divided by the output level. Marginal costs equal the change in total costs divided by the change in the output level. Total cost equals average total cost multiplied by the output level. See pages 183-184.

12. c Average total cost is total cost divided by output ($800/100 = $8). Average fixed cost is average total cost minus average variable cost ($8 $5 = $3). See pages 183-184.

13. b 5 workers times 40 hours times $15 is $3,000. These are variable costs. Add this to fixed cost to get total cost. Average total cost is $7,000 divided by 4,000, or $1.75. Average fixed cost is $4,000 divided by 4,000, or $1. See pages 183-184.

14. b Average fixed costs equal total fixed costs divided by output. If the firm's total fixed costs are $100 and average fixed costs are $20, the quantity must be 100/20 = 5. See pages 183-184.

15. a The *ATC* curve is above the *AVC* curve and the *MC* curve goes through the minimum points of the *AVC* and the *ATC* curves. The *AFC* curve is always falling. See Figure 8-2, pages 185-186.

16. c Only the average fixed cost curve falls continuously. See Figure 8-2 on pages 185-186.

17. c $AFC = ATC - AVC$. See pages 183-186.

ANSWERS

SHORT-ANSWER QUESTIONS

1. Accounting profit = revenue − explicit cost. Economic profit = revenue − (explicit *and* implicit cost). Implicit costs include the opportunity cost of time and capital provided by the owners of the firm. Accountants do not include these implicit costs in their calculations of profit. (179)

2. In a long-run planning decision, a firm chooses among all possible production techniques. In a short-run planning decision, the firm has fewer options. (180)

3. This is obviously not true because each additional seed you are adding will produce fewer and fewer berries. Eventually, the yield will even decline as the plants choke one another out. This follows from the law of diminishing marginal productivity: as more and more of a variable input is added to an existing fixed input, after some point, the additional output one gets from the additional input will fall. (181-182)

4. $TC = VC + FC$. $ATC = AVC + AFC$. $MC = \Delta TC/\Delta Q$ (183-184)

5. A marginal cost curve measures the change in total cost associated with a change in output. (184)

6. An average variable cost curve measures variable cost averaged over total output. (183-184)

7. An average fixed cost curve measures fixed costs averaged over total output. (183-184)

8. An average total cost curve measures total cost (variable plus fixed) averaged over total output. (183-184)

9. The law of diminishing marginal productivity means that eventually marginal productivity falls. When that happens, short run costs begin to rise. When marginal and average productivity are rising, then marginal and average cost curves are falling. When marginal and average productivity are falling, then marginal and average cost curves are rising. (182)

10. The marginal cost curve intersects the average total and average variable cost curves at their minimum points. The marginal cost curve intersects these average cost curves at their minimum points because when marginal cost exceeds average total cost, average total cost must be rising; and when marginal cost is less than average total cost, average total cost must be falling. (186)

11. Typical *AFC, AVC, ATC,* and *MC* curves are graphed below. Since fixed costs are the same for all levels of output, the *AFC* curve is always falling as the same fixed costs are spread over larger and larger levels of output. The *MC* curve first declines because of increasing marginal productivity, but then rises because decreasing marginal productivity, eventually sets in. The *MC* curve intersects the *AVC* and *ATC* curves at their minimum points. This is true because if the marginal cost is below average cost, average cost must be falling and if marginal cost is above average cost, average cost must be rising. (185-189)

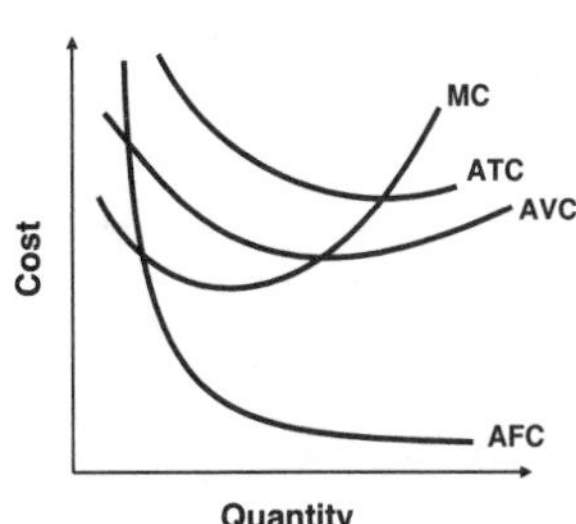

ANSWERS

PROBLEMS AND APPLICATIONS

1. **a.** Accounting profit = revenue − explicit cost = \$33,000 − (\$9,000 + \$1,000 + \$8,000) = \$15,000 accounting profit. (200-201)
   b. Economic profit = revenue − explicit and implicit cost = \$33,000 − (\$7,000 + \$7,000 + \$9,000 + \$1,000 + \$8,000 + \$1,500) = − \$500; \$500 economic loss. (179)

2. By definition, $TC = FC + VC$, $AFC = FC/Q$, $AVC = VC/Q$, $ATC = AFC + AVC$, and MC = the change in TC. Using this information, we completed the following table. (Marginal cost refers to the marginal cost of increasing output to that row, e.g., the marginal cost of going from 0 to 1 is 90.) (183-185)

Units	TC	MC	AFC	AVC	ATC
0	50	—	—	—	—
1	140	90	50.00	90	
2	170	30	25.00	60	
3	215	45	16.67	55	
4	270	55	12.50	55	
5	340	70	10.00	58	

The total cost curve is shown below. The *ATC*, *AVC*, *MC*, and *AFC* curves are also shown below.

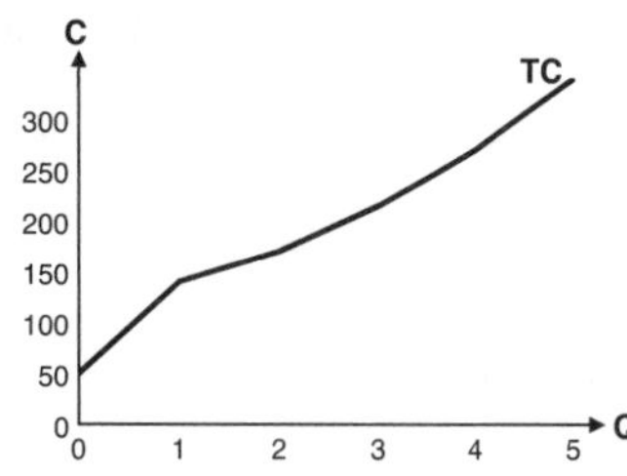

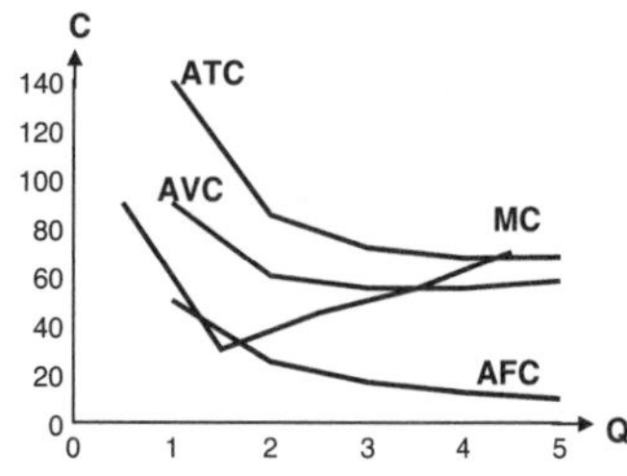

3. **a.** $AP = TP/Q$, MP = change in TP ÷ change in Q, TC is (Labour × \$20) + FC, MC = change in TC per unit change in product. AVC is VC/Q. Using these definitions, we completed the following table. (Marginal cost refers to the marginal cost of increasing to that row, e.g., the marginal cost of increasing total product from 2 to 6 is 5.00.) (181)

Labour	TP	MP	AP	TC	MC	AVC
1	2	—	2.0	70	—	10.00
2	6	4	3.0	90	5.00	6.67
3	15	9	5.0	110	2.22	4.00
4	20	5	5.0	130	4.00	4.00
5	23	3	5.6	150	6.67	4.35
6	24	1	4.0	170	20.00	5.00

   b. The average variable cost curve is shown below. (183-185)

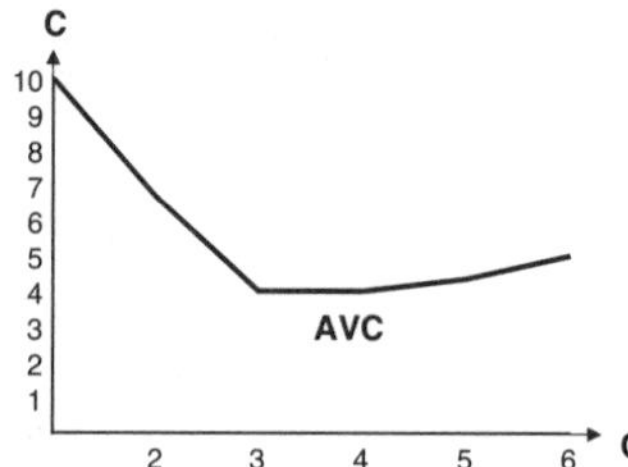

   c. The AP and AVC curves are shown below. They are the mirror images of one another. The maximum point on the AP curve occurs at the minimum point on the AVC curve. When AP curve is falling, AVC is rising, and vice versa. This is because as productivity falls, costs per unit rise, and as productivity increases, costs per unit decrease. (186-187)

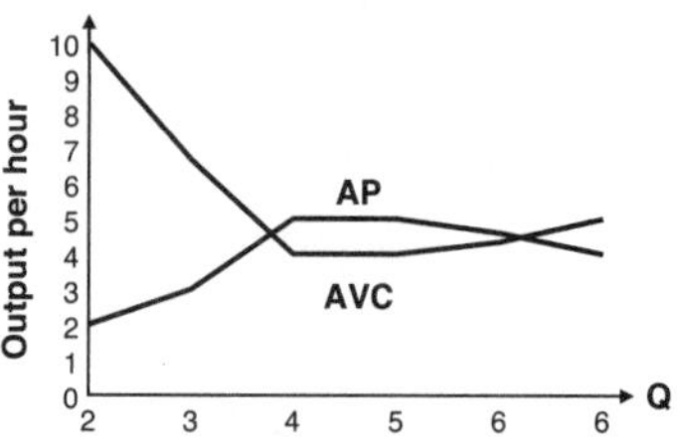

d. The marginal cost and marginal productivity curves are shown below. The maximum point on the *MP* curve occurs at the minimum point on the *MC* curve. When the *MP* curve is falling *MC* is rising, and vice versa. This is because as productivity falls, costs per unit rise and as productivity increases, costs per unit decrease. (186-187)

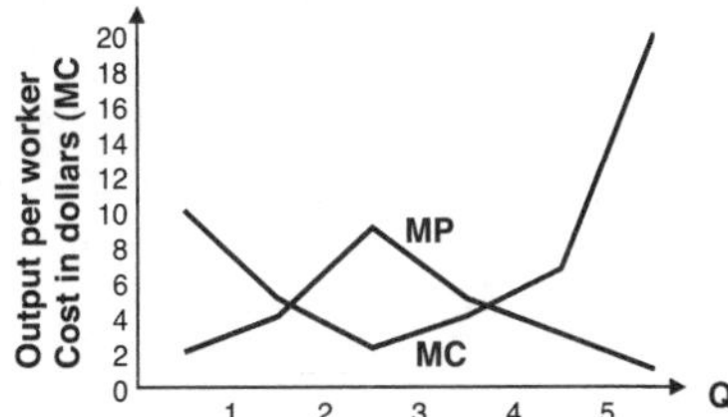

e. When the *MC* curve is below the *AVC* (or *ATC*) curve, the *AVC* (or *ATC*) curve is falling. The *MC* curve intersects with the *AVC* (and *ATC*) curve at its minimum point. When the *MC* curve is above the *AVC* (or *ATC*) curve, the *AVC* (*ATC*) is rising. The same goes for marginal product and average product. When marginal product is below average product, average product is falling and when marginal product is above average product, average product is rising. (183-185)

4. a. To graph the *ATC*, *AFC*, *AVC*, and *MC* curves, first determine the values of these curves for units 1 through 6. $TC = FC + VC$, $AFC = FC/Q$, $AVC = VC/Q$, $ATC = AFC + AVC$, and $MC =$ the change in *TC*. These values are shown in the table below. The curves are also shown below. (Marginal cost refers to the marginal cost of increasing to that row, e.g., the marginal cost of going from 0 to 1 is 75.) (183-185)

Units	VC	ATC	AVC	AFC	MC
1	75		75	50	75
2	110		55	25	35
3	150		50	16.67	40
4	200		50	12.5	50
5	260		52	10	60
6	335		55.83	8.33	75

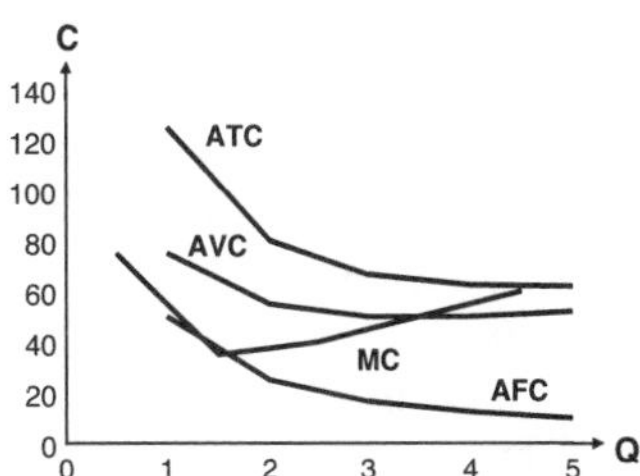

b. The *MC* curve goes through the minimum points of both *ATC* and *AVC* curves, which are rising when they are below the *MC* curve, and which are falling when they are above the *MC* curve. *ATC* and *AVC* curves are both U-shaped. Because of fixed costs, the *AVC* curve is always below the *ATC* curve, but the two curves converge as output increases. (185-186)

c. The curves are shown below.

Units	VC	ATC	AVC	AFC	MC
1	75	95	75	20	75
2	110	65	55	10	35
3	150	56.67	50	6.67	40
4	200	55	50	5	50
5	260	56	52	4	60
6	335	59.17	55.83	3.33	75

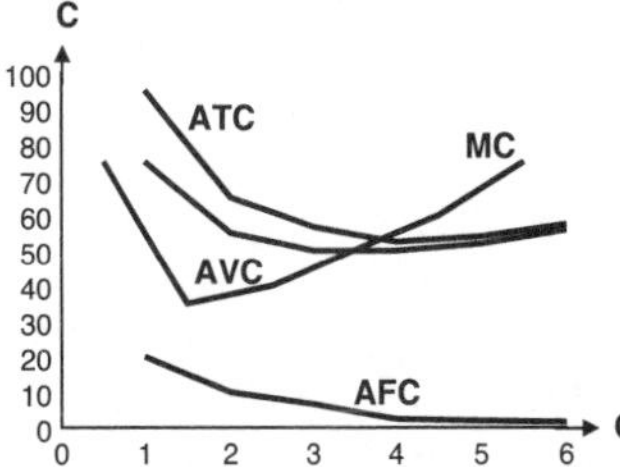

d. Only the *AFC* and *ATC* curves shifted because they are the only curves that depend upon fixed costs. All the others are based upon only variable costs. Because the fixed cost falls to $20, the average fixed cost must fall as well. (184-186)

5. **a.** Labour and material costs are variable costs since they will rise and fall as production of Wheaties rises and falls. (183-184)
   b. Sales, advertising, research and development, and rent on factory building and equipment are fixed cost since they are most likely independent of the level of Wheaties produced. (183-184)
   c. Because fixed cost is high in this production process, almost equal to half of the revenue, an increase in output is likely to reduce *AFC*, and thus, *ATC* would likely fall as well. (183-184)

ANSWERS

A BRAIN TEASER

1. **a.** MC for the 100th unit of output is equal to \$13 (the extra cost of producing that 100th unit is \$13), or line segment OM. (The line segment OM simply represents the distance or amount of \$13). (183-184)
   b. ATC = \$9, or line segment OT, when output is 100. (183-184)
   c. AVC = \$5, or line segment OV, when output is 100. (183-184)
   d. AFC = \$4. Note that AFC = ATC − AVC. The line segment representing AFC is line segment AB, which is also equal to line segment VT. Recall that, at a given output level, the vertical distance between the ATC and AVC curves equals AFC at that particular output level. (183-184)
   e. TC = \$900. (Note that TC = ATC × Q = \$9 × 100 = \$900). The geometric area representing TC is area OTBQ. (Note that like any area, the area OTBQ is equal to a width multiplied by a length. Think of the width as line segment OT, representing ATC. Think of the length as line segment OQ, representing the output level, Q. OT multiplied by OQ equals area OTBQ.) (183-184)
   f. VC = \$500 (VC = AVC × Q = \$5 × 100 = \$500), or area OVAQ (OVAQ = line segment OV multiplied by line segment OQ). (183-184)
   g. FC = \$400 (FC = AFC × Q = \$4 × 100 = \$400; or, FC = TC × VC = \$900 − \$500 = \$400). The area representing FC is area VTBA. (FC = TC − VC = OTBQ − OVAQ = VTBA). (183-184)
   Note that one can obtain all seven (7) short-run cost numbers when only provided with the MC, AVC, and ATC curves! Remember how to do this. It will come in handy later.
   h. Because the vertical distance between the ATC and AVC curves equals AFC, and AFC decreases as output increases, then the vertical distance between the ATC and AVC curves decreases as output increases. (183-184)

ANSWERS

POTENTIAL ESSAY QUESTIONS

The following are annotated answers. They indicate the general idea behind the answer.

1. When marginal productivity is increasing, then costs of production (except fixed cost which do not vary with the output level) are falling. When marginal productivity is decreasing, then costs of production (except fixed cost which do not vary with the output level) are rising.

2. When productivity is falling, then marginal cost and therefore average variable (and average total) costs must be rising.

Know how to calculate all 7 short-run costs!

PRODUCTION AND COST ANALYSIS II

9

CHAPTER AT A GLANCE

This chapter expands the discussion of long run production decisions. The long run cost curve is introduced. There are essentially three segments to this curve, each of which relate to several important concepts—economies of scale, diseconomies of scale and constant returns to scale.

In real life, cost analysis is difficult because actual production processes are influenced by a number of issues—economies of scope, learning by doing, by technological change and by many unmeasured opportunity costs. These issues are highlighted at the end of the chapter.

This review is based upon the learning objectives that open the chapter.

1. Technical efficiency is efficiency that does not consider costs of inputs. The fewest possible inputs are used. The least-cost technically efficient process is the economically efficient process. (194-195)

Firms try to be economically efficient because they want to minimize costs.

2a. There is a relationship between long-run and short-run average total costs. The long-run ATC curve is an envelope of short-run ATC curves. (195-196)

Each short-run ATC curve touches the long-run ATC curve at only one point.

2b. In the long run, all inputs are variable, so only economies and diseconomies of scale can influence the shape of the long-run cost curve. (196-199)

2c. Know the concepts increasing returns to scale, constant returns to scale and decreasing returns to scale.

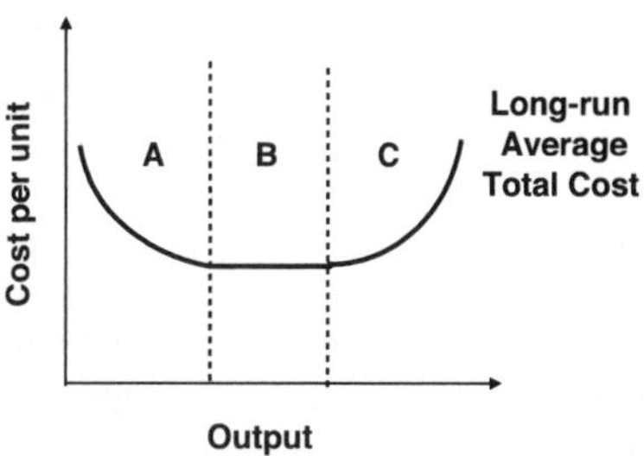

Note that, in the long run, as quantity of production increases, the firm is using ever-larger scales of operation (larger plant or factory sizes).

If you double all inputs and <u>per-unit</u> costs fall (rise), then you experience economies (diseconomies) of scale.

If per-unit (or average) costs do not change then the firm is experiencing constant returns to scale, referred to the "c" section of the long run ATC curve.

Economies of scale refers to the "A" section of the long run ATC curve, while diseconomies of scale refers to the "B" section.

Don't get short-run costs confused with long-run costs. The U-shape of short-run average variable and average total cost curves reflects increasing and diminishing marginal productivity. The U-shape of the long-run average total cost curve reflects economies and diseconomies of scale.

2d. At the planned output level, short-run ATC equals long-run ATC, but at all other levels of output, short-run ATC is higher than long-run ATC. (195-196)

See Figure 9-2 in the textbook (page 198)

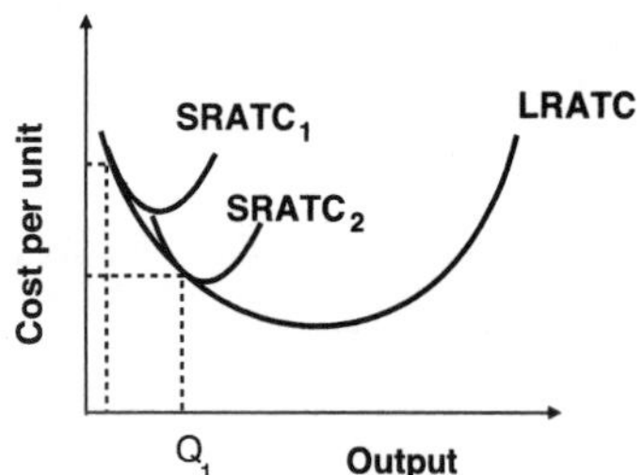

$SRATC_2$ is the appropriate plant size to produce Q_1 because costs per unit are lowest.

3a. The difference between the expected price of a good and the expected average total cost of producing it is the supplier's expected economic profit per unit. The expected profit per unit must exceed the opportunity cost of supplying the good for a good to be supplied. (201)

Potential economic profit motivates entrepreneurs to supply those goods demanded by consumers. The greater the demand, the greater the price, the greater the profit potential, and the greater the quantity supplied.

3b. Some of the problems of using cost analysis in the real world include: (201-205)

- Economies of scope;
- Learning by doing and technological change;
- Many dimensions; and
- Unmeasured costs such as opportunity costs.

See also, Appendix A: "Isocost/Isoquant Analysis.

MATCHING THE TERMS
Match the terms to their definitions

All of these key terms are found at the end of the chapter.

___ **1.** constant returns to scale
___ **2.** diseconomies of scale
___ **3.** decreasing returns to scale
___ **4.** economically efficient
___ **5.** economies of scale
___ **6.** economies of scope
___ **7.** entrepreneur
___ **8.** envelope relationship
___ **9.** external economies
___ **10.** indivisible setup cost
___ **11.** increasing returns to scale
___ **12.** learning by doing
___ **13.** learning curve
___ **14.** minimum efficient scale of production
___ **15.** monitoring costs
___ **16.** team spirit
___ **17.** technical efficiency
___ **18.** technological change

a. When long-run average total costs decrease as output increases.
b. An increase in per-unit cost as a result of an increase in output.
c. An increase in the range of production techniques that provides new ways of producing goods.
d. Becoming more proficient at doing something by actually doing it.
e. Where long-run average total costs do not change with an increase in output.
f. Individual who sees an opportunity to sell an item at a price higher than the average cost of producing it.
g. The costs of producing products are interdependent so that it is less costly for a firm to produce one good when it is already producing another.
h. Output at which all economies of scale have been captured..
i. The cost of an indivisible input for which a certain minimum amount of production must be undertaken before the input becomes economically feasible to use.
j. Using the method of production that produces a given level of output at the lowest possible cost.
k. A situation where the fewest inputs as possible are used to produce a given output.
l. Costs incurred by the firm to ensure that employees do what they are supposed to.
m. The feelings of friendship and being part of something that brings out people's best efforts.
n. The doubling of inputs results in a less-than-doubling of output.
o. Force beyond the control of the individual firm.
p. Doubling the inputs, more than doubles the output.
q. Represents the process of workers becoming better (more productive) at a specific job as they gain experience from doing it repeatedly.
r. The relationship between long-run and short-run average total costs.

MULTIPLE CHOICE

Circle the one best answer for each of the following questions:

1. Which of the following concerning technical and economic efficiency is true?
   a. Many different production processes can be economically efficient, but only the method that involves the lowest possible cost is technically efficient.
   b. To achieve technical efficiency, managers must use the most up-to-date technology.
   c. The economically efficient method of production is the same in all countries.
   d. To achieve economic efficiency, managers need to use the least costly input combination.

2. The long run average total costs of production
   a. rises as output increases when we experience economies of scale.
   b. is explained by decreasing marginal productivity.
   c. passes through the minimum point of each short-run average total cost curve.
   d. is considered to be an envelope curve because each short-run average total cost curve touches it at only one level of output.

3. Indivisible setup costs refer to
   a. the cost of an indivisible input for which a certain minimum amount of production must be undertaken before production becomes economically feasible.
   b. the cost of an indivisible input for which a certain maximum amount of production must be undertaken before production becomes economically feasible.
   c. the cost of an indivisible input whose cost is invisible.
   d. the cost of an indivisible input whose cost of production is lower because an interdependent good is also being produced.

4. Economies of scale:
   a. account for the upward-sloping portion of the long-run average total cost curve.
   b. exist because of the difficulties in coordinating and managing a large business enterprise.
   c. imply an increase in per-unit costs of production associated with an increase in output.
   d. arise because large indivisible setup costs are spread out among a larger level of output and because of the efficiencies of greater labour and management specialization.

5. Refer to the graph below. The section of the long-run average total cost curve marked as "A" represents

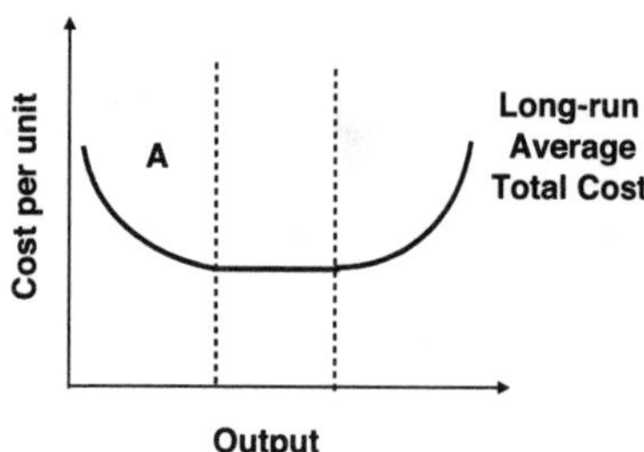

   a. economies of scale.
   b. diseconomies of scale.
   c. diminishing marginal productivity.
   d. increasing marginal productivity.

6. Explanations for diseconomies of scale include all of the following *except*
   a. as firm size increases, monitoring costs generally increase.
   b. as firm size increases, team spirit or morale generally decreases.
   c. as firm size increases, monitoring costs generally decrease, thereby increasing other costs.
   d. All of the above are explanations.

7. Which of the following is associated with diseconomies of scale?
   a. Producing 1,000 lawn mowers costs $100,000 while producing 2,000 lawn mowers costs $220,000.
   b. 50 workers and 5 machines produces 1,000 units of output while 100 workers and 10 machines produces 2,500 units of output.
   c. 50 workers and 5 machines produces 1,000 units of output wile 60 workers and 5 machines produces 1,200 units of output.
   d. Producing 1,000 lawn mowers costs $100,000 while producing 2,000 lawn mowers costs $150,000.

8. Refer to the graph below. Which of the following statements about the graph is true?

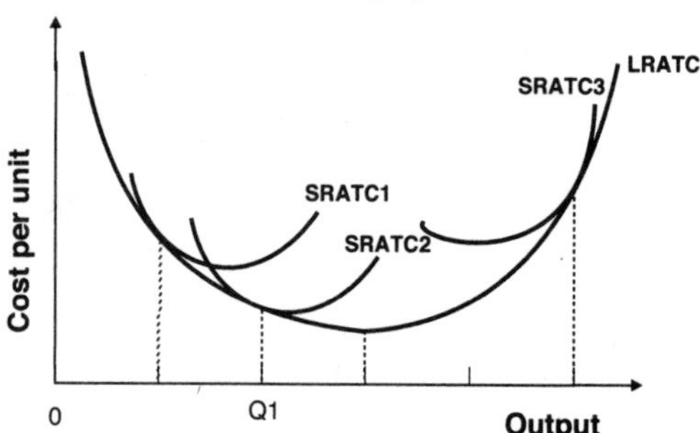

   a. The scale of operation associated with $SRATC_3$ is realizing some economies of scale.
   b. $SRATC_2$ is a smaller scale of operation than $SRATC_1$.
   c. The lowest-cost scale of operation to produce Q_1 is $SRATC_1$.
   d. The lowest-cost scale of operation to produce Q_1 is $SRATC_2$.

9. Constant returns to scale
   a. refer to the upward sloping portion of the long run ATC curve.
   b. refer to the downward sloping portion of the long run ATC curve.
   c. means long-run average total costs do not change with an increase in output.
   d. are a result of rising monitoring costs and a loss of team spirit.

10. The envelope relationship refers to the fact that the
   a. short-run average cost curve forms an envelope around long-run average cost curves.
   b. long-run average cost curve forms an envelope around short-run average cost curves.
   c. average cost curve forms an envelope around the marginal cost curve.
   d. marginal cost curve forms an envelope around the average cost curve.

11. Economies of scope occur when
   a. firms increase production of a good, that good's cost falls.
   b. firms increase their long-run vision and costs fall.
   c. the costs of production of one product fall when the firm increases the production of another product.
   d. technological change lowers cost of production.

12. Learning by doing and increases in technology cause the long-run
   a. average cost curve to be downward sloping.
   b. average cost curve to be upward sloping.
   c. average cost curve to shift down.
   d. marginal cost curve to be downward sloping.

13. Total revenue is $1,000; explicit measurable costs are $500.
   a. Accounting profit is $1,000.
   b. Accounting profit is $500.
   c. Accounting profit is $200.
   d. Accounting profit cannot be determined from the figures given.

14. A business owner makes 400 items by hand in 500 hours. She could have earned $20 an hour working for someone else. If the item sells for $50 each and the explicit costs total $12,000, then
   a. total revenue equals $10,000.
   b. implicit costs equal $20,000.
   c. the accounting profits equals $10,000.
   d. the economic loss equals $2,000.

A1. Refer to the graph below. The isocost curve shown above represents a price of machinery (in terms of labour) of
   a. one-eighth unit of labour.
   b. one-fourth unit of labour.
   c. one-half unit of labour.
   d. two units of labour.

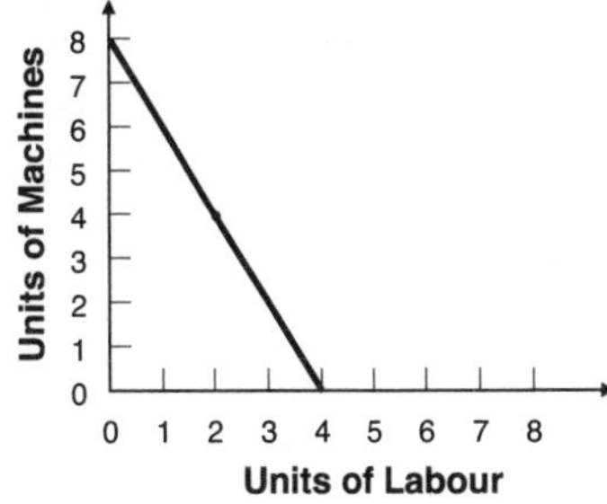

A2. Refer to the graph for Question A1. If the price of machinery increases, the isocost curve will rotate
   a. in and become flatter
   b. in and become steeper
   c. out and become flatter.
   d. out and become steeper.

A3. The economically efficient point in the isoquant model in the graph below is at point
   a. A.
   b. B.
   c. C.
   d. D.

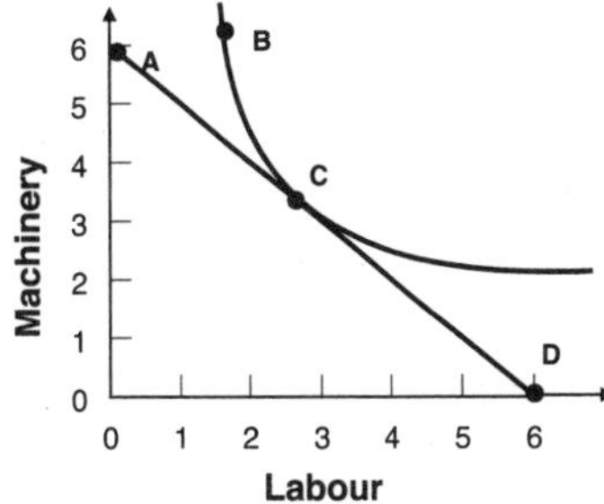

SHORT-ANSWER QUESTIONS

1. You are consulting for a firm. Through analysis, the firm has determined that the best it can do is produce 100 tons of wheat per day with 10 workers and 1 acre of land or 100 tons of wheat per day with 10 acres of land and 1 worker. You are asked to choose the most efficient method of production. What do you advise?

2. After having read your report, the executives come running after you. They tell you that they have forgotten to tell you that an acre of land costs $40 an acre per day and workers can be hired for $100 a day. They wonder whether your answer to Question 1 changes.

3. The cost of developing a typical introductory economics textbook is well over $1 million. Once the textbook is developed and ready to print, the actual print costs for large runs are about $6 per book. What do these facts suggest about the shape of the long-run average total cost curve of producing textbooks?

4. What is the envelope relationship between short-run cost curves and long-run cost curves?

5. How do returns to scale affect a firm's long-run production decision?

6. Why does an entrepreneur start a business? How are the decisions by the entrepreneur central to all supply decisions?

7. Suppose you are giving a talk on costs to decision-makers at firms. You have presented the cost curves as taught to you in this text without caveat. What would be some of the problems your audience might have with your presentation?

PROBLEMS AND APPLICATIONS

1. In some developing countries, relatively primitive labour-intensive production processes are often used. For example, in farming. Why might a firm be economically efficient by not using the latest technology in the production process?

2. The following table represents long-run total costs:

Q	TC	LRATC
1	60	
2	66	
3	69	
4	72	
5	75	
6	90	
7	126	
8	184	
9	297	
10	600	

   a. Calculate the long-run average total cost in the column provided.

   b. Graph the *LRATC* curve on the graph below.

   c. Label the area of economies of scale and the area of diseconomies of scale on the graph.

3. How can the extent to which the presence of economies and diseconomies of scale in an industry help account for the size and the number of firms in that industry? That is, if economies of scale were quite extensive in a particular industry, would you expect a large number of relatively small firms, or a small number of relatively large firms to be operating within that industry? What if diseconomies of scale set in at a relatively small output level?

4. What could help account for computer hardware manufacturers getting increasingly more involved with the development and production of computer software? Or, the airline passenger service businesses getting involved in air parcel and small package delivery service, and soft drink manufacturers buying up fast food restaurants (e.g. Pepsi-Cola company buying up Kentucky Fried Chicken and Pizza Hut—to name a few)?

A1. Suppose the following table depicts the combinations of factors of production that results in the production of 100 units of bhindi.

	Labour	Machinery
A	25	4
B	20	5
C	10	10
D	5	20
E	4	25

a. Graph the isoquant curve for this table on the graph below, with machinery on the vertical axis and labour on the horizontal axis.

b. What is the marginal rate of substitution between combinations C and D?

A2. Suppose you had $120 available to produce the same product (bhindi) as in the previous question. Labour costs are $4 per person and machinery costs are $8 per unit. Draw the isocost line with machinery on the vertical axis and labour on the horizontal axis.

a. What is the slope of the line?

b. What happens to the isocost line if you frivolously spend $40 of your $120 on entertaining your good for nothing boyfriend Kyle? What is the slope of your new cost constraint? Show this graphically.

c. Suppose the labour unions manage to raise labour costs to $10 per person. What happens to the isocost line? Show this graphically.

d. Combine the isoquant curve from *A1* with the original isocost line from *A2* on the graph below. What combination of labour and machinery will you choose for the economically efficient point of production?

A BRAIN TEASER

1. Explain why when long-run average total costs are decreasing, and economies of scale are experienced, it may be better for a firm to operate a larger plant with some excess capacity (not operating at that scale of operation's minimum average total costs); as opposed to using a smaller plant that is operating at peak efficiency (at that plant's minimum average total costs). *(Hint: You may want to graph a long-run average cost curve as an envelope of short-run average cost curves and use that graph as a visual aid in helping you answer this question.)*

POTENTIAL ESSAY QUESTIONS

You may also see essay questions similar to the "Problems & Applications" and "Brain Teaser" exercises.

1. What are economies and diseconomies of scale? Why do they exist?

2. Discuss some of the problems of using cost analysis in the real world.

ANSWERS

MATCHING

1-e; 2-b; 3-n; 4-j; 5-a; 6-g; 7-f; 8-r; 9-o; 10-i; 11-p; 12-d; 13-q; 14-h; 15-l; 16-m; 17-k; 18-c.

ANSWERS

MULTIPLE CHOICE

1. d Economic efficiency means producing with least cost, while technical efficiency means producing with the least number of inputs. Many combinations are technically efficient. Which is economically efficient depends upon the costs of each input. Because inputs to production have different costs in various countries, an economically efficient method of production in one country might not be the same method in another country. See page 195.

2. d Economies of scale cause the LRATC curve to decrease (slope downward). Long run costs are *not* related to marginal productivity. The curve is not tangent to the low points of all SRATC curves. See pages 195-197.

3. a See the definition of indivisible setup costs on pages 195-197.

4. d Economies of scale cause the LRATC curve to slope downward. Per unit production costs fall. Difficulties in coordinating and managing a large business cause *dis*economies of scale. See pages 195-197.

5. a Economies of scale cause the LRATC curve to slope downward. The law of diminishing marginal productivity relates to short-run curves only. See Figure 9-1 on page 196.

6. c Monitoring costs generally rise as a firm enlarges. Moreover, there is no reason to assume that decreasing monitoring costs will cause other costs to increase. See page 198.

7. a Economies and diseconomies of scale relate to instances where all inputs are varied. That eliminates the option where only the number of workers is increased as a possibility. Diseconomies of scale exist when *average* costs rise. Average costs rise in (a) from $100 to $110. See pages 198-199.

8. d The lowest-cost scale of operation is on the SRATC curve that is tangent to the LRATC curve at that level of output. The scale of operation represented by $SRATC_3$ suffers from diseconomies of scale. See page 198, especially Figure 9-2.

9. c Constant returns to scale refer to the flat portion of the LRATC curve where long-run average total costs remain constant when output increases. See page 199.

10. b As discussed on pages 195-196 (including Figure 9-2), the long-run average total cost curve forms an envelope around short-run average cost curves.

11. c As discussed on pages 202-203, c is the definition of economies of scope.

12. c Learning by doing reduces average costs at every level of output. This is shown by a downward shift in the average cost curve. See pages 203-204.

13. b Accounting profit is total revenue minus explicit measurable costs. See pages 201-202.

14. d Total revenue equals $20,000. Implicit costs plus explicit costs equals $22,000. Economic loss is $2,000. Accounting profit equals $8,000. See pages 201-202.

A1. c To get one unit of machinery, one must give up one-half units of labour. See pages 209-211.

A2. a A rise in the price of machinery means that the same amount of funds will purchase less machinery, so the isocost line rotates down from the intersection of the labour axis, hence becoming flatter. See pages 209-211.

A3. c The economically efficient point is where the isoquant curve is tangent to the isocost line. See pages 211-212.

ANSWERS

SHORT-ANSWER QUESTIONS

1. You tell them that both methods are of equal technical efficiency, but you cannot determine which is more economically efficient. To make this decision, you would need to know the relative prices of each input. (194-195)

2. You smile and say that is exactly the information you need to tell them the most economically efficient method of production. At these prices, the first method of production costs $1,040 per 100 tons and the second method costs $500 per 100 tons. The second method is the economically efficient method. Technical efficiency means as few inputs as possible are used to produce a given output. It does not consider the costs of inputs. Economic efficiency means using that combination of inputs with the lowest possible cost for a given output. (194-195)

3. Because of the large indivisible setup costs, large economies of scale are possible in printing books. These economies of scale suggest that the long-run average total cost curve is steeply downward sloping. As production expands, economies of scale predominate and cost per unit declines. After some point, as output increases, however, diseconomies could set in and cost per unit rise. This would lead to a U-shaped average total cost curve in the long run. (194-195)

4. The envelope relationship is the relationship explaining that, at the planned output level, short-run average total cost equals long-run average total cost, but at all other levels of output, short-run average total cost is higher than long-run average total cost. (195-196)

5. The firm first needs to determine how much produce it can sell and then decide on the appropriate size of plant to produce at the lowest possible cost. (200)

6. An entrepreneur will supply a good if the difference between the expected price of the good exceeds the cost of producing it. This difference is the entrepreneur's expected profit. It is the profit incentive that underlies production in an economy. (201-202)

7. Since your audience is working with the real world, they will see that actual production processes diverge from textbook analysis. Some of the problems the audience might list are (1) economies of scope; (2) learning by doing and technological change; (3) the supply decision is multidimensional; and (4) the relevant costs are not the ones you find in a firm's accounts. (201-202)

ANSWERS

PROBLEMS AND APPLICATIONS

1. Using the latest technology in the combination of inputs employed may be a more costly production process than using more primitive techniques—especially when labour is cheap. What a firm wants to do is to use whatever combination of inputs that will minimize costs of production so that it can remain price competitive in the market. (195-198)

2. Before graphing *LRATC*, first calculate the figures. *LRATC* = *TC*/*Q*. (195-198)

   a.

Q	TC	LRATC
1	60	60
2	66	33
3	69	23
4	72	18
5	75	15
6	90	15
7	126	18
8	184	23
9	297	33
10	600	60

   b. The graph shown below plots the values from the table above to show the *LRATC* curve. (See Figure 9-1 on page 196.)

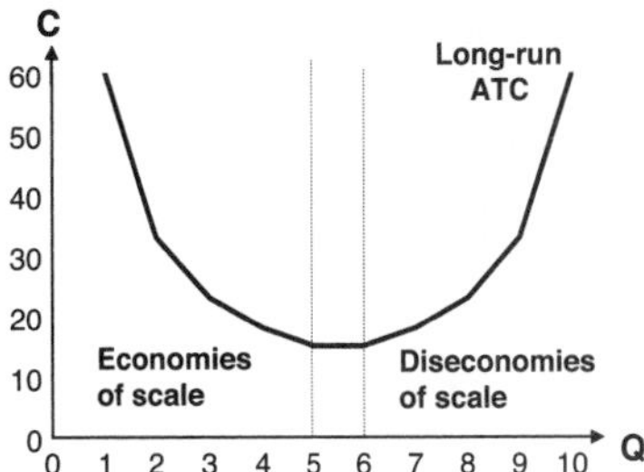

c. As shown in the figure, economies of scale is to the left of $Q = 5$, where $LRATC$ is falling. Diseconomies of scale is to the right of $Q = 6$, where $LRATC$ is rising. (195-199)

3. If economies of scale are quite extensive in an industry (i.e. larger and larger scales of operation result in lower and lower long-run average total costs of production), one would expect a relatively few number of very large firms. This is because all firms will be trying to reduce their costs, to lower their prices, and to gain a greater share of the market. You have to get big or get out—or be driven out of business by your competitor's lower prices. On the other hand, if diseconomies of scale set in at a relatively small output level then you would expect a relatively large number of relatively small firms. (199-200)

4. Economies of scope can explain this. It is cheaper for these firms to produce, market, or distribute these goods or services when they are already involved in producing the other. Indeed, this concept seems to explain best why firms produce multiple rather than single products. (202-203)

A1. a. To graph the isoquant curve, plot each of the combinations of labour and machinery which generate the same (100) units of production of bhindi, as is done in the graph below. (209-212)

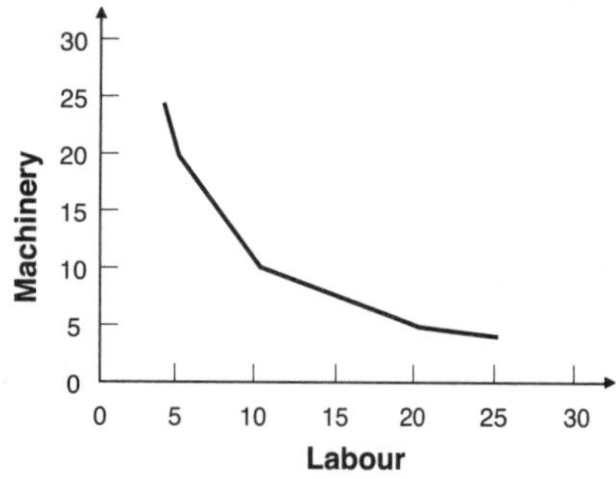

b. The marginal rate of substitution between combinations C and D is equal to the absolute value of the slope between C and D, $MP_{labour}/MP_{machinery} = 2$. (209-212)

A2. a. The slope of the line is $P_{labour}/P_{machinery} = 4/8 = 1/2$. It is shown in the graph below. (209-212).

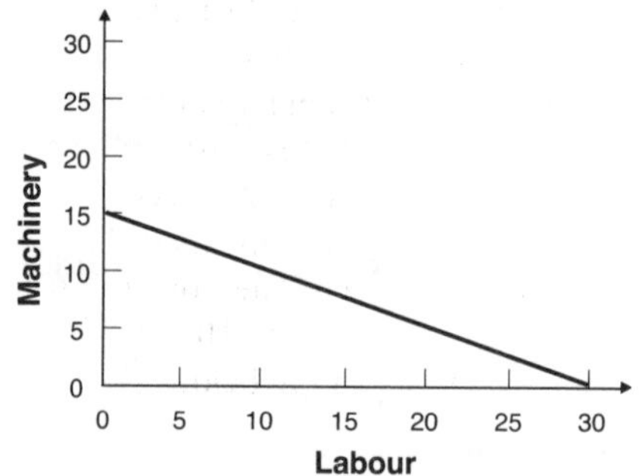

b. The isocost line shifts in as money available for production is reduced to $80. Now maximum 20 units of labour or 10 units of machinery can be purchased. Since the relative price of labour and machinery doesn't change, the slope of the isocost line remains 1/2. It is shown in the graph below. (209-212)

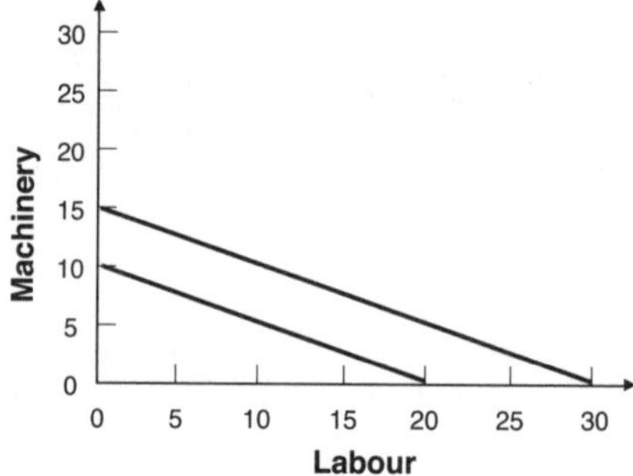

c. Now because relative prices change, the isocost line rotates. To find the new isocost line, find first how many units of labour can be purchased for $120 at the new price $10. The y intercept remains the same at 15 since the price of machinery did not change. The isocost line rotates along the labour axis and intersects it at 12 units of labour. Since labour becomes more expensive, the slope becomes steeper. The slope of the line now is $P_{labour}/P_{machinery}$ = 10/8 = 1.25. This is shown in the graph below. (209-212)

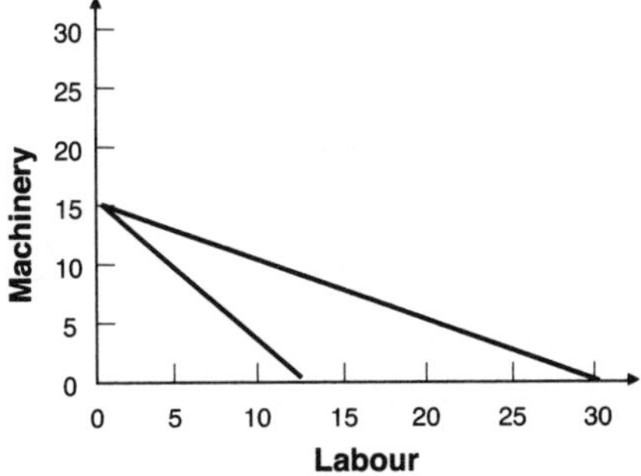

d. To find where you are most economically efficient, find that point where the slope of the isocost line equals the slope of the isoquant curve (which is the marginal rate of substitution between labour and machinery). This is at points between B and C where $-MP_{labour}/MP_{machinery}$ = 1/2 = $P_{labour}/P_{machinery}$. The isocost line is tangent to the isoquant curve at points between B and C. This implies that any other isoquant curve that intersects the isocost line is less economically efficient. It is shown in the graph below. (209-212)

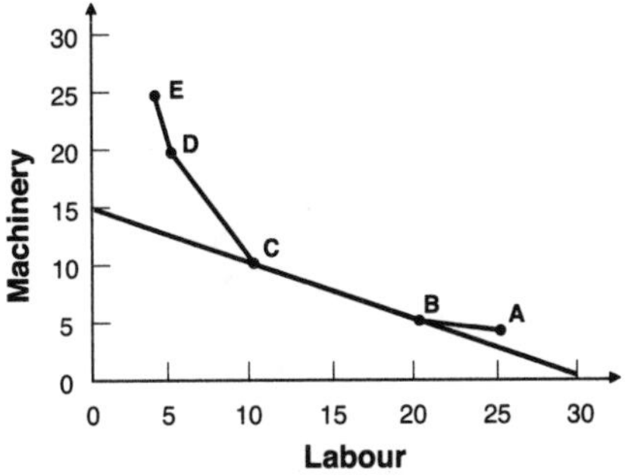

ANSWERS

A BRAIN TEASER

1. This is best explained by viewing a long-run average total cost (LRATC) curve. See the graph below. Note that the downward sloping portion of the LRATC curve indicates decreasing LRATC and, therefore, economies of scale. Also, one needs to keep in mind that a LRATC curve is really an envelope of short-run average total cost (SRATC) curves, and that each SRATC curve is associated with a larger scale of operation (or plant size) as the quantity increases. Also note that a firm's objective is to find that scale of operation (or plant size) which minimizes LRATC given the targeted output level it wishes to produce. This is shown as that scale of operation where its SRATC curve is just tangent to the LRATC curve at the targeted output level.

    Now suppose that a firm has determined that the profit maximizing quantity it should produce, given the market demand for its product, is Q_1—this is the targeted output level. To produce Q_1, the firm should use the plant size associated with $SRATC_2$—this curve is just tangent to the LRATC curve. No other plant size can produce Q_1 cheaper, even though this scale of operation is not operating at its minimum average total costs (we are not at the low point on $SRATC_2$). Notice that $SRATC_1$ is a smaller plant size. It could produce Q_1 at its minimum average total costs (at the low point on $SRATC_1$). But, the per-unit costs associated with this smaller plant size are higher (note that $SRATC_1$ lies above $SRATC_2$).

    The idea, in the long run, is to minimize long-run average total costs (even if that means operating with a scale of operation which has some excess productive capacity—not operating at its SRATC curve's low point). (195-198)

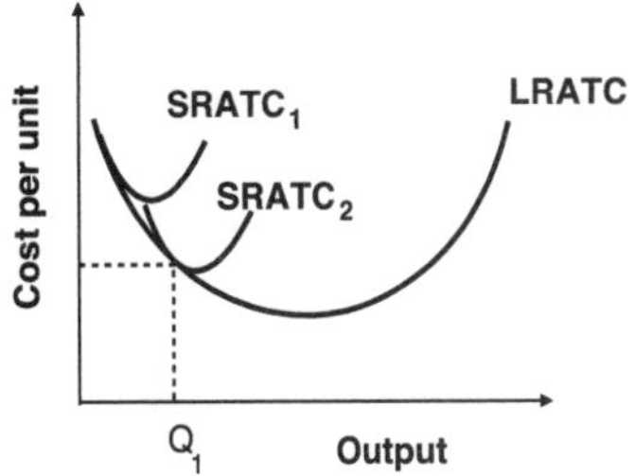

ANSWERS

POTENTIAL ESSAY QUESTIONS

The following are annotated answers. They indicate the general idea behind the answer.

1. Economies of scale are lower average total costs of production as larger scales of operation are used. They result from greater specialization of labour and management. Diseconomies of scale arise when larger scales of operation are used and higher average total costs of production are experienced. Diseconomies of scale arise because management loses control over operations. That is, monitoring costs rise and there is often a loss of team spirit.

2. Some of the problems of using cost analysis in the real world include:
(1) Economies of scope; (2) Learning by doing and technological change (3) Many dimensions; and (4) Unmeasured costs such as opportunity cost.

PERFECT COMPETITION

10

CHAPTER AT A GLANCE

Chapters 10, 11 and 12 discuss how firms determine price and output under different market structures of which there are four of them—perfect competition, monopoly, monopolistic competition and oligopoly. Each market structure has unique features and depending on which market structure a firm is located, it will behave differently. Each firm's pricing and output decisions will be based on the number of competitors it has, the type of product or service it produces, the barriers to entry and exit, and the amount of non-price competition that is available to them. The basic characteristics of each particular market structure should be understood.

This chapter highlights six conditions for a model to be perfectly competitive as well as how to determine the level of output that will yield profit maximization—this can be determined both numerically or graphically. Be sure to be able to comfortably draw the demand curve and cost structure for the perfectly competitive market structure and be able to determine a profit, a loss, and the shutdown point.

The issue of the long run and the short run will be addressed again. A perfectly competitive firm will behave differently depending upon which time frame it is operating in. Be sure to understand the adjustment process of going from a short-run equilibrium to a long-run equilibrium.

This review is based upon the learning objectives that open the chapter.

1. Six conditions for a market to be perfectly competitive are: (233)

- Large number of firms.
- Identical product.
- Free entry and free exit.
- Complete information.
- Profit-maximizing entrepreneurial firms.
- Both buyers and sellers are price takers.

Compare these with the non-competitive markets (next 2 chapters).

2a. If marginal revenue does not equal marginal cost, a firm can change profit by changing output. Therefore, profit is maximized when MC = MR = P. (217-219)

P = MR for a perfectly competitive firm.

In general, if

MR > MC then increase Q.
MR = MC then *maximizing profit.*
MR < MC then decrease Q.

2b. The marginal cost curve tells us how much of a produced good a firm will supply at a given price, so the marginal cost curve is the firm's supply curve. (219-220)

A firm's short-run supply curve is its MC curve above minimum AVC. This is because at any P greater than minimum AVC, a competitive firm will produce where P = MR = MC.

3a. The profit-maximizing output can be determined in a table (as in Table 10-1 on page 223) or in a graph (as in Figure 10-5 on page 224).

Just find that output level at which MR = MC. This is shown graphically where the two curves intersect. (Remember: the demand curve facing the firm is also its MR curve and it is horizontal at the market price. This reflects the fact that the price is given and perfectly competitive firms can produce as little or as much as they wish without influencing the price.)

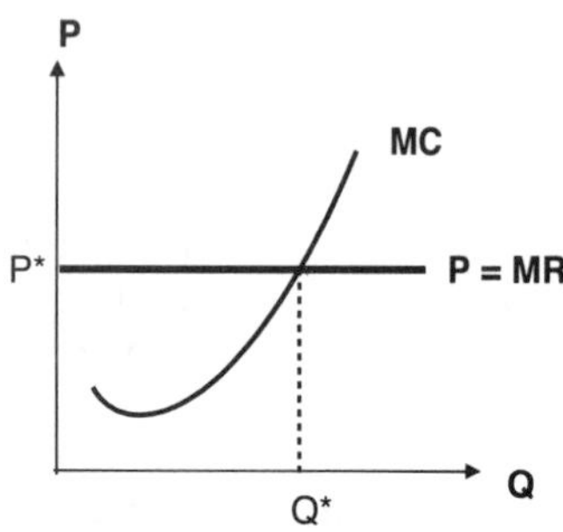

3b. Profits act as market signals: (225)

a. If there are positive economic profits, this is a market signal for new firms to enter the industry, while existing firms expand output.
b. If there are zero economic profits (normal profits), this is a market signal for no entry or exit of the industry.
c. If there is an economic loss, there is a market signal for existing firms to exit the industry or reduce output.

4a. The market supply curve is the horizontal sum of all the firms' marginal cost curves, taking account of any changes in input prices that might occur. (227)

At each price, bounce off of the marginal cost curve to determine the quantity supplied by each firm in the market. Then add the quantity supplied by each firm at each price to obtain the market supply curve.

4b. Since profits create incentives for new firms to enter, output will increase, and the price will fall until zero profits are being made. (228-229)

Over time, if economic profits are earned then the number of sellers increases, which increases market supply and puts downward pressure on the market price. The lower market price decreases firms' profits until the economic profits are competed away. Note that a zero economic profit (a normal profit) is earned by competitive firms in the long run.

5. The long-run market supply curve may be upward sloping, horizontal, or downward sloping, depending on what happens to input prices as an industry expands. (229-231)

If the demand for an industry's product increases, then the industry will expand (more of the good is produced).

- *An increasing-cost industry has an upward-sloping long-run market supply curve reflecting higher input prices as the industry expands.*
- *A constant-cost industry has a horizontal long-run market supply curve reflecting no change in input prices as the industry expands.*
- *A decreasing-cost industry has a downward-sloping long-run market supply curve reflecting lower input prices as the industry expands.*

MATCHING THE TERMS
Match the terms to their definitions

All of these key terms are found at the end of the chapter.

___ **1.** barriers to entry
___ **2.** constant-cost industry
___ **3.** decreasing-cost industry
___ **4.** economic profit
___ **5.** firm's supply curve
___ **6.** free entry
___ **7.** free exit
___ **8.** increasing-cost industry
___ **9.** marginal cost
___ **10.** marginal revenue
___ **11.** market supply curve
___ **12.** normal profit
___ **13.** perfectly competitive
___ **14.** price taker
___ **15.** profit maximizing condition
___ **16.** rent
___ **17.** shutdown point
___ **18.** zero economic profit

a. Firm or individual who takes the price determined by market supply and demand as given.
b. Social, political, or economic impediments that prevent other firms from entering a market.
c. The change in total cost associated with a change in quantity.
d. The change in total revenue associated with a change in quantity.
e. A market in which economic forces operate unimpeded.
f. Point at which the firm will gain more by temporarily shutting down than it will by staying in business.
g. The horizontal sum of all the firms' marginal cost curves, taking account of any changes in input prices that might occur.
h. Where revenues are sufficient to cover all opportunity costs.
i. Produce where MC = MR.
j. Profit greater than normal profit.
k. Free to enter a market or to expand within a market.
l. Cannot exit from an industry without incurring a substantial loss on its investment.
m. A normal profit.
n. That portion of the firm's short-run marginal cost curve above the average variable cost curve.
o. Factor prices do nor increase as industry output increases.
p. Factor prices rise as more firms enter the market and existing firms expand production and compete for the available resources.
q. Factor prices fall as industry output expands.
r. A payment greater than the factor's opportunity cost.

MULTIPLE CHOICE

Circle the one best answer for each of the following questions:

1. All the following are requirements of a perfectly competitive market *except*
   a. buyers and sellers are price takers.
   b. there are no barriers to entry.
   c. there is complete information.
   d. selling firms maximize sales.

2. In a perfectly competitive market
   a. firms sell a differentiated product where one firm's output can be distinguished from another firm's output.
   b. there are so many firms selling output in the market that no one individual firm has the ability to control the market price.
   c. economic profits can be earned in the long run.
   d. there are very strong barriers to entry which can prevent potential competitors from entering the market.

3. Refer to the graph below. The perceived demand curve faced by an individual firm in a competitive market is best represented by which of the following?
   a. A.
   b. B.
   c. C.
   d. D.

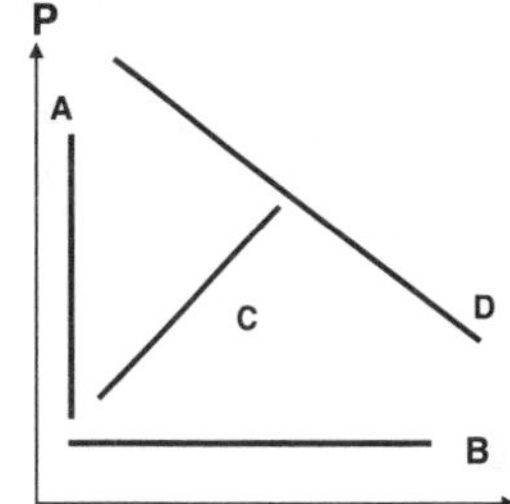

4. Refer to the graph below. The market demand curve in a competitive market is best represented by which of the following?
   a. A.
   b. B.
   c. C.
   d. D.

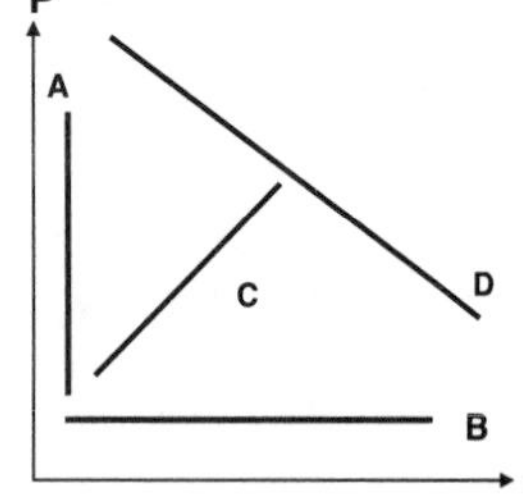

5. Refer to the graph below. A competitive firm is producing at output A.

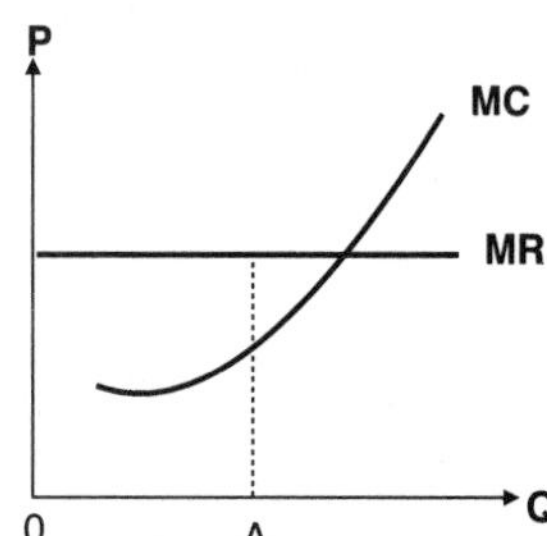

   a. It could increase profits by increasing output.
   b. It could increase profits by decreasing output.
   c. It cannot increase profits.
   d. One can say nothing about profits from the diagram below.

6. Refer to the graph below. A competitive firm is producing at output A.

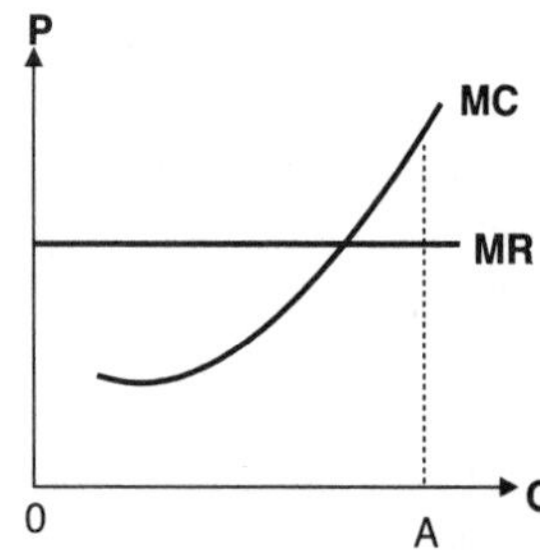

   a. It could increase profits by increasing output.
   b. It could increase profits by decreasing output.
   c. It cannot increase profits.
   d. One can say nothing about profits from the diagram below.

7. In order to maximize profits (or minimize losses), a firm should produce at that output level in which
   a. total revenue is maximized.
   b. average total cost are minimized.
   c. marginal revenue equals marginal cost.
   d. marginal revenue exceeds marginal cost by the greatest amount.

8. Price in a competitive market is \$6. The firm's marginal cost is \$4 and the marginal cost curve has the normal shape. What would you advise the firm to do?
   a. Raise its price.
   b. Increase its output.
   c. Decrease its output.
   d. Lower its price.

9. In a competitive market, which of the following is the firm's supply curve?
   a. The average variable cost curve.
   b. The marginal cost curve.
   c. The average total cost curve.
   d. The average revenue curve.

10. If a firm is producing at an output level at which:
    a. marginal revenue exceeds marginal cost then the firm should reduce its output level to maximize profits.
    b. marginal revenue is less than marginal cost then the firm should expand its output level to maximize profits.
    c. price exceeds average total costs then the firm is earning an economic profit.
    d. price is less than minimum average total cost but greater than average variable cost then the firm should shut down.

11. Refer to the graph below. The firm's profit in this case will be measured by

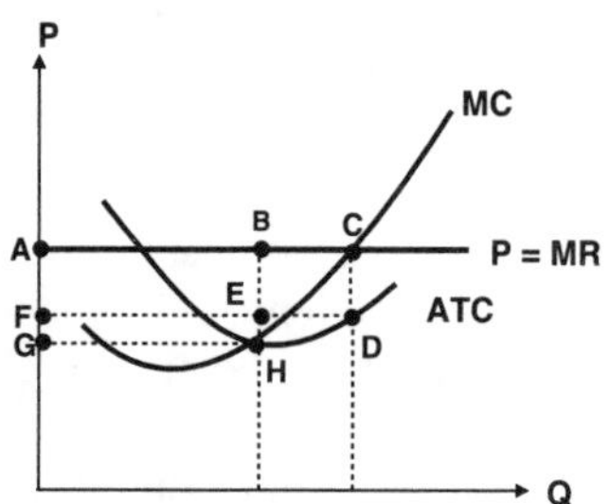

    a. the rectangle ABEF.
    b. the rectangle ACDF.
    c. the rectangle ABHG.
    d. the rectangle BCDE.

12. Refer to the graph below. How low must the price fall before the firm will decide to shut down?

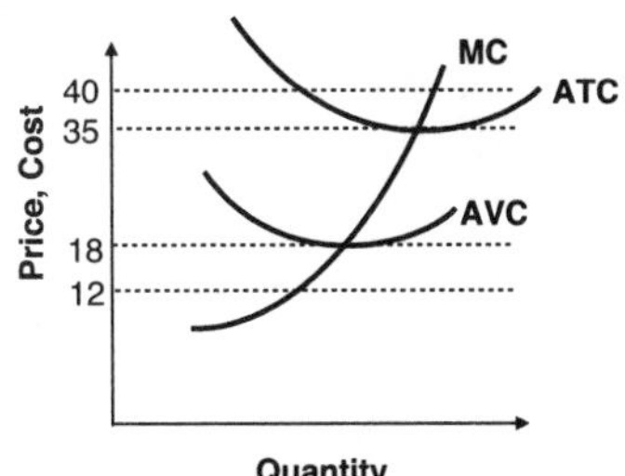

a. Approximately $40.
b. Approximately $35.
c. Approximately $18.
d. Approximately $12.

13. Refer to the graph below. This firm

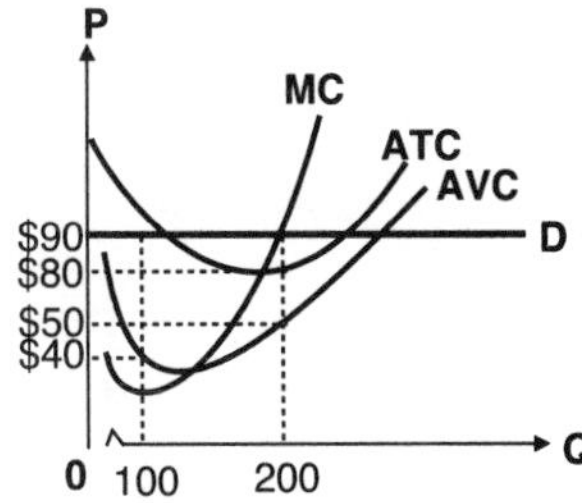

a. is earning an economic profit equal to $2,000.
b. should produce 100 units of output and charge a price of $40.
c. is incurring total costs equal to $80.
d. should shut down because price is less than minimum average variable cost.

14. In the graph below for a perfectly competitive firm,

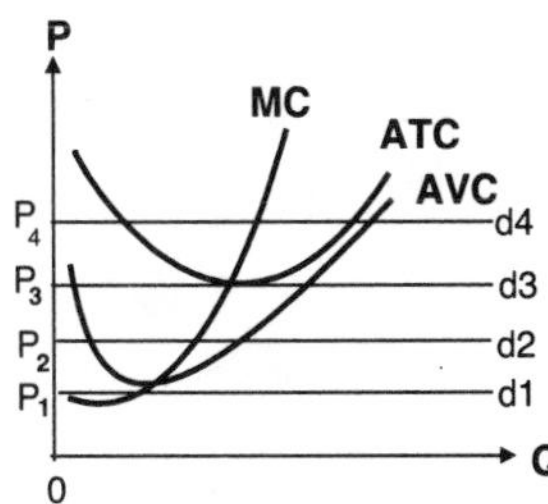

a. at P_2 the firm is incurring an economic loss but should remain in operation to minimize losses.
b. at P_3 a zero economic profit is being earned.
c. at P_4 an economic profit is earned.
d. All of the above.

15. Normal profits are
a. approximately 6 percent of costs.
b. approximately 8 percent of costs.
c. returns to the owners of business for the opportunity cost of their implicit inputs.
d. generally larger than accounting profits.

16. In long-run competitive equilibrium, the average firm
a. will be going out of business.
b. will be expanding.
c. will be making only normal profit.
d. won't even be making normal profit.

17. In a competitive market for good X, the price of a complementary good falls. If it is a constant-cost industry, we know that in the long run, equilibrium quantity will
a. increase and equilibrium price will remain the same.
b. increase and equilibrium price will increase.
c. decrease and equilibrium price will increase.
d. decrease and equilibrium price will remain the same.

18. In an increasing-cost industry, the long-run market supply curve will be
a. upward sloping.
b. horizontal.
c. vertical.
d. downward-sloping.

SHORT-ANSWER QUESTIONS

1. How is competition as a process different from competition as a state?

2. What are six necessary conditions for perfect competition?

3. You are advising a vendor of ice cream at a beach. There are plenty of vendors on the beach and plenty more waiting to begin selling. Your client can't seem to change the market price for ice cream, but she still wants to make sure she maximizes profits. What do you advise she do? She knows all her costs of doing business.

4. You are given a competitive firm's marginal cost curve and asked to determine the supply curve for that firm. What do you say?

5. Given the following table, what is the output and profit of a perfect competitor?

P=MR	Q	FC	VC
35	0	10	0
35	1	10	20
35	2	10	38
35	3	10	50
35	4	10	77
35	5	10	112
35	6	10	156

6. On the graph below, show the output and short-run profit of a perfect competitor

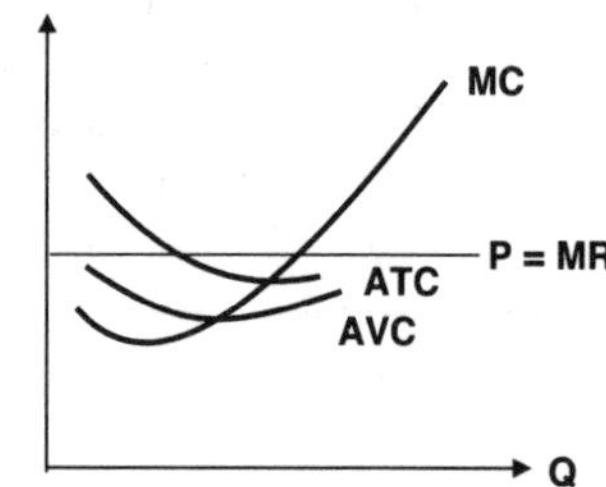

7. When should a firm shut down?

8. How are firm's marginal cost curves and the market supply curve related?

9. Given the graph below, showing a representative firm in a competitive market, what will happen in the long run? Explain using the graph and words.

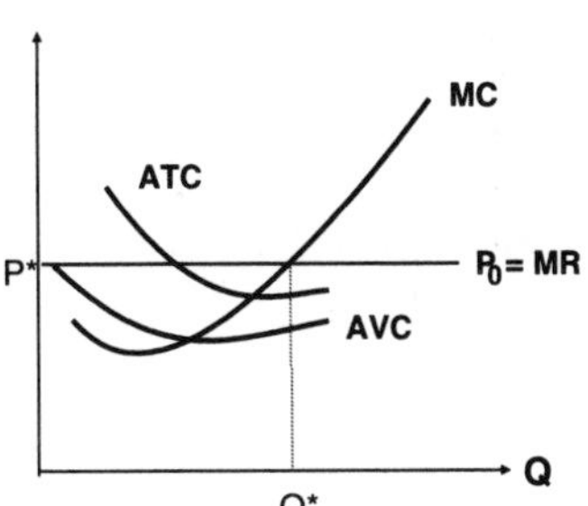

10. Suppose the owners of a small drug store decided to close their store after Wal-Mart opened a store nearby. Assuming the market was competitive before and after Wal-Mart opened its store, show graphically and explain with words the likely conditions for the small drug store before and after Wal-Mart opened.

11. What does the long-run market supply curve look like in an increasing-cost industry? Why? What about the constant-cost and decreasing-cost industries?

PROBLEMS AND APPLICATIONS

1. The following table shows the total cost for a product that sells for $20 a unit.

Q	TC
0	30
1	55
2	75
3	85
4	100
5	120
6	145
7	185
8	240
9	310
10	395

a. What is the output level for a profit-maximizing firm? Use the space to the right of the table to work out your answer.

b. How does your answer change if price rises to $25?

c. Calculate profit in part *a* and *b* above.

d. Should the firm stay in business at P = $20? At $25?

e. Suppose P = $15, what output level maximizes profit? What is the profit? Should the firm stay in business?

2. The cost curves below are for a representative firm in a competitive market.

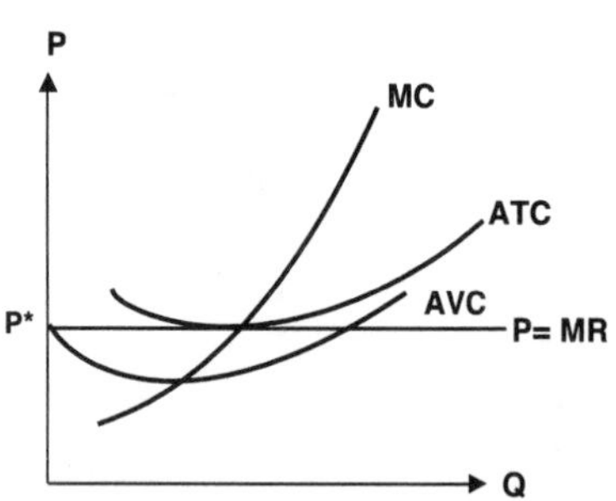

a. Label the minimum point of the *ATC* and *AVC* curves as A and B respectively. Explain your answer.

b. Draw a demand curve for this firm on that same graph and explain why you have drawn it this way.

c. Illustrate the long-run equilibrium price and quantity for the firm on that same graph. Is the firm earning economic profit? Explain your answer.

3. Consider the market demand and supply curves below on the left and a representative firm's cost curves below on the right.

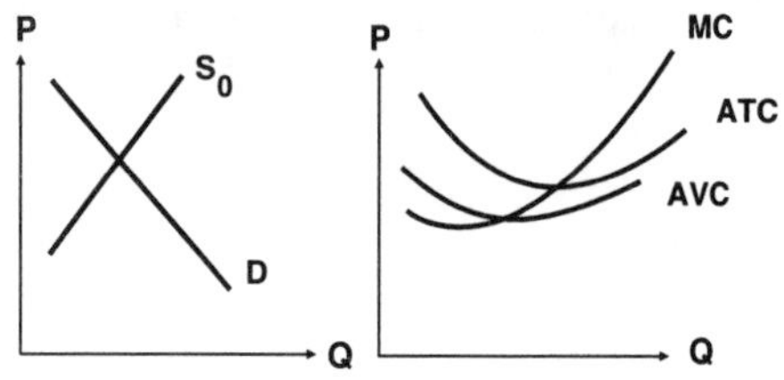

a. Is this representative firm earning economic profit, loss, or zero profit? Shade the area for profit or loss, or label the point of zero profit.

b. In the long run, what will happen?

c. Beginning with the long-run equilibrium in *b*, show the effect of a decrease in demand on profit. What will happen in the long run to supply, price, and profit?

4. What is wrong with each of the following graphs?

a.

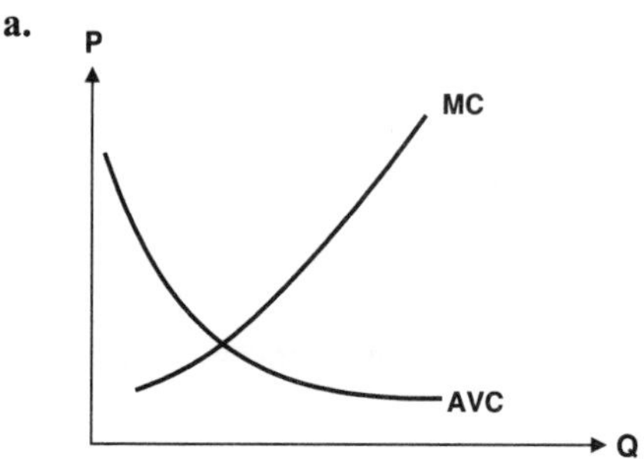

b.

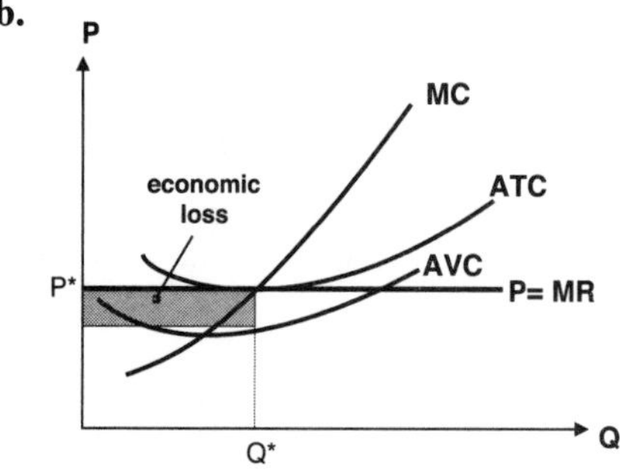

c.

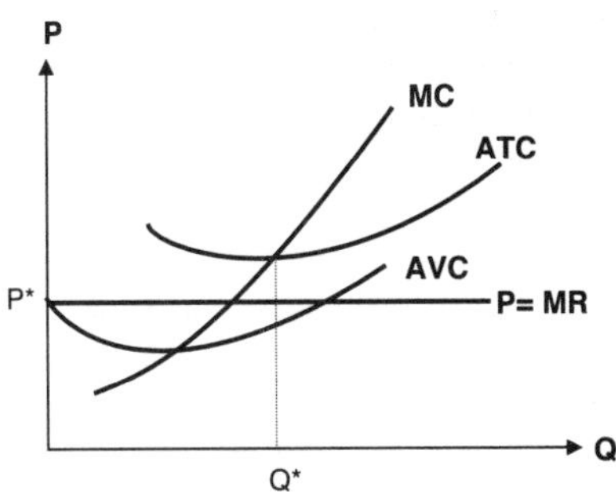

d.

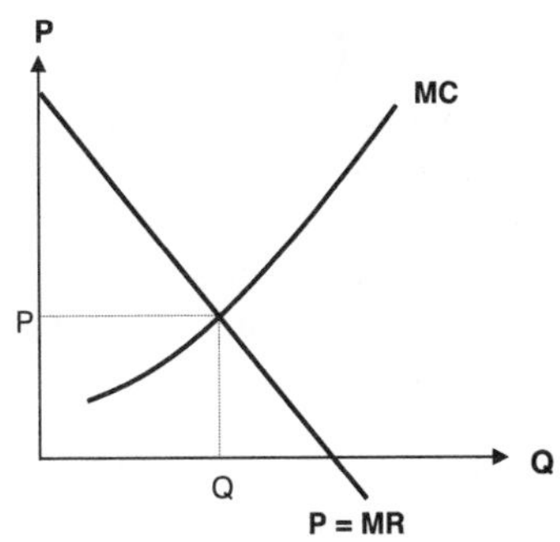

A BRAIN TEASER

1. Suppose a perfectly competitive firm experiences a sudden increase in its fixed costs. For example, suppose property taxes increase dramatically. What impact, if any will this have on the firm's profit-maximizing quantity to produce? What will happen to the firm's profit?

POTENTIAL ESSAY QUESTIONS

You may also see essay questions similar to the "Problems & Applications" and "Brain Teasers" exercises.

1. Describe how to find a competitive firm's price, level of output, and profit given the firm's marginal cost curve and average total cost curve.

2. According to the textbook author, there are four major things to remember when considering a perfectly competitive industry. What are these four things?

ANSWERS

MATCHING

1-b; 2-o; 3-q; 4-j; 5-n; 6-k; 7-l; 8-p; 9-c; 10-d; 11-g; 12-h; 13-e; 14-a; 15-i; 16-r; 17-f; 18-m.

ANSWERS

MULTIPLE CHOICE

1. d In a competitive market, firms are profit-maximizing, not sales maximizing firms. See pages 214-215.

2. b Competitive firms sell a homogenous (identical) product, there are no barriers to entry and they cannot earn economic profits in the long run. See pages 214-215 and 228-229.

3. b Although the market demand curve is downward sloping, individual firms are so small in relation to the market that they perceive their demand curves as horizontal. See page 217 and Figure 10-1.

4. d The market demand curve is downward sloping as the industry as a whole can influence price. See page 217 and Figure 10-1.

5. a For the perfectly competitive firm P = MR. If P > MC, increase output to increase profits. See page 217-219 (especially Figure 10-2).

6. b For the perfectly competitive firm P = MR. If P < MC, decrease output to increase profits. See page 217-219 (especially Figure 10-2).

7. c Any firm maximizes profit by producing where marginal revenue equals marginal cost. Also note, for the perfectly competitive firm, price equals marginal revenue. See pages 217-219.

8. b Since P > MC, increase output to until MC = P = MR, the profit-maximizing level of output. See pages 217-219.

9. b Since a perfect competitor chooses to produce where P = MC, the marginal cost curve is the firm's supply curve. See pages 217-219.

10. c Profit per unit = (P − ATC). Total profit equals profit per unit times quantity. See pages 220-224.

11. b Output is determined where marginal cost equals price (and price equals marginal revenue for the competitive firm). To determine profit one finds the rectangle formed by ATC at the output level and price determined by where marginal cost equals price. See Figure 10-5, page 224.

12. c The shutdown point is where the marginal cost equals minimum average variable cost. See pages 225-227.

13. a Quantity is where P = MR = MC. Profit is (P − ATC) times quantity produced. Total cost is ATC times quantity. See pages 224-225.

14. d If P > ATC an economic profit is earned, If P = ATC a zero economic profit (a normal profit) is earned. If P < ATC but above minimum AVC then the firm is incurring an economic loss but should remain in operation to minimize losses. See pages 223-225.

15. c See definition of normal profit in the textbook on page 228.

16. c The zero profit condition discussed in the text includes normal profit. See page 228.

17. a If the price of a complement falls, the demand for X will increase, increasing quantity and increasing price in the short run. Economic profits will induce new firms to enter the market over time and the supply curve will shift to the right. Since it is a constant cost industry, the long-run supply curve is horizontal—price remains the same while output rises. See pages 229-231.

18. a If an industry expands and this increases input prices then the long-run market supply will be upward sloping. See pages 229-231.

ANSWERS

SHORT-ANSWER QUESTIONS

1. Competition as a process is a rivalry among firms, with one firm trying to take away market share from another firm. Competition as a state is the end result of the competitive process under certain conditions. (214-215)

2. The six conditions necessary for perfect competition are that (1) the number of firms is large, (2) firms' products are identical, (3) free entry and free exit, (4) there is complete information, (5) selling firms are profit maximizing entrepreneurial firms, and (6) buyers and sellers are both price takers. (214-215)

3. It is clear that she is in a competitive market. She has no control over prices—she is a price-taker. I would advise that she calculate her marginal cost at various levels of output and sell the number of ice creams where marginal cost equals price. This will maximize her profit. To see why, for a perfect competitor, producing where $MC = P$ maximizes total profit, you must first understand that $MR = P$ for a perfect competitor. By definition, a competitive firm takes price as given, so the incremental revenue, marginal revenue, of selling an additional unit is that unit's price. If we prove that a perfect competitor maximizes profit when $MC = MR$, we simultaneously prove that profit is maximized at output where $MC = P$. If marginal revenue does not equal marginal cost, a firm can increase profit by changing output. If a firm produces where $MC < MR$, it is earning a profit per unit and the firm can increase total profits by producing more until MC is no longer less than MR. If $MC > MR$, the firm is incurring a loss for that last unit; it can increase profits by reducing output until MC is no longer greater than MR. Given these conditions, the firm maximizes profit where $MC = MR$ or $MC = P$. (219)

4. The marginal cost curve is the supply curve for a perfectly competitive firm because the marginal cost curve tells us how much of a produced good a firm will supply at a given price. Specifically; the marginal cost curve is the firm's supply curve only if price exceeds average variable cost. If price is less than minimum AVC, shutdown will occur. (219-220, especially Figure 10-3)

5. To find where the profit-maximizing competitive firm produces, we need to know MR and MC. We know MR. We need to calculate MC. We do this in column 5 in the table below. To calculate profit, we need to know ATC. It is the sum of FC and VC divided by Q and is shown in column 7. (Marginal cost refers to the marginal cost of increasing to that row, e.g., the marginal cost of going from 0 to 1 is 20.)

P= MR	Q	FC	VC	MC	TC	ATC	TR	Profit
35	0	10	—	—	10	—	0	10
35	1	10	20	20	30	30	35	5
35	2	10	38	18	48	24	70	22
35	3	10	50	12	60	20	105	45
35	4	10	77	27	87	21.75	140	53
35	5	10	112	35	122	24.4	175	53
35	6	10	156	44	166	27.67	210	44

Looking at the table, we see that $MC = MR$ at Q = 5. Profit is $(P - ATC) \times Q = 10.6 \times 5 = 53$. Alternatively, Profit = TR − TC = (P × Q) − TC = (35 × 5) − 122 = 175 − 122 = 53. Notice that when producing where MR = MC profit is as high, or higher than at any other level of output. Increase output until MR = MC. This way you know you will be maximizing profits (minimizing losses). (222-224, especially Table 10-1)

6. The output of a perfect competitor is shown by the intersection of the marginal cost curve and the marginal revenue curve. On the graph below, it is at Q^*. Profit for a perfect competitor is the profit per unit, the difference between the price for which each unit is sold and the average cost of each unit, times the number of units sold. Graphically, profit per unit is the vertical distance from the MR curve to the ATC curve. Multiply this by Q^* to get profit. It is the shaded region in the graph. (222-224)

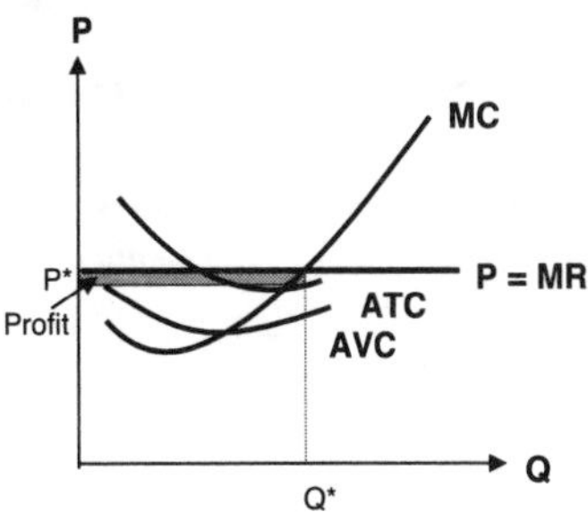

7. A firm should shut down if P ≤ minimum AVC. (Alternatively, a firm should shut down if losses are greater than total fixed costs; or, total revenue is less than total variable costs.) (228-230)

8. The market supply curve is the horizontal sum of all firms' marginal cost curves, taking account of any changes in input prices that might occur. (227-228)

9. The graph below shows that the representative firm in a competitive market is making an economic profit when price is P^*. Since profits create incentives for new firms to enter, output will increase and the price will fall to P_1 until zero profits are being made. (228-230)

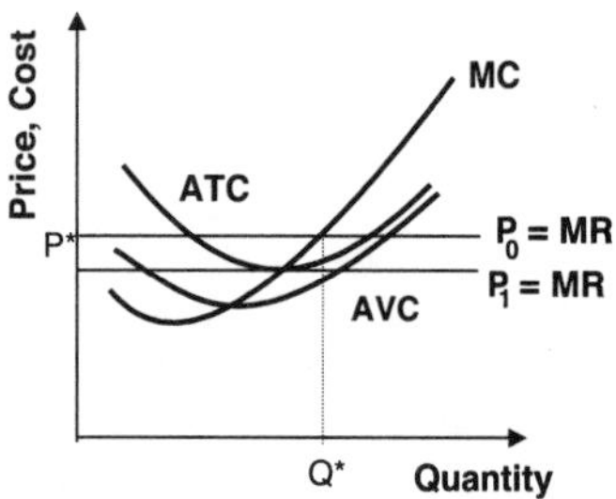

10. Before Wal-Mart opened a store, the small drug store produced Q^* given competitive price of P^* and earned normal profits. Since Wal-Mart is a discount drug store, opening its store in the market most likely pushed prices down to P_1. Given the new price level, the small drug store now reduced output to Q_1 and incurred a loss. Eventually, all costs are variable and the *ATC* curve becomes the *AVC* curve and prices were below the shutdown point. This is shown in the graph below. (228-230)

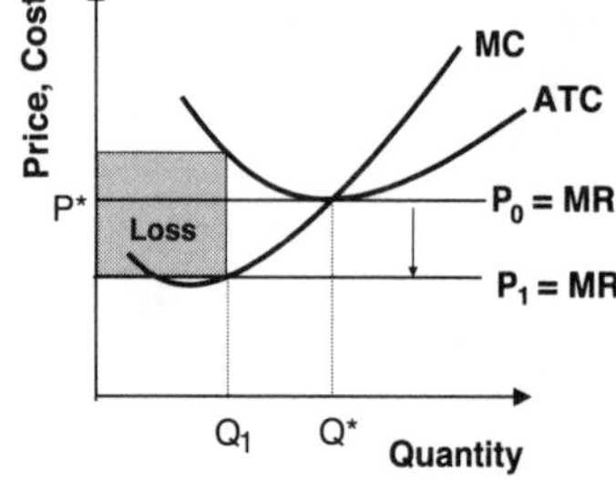

11. In an increasing-cost industry, the long-run market supply curve is upward sloping because of higher input prices as the industry expands. The constant-cost industry's long-run market supply curve is horizontal because of constant input prices as the industry expands. The decreasing-cost industry's long-run market supply curve is downward sloping because of lower input prices as the industry expands. (230-231)

ANSWERS

PROBLEMS AND APPLICATIONS

1. To find the profit-maximizing level of output, first we determine marginal costs for the firm. Here we show the values for a number of costs. We use the formulas for the cost curves: *MC* = change in total cost/change in output, *FC* = $30 (costs when *Q* = 0); VC = *TC* − *FC*, *AVC* = *VC*/*Q*. (Marginal cost refers to the marginal cost of increasing to that row, e.g., the marginal cost of going from 0 to 1 is 25.) (222-224)

Q	TC	MC	VC	FC	AVC
0	30	0	0	30	0
1	55	25	25	30	25
2	75	20	45	30	22.5
3	85	10	55	30	18.3
4	100	15	70	30	17.5
5	120	20	90	30	18
6	145	25	115	30	19.2
7	185	40	155	30	22.1
8	240	55	210	30	26.25
9	310	70	280	30	31.1
10	395	85	365	30	36.5

a. A profit-maximizing firm will produce at the output level where *MC* = *MR*. Since *MR* = market price for the competitive firm, *MR* =$20. *MC* = 20 at 2 units and 5 units. It will not choose to produce 2 units because marginal costs are declining and the firm would make additional profit by increasing output above 2. So, the profit maximizing output level is at 5 units. (222-224)

b. If price rises to $25, so does *MR*. *MC* = *25* at 6 units. (222-224)

c. In (a), profit = total revenue total costs at 5 units: (5 $20) $120 = $20, an economic loss. In (b), profit = total revenue total costs at 6 units: (6 $25) $145 = $5. (222-224)

d. The firm will stay in business at P = $20 or $25, since $P >$ minimum AVC at both these prices. (225-226)

e. At P = $15, the profit-maximizing level of output is 4 units. The profit in this case is $40 (loss of $40). Since $P <$ minimum AVC in this case, the firm should temporarily shut down its business. (225-226)

2. a. As shown in the graph below, points A and B are the minimum of the ATC and AVC curves. It is where they intersect the MC curve. From an earlier chapter, we know that the MC curve goes through the ATC and AVC curves at their minimum points. (225-226)

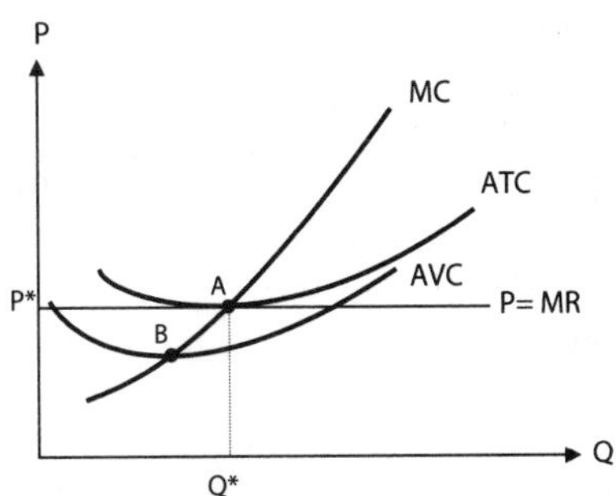

b. A demand curve for the representative firm is drawn in the graph above. It is a horizontal line because an individual firm in a competitive market is a price taker; the demand for its product is perfectly elastic. (216-217)

c. As illustrated above, the long-run equilibrium position occurs when the demand curve is tangent to the ATC curve because it is only at this point that economic profit for the firm is equal to zero. There is no incentive for new firms to enter the market, nor would existing firms exit the market. The long-run equilibrium is reached. (228-231)

3. a. As shown by the shaded region on the graph below, the representative firm is earning an economic profit. (228-231)

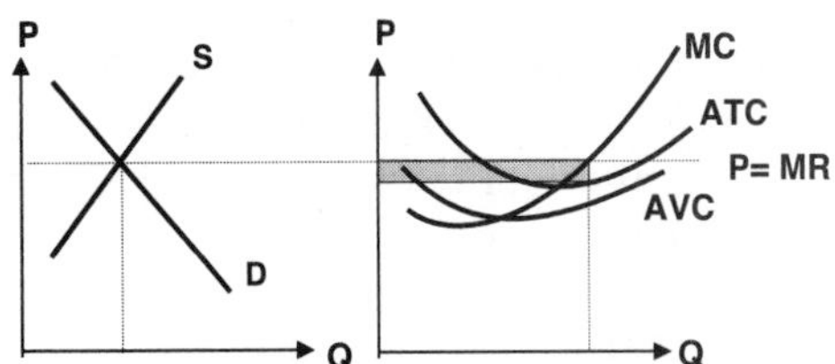

b. Refer to the graphs below. More firms will enter the market to share the profit. But as market supply increases from S_0 to S_1, the market price falls which, in turn, reduces the profit margin for all the firms. This process continues until price falls to P_1 where there is no more economic profit. This assumes a constant-cost industry. (228-231)

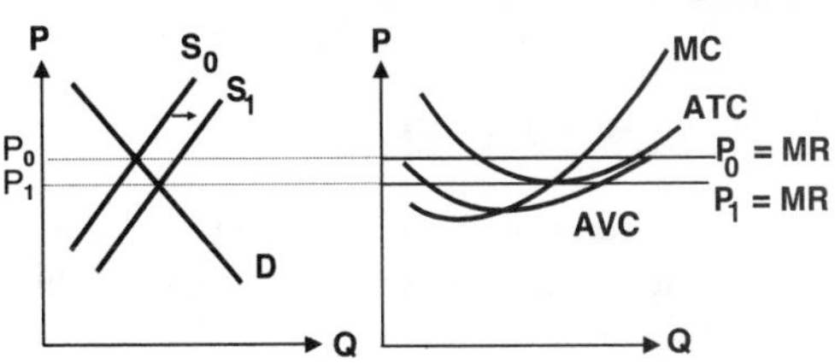

c. As shown on the graphs below, a decrease in market demand from D_0 to D_1, results in a fall of market price from P_0 to P_1 which in turn reduces the profit for each firm in the market to a loss. The losses will cause some firms to exit the market. Hence, market supply shrinks from S_0 to S_1, until prices rise from P_1 to P_0. In the long run, price returns to the original level while output in the market is reduced. Each firm still has zero economic profit. This assumes a constant-cost industry. (228-231)

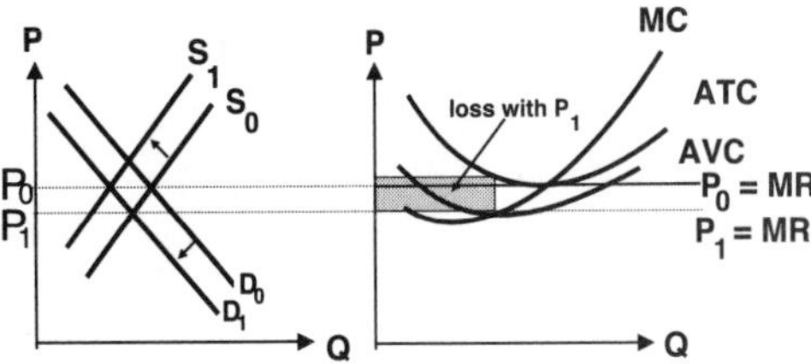

4. **a.** The curve labeled *AVC* is really an *AFC* curve. The correct *AVC* curve would intersect the *MC* at the minimum point of the *AVC* curve and rise thereafter. (224)
   b. Loss is mis-labeled in the graph. Loss and profit are measured by the vertical difference between price and average total costs, not average variable costs. Here, economic profit is zero (there is no loss). (224)
   c. Output should be where *MC* = *MR* = *P*, not where *ATC* = *MC*. A competitive firm will maximize profits where *MC* = *MR* = *P*. (224)
   d. A competitive firm faces a horizontal demand curve, since it cannot affect prices. Here, it is downward-sloping. (224)

ANSWERS

A BRAIN TEASER

1. An increase in fixed costs (FC) will increase average total cost (ATC). Average variable cost (AVC) and marginal cost (MC) will remain unchanged. The ATC curve will be the only curve that shifts up. Because MC has not changed (the MC curve has not shifted), and assuming the price in the competitive market (MR for the firm) has not changed, then the profit- maximizing output level will not change for the firm. However, its profits will decrease because of higher costs

ANSWERS

POTENTIAL ESSAY QUESTIONS

The following are annotated answers. They indicate the general idea behind the answer.

1. To find a competitive firm's price, level of output, and profit given the firm's marginal cost curve and average total cost curve, do the following: (See the "Knowing the Tools" box on page 227)
   1. Determine the market price where market supply and demand curves intersect. This is the price the competitive firm accepts for its products. Draw a horizontal marginal revenue (MR) curve at the market price.
   2. Determine the profit-maximizing level of output by finding the level of output where the MR and MC curves intersect.
   3. Determine profit by subtracting average total costs at the profit-maximizing level of output from the price and multiplying by the firm's output.

   If you are determining profit graphically, find the point at which MR = MC. Extend a line down to the ATC curve. Extend a line from that point to the vertical axis. To complete the box indicating profit, go up the vertical axis to the market price.
2. Four things to remember when considering a perfectly competitive industry: (See "Knowing the Tools" box on page 230)
   1. The profit-maximizing condition for perfectly competitive firms is MC = MR =P.
   2. To determine profit or loss at the profit-maximizing level of output, subtract average total cost at that level of output from price and multiply the result by the output level.
   3. Firms will shut down production if price is equal to or falls below the minimum of their average variable costs.
   4. A firm is in long-run equilibrium only when it is earning zero economic profit, or where price equals the minimum of long-run average total costs.

MONOPOLY

CHAPTER AT A GLANCE

Chapter 11 is the second chapter devoted to analyzing market structures. After this chapter, one will have enough background to be able to compare monopoly with perfect competition.

The characteristics of a monopoly are different from that of perfect competition, yet the profit maximizing rule is the same — MR=MC. As with perfect competition, one has to be able to draw the demand and marginal revenue curves and the cost structure of the firm in order to determine a profit or a loss.

The last part of the chapter highlights a distinct feature of monopolies, price discrimination, that is, charging different prices to different individuals or groups of individuals in order to increase profits and output. As well, the regulation of natural monopolies is explored. Regulation is important in order to ensure efficiency from a society's point of view.

This review is based upon the learning objectives that open the chapter.

1. For a competitive firm, marginal revenue equals price. For a monopolist, it does not. The monopolist must take into account the fact that its production decision affects price. (238-239)

The monopolist faces the market demand curve, which is downward sloping. It must reduce P to sell more. Hence, MR < P.

2a. The general rule that any firm must follow to maximize profit is: Produce at an output level at which MC = MR. (242)

If MR > MC, then increase Q.

If MR = MC, then the firm is maximizing profit or minimizing losses.

If MR < MC, then decrease Q.

2b. To find a monopolist's level of output, price and profit, follow these four steps: (243-245)

1. Draw the marginal revenue curve.

2. Determine the output the monopolist will produce: The profit-maximizing level of output is where the *MR* and *MC* curves intersect. *(See the graph below.)*

3. Determine the price the monopolist will charge: Extend a line from where the profit maximizing output level (Q*) up to the demand curve. Where this line intersects the demand curve is the monopolist's price. *(See the graph below.)*

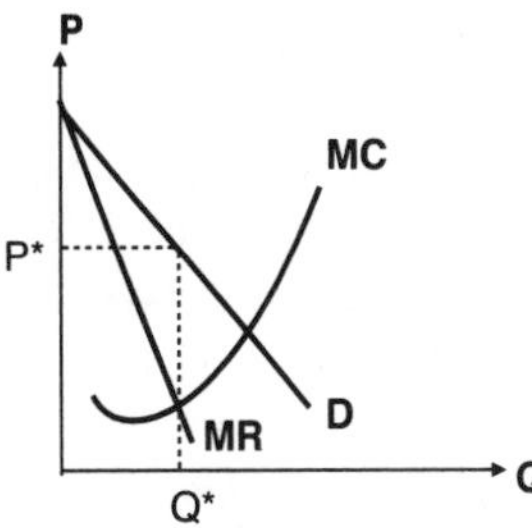

4. Determine the profit the monopolist will earn: Subtract the *ATC* from price at the profit-maximizing level of output to get profit per unit. Multiply profit per unit by quantity of output to get total profit. *(See the graph below.)*

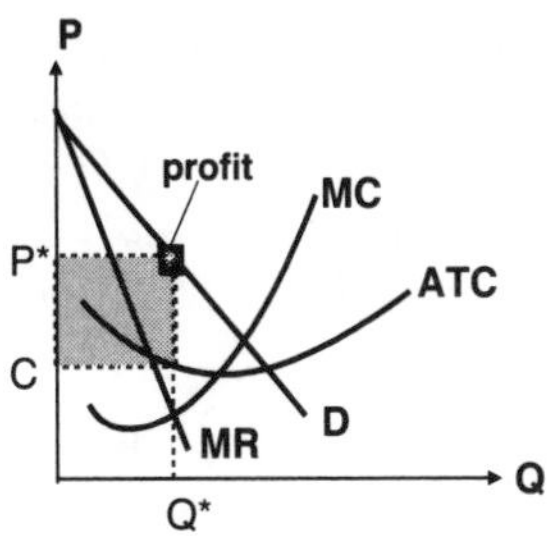

3. In the short run, a monopolist can make profits, breakeven and even earn a loss. It depends on the level of its ATC relative to price. If price exceeds ATC at the output it chooses, the monopolist will make a positive economic profit (242-243)

4. The welfare loss from monopoly is the triangle in the graph below. (245-246)

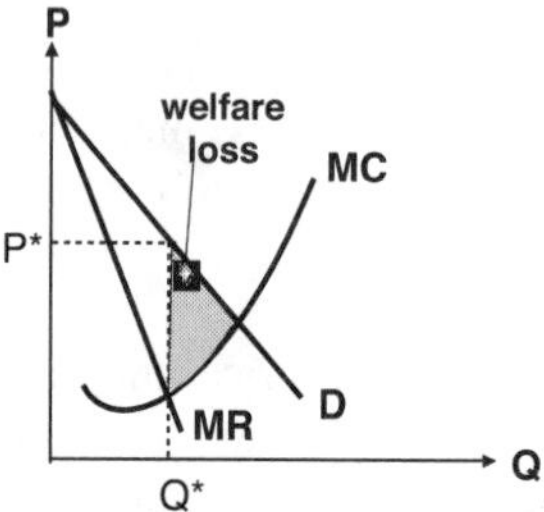

Because monopolists reduce output and charge a price that is higher than marginal cost, monopolies create a welfare loss to society.

5. When a monopolist price discriminates, it charges individuals high up on the demand curve higher prices and those low on the demand curve lower prices. (246)

If a monopolist can (1) identify groups of customers who have different elasticities of demand, (2) separate them in some way and (3) limit their ability to re-sell its product between groups, it can price discriminate.

A price discriminating monopolist earns more profit than a normal, single-price monopolist because it can charge a higher price to those with less elastic demands and a lower price to those with more elastic demands. Price discrimination leads to a larger output, no deadweight loss, no consumer surplus, and a larger profit.

6. If there were no barriers to entry, profit-maximizing firms would always compete away monopoly profits. (248)

Know the different types of barriers to entry. The stronger the barriers to entry, the stronger the monopoly power (the greater the ability to charge a higher price).

7. Normative arguments against monopoly include:
- monopolies are unfair and inconsistent with freedom,
- the income distributional effects associated with monopoly are unfair, and
- monopolies encourage people to waste resources and money trying to get monopolies. (251-253)

Possible economic profits from monopoly lead potential monopolists to spend money to get government to give them a monopoly.

8. Our society's legal system is designed to attract large research companies and create monopolies. The current patent system allows companies to engage in important research and development that will benefit society and to allow firms to recoup their high research and development costs. However, it also allows firms to generates large profits if these firms are successful. Firms developing important goods for society are forcing society to bare the burden through very high prices. The debate is whether or not this is appropriate. (253-254)

See also, Appendix A: "The Algebra of Competitive and Monopolistic Firms."

MATCHING THE TERMS

Match the terms to their definitions

All of these key terms are found at the end of the chapter.

___ 1. monopoly
___ 2. natural monopoly
___ 3. patent
___ 4. price discriminate
___ 5. setup costs
___ 6. welfare loss
___ 7. single-price monopoly

a. A legal protection of a technical innovation which gives the person holding that protection a monopoly on using that innovation.
b. A firm that charges all customers the same price.
c. An industry in which a single firm can produce at a lower cost than can two or more firms.
d. To charge a different price to different individuals or groups of individuals.
e. A market structure in which one firm makes up the entire supply side of the market.
f. Net loss to society from the existence of monopoly.
g. Large costs involved in getting industry ready for protection.

MULTIPLE CHOICE

Circle the one best answer for each of the following questions:

1. Monopoly is the market structure in which:
a. one firm makes up the entire market.
b. two firms make up the entire market.
c. the market is made up of a few big firms.
d. firms make a supernormal profit.

2. Which of the following is *not* a significant difference between a monopolist and a competitive firm?
a. A monopoly is a price-maker, whereas a competitive firm is a price-taker.
b. The monopolist produces where MR = MC while the perfect competitor does not.
c. The monopoly's marginal revenue curve lies below the demand curve whereas the competitive firm's marginal revenue curve is horizontal at the market price.
d. A monopolist is protected by barriers to entry whereas a competitive firm is not.

3. A profit-maximizing monopolist will:
a. produce an output level at which MR > MC.
b. produce an output level at which P > MC.
c. always earn an economic profit in the short run.
d. increase production when MR < MC.

4. Refer to the graph below. Which curve is the marginal revenue curve for the market demand curve?
a. Curve A.
b. Curve B.
c. Curve C.
d. Curve D.

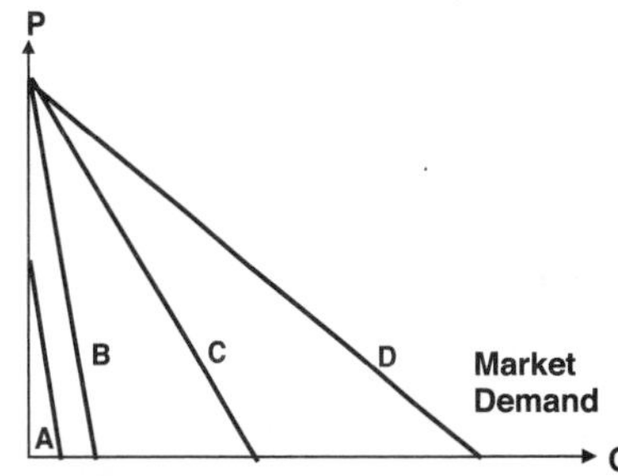

5. Refer to the graph below. A monopolist would most likely produce quantity shown by:
a. A.
b. B.
c. C.
d. D.

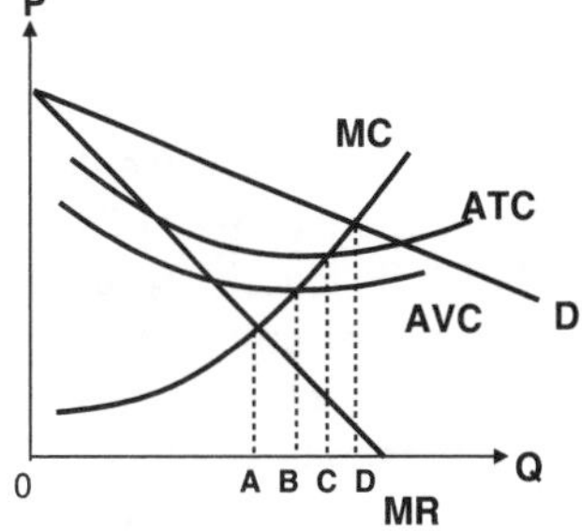

6. Refer to the graph below. Which rectangle represents the monopolist's profit?
   a. A.
   b. A + B + C.
   c. C + D.
   d. None of the above.

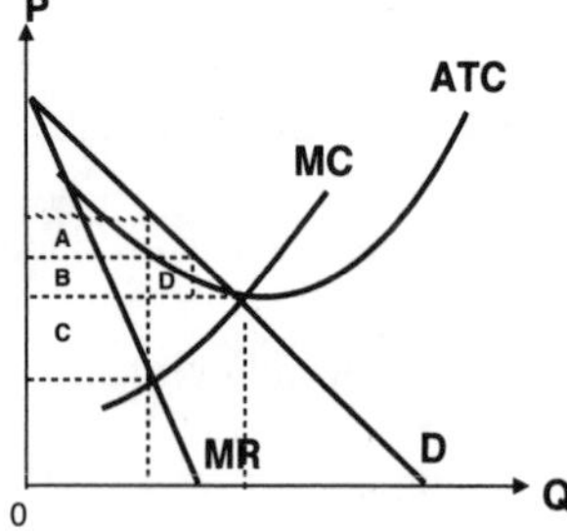

7. Refer to the graph below. The monopolist represented is:

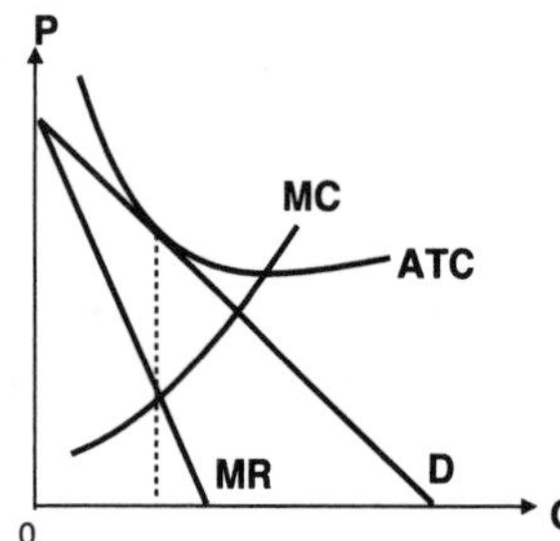

   a. making a profit.
   b. making a loss.
   c. making zero profit.
   d. unable to determine what kind of profit the monopolist is making.

8. Refer to the graph below. Which of the following statements about the market represented is true?

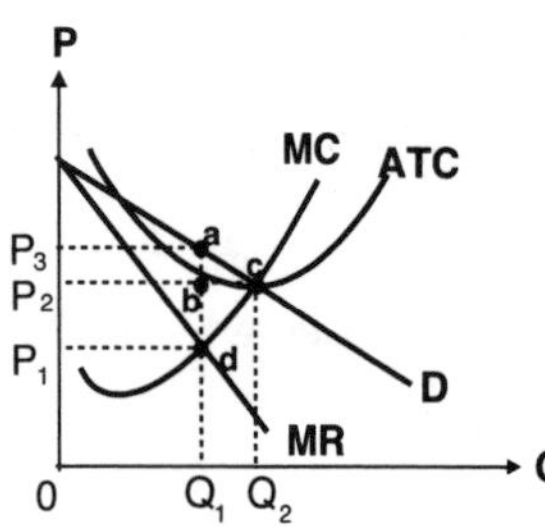

   a. A monopolist would charge price P_2 and produce output Q_2.
   b. A monopolist would charge price P_1 and produce output Q_1.
   c. A competitive market would charge price P_2 and produce output Q_2.
   d. A monopolist would earn a profit per unit equal to P_3 minus P_2.

9. Refer to the graph for Question #8. Which of the following statements about the effect of the monopolist represented is true?
   a. Triangle *bac* represents the lost producer surplus to society due to the monopoly.
   b. Triangle *dbc* represents the lost consumer surplus to society due to the monopoly.
   c. Triangle *dac* represents the welfare loss to society due to the monopoly.
   d. Lost production due to the monopoly is equal to Q_1.

10. A price-discriminating monopolist:
    a. charges different prices to customers with different elasticities of demand.
    b. will earn a lower profit than a non-price-discriminating monopolist.
    c. will have a marginal revenue curve which lies above its demand curve.
    d. is trying to allow some people to purchase the good who could not normally afford to do so.

11. Price discrimination requires:
    a. identifying groups of customers with different elasticities.
    b. separating customers in some way.
    c. limiting customers' ability to re-sell the product between different groups.
    d. all of the options listed to be successful.

12. A natural monopoly is a monopoly:
    a. that exists because of economies of scale.
    b. that is created by natural law.
    c. where natural legal barriers prevent entry.
    d. in which patents exist.

13. Refer to the graph below. Which area represents the welfare loss due to a monopolist?
    a. A.
    b. A + B.
    c. B + C.
    d. A + B + C.

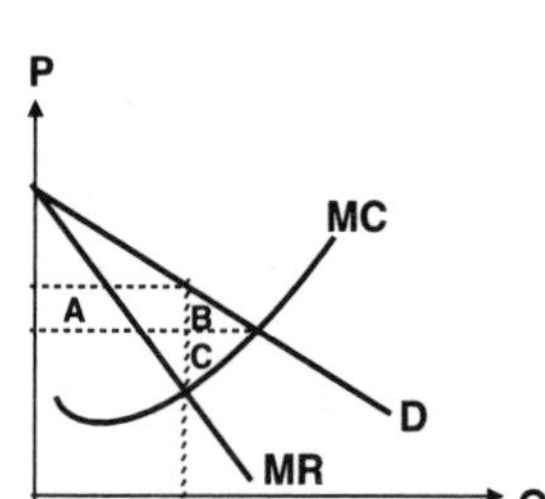

14. For a monopolist to earn an economic profit in the long run, which of the following must happen?
   a. There are barriers to entry.
   b. Average total costs must fall.
   c. Welfare loss due to monopoly must increase.
   d. Fixed costs must be eliminated.

A1. Suppose the marginal costs, and, therefore, the market supply, for ketchup in Mexico is given by $P = Q_s/2 + 1$. The market demand is given by, $Q_d = 20 - 4P$. If there is a monopoly in the ketchup market, the price and the quantity produced is
   a. P = 11/3, Q= 16/3.
   b. P = 11/3, Q= 4.
   c. P = 3, Q= 4.
   d. P = 4, Q= 4.

SHORT-ANSWER QUESTIONS

1. What is the key difference between the decisions by monopolists and the collective decisions of competing firms with regard to setting price and production levels?

2. The president of Corning Fiberglass comes to you for advice. The firm has patented its pink fiberglass. It seems to be able to set its own price. In fact, you can say it has a monopoly on its shade of pink fiberglass. It wants you to tell it how to maximize profits. What information would you ask the president for, and what would you do with that information?

3. Calculate a monopolist's price, output, and profit using the following table:

Q	Price	Total cost
0	$36	$47
1	33	48
2	30	50
3	27	58
4	24	73
5	21	89
6	18	113
7	15	153
8	12	209
9	9	289

4. Show a monopolist's price, output, and profit using the graph below.

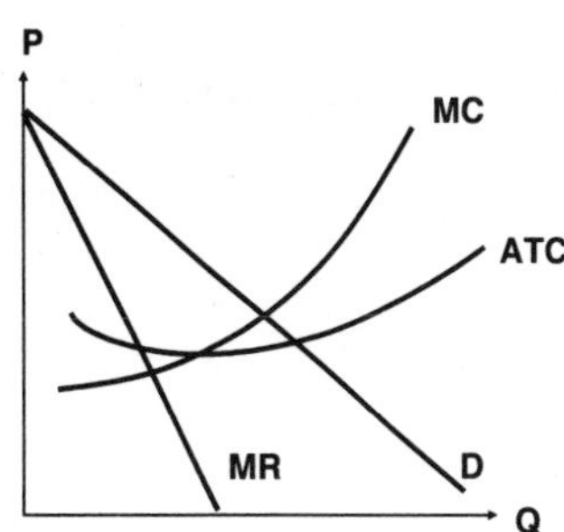

5. Why will a price discriminating monopolist earn more profit than a normal monopolist?

6. Show graphically the welfare loss from monopoly on the axes below.

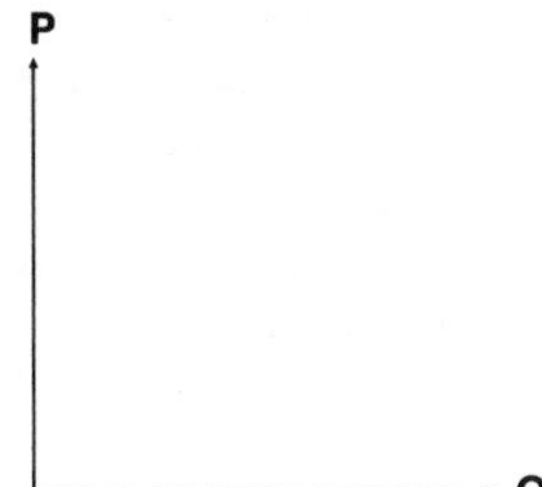

7. Why, without barriers to entry, would there be no monopoly?

8. After seeing your answer to question 6, a group of consumers are outraged. "Why," they say, "that doesn't come close to the harm monopolists inflict on us." Why might the welfare loss from monopoly you demonstrated underestimate their view of the loss from monopoly?

PROBLEMS AND APPLICATIONS

1. What are some real-world examples of monopolies?

2. Consider the following graph for a monopoly.

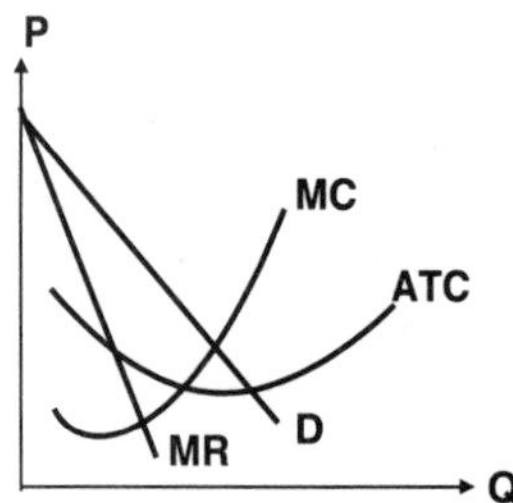

a. Indicate on the graph the monopolist's output and price. Shade the area representing any economic profit (or loss).

b. If this monopolist earns economic profits, then what is expected to happen over time? What if economic losses were incurred?

3. Consider the following graph for a monopoly.

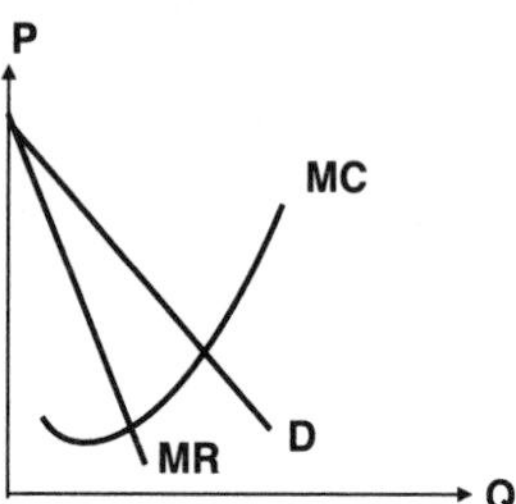

a. Illustrate the output level and price charged by the monopoly on the graph.

b. What would the price and output level be if this were a competitive market?

c. Illustrate the area representing welfare loss on the graph. Explain what is meant by "welfare loss" associated with a monopoly.

4. The following table represents the market for Corning Fiberglass. Corning is the sole producer of fiberglass.

Q	Price	TC
0	—	60
1	46	65
2	42	81
3	38	111
4	34	145
5	30	189
6	24	249

   a. Determine the profit-maximizing price and output.

   b. What is the monopolist's profit?

   c. Suppose the market is competitive, what is output and price? Would this company stay in business?

A1. Suppose the marginal costs, and, therefore, the market supply, for Mimi Chocolates is given by $P = Q_s/2 + 3$. The market demand is given by, $Q_d = 10 \quad 2P$.

   a. What is the equilibrium price and quantity if the market for chocolates is perfectly competitive?

   b. If Mimi Chocolates has a monopoly in the markets, what will be the price in the market and the quantity produced?

A BRAIN TEASER

1. Suppose you are in the business of staging concerts. You have just contracted to stage a concert featuring a red-hot rock group. The total cost of staging the concert is $10,000. This total cost is independent of how many people attend the concert. Your market research indicates that attendance at the concert will vary depending on the price of an admission ticket, as shown below. What ticket price should you charge to maximize profit? Briefly explain.

Ticket Price	Attendance
$20	771
$18	979
$16	1,133
$14	1,327
$12	1,559
$10	1,625
$ 8	1,803

POTENTIAL ESSAY QUESTIONS

You may also see essay questions similar to the "Problems & Applications" and "Brain Teasers" exercises.

1. What is the objective of price discrimination? What conditions must be present for a firm to be able to price discriminate?

2. What are three normative arguments against monopoly?

ANSWERS

MATCHING

1-e; 2-c; 3-a; 4-d; 5-g; 6-f;7-b.

ANSWERS

MULTIPLE CHOICE

1. a Monopoly means one firm; that firm may or may not make a supernormal profit. See page 238.

2. b Both monopolies and competitive firms produce where MR = MC. See pages 238-239.

3. b A monopolist produces where MR = MC. Since MR is below the demand curve, this means the monopolist produces where P > MC. If MR > MC, it will increase production. See pages 239-240.

4. c The marginal revenue curve equals the demand curve at the vertical axis but it falls twice as fast as the demand curve, cutting the horizontal space in half, and intersecting the quantity axis at a point half the distance from where the demand curve intersects the quantity axis. See page 241 "Knowing the Tools."

5. a Output is determined where marginal revenue equals marginal cost. See pages 239-240, especially Figure 11-1 on page 241.

6. a Output is determined where marginal revenue equals marginal cost. Profit is determined by the rectangle created by the relevant price and average total cost at that output. See pages 244-245, and "Knowing the Tools" on page 241.

7. c A monopolist produces where MC = MR and charges a price determined by the demand curve. Since P = ATC, the monopolist is earning no profit. See Figure 11-4a on page 245.

8. d A monopolist produces where MC = MR and charges a price determined by the demand curve. A perfectly competitive market produces where MC intersects the market demand curve (at P_2 and Q_2). See Figure 11-1 on page 241.

9. c A monopolist produces where MC = MR and charges a price determined by the demand curve. A perfectly competitive market produces where MC intersects the market demand curve. Welfare loss is lost consumer and producer surplus due to the decline in output. This is the triangle above the MC curve, below the demand curve and between Q_1 and Q_2 . See pages 245-246, especially Figure 11-5.

10. a By segmenting the market into groups of customers with different elasticities of demand, a price-discriminating monopolist can charge different prices to various consumers. See pages 246-247.

11. d By segmenting the market into groups of customers with different elasticities of demand a price-discriminating monopolist can charge different prices to various consumers. This requires all the options listed. See pages 246-247.

12. a Large fixed costs create barriers to entry for an industry. Average total costs decline as output rises so that it is more efficient for there to be one producer. This industry is known as a natural monopoly. See pages 249-250.

13. c A monopolist produces where MC = MR and charges a price determined by the demand curve. A perfectly competitive market produces where MC intersects the market demand curve. Welfare loss is lost consumer and producer surplus due to the decline in output. This is the triangle above the MC curve, below the demand curve and between the two levels of output. See pages 245-246, especially Figure 11-5.

14. a If there were no barriers to entry, competitors would enter the market and drive down price until only normal profits were earned. See pages 248-249.

A1. d Specifying the demand curve in terms of quantity produced gives: P = 5 − Q/4. Multiplying this by Q gives total revenue TR = 5Q 2 $Q^2/4$. The marginal revenue is the first derivative of this. (This is not something you need to know for this course.) Thus, MR = 5 − Q/2. By setting MR = MC and solving for Q, we get the quantity produced: 5 − Q/2 = Q/2 + 1; Q = 4. The monopolist charges the price that consumers are willing to pay for that quantity. Substituting Q = 4 into the demand equation gives P = 4. Thus, *d* is the correct answer. See pages 258-259.

ANSWERS

SHORT-ANSWER QUESTIONS

1. For a competitive firm, marginal revenue equals price regardless of output. But for a monopolist, price depends upon output. A monopolist must take into account the fact that its output decisions can affect price. The monopolist can only sell more if it lowers the price. Its marginal revenue does not equal the price it charges. Instead, MR < P for the monopolist. (238-239)

2. You tell the president that the firm needs to know its marginal costs and its marginal revenues. To maximize profits, it should produce where *MR* = *MC*. A monopolist produces where *MC* = *MR* to maximize total profit for the same reasons a perfectly competitive firm does. If *MC* < *MR*, it can increase total profits by producing more. If *MC* > *MR*, it can increase total profits by decreasing output. It is only where *MC* = *MR* that it cannot increase profits by changing output. (239-242)

3. To calculate a monopolist's output, first calculate total revenue (*P* × *Q*) for each output level. Then calculate marginal revenue (the change in total revenue/the change in *Q*). Find where *MR* = *MC*. This is at 4 units and a price of $24. Profit is calculated as total revenue minus total cost: $23. Notice that profit is maximized at an output where *MR* = *MC*. Profits are as high, or higher here than at any other output level. (Marginal cost refers to the marginal cost of increasing to that row, e.g., the marginal cost of going from 0 to 1 is 1. The same goes for marginal revenue.) (239-242)

Q	Price	Total revenue	Marginal revenue	Total cost	Marginal cost
0	$36	0	—	$47	—
1	33	33	33	48	1
2	30	60	27	50	2
3	27	81	21	58	8
4	24	96	15	73	15
5	21	105	9	89	16
6	18	108	3	113	24
7	15	105	–3	153	40
8	12	96	–9	209	56
9	9	81	–15	289	80

4. A monopolist's output is set where *MC* = *MR* (where the *MC* and *MR* curves intersect). Extend a line vertically from the profit maximizing output level (Q^*) to the demand curve; it sets price where that line intersects the demand curve, here at P^*. Profit is determined by dropping a vertical line from the price the monopolist charges to the *ATC* curve and multiplying by Q^*. This is the shaded region in the graph below. (239-246; especially page 246 "Knowing the Tools")

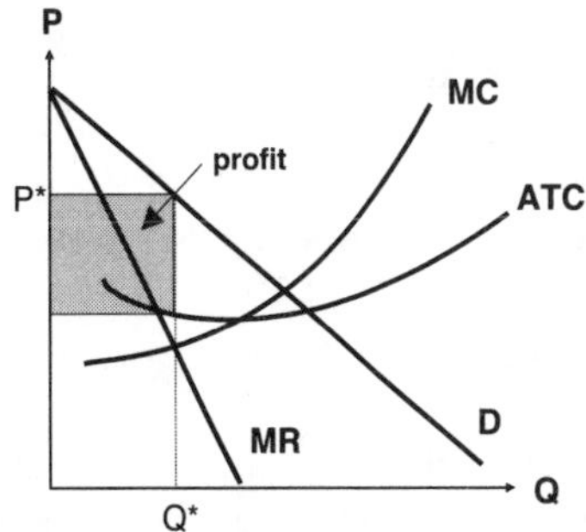

5. If a monopolist can (1) identify groups of customers who have different elasticities of demand, (2) separate them in some way and (3) limit their ability to re-sell its product between groups, it can price discriminate. A price discriminating monopolist earns more profit than a normal single-price monopolist because it can charge a higher price to those with less elastic demands and a lower price to those with more elastic demands. Price discrimination leads to larger output, no deadweight loss, no consumer surplus and a larger profit. (246-248)

6. Welfare loss from monopoly is shown as the shaded region on the graph below. (246)

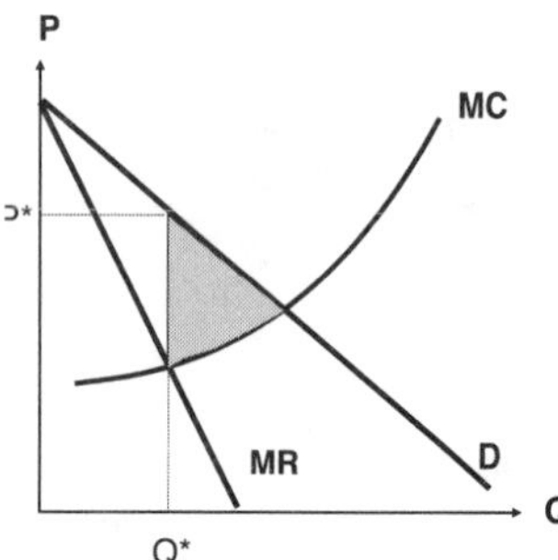

7. Without barriers to entry, there would there be no monopoly because profit-maximizing firms would always enter to compete away monopoly profits. (248-249)

8. You first think that they are wrong. They simply do not understand the model. Upon further reflection, you realize that your model does not capture normative arguments against monopoly. The welfare loss from monopoly shown in question 6 does not capture normative arguments against monopoly. These include: (1) monopolies are unfair and inconsistent with freedom, (2) the income distributional effects associated with monopoly are unfair, and (3) monopolies encourage people to waste resources and money trying to get monopolies. (251-253)

ANSWERS

PROBLEMS AND APPLICATIONS

1. Your local cable television, water, gas and electric companies are a few examples. In some small towns, the only grocery store in town will behave as a monopoly. Note that it may be helpful to think in terms of regional markets, and in terms of the number of suitable substitutes available for the good or service. The smaller the number of suitable substitutes, the greater the monopoly power. (238-239)

2. a. The monopolist will produce Q* and charge price P*. Because $P > ATC$, the monopoly is earning an economic profit shown as the shaded area in the graph below. (239-245)

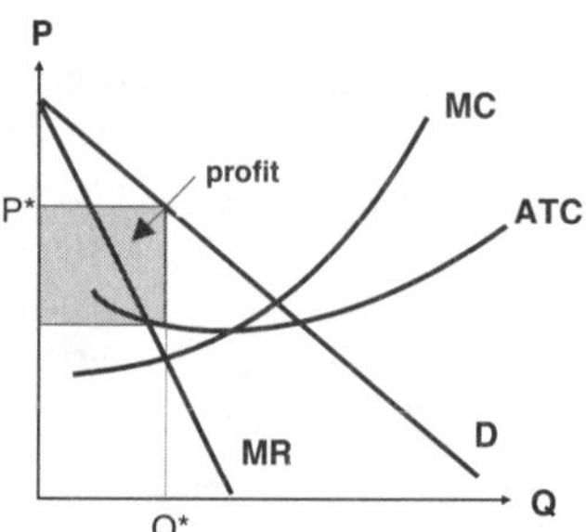

b. Economic profits always attract other businesses. However, because the barriers to entry in a monopoly are so strong, potential competitors will find it very difficult to enter this market. Therefore, economic profits are likely to persist for some time. If losses are incurred by a monopolist then like any other firm, the monopolist will shut down if $P <$ minimum AVC in the short run. No firm can sustain losses in the long run. (239-245)

3. a. See the graph below. The monopoly would produce Q_m and charge price P_m. (239-245)

b. See the graph below. The competitive outcome would be Q_c and P_c. (As you would expect, the monopolist charges a higher price and produces less than if the market were competitive.) (See page 245 and Figure 11-1 on page 241)

c. The shaded area in the graph below illustrates welfare loss. Welfare loss is the amount by which the marginal benefits to society (measured by the prices people are willing to pay along the demand curve) exceed the marginal costs to society (measured by points along the marginal cost curve) for those units which would be produced in a competitive market but are not produced in a non-competitive market. (245-246)

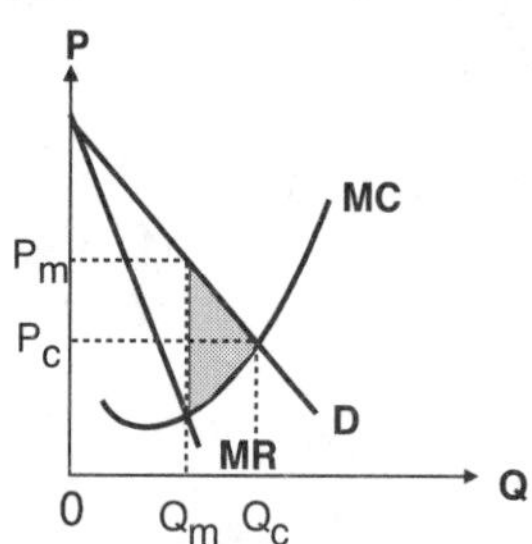

4. To answer the following questions, first calculate *MC*, *MR*, and *AVC*. *MC* is the change in *TC* as *Q* changes, *AVC* is *VC*/*Q*, and *MR* is the change in *TR* as *Q* changes, where *TR* is $P \times Q$. This is shown below. (Marginal cost refers to the marginal cost of increasing to that row, e.g., the marginal cost of going from 0 to 1 is 5. The same goes for marginal revenue.) (239-245)

Q	Price	TC	MC	MR	AVC
0	—	60	—	—	0
1	46	65	5	46	5
2	42	81	16	38	10.5
3	38	111	30	30	17.00
4	34	145	34	22	21.25
5	30	189	44	14	25.8
6	24	249	60	−6	31.5

a. Monopolists maximize profits where *MR* = *MC*. *MR* = *MC* at 3 units. Corning will charge a price of $38. (239-245)

b. Profit = total revenue minus total costs = $3. (239-245)

c. If the market were competitive, then the firm would produce where *MC* = *P*. So *Q* is 4 units and *P* = 34. Profit = total revenue − total costs = −$9. The firm will still stay in business since *P* > minimum *AVC*. (239-245)

A1. a. Rewriting the marginal cost equation with quantity supplied on the left gives: $Q_S = 2P - 6$. Setting this equal to quantity demanded gives equilibrium price at 4 and quantity at 2. (258-259)

b. Specifying the demand curve in terms of quantity produced gives: $P = 5 - Q/2$. Multiplying this by Q gives total revenue $TR = 5Q - Q^2/2$. The marginal revenue is the first derivative of this. Thus, $MR = 5 - Q$. By setting MR = MC and solving for Q we get the quantity that would be produced if the chocolate market were a monopoly. (258-259)

$5 - Q = Q/2 + 3$

$3/2Q = 2$

$Q = 4/3$.

The monopolist charges the price that consumers are willing to pay for that quantity. Substituting $Q = 4/3$ into the demand equation gives $P = 13/3$. You can see that if there is a monopoly in the market, the price charged is higher than the competitive market price; also, the quantity produced is lower.

ANSWERS

A BRAIN TEASER

1. The profit-maximizing price is $12. It generates maximum revenues of $18,708. Since all costs of staging the concert are fixed costs, a price which maximizes revenues also maximizes profit. Profit will equal $8,708 (TR TC = $18,708 $10,000). (259-259)

ANSWERS

POTENTIAL ESSAY QUESTIONS

The following are annotated answers. They indicate the general idea behind the answer.

1. The objective of price discrimination is to increase profits. In order to price discriminate, a firm must be able to segment its markets or customers. It must also be able to determine which markets or customers have the more inelastic demand for the good or service, and then charge those people the higher price. Finally, the product cannot be easily resold.

2. Normative arguments against monopoly include (1) monopolies are unfair and inconsistent with freedom, (2) the income distributional effects associated with monopoly are unfair, (3) monopolies encourage people to waste resources and money trying to get monopolies.

MONOPOLISTIC COMPETITION, OLIGOPOLY, AND STRATEGIC PRICING

12

CHAPTER AT A GLANCE

This is the last chapter dealing with market structures. This one deals with two of them — monopolistic competition and oligopoly. Again, knowing the different characteristics, behaviour, and pricing and output decisions, and how to graphically determine a profit or loss for each is very important. We will also see that these two market structures lead to a less than efficient solution compared to the perfectly competitive market structure from a society's point of view.

An important feature of oligopoly is the kinked demand curve, which is based on the fact that there are different reactions from the competitors depending on if the market price is increased or lowered. Another model of oligopoly is introduced, the cartel model, which assumes that competitors can be made better off if they collude (agree on price and output). A classic example of a collusive arrangement is the OPEC (Organization of Petroleum Exporting Countries) cartel.

The chapter introduces the notion of game theory — the appreciation of economic principles and reasoning to decision making. It outlines under what conditions, with imperfect information, firms can maximize profits.

The last part of the chapter makes a comparison of the various market structures and highlights the important issues raised in the past few chapters. This should be considered an important review of the theories and concepts associated with the four market structures.

This review is based upon the learning objectives that open the chapter.

1. To measure industry structure, economists use one of two methods: the concentration ratio or a Herfindahl index. (262)
A concentration ratio is the percentage of total industry sales by the top few firms of the industry. For example, a four-firm concentration ratio of 60% means the four largest firms account for 60% of industry sales.

A Herfindahl Index is a method used by economists to classify how competitive an industry is. A Herfindahl Index has 2 advantages over a concentration ratio: (1) it takes into account all firms in an industry, and (2) it gives extra weight to firms with especially large shares of the market.

2. Four distinguishing characteristics of monopolistic competition are: (263)

1. Therre are many sellers.
2. Firms sell differentiated products.
3. There are multiple dimensions of competition.
4. There is easy entry of new firms in the long run.

Know these as well as the distinguishing characteristics of all 4 market stuctures.

3a. The equilibrium of a monopolistic competitor is: (265-266)

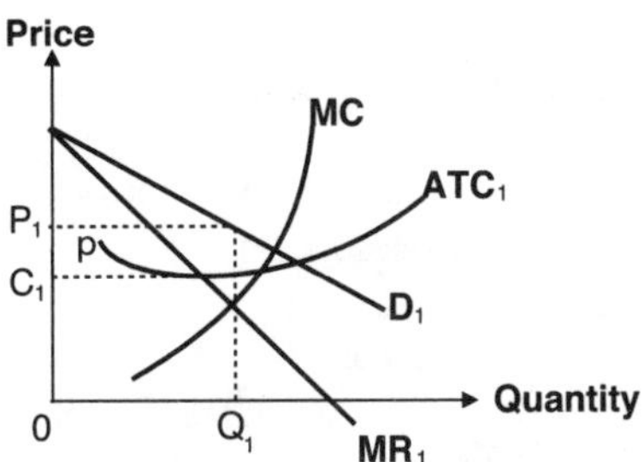

Notice that the profit maximizing output (Q) is determined by MR = MC (just as with pure monopoly). Profit is the difference between P* and ATC multiplied by the output. But because P>MC, this implies underproduction from society's perspective.*

3b. A monopolistically competitive firm has productive capacity that it does not use in long-run equilibrium. This is because its output is less than the output at minimum average total cost. This is called the Excess Capacity Theorem and it occurs because monopolistically competitive firms have downward sloping demand curves. (266-267)

4. The central element of oligopoly is that the industry is made up of a small number of very large firms so that, in any decision it makes, each firm must take into account the expected reaction of other firms. (269)

Oligopolistic firms are mutually interdependent and can be collusive or non-collusive. If oligopolies can collude and form a cartel, they increase the profits going to the combination of firms in the cartel. Although there is an inherent tendency for collusion (getting together to avoid competing), holding firms together is difficult because of a tendency for each of them to cheat.

5a. One characteristic of informal collusive behaviour is that prices tend to be sticky, that they don't tend to change much. (270-272)

One explanation of why prices are sticky is that firms face a linked demand curve. If the firm increases its price, rival firms will not match the price increase, but if the firm lowers its price, other firms will match the price decrease. In either case, the firm is worse off and, as a result, won't change its price in either direction.

5b. In the contestable market model of oligopoly, pricing and entry decisions are based only on barriers to entry and exit, not on market structure. Thus, even if the industry contains only one firm, it could still be a competitive market if entry is open. (272)

Two extreme models of oligopoly behavior:

- Cartel model: Firms set a monopoly price.
- Contestable market model: An oligopoly with no barriers sets a competitive price.

Most real-world oligopolies are in between.

6. In the prisoner's dilemma, while trust gets one out of the dilemma, confessing is the rational choice. (273)

When firms collude, they maximize joint profits. However, the threat of cheating results in all firms cheating and we get a competitive result.
Also notice the table on page 278 which compares the various market structures. Study this table! (It makes for "nice" exam questions.)

MATCHING THE TERMS

Match the terms to their definitions

All of these key terms are found at the end of the chapter.

___ 1. brand proliferation
___ 2. cartel
___ 3. cartel model of oligopoly
___ 4. concentration ratio
___ 5. contestable market model
___ 6. dominant-firm cartel model
___ 7. dominant strategy
___ 8. duopoly
___ 9. excess capacity theorem
___ 10. fringe firms
___ 11. game theory
___ 12. Herfindahl Index
___ 13. implicit collusion
___ 14. market structure
___ 15. monopolistic competition
___ 16. Nash equilibrium
___ 17. North American Industry Classification System (NAICS)
___ 18. oligopoly
___ 19. payoff matrix
___ 20. prisoner's dilemma
___ 21. sticky prices
___ 22. strategic decision making
___ 23. strategic pricing

a. A market structure in which many firms sell differentiated products.
b. A market structure in which there are only a few firms.
c. A well-known game that demonstrates the difficulty of cooperative behavior in certain circumstances.
d. A combination of firms that acts like a single firm.
e. A model that bases pricing and output decisions on entry and exit conditions, not on market structure.
f. The physical characteristics of the market within which firms interact.
g. An index of market concentration.
h. An industry classification that categorizes firms by type of economic activity and groups firms with similar production processes.
i. An oligopoly with only two firms.
j. Firms set their price based upon the expected reactions of other firms.
k. Multiple firms making the same pricing decisions even though they have not consulted with one another.
l. A model that assumes that oligopolies act together as if they were monopolists that have assigned output quotas to individual member firms of the oligopoly so that total output is consistent with joint profit maximization.
m. Taking explicit account of a rival's expected response to a decision it is making.
n. The application of economic principles to interdependent situations.
o. The percentage of total industry sales that a specific number of the largest firms of the industry have.
p. Where firms produce many competing varieties of a product.
q. A firm has extra productive capacity that it does not use in long-run equilibrium.
r. A single firm, often the largest or dominant firm, takes the lead in pricing and output decisions.
s. The smaller members of the industry that usually act as price takers.
t. Prices that tend not to change much.
u. A box that displays the actions and outcomes of a strategic game.
v. A non-competitive equilibrium where no player can achieve a better outcome by switching strategies, given the strategy of the other player.
w. A strategy that always yields the highest payoff, no matter what the other player does.
x. Multiple firms make the same pricing decisions even though they have not explicitly consulted with one another.

MULTIPLE CHOICE

Circle the one best answer for each of the following questions:

1. In a market, there are many firms selling differentiated products. This market is
   a. a competitive market.
   b. a monopolistically competitive market.
   c. an oligopoly.
   d. a monopoly.

2. Several firms are operating in a market where they take the other firms' response to their actions into account. This market is
   a. a competitive market.
   b. a monopolistically competitive market.
   c. an oligopolistic market.
   d. a monopoly.

3. In the NAICS classification system, the broadest classification would be
   a. a two-digit industry.
   b. a three-digit industry.
   c. a four-digit industry.
   d. a five-digit industry.

4. The top four firms in the industry have 10 percent, 8 percent, 8 percent, and 6 percent of the market. The four-firm concentration ratio of this market is
   a. 8.
   b. 32.
   c. 66.
   d. 264.

5. The top four firms in the industry have 10 percent, 8 percent, 8 percent, and 6 percent of the market. The Herfindahl index of this market is closest to which of the following?
   a. 8.
   b. 32.
   c. 66.
   d. 264.

6. Brand proliferation is where:
   a. many firms produce many different products.
   b. many products have easy entry into the industry.
   c. firms produce many competing varieties of a product.
   d. several firms produce same products.

7. Strategic decision making is most important in
   a. competitive markets.
   b. monopolistically competitive markets.
   c. oligopolistic markets.
   d. monopolistic markets.

8. At the equilibrium output for a monopolistic competitor
   a. price equals marginal cost equals marginal revenue.
   b. price equals average total cost equals marginal revenue.
   c. marginal cost equals marginal revenue equals average total costs.
   d. marginal costs equals marginal revenue.

9. Refer to the graph below. Which of the following is the output chosen by the monopolistically competitive firm?

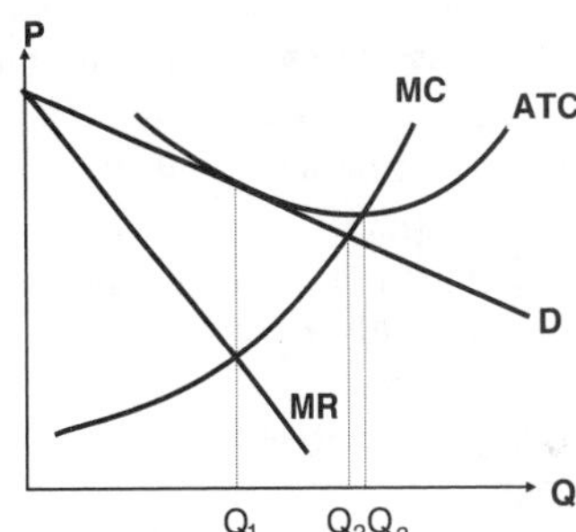

   a. Q_1.
   b. Q_2.
   c. Q_3.
   d. Output cannot be determined.

10. In long-run equilibrium, a monopolistically competitive firm
    a. makes a loss.
    b. makes only a normal profit.
    c. makes a monopolistic profit.
    d. may make a loss or a profit.

11. Advertising adds cost to producing a good. Therefore, it
    a. increases the average total cost of production.
    b. decreases the average total cost of production.
    c. sometimes increases and sometimes decreases the average total cost of production.
    d. has no effect on the average total cost of production.

12. In the cartel model of oligopoly, the firms would decide how much to produce where
 a. marginal cost equals marginal revenue.
 b. marginal cost equals price.
 c. marginal cost equals average total cost.
 d. where the kink in the demand curve is.

13. In a contestable market model of oligopoly, prices are determined by
 a. costs and barriers to exit.
 b. costs and barriers to entry.
 c. costs, barriers to entry, and barriers to exit
 d. costs alone.

14. There is only one firm in the market. The economist analyzing that market has said she would expect the price to equal the firm's average total costs.
 a. She must be analyzing this market using a contestable market model.
 b. She must be analyzing this market using a game theory model.
 c. She must be analyzing this market using a cartel model.
 d. She must not be an economist, because that answer is clearly wrong.

15. The prisoner's dilemma is a well-known game in which
 a. cooperation is costly.
 b. independent action is costly.
 c. firms always cheat.
 d. firms never cheat.

16. The market has the following characteristics: There is strategic pricing, output is somewhat restricted, there is interdependent decision-making, and some long-run economic profits are possible. This market is
 a. a monopoly.
 b. an oligopoly.
 c. monopolistically competitive.
 d. perfectly competitive.

SHORT-ANSWER QUESTIONS

1. What is the 4-firm concentration ratio for an industry in which 10 firms all have 10% of the market?

2. What is a Herfindahl index for an industry in which 10 firms all have 10% of the market?

3. The soap industry is characterized by monopolistic competition. There are many types of soap: Ivory, Irish Spring, Lever, and so on. When one firm lowers its price, it won't calculate the reaction of the other firms. In the automobile market, which is oligopolistic, GM does worry about how Chrysler prices its cars. Based on level of competition, what distinguishes these two (monopolistically competitive vs. oligopolistic) markets?

4. Show graphically the equilibrium of a monopolistic competitor.

5. What is the Excess Capacity Theorem?

6. State the central element of oligopoly and the two basic types of oligopolies?

7. Major oil producers in the world have formed a tight cartel, OPEC. At times, the cartel has fallen apart. What are the reasons the major oil producers have a strong desire to keep OPEC strong?

8. How does the contestable market theory lead to determining competitiveness by performance rather than structure?

9. How is the prisoner's dilemma related to an oligopoly?

PROBLEMS AND APPLICATIONS

1. For each of the following calculate the four-firm concentration ratio and the Herfindahl index.

   a. 20 firms in the market each having equal shares.

   b. 10 firms are in the market. One firm has 91% of market share. The remaining 9 firms share the remaining market equally.

   c. The industry's top firm has 31% of the market and the next three have 2% apiece. There are 63 remaining firms, each with a 1% share.

   d. 4 firms equally share the market.

   e. Rank the markets by how competitive the market is, from more competitive to less competitive, first using the concentration ratio and then the Herfindahl index. Do they differ? Why or why not?

2. Given the following demand curve and marginal revenue curve, add a marginal cost curve.

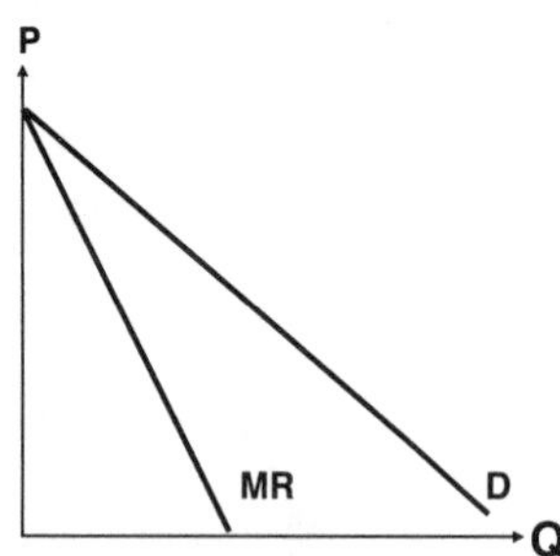

a. Label profit-maximizing price and output for a monopolist. Label profit-maximizing price and output for a monopolistically competitive firm.

b. Add an average total cost curve that is consistent with long-run equilibrium in a market characterized by monopolistic competition. What is the economic profit? Explain your answer.

3. For each of the following graphs, state whether it characterizes perfect competition, monopoly, or monopolistic competition in the long run. Explain your answer.

(a)

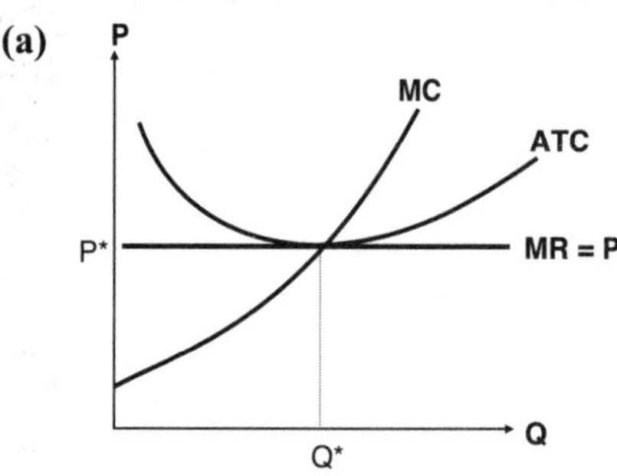

(b)

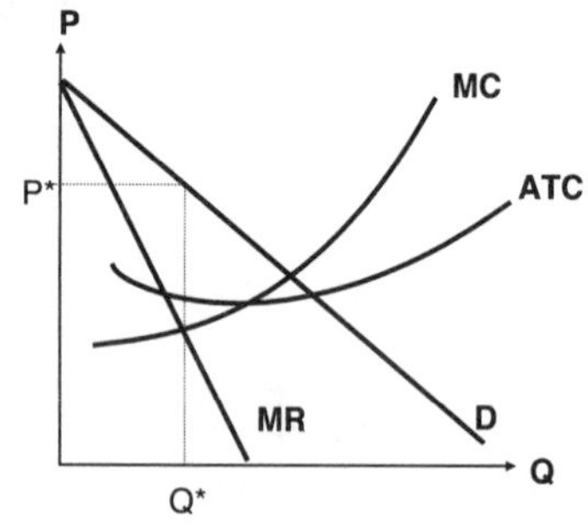

(c)

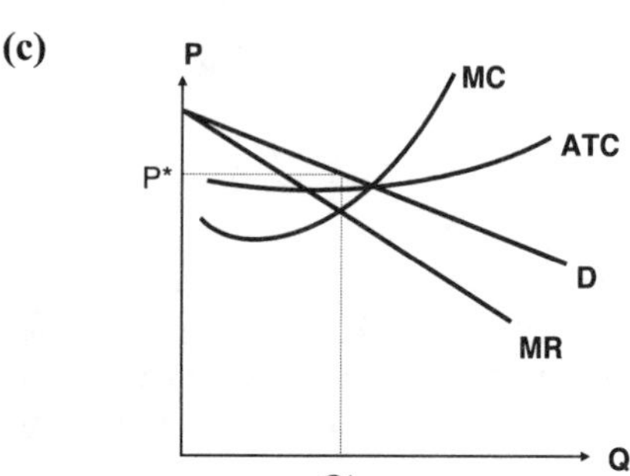

(d)

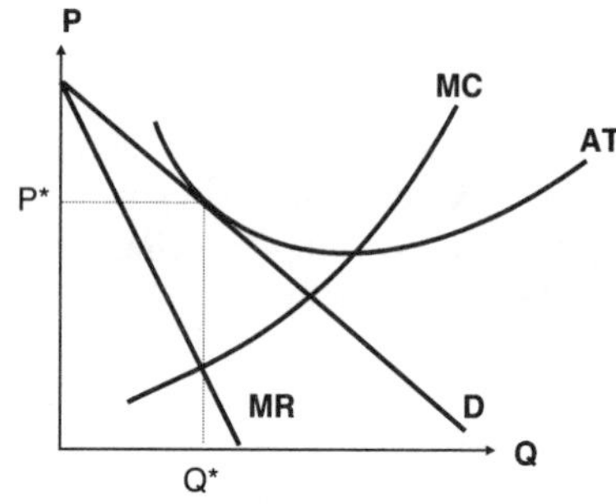

4. Suppose there are two ice-cream stands on opposite sides of the road: Ben's stand and Jerry's stand. Each has identical costs of 25 cents a cone. Each has the option of charging $1 a cone or $1.50 a cone. If Ben and Jerry collude, both charging $1.50 a cone, each will sell 50 cones each day. Ben thinks that he would sell more cones if he sells his at $1 a cone. If he does this, he will sell 80 cones and Jerry will sell 20. Jerry is considering the same strategy. If they both charge $1, each will sell 50 cones per day.

a. Construct a payoff matrix for Ben and Jerry.

b. If the stand is to be in business only one day, what would you advise Ben?

c. If the stands are to be in business all summer long, what would you advise Ben?

5. Fill in the following table, which captures the central differences among various market structures.

	Monopoly	Oligopoly	Monopolistic competition	Perfect Competition
Number of Firms				
Pricing Decisions				
Output Decisions				
Profit				

A BRAIN TEASER

1. In a recent consent decree, airlines agreed to stop a practice in which they had signaled planned fare increases in the computer reservation system and then waited to see if other airlines would follow suit. After this consent decree, travel agents have noticed that airlines often raise their prices on Friday nights and often, but not always, lower those prices on Monday morning. Can you give a likely explanation for this airline action?

POTENTIAL ESSAY QUESTIONS

You may also see essay questions similar to the "Problems & Applications" and "Brain Teasers" exercises.

1. What is the "monopolistic" element and the "competitive" element of monopolistic competition?

2. What is the difference between the contestable market model and the cartel model of oligopoly? How are they related?

ANSWERS

MATCHING

1-p; 2-d; 3-l; 4-o; 5-e; 6-r; 7-w; 8-i; 9-q; 10-s; 11-n; 12-g; 13-x; 14-f; 15-a; 16-y; 17-h; 18-b; 19-u; 20-c; 21-t; 22-m; 23-j.

ANSWERS

MULTIPLE CHOICE

1. b A monopolistically competitive market has many firms selling differentiated products. See page 263.

2. c An oligopoly is a market in which a few firms engage in strategic decision making. See page 269.

3. a In the North American Industry Classification System (NAICS), the more numbers, the greater the particular subdivisions, so the answer is a two-digit sector. See page 261.

4. b The concentration ratio is calculated by summing the market shares of the top four firms. See page 262.

5. d The Herfindahl index sums the squares of the market shares of firms in the industry. Squaring these market shares and adding them gives 264, so the Herfindahl index must be exceed 264 assuming there are more than four firms. See page 262.

6. c There are many examples of monopolistically competitive firms producing many competing varieties of a product – soap, jeans, cookies and games. See page 264.

7. c It is within oligopolies that firms take other firms' expected reactions into account, so it is oligopoly where strategic decision making is most important. See page 269.

8. d The equilibrium output is determined where marginal costs equal marginal revenue. It is only in the long run,where P = ATC and the firm earns a normal profit. See pages 265-266.

9. a The equilibrium output is determined by where marginal cost equals marginal revenue. See page 266 and Figure 12-1.

10. b In long-run equilibrium, a monopolistically competitive firm must make zero profit, so that no entry is induced. See page 267.

11. c The answer is "sometimes increases and sometimes decreases the average total cost of production." Although advertising costs rise, depending on how many economies of scale the advertising allows, average total costs may increase or decrease. See pages 268-269.

12. a The cartel model has the oligopoly acting like a monopolist. See pages 270-271.

13. c Costs determine reference price, and barriers to both entry and exit determine the degree to which price deviates from cost. The higher the barriers, the more the price exceeds cost. See page 272.

14. a In a contestable market model, exit and entry conditions determine the firm's price and output decisions. Thus, if there are no barriers to entry and exit, even if there is only one firm in the industry, the firm will produce where price equals the firm's average total costs. See page 272.

15. b In the prisoner's dilemma game, cooperation is beneficial for both prisoners, but difficult to achieve. Firms do not always get together. There may or may not be cheating, but firms expect others to cheat. See pages 273-276.

16. b An oligopoly is a market in which a few firms operate, each taking into consideration other firms' behavior when making decisions. Because output is somewhat restricted, some long-run profit is possible. See page 278.

ANSWERS

SHORT-ANSWER QUESTIONS

1. A concentration ratio is the percentage of industry by the top few firms of the industry. A 4-firm concentration ratio is calculated by adding together the market shares of the four firms with the largest market shares. In the case given, the 4-firm concentration ratio is 40. (262)

2. A Herfindahl index is a method used by economists to classify how competitive an industry is. It is calculated by summing the squares of the market shares of all the firms in the industry. In this case, the Herfindahl index is 10 $10^2 = 1000$. (262)

3. The distinguishing characteristics are: (1) In the soap industry, there are many sellers in a highly competitive market. In the automobile industry there are about 5 big producers. (2) In the soap industry, the different labels are distinct, but firms still act independently. In the automobile industry, the products are distinct and the firms do not act independently. (3) In the soap industry, there is easy entry of new firms in the long run, so there are no long-run profits. In the auto industry, entry is not easy. In both industries firms compete on more than price; they also compete on image. (263-265)

4. The equilibrium of a monopolistic competitor is shown in the graph below.

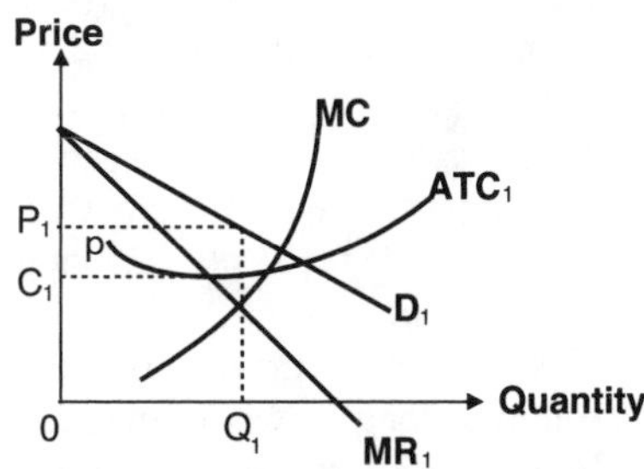

5. In the long run, monopolistically competitive firms tend to produce at a price that exceeds the minimum point of the ATC curve. This reflects a lower output than could be produced causing the output to be less than the output at minimum ATC. (266-267).

6. The central element of oligopoly is that the industry is made up of a small number of very large firms so that, in any decision it makes, each firm must take into account the expected reaction of other firms. Oligopolistic firms are mutually interdependent and can be collusive or non-collusive. (269)

7. Since there are only a few large oil-producing nations, together they are an oligopoly. Oil-producing nations have a powerful desire to keep OPEC strong because as a cartel it can increase the profits going to the combination of oil-producing nations by reducing output. (269-273)

8. In the contestable market theory, pricing decisions are based on the threat of new entrants into the market, not market share. Thus, even if the industry has only one firm, it could still price competitively. (272)

9. When firms collude, they maximize joint profits. However, the threat of cheating results in all firms cheating and we get a competitive result. (273-276)

ANSWERS

PROBLEMS AND APPLICATIONS

1. A four-firm concentration ratio is the percentage of the total industry output that the top four firms have. It is calculated by adding together the top four firms' market shares. The Herfindahl index is calculated by adding the squared value of the market shares of all the firms in the industry. (262)
   - **a.** Four-firm concentration ratio = 5+5+5+5 = 20. Herfindahl index is $20 \times 5^2 = 500$. (262)
   - **b.** Four-firm concentration ratio = 91+1+1+1 = 94. Herfindahl index is $91^2+1^2+1^2+1^2+1^2+1^2+1^2+1^2+1^2+1^2 = 8290$. (279)
   - **c.** Four-firm concentration ratio = 31+2+2+2 = 37. Herfindahl index is $31^2+2^2+2^2+2^2+63 \times 1^2 = 1036$. (262)
   - **d.** Four-firm concentration ratio = 25+25+25+25 = 100. Herfindahl index is $25^2+25^2+25^2+25^2 = 2500$. (262)

e. A higher concentration ratio and Herfindahl index indicates that the market is less competitive. The ranking using the four-firm concentration ratio is *a* (20), *c* (37), *b* (94), *d* (100). Using the Herfindahl index, the ranking is *a* (500), *c* (1036), *d* (2500), *b* (8290). They differ because the Herfindahl index takes into account all the firms in the market and gives extra weight to a single firm with an especially large share of the market (this accounts for the difference in the ranking of *b*). (262)

2. a. The graph below shows a typical marginal cost curve for a firm. The profit-maximizing level of output for a monopolist is where $MC = MR$. It will set price by extending the quantity line to the demand curve and extending a horizontal line to the price axis. This is the price a monopolist would charge. This is labeled as Q^* and P^* respectively. The profit maximizing price and output procedure for a monopolistically competitive firm is the same as for a monopolist. (265-266)

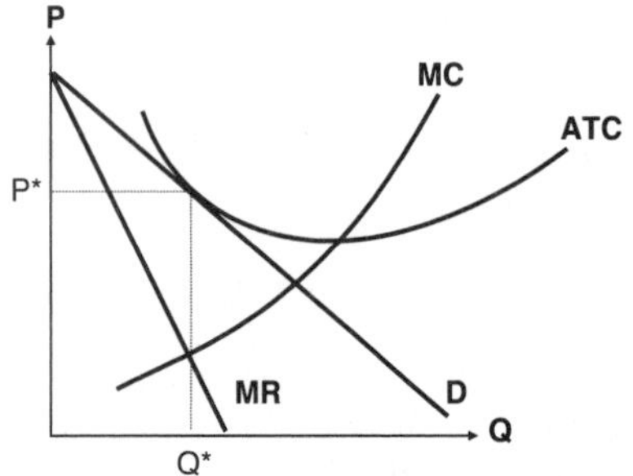

b. The average total cost curve consistent with long-run equilibrium in a market characterized by monopolistic competition is drawn on the graph above. It is tangent to the demand curve at the profit-maximizing price and quantity combination. Economic profit is zero. It is drawn this way because competition implies zero economic profit in the long run. (265-266)

3. a. This graph depicts perfect competition because the demand curve facing the firm is horizontal and no economic profit is earned. (It could also depict a monopolist and a monopolistic competitor in the special case where demand is perfectly elastic.) (266-267)

b. This graph depicts a monopolist because it faces a downward-sloping demand curve and it is earning economic profit. (266-267)

c. This graph depicts a monopolistic competition. The demand curve is downward sloping but more elastic than under pure monopoly. This reflects the firm's limited pricing power due to heavy competition in the long run. (266-267)

d. This graph depicts a monopolistic competitor in the long run because it faces a downward-sloping demand curve and it is not earning any economic profit. (It could also depict a monopolist if it so happens that the *ATC* curve is drawn as given.) (266-267)

4. a. The payoff matrix is shown below. Ben's strategies are listed vertically. Jerry's strategies are listed horizontally. The first number in each cell is Ben's profits calculated as quantity times profit per unit. The second number is Jerry's profit calculated in the same way. (276)

		Jerry's Price	
		$1.50	$1.00
Ben's	$1.50	$62.50/$62.50	$25/$60
Price	$1.00	$60/$25	$37.50/$37.50

b. If the stand is to be in business only one day, I would tell Ben that his profit-maximizing strategy is to charge $1. Expected profit of charging $1.50 is $43.75 ((62.5+25)/2), assuming it is equally likely that Jerry will charge $1.50 or $1.00. Expected profit of charging $1.00 is $48.75 ((60+37.5)/2), assuming it is equally likely that Jerry will charge $1.50 or $1.00. He should charge $1.00. (276)

c. If they were going to sell ice cream all summer long I would recommend that Ben and Jerry develop some level of trust between themselves and collude to charge $1.50 each. This way, they maximize joint profits. (276)

5. See the following table.

	Monopoly	**Oligopoly**	**Monopolistic competition**	**Perfect Competition**
Number of Firms	One	Few	Many	Almost Infinite
Pricing Decisions	MC=MR	Strategic pricing between mo-nopoly and perfect competition	MC=MR	MC=MR=P
Output Decisions	Most output restricted	Output somewhat restricted	Output restricted somewhat by product differentiation	No output restriction
Profit	Possibility of long-run eco-nomic profit	Some long-run economic profit	No long-run eco-nomic profit	No long-run eco-nomic profit possible

ANSWERS

A BRAIN TEASER

1. The airline industry is an oligopoly. The demand curve for airline services appears from this action to be kinked around the "going-market price." Before the consent decree, many airlines which had signaled a price increase may have often found that the other airlines did not follow suit. Consequently, an airline's signaled price increase could cause a significant reduction in its ticket sales and its revenues. After the consent decree, an airline which increases its ticket prices Friday night can reduce its air fares back to where they were come Monday morning before too many ticket sales and revenues are lost if other airlines do not follow with their own price increases. (270-272)

ANSWERS

POTENTIAL ESSAY QUESTIONS

The following are annotated answers. They indicate the general idea behind the answer.

1. The "monopolistic" element is the ability to charge a higher-than-competitive price that is directly related to the success the firm has in differentiating its product from its competitors. The "competitive" element is that there are many sellers who are able to earn only a zero economic profit in the long run because of the weak barriers to entry into the market (the only real barrier to entry is the ability to differentiate the product).

2. The cartel model argues that oligopolists will come together to behave as a monopoly in terms of their pricing and output decisions because it is in their self-interest to do so—they'll make more money. (However, there is always a tendency for a firm to want to "cheat" and the mere rumor of cheating can cause a breakdown of the collusion.) The contestable market model argues that an industry that looks like an oligopoly (because there are a few dominant firms in the industry) could set highly competitive prices and produce a competitive output level. What is important in pricing and output decisions, according to the contestable market model, is not the number of firms in the industry, but the strength of the barriers to entry that exist in the market. If there are few, if any, barriers to entry, then a competitive price and output level will be observed. These two models are related in that the stronger the barriers to entry, usually the fewer the number of firms, and, therefore, the greater the probability for collusion.

COMPETITION, GLOBALIZATION AND TECHNOLOGY

13

CHAPTER AT A GLANCE

In discussing the four market structures, distinctions were made regarding a firm's behaviour in the short run versus the long run. However, little was mentioned about the factors influencing how the long run will look.

This chapter discusses two issues that are very much in the news — technology and globalization — and how they can influence the long run. These issues can alter a firm's behaviour and profitability in the long run, depending on the nature of technological advances, its impact on efficiency, and the degree of competitive pressures in existence.

Monopolies, for example, may exhibit lazy behavior in that the lack of competitive pressures leads to a lack of research and development and for the firm to perform only as efficiently as necessary. Economists use the term X-inefficiency to describe firms operating far less efficiently than technically they could. Other firms in the market do have recourse for this behaviour. Firms can break down a monopoly through political and through economic means, such as by lobbying for slight modifications to existing patent laws. As well, new technologies by others can compete with and undermine natural monopolies. In addition, the global economy increases the number of competitors for the firm.

The discussion begs the question as to whether one particular market structure is more condusive to technological progress. A case can be made that oligopoly seems to be that market structure as it has the incentive to innovate and because they have long run profits to devote to the development of new technologies.

This review is based upon the learning objectives that open the chapter.

1. The monitoring problem is that managers' incentives differ from the owner's (shareholders') incentives. By changing managers' incentives, the efficiency of the firm can sometimes be improved. (285)

Shareholders (owners) of the firm are interested strictly in profit maximizing, however, self-interested managers are interested in maximizing the firm's profit only if the structure of the firm requires them to do so.

An incentive-compatible contract is needed to match the goals of managers with owners.

2. X-inefficiency is a firm operating far less efficiently than technically it could. Corporate takeovers, or simply, the threat of a takeover, can improve firms' efficiency. (287-288)

The competitive pressures a firm faces limit its laziness and its X-inefficiency.

3a. When competitive pressures get strong, individuals often fight back through social and political pressures. Competition is a process—a fight between the forces of monopolization and the forces of competition. (289)

Everyone applauds competition, except for themselves.

Competitive markets will exist only if producers or consumers don't collude.

3b. Actions firms take to break down monopoly include (1) lobbying government to change the law which maintains that monopoly if the monopoly is a legal monopoly and (2) to make slight modifications to a monopolist's patent within the limits of the law. (290)

4. Firms protect their monopolies by (1) advertising and lobbying government, (2) producing products as nearly unique as possible, and (3) charging low prices. (292)

   Firms will spend money and time to obtain monopoly power until the marginal cost equals the marginal benefit.

5. Modern competition is different because of globalization and technology. (293-294)

   Technological advance and globalization go together. Globalization, which is the integration of world markets, leads to specialization, which leads to technological advance and increased productivity. This interplay results in intense price competition.

6. Oligopoly tends to be most conducive to technological change. (298)

   Since the typical oligopolist realizes on-going economic profit, it has the necessarily large funds required to carry out significant research and development. Moreover, the belief that its competitors are innovating also forces it to do so.

   Oligopolists are constantly searching for new ways to get an edge on competitors, so most technological advance takes place in oligopolistic industries.

7. The threat of competition keeps firms behaving competitively which leads to technological progress. (298)

   Some argue that technological advances lead to the formation of oligopolies rather than oligopolies developing technological advances.

MATCHING THE TERMS
Match the terms to their definitions

All of these key terms are found at the end of the chapter.

___ **1.** corporate takeover
___ **2.** dynamic efficiency
___ **3.** globalization
___ 4. incentive-compatible contract
___ **5.** industrial organization
___ **6.** lazy monopolist
___ **7.** monitoring problem
___ **8.** network externality
___ **9.** patent
___ **10.** reverse engineering
___ **11.** technological development
___ **12.** technological lock-in
___ **13.** X-inefficiency

a. Problem that employees' incentives differ from the owner's incentives.
b. An agreement in which the incentives of both parties match as closely as possible.
c. Firm that does not push for efficiency, but merely enjoys the position it is already in.
d. Operating less efficiently than technically possible.
e. A firm or a group of individuals issues an offer to buy up the stock of a company to gain control and to install its own managers.
f. The ability to promote cost-reducing or product-enhancing technological change.
g. A legal right to be the sole supplier of a good.
h. Firm buying up other firms' products, disassembling them, figuring out what's special about them, and then copying them within the limits of the law.
i. When greater use of a product increases the benefit of that product to everyone.
j. When prior use of a technology makes the adoption of subsequent technologies difficult.
k. The discovery of new or improved products or methods of production.
l. A branch of economics that studies the organizational structure, behavioral strategies, and efficiency of markets.
m. The integration of world markets.

MULTIPLE CHOICE

Circle the one best answer for each of the following questions:

1. The *best* definition of an incentive-compatible contract is
a. a contract with sympathetic incentives.
b. a contract with compatible incentives.
c. a contract in which the incentive structure corresponds to the firm's goals and managers' goals as much as possible.
d. a contract that pays bonuses.

2. A firm is making no profit. If there is X-inefficiency, what can we conclude?
a. The firm is operating at least cost.
b. The firm is operating using the fewest inputs possible.
c. The firm is operating less efficiently than economically possible.
d. We can say nothing about the efficiency of the firm.

3. The goals of managers are generally
a. identical to the goals of owners.
b. identical to the goals of workers.
c. totally inconsistent with the goals of owners.
d. somewhat inconsistent with the goals of owners.

4. When there is little competitive pressure, large organizations have a tendency to make decisions that
a. benefit the consumer.
b. benefit the managers.
c. benefit the government.
d. do not benefit anyone.

5. Economists would expect that generally
a. for-profit firms operate more efficiently than nonprofit firms.
b. nonprofit firms operate more efficiently than for-profit firms.
c. for-profit firms operate equally efficiently as nonprofit firms.
d. nonprofit firms cannot exist because they operate so inefficiently.

6. Refer to the graph below. If suppliers restrict output to OL, what area represents the welfare loss to society?
a. A + B.
b. B + C.
c. C + D.
d. A + D.

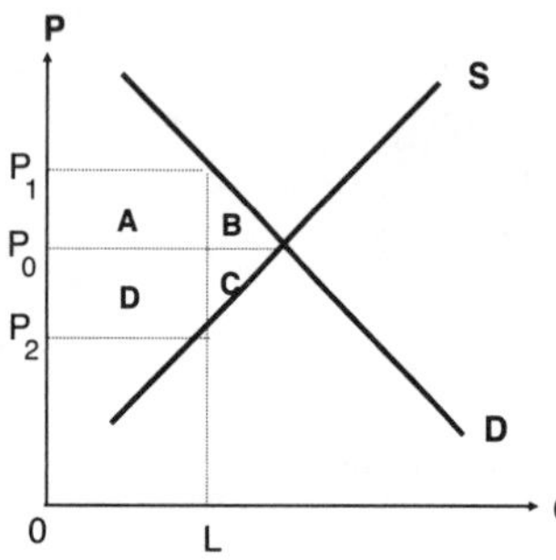

7. A patent is
a. a type of reverse engineering.
b. a type of natural monopoly.
c. a type of corporate takeover.
d. a type of legal monopoly.

8. If average total costs are decreasing throughout the relevant range of production, the industry will be
a. a natural monopoly.
b. a prime target for rent-seeking.
c. a lazy monopolist.
d. an example of monitoring problems.

9. When firms are allowed to pass on all cost increases to earn a normal profit, they
a. have a strong incentive to operate efficiently.
b. have little incentive to operate efficiently.
c. become a focal point of reverse engineering.
d. will apply for a patent.

10. Ways in which firms try to protect their monopoly include all the following *except*
a. advertising and lobbying.
b. charging low prices.
c. making their product unique.
d. reverse engineering.

11. Many economists consider competition today to be more intense than competition ten or twenty years ago because of
a. globalization and technological development.
b. greater governmental regulation and more reverse engineering.
c. more corporate takeovers and higher trade barriers.
d. greater political tensions among governments and lower taxes.

12. Globalization generally
a. decreases competition.
b. is a result of higher trade barriers.
c. results in lower prices to consumers.
d. reduces technological advances.

13. The market structure most conducive to technological advance is
a. perfect competition.
b. monopolistic competition.
c. oligopoly.
d. monopoly.

14. Technological advances are most likely for markets that
a. earn economic profits.
b. have one firm supplying all the output.
c. are protected by government regulation.
d. produce where MR = MC.

15. Network externalities
a. occur when greater use of a product increases the benefit of that product to everyone.
b. inhibit the development of industry standards.
c. make it more likely that the most efficient standards will be adopted.
d. reduce the likelihood that an industry becomes a "winner takes all" industry.

SHORT-ANSWER QUESTIONS

1. Is the high pay that top-level management receives an example of the monitoring problem?

2. What are the implications of the monitoring problem for economics?

3. How can corporate takeovers improve firms' efficiency?

4. What is meant by the phrase "Competition is a process, not a state"?

5. List two actions firms take to break down monopoly.

6. List three ways in which firms protect their monopoly.

7. Explain how globalization and technology have changed competition.

8. Which market structure is most conducive to technological advance? Why?

PROBLEMS AND APPLICATIONS

1. College Retirement Equities Fund (CREF) is a pension fund for college teachers, which has billions of dollars invested in the stock market. A few years ago, fund participants voted on a proposal that would have placed strict limits on the amount of compensation paid to CREF executives. Why do you think 75 percent of the participants voted against the proposal?

2. Demonstrate, using the graph below, the net gain to producers and the net loss to consumers if suppliers are able to restrict their output to Q_R. What is the net deadweight loss to society?

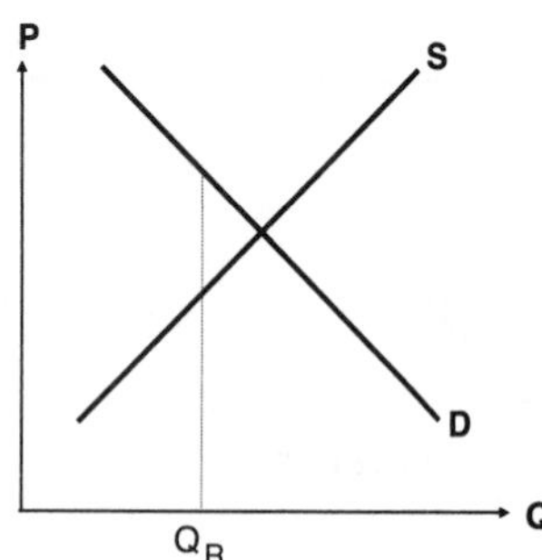

3. a. What is one positive and one negative effect of globalization on firms?

   b. What is one positive and one negative effect of globalization for a nation?

   c. Do the benefits of globalization for a nation outweigh the costs, or do the costs outweigh the benefits?

A BRAIN TEASER

1. Consider the graph below representing a natural monopoly.

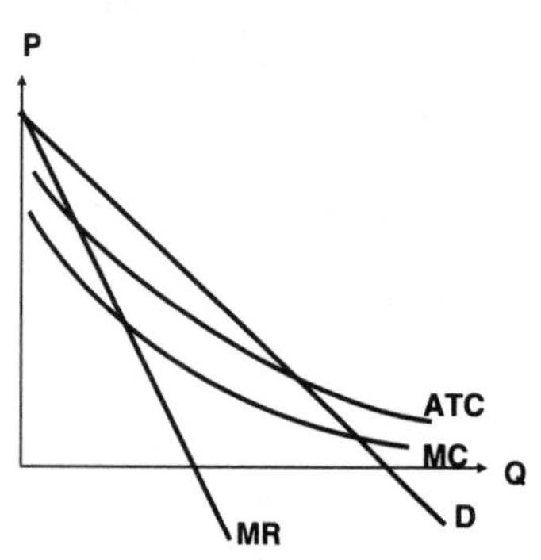

   a. What price would the firm charge if it were unregulated?

   b. What price would you advise to the government that the firm should be allowed to charge? Explain your answer.

   c. What potential problem might your advice create over time?

POTENTIAL ESSAY QUESTIONS

You may also see essay questions similar to the "Problems & Applications" and "Brain Teasers" exercises.

1. Describe two actions firms take to break down monopoly and three they take to protect monopoly.

2. Explain how globalization and technology have changed competition.

ANSWERS

MATCHING

1-e; 2-f; 3-m; 4-b; 5-l; 6-c; 7-a; 8-i; 9-g. 10-h; 11-k; 12-j; 13-d

ANSWERS

MULTIPLE CHOICE

1. c While incentive-compatible contracts could pay bonuses, they do not necessarily have to, which rules out this option. The contract with compatible incentives doesn't say what it is compatible with. See the definition of incentive compatible contract on page 285.

2. c Whenever there is X-inefficiency, the firm is not operating at least cost. That is, it is not economically efficient. See page 287.

3. d Managers' goals are quite inconsistent with the goals of the owners. However, the managers do not want to get fired and the competitive pressures out there mean those managers must make sufficient profits so they don't get fired. To that degree, their goals are consistent with the goals of the owners. See pages 284-287.

4. b When there are no competitive pressures, organizations tend to make decisions that benefit employees or the decision-makers rather than consumers. See pages 284-287.

5. a While for-profit firms can exhibit inefficiency, the market limits that inefficiency. See pages 287-289.

6. b The welfare loss is the triangle made up of areas *B* and *C*. This area represents the producer and consumer surplus lost by both but not gained by the other. The other areas represent transfers. See page 290 and Figure 13-2.

7. d A patent is the legal right to be the sole supplier of a product. It is a type of legal monopoly. See page 290.

8. a A "natural monopoly" is the best answer. The other answers fit, but nowhere near as closely. The statement you are asked to complete is essentially the definition of a natural monopoly. See pages 291-292.

9. b When you can pass on cost increases, why try to hold costs down? See pages 291-292.

10. d Reverse engineering is a method firms use to try to break down other firms' monopolies. See pages 291-292.

11. a Globalization has increased the number of competitors domestic firms face and technological development increases competition by providing more products. See pages 293-294.

12. c Globalization increases the competition domestic firms face. Firms can also move production to lower-cost parts of the world. Both of these result in lower product prices for consumers. See pages 293-294.

13. c Oligopoly provides the best market structure for technological advance because firms have an incentive to innovate (they face competition) and they also have the profits to devote to research and development. See page 298.

14. a Technological advance requires large amounts of investment. Only firms that earn economic profit can afford to invest in research and development. See page 298.

15. a Network externalities promote industry standards, although those standards may not be the most efficient. They also increase the likelihood that an industry becomes a "winner takes all" industry. See pages 298-300.

ANSWERS

SHORT-ANSWER QUESTIONS

1. The monitoring problem is the problem of seeing that self-interest-seeking individuals working for an organization follow the goals of the organization rather than their own goals. The high pay that top-level management gets might be pay for performance, or it might be an example of the monitoring problem. To determine which it is, one would need to consider the specific case and determine whether there are incentive-compatible contracts (probably low base pay and high option bonuses) that make the managers' goals consistent with the goals of the firms' owners. (285)

2. Economics assumes that firms and the economy operate efficiently because firms maximize profits. The monitoring problem undermines that assumption since managers, to some degree, will follow their own goals rather than the profit-maximizing goal. Firms may become lazy monopolists and exhibit X-inefficiency. So the monitoring problem has significant implications. The degree to which firms become lazy monopolists will be limited, however, by competitive pressures. (287-288)

3. Answer *2* above pointed out that when there is a monitoring problem a firm can exhibit X-inefficiency—it can have higher costs than necessary and firms operating far less efficiently than technically they could. When that happens, the firm's stock price will fall and it may be worthwhile for another firm to come in and take the inefficient firm over, eliminate the inefficiency, and develop better incentive-compatible contracts. Often, these takeovers are financed by large amounts of debt, which means that the resulting firm must make high interest payments. So even if the new firm does not establish incentive-compatible contracts, the high debt can force the firm to operate more efficiently. (288-289)

4. Competition is a process—a fight between the forces of monopolization and the forces of competition. The basic idea of economics is that self-interest-seeking individuals try to do the best they can for themselves—to make life as easy as possible for themselves. One of the important ways in which they can do that is to create a monopoly for themselves. When they do that they create the possibility of profits for other individuals who come in and steal their market—thereby breaking down their monopoly. This process of monopolization and competition breaking down the resulting monopoly is pervasive in our economy and is what is meant by the phrase: "competition is a process, not a state." (289-290)

5. To soak up monopoly profits for themselves, firms will break down monopoly through political and through economic means. If the monopoly is a legal monopoly, high profit will lead potential competitors to lobby to change the law which maintains that monopoly. If the law can't be changed—say, the monopolist has a patent—potential competitors will generally get around the obstacle by developing a slightly different product or by working on a new technology that avoids the monopoly but satisfies the relevant need. (290)

6. Three ways in which firms protect their monopoly are (1) advertising and lobbying; (2) producing products as nearly unique as possible, and (3) charging low prices that discourage entry. All these methods cost the firms money in the short run, but increase their monopoly rents (profits) in the long run. (290)

7. Globalization leads to specialization, technological advance, increased productivity, and lower costs of production that result in intense competition. (293-296)

8. Oligopoly tends to be most conducive to technological change. Since the typical oligopolist realizes on-going economic profit, it has the necessarily large funds required to carry out significant research and development. Moreover, the belief that its competitors are innovating also forces it to do so. Oligopolists are constantly searching for new ways to get an edge on competitors, so most technological advance takes place in oligopolistic industries. (298)

ANSWERS

PROBLEMS AND APPLICATIONS

1. The fund participants are aware of incentive-compatible contracts. Structuring CREF executive pay based on the fund's performance in the stock market increases the chances that the interests of the owners and the managers of the fund are compatible. (285-286)

2. As shown on the graph below, if suppliers restrict supply to Q_R, they will be able to charge a price of P_R, which is higher than competitive price, P_C. This gives suppliers supplying Q_R additional income, labeled A. Some suppliers are excluded from the market ($Q_c - Q_R$). They lose area C in producer surplus. Consumers who cannot purchase goods lose consumer surplus represented by area B. Those who can buy goods pay the higher price. Higher expenditures are represented by area A (the additional income to firms). Since A is transferred from consumers to producers, this is not a loss to society. Areas B and C are lost by consumers and producers, respectively, but not transferred to anyone. Those areas are the deadweight loss to society. (290)

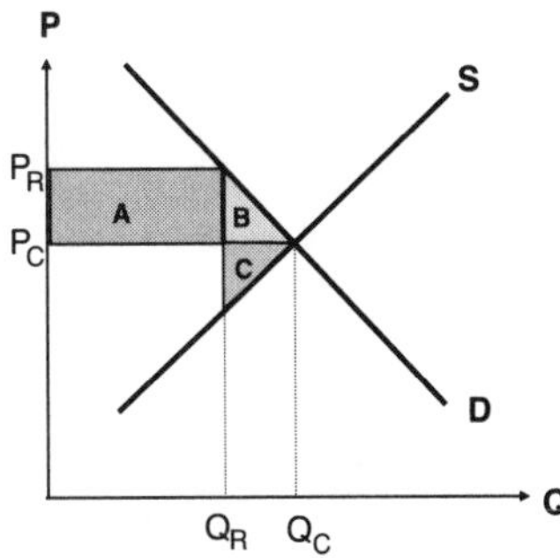

3. **a.** Globalization increases the size of the gain to the firm that is a winner, but makes it harder to win, or to even stay in business. (293-296)
   b. A positive effect of globalization for a nation is increased competition. Greater competition results in a wider variety of higher quality products at lower prices. This ultimately means a higher average absolute standard of living for the nation. However, globalization may result in some temporary loss of jobs or business failures as a result of the more intense global competition. (293-296)
   c. The benefits of globalization outweigh the costs for a nation over time. This is why so many nations are more aggressively pursuing greater participation in the global economy. (293-296)

ANSWERS

BRAIN TEASER

1. **a.** The natural monopolist would produce quantity where $MC = MR$ and charge the price that corresponds to that quantity from the demand curve. This combination is shown on the graph below as (Q_M, P_M). (291-292)

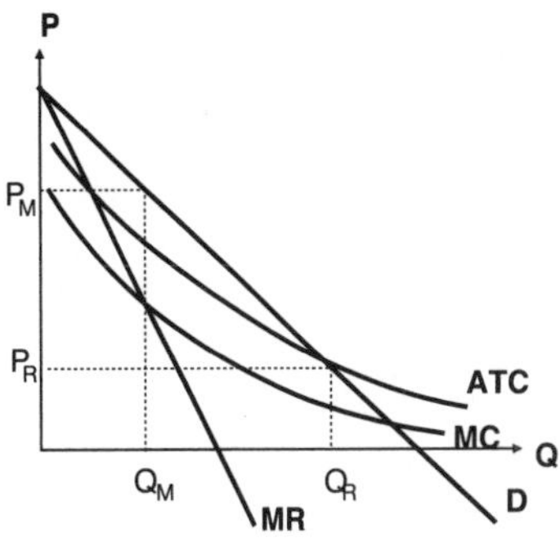

   b. I would advise the government that the natural monopolist should be regulated to charge a price where average total costs intersects the demand curve. This way, the monopolist earns normal profit. You cannot require that $MC = P$ because at that price $MC < ATC$, losses would be incurred, and the monopolist would not be able to survive under these circumstances. (291-292)
   c. The problem with this advice is that there is little incentive for the firm to keep its costs down. Why should it keep costs down if it knows it can raise the price sufficiently to cover its costs? (291-292)

ANSWERS

POTENTIAL ESSAY QUESTIONS

The following are annotated answers. They indicate the general idea behind the answer.

1. Actions firms take to break down monopoly include (1) lobbying government to change the law which maintains that monopoly if the monopoly is a legal monopoly and (2) to make slight modifications to a monopolist's patent within the limits of the law. Firms protect their monopolies by (1) advertising and lobbying government, (2) producing products as nearly unique as possible, and (3) charging low prices.

2. Globalization leads to specialization, technological advance, increased productivity, and lower costs of production that result in intense competition.

MARKET FAILURES AND GOVERNMENT POLICY

CHAPTER AT A GLANCE

Now that we have a foundation of supply and demand and an understanding of various market structures, we can explore policy questions more deeply and develop a greater understanding of some of the roles of government. Markets are not entirely efficient. They tend to fail to operate efficiently and in the best interests of society. One important area of analysis will be how government reacts to market failures – when activities within the market do not lead to socially desirable outcomes.

There are essentially four sources of market failure that are explored– externalities, public goods, moral hazard and asymmetric information. Sometimes governments intervene to provide those goods and services not provided in the private sector (public goods), to address externalities such as pollution or environmental damage, or to ensure that consumers and producers have complete information when making decisions. Government intervention can take many forms such as taxation, providing subsidies, and the implementation of regulations.

The chapter discusses a number of methods of dealing with externalities from direct regulation, to incentive policies, which could include tax incentive and market incentive policies, and to voluntary solutions. Economists tend to like incentive policies as they are more efficient.

This review is based upon the learning objectives that open the chapter.

1. Market failure is where the natural market forces of demand and supply do not function to create an efficient market equilibrium. (304)

2a. An externality is an effect of a decision on a third party not taken into account by the decision maker. They can also occur when a market transaction has a beneficial or detrimental effect on others. (306)

Externalities can either be negative (have undesirable social side effects in which case society would want less of the good) or positive (have desirable social side effects in which case society would want more of the good). Externalities are only one source of market failure.

2b. When there are externalities, the social marginal cost differs from the private marginal cost. (305-306)

4 sources of market failure:
- *Externalities*
- *Public goods*
- *Asymmetric information*
- *Moral hazard*

Any time a market failure exists, there is a reason for possible government intervention to improve the outcome. However, government failure (government intervention in the market to improve the market failure actually making matters worse) is always a possibility.

Economic policy is often a choice between market failure and government failure.

3. Ways to deal with externalities include (1) direct regulation (2) incentive policies (tax incentive policies and market incentive policies), and (3) voluntary solutions. (308-311)

Economists tend to like incentive policies to deal with externalities.

The optimal policy is one in which the marginal cost of undertaking the policy equals the marginal benefit of that policy.

4. *Coase Theorem states that an optimal allocation of resources (efficient market solution) can always be achieved through market forces regardless of the initial assignment of property rights. When* *externalities are present, the performance of the market economy to allocate goods efficiently can be impaired. Four types of goods are highlighted. – rival goods, excludable goods, nonrival goods, and nonexcludable goods. (312-314)*

5. A public good is a good that is nonexcludable (no one can be excluded from its benefits) and nonrival (consumption by one does not preclude consumption by others). (314)

   It is difficult for government to decide the efficient quantity of a public good. If the public good is to be financed by a tax on citizens who benefit from it, individuals have an incentive to conceal their willingness to pay for it.

   Similarly, if citizens think they will not be the ones taxed to fund the public good, but will benefit from it, they have an incentive to exaggerate their willingness to pay. We get the free rider problem with public goods.

6. Real-world markets often involve inaccurate or concealed information, and outright cheating and deception = asymmetric information. Adverse selection problems can occur when buyers and sellers have different amounts of information about the good for sale. Moral hazard occurs when one party is able to misrepresent his intentions and behaves differently than what was agreed to. (318)

   When there is a lack of information or buyers and sellers don't have equal information, markets in some goods may not work well (hence, market failure).

7. 2 general policies to deal with informational problems are:

   - *Regulatory approach*
   - *Market approach*

8. Should government intervene in the market? It depends. (319)

   We need to weight the benefits against the costs of government intervention on a case-by-case basis and remain as objective as possible in the measurement of those benefits and costs.

   Government failure may occur because sometimes:

   - *Governments don't have an incentive to correct the problem.*
   - *Governments don't have enough information to deal with the problem.*
   - *Intervention in markets is almost always more complicated than it initially seems.*
   - *The bureaucratic nature of government intervention does not allow fine-tuning.*
   - *Government intervention often leads to more government intervention.*

MATCHING THE TERMS

Match the terms to their definitions

All of these key terms are found at the end of the chapter.

___ **1.** adverse selection problem
___ **2.** asymmetric information
___ **3.** Coase theorem
___ **4.** complete contract
___ **5.** consumer sovereignty
___ **6.** direct regulation
___ **7.** efficient
___ **8.** effluent fees
___ **9.** excludable good
___ **10.** experienced good
___ **11.** externality
___ **12.** free rider problem
___ **13.** government failure
___ **14.** inefficient
___ **15.** market failure
___ **16.** market incentive plan
___ **17.** market outcome failure
___ **18.** moral hazard
___ **19.** negative externality
___ **20.** non-excludable good
___ **21.** nonrival good
___ **22.** optimal policy
___ **23.** positive externality
___ **24.** private marginal benefit
___ **25.** private marginal cost
___ **26.** property rights
___ **27.** public good
___ **28.** rival good
___ **29.** social marginal benefit
___ **30.** social marginal cost
___ **31.** tax incentive program

a. A situation in which the invisible hand pushes in such a way that individual decisions do not lead to socially optimal outcomes.
b. The sum of the private marginal costs of production plus the cost of the negative externalities associated with that production.
c. The effect of a decision on a third party that is not taken into account by the decision maker.
d. The amount of a good people are allowed to use is directly limited by the government.
e. When the effect of a decision not taken into account by the decision maker is detrimental to others.
f. Charges imposed by government on the level of pollution created.
g. When the effect of a decision not taken into account by the decision maker is beneficial to others
h. A plan requiring market participants to certify that they have reduced total consumption—not necessarily their own individual consumption—by a specified amount.
i. A good that is nonexcludible (no one can be excluded from its benefits) and nonrival (consumption by one does not preclude consumption by others).
j. Achieving a goal at the lowest cost in total resources.
k. A problem that occurs when buyers and sellers have different amounts of information about the good for sale.
l. When government intervention in the market to improve a market failure makes the situation worse.
m. Individuals' unwillingness to share in the cost of a public good.
n. Equals the private marginal benefit of consuming a good plus the benefits of the positive externalities resulting from consuming that good.
o. Achieving a goal in a more costly manner than necessary.
p. A policy in which the marginal cost of undertaking the policy equals the marginal benefit of that policy.
q. A program using a tax to create incentives for individuals to structure their activities in a way that is consistent with the desired ends.
r. Occurs when one person has information which is relevant to the exchange, but the other person does not.
s. Persons can be prevented from consuming the good.
t. Persons cannot be prevented from consuming the good and no one can be excluded from its benefits.
u. Can be jointly consumed; one person's use of the good does not diminish another person's use of it.
v. The benefit that is captured by the person consuming the good.
w. The cost that is borne by the firm producing the good.
x. A set of use and ownership rules in society.
y. When one person consumes it, another person cannot consume the same unit.
z. Where the market forces produce an efficient equilibrium, but society does not prefer the equilibrium that naturally emerges.
Z1. An optimal allocation of resources can always be achieved through market forces regardless of the initial assignment of property rights.
Z2. A person learns the characteristics of a good through experience with it.
Z3. Occurs when one party is able to misrepresent his intentions and behaves differently than what was agreed to.
Z4. A contract where everything is specified so that expected behaviour is clear to both parties.
Z5. The right of the individual to make choices about what is consumed and produced.

MULTIPLE CHOICE

Circle the one best answer for each of the following questions:

1. All of the following are market failures *except*
   a. positive externalities.
   b. imperfect information.
   c. negative externalities.
   d. the invisible hand.

2. An externality is
   a. the effect of a decision on a third party not taken into account by a decision maker.
   b. another name for exports.
   c. events that happen that are external to the economy.
   d. the external effect of a government policy.

3. Refer to the graph below. The S curve represents the private marginal cost of production, and the D curve represents the private marginal benefit to consumers of the good. If there is a negative externality of production, and one wants to adjust the curves so that the equilibrium demonstrates the appropriate marginal social benefits,

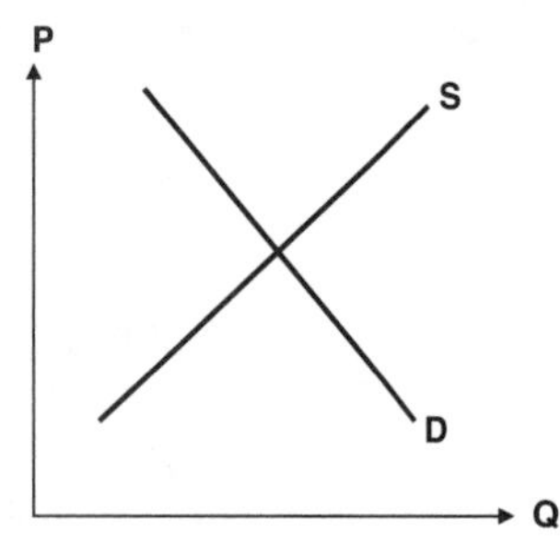

   a. the D curve should be shifted out to the right.
   b. the D curve should be shifted in to the left.
   c. the S curve should be shifted out to the right.
   d. the S curve should be shifted in to the left.

4. Refer to the graph for Question #3. The S curve represents the private marginal cost of production, and the D curve represents the private marginal benefit to consumers of the good. If there is a positive externality of consumption, and one wants to adjust the curves so that the equilibrium demonstrates the appropriate social marginal benefits,
   a. the D curve should be shifted out to the right.
   b. the D curve should be shifted in to the left.
   c. the S curve should be shifted out to the right.
   d. the S curve should be shifted in to the left.

5. Which of the following is *not* one of the ways to deal with negative externalities?
   a. Regulation.
   b. Subsidizing producers.
   c. Creating a market in the externality.
   d. Voluntary solutions.

6. Refer to the graph below. If the government were attempting to set an effluent fee, the amount of that effluent fee should be
   a. P_1.

   b. P_2.
   c. $P_1 - P_2$.
   d. $P_1 - P_3$.
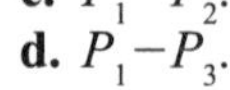

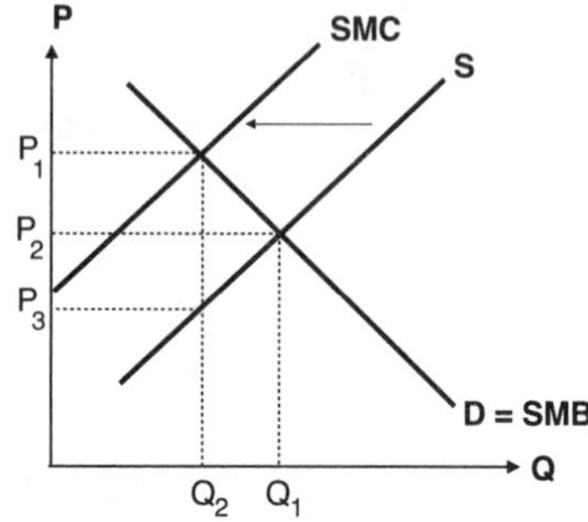

7. Mr. A is using 10 gallons of gas a day and Mr. B is using 20 gallons of gas a day. The marginal cost of reducing gas consumption by 3 gallons a day is \$8 for Mr. A and \$4 for Mr. B. The government places a tax on the use of gasoline. Economists would expect
   a. Mr. A to reduce his consumption by the same amount as Mr. B.
   b. Mr. A to reduce his consumption by more than Mr. B.
   c. Mr. B to reduce his consumption by more than Mr. A.
   d. both to reduce their consumption to zero.

8. Refer to the graph below, which shows the private and social marginal cost of fishing and the demand for fishing, the socially efficient price of fishing would be
   a. 0.
   b. P_1.
   c. P_2.
   d. P_3.

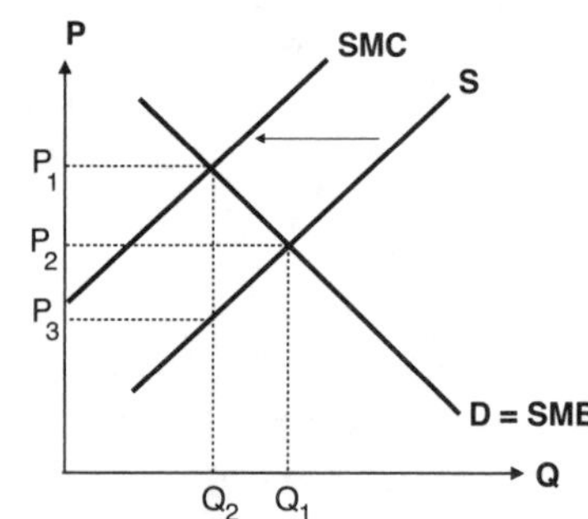

9. In addressing pollution problems, economists would most likely prefer
  a. direct regulation.
  b. subsidies provided to suppliers.
  c. a market incentive plan.
  d. banning the production of those products that pollute.

10. A public good is
  a. any good traded in markets.
  b. a good that is nonexcludable and nonrival.
  c. a good provided only to those who pay for it.
  d. rarely provided by government.

11. Economists are concerned about the effectiveness of voluntary solutions because, while voluntary solutions may be temporarily successful, in the long run, voluntary solutions generally experience
  a. free rider problems.
  b. too much government intervention problems.
  c. TANSTAAFL problems.
  d. opportunity cost problems.

12. The optimal level of pollution control, or any other government policy, exists when the
  a. marginal benefit exceeds the marginal cost.
  b. marginal benefit equals the marginal cost.
  c. marginal benefit is less than the marginal cost.
  d. marginal benefit is maximized.

13. The market demand curve for a public good is
  a. the vertical sum of the individual demand curves at every quantity.
  b. the horizontal sum of the individual demand curves at every price.
  c. vertical at the quantity desired.
  d. always horizontal.

14. If health insurers cannot distinguish between people who have a high-risk and low-risk of medical needs, but those buying the health insurance can, the price at which insurers are willing to provide insurance to cover health care costs will be:
  a. low enough so that at least one-half of all those covered are low-insurance risks.
  b. set in expectations that high-risk people will not purchase coverage.
  c. so low that insurers will be unwilling to provide health coverage.
  d. so high that many of those in good health will be unwilling to buy insurance.

15. Government failure
  a. always outweighs market failure.
  b. sometimes outweighs market failure.
  c. never outweighs market failure.
  d. is the same as market failure.

SHORT-ANSWER QUESTIONS

1. What are three sources of market failures?

2. Suppose a steel plant begins production near your home. The resulting smoke pollutes the air you breathe. You bring a complaint to the local town board saying, "I didn't ask for that factory to be built, but I'm having to endure polluted air." The basis of your complaint is an example of what concept in economics?

3. Briefly describe the three methods of dealing with externalities.

4. Which of the methods you state in Question #3 do most economists prefer to use when dealing with externalities?

5. What is an optimal policy?

6. Why is it difficult for government to decide the efficient quantity of a public good to provide?

7. What are two ways society can deal with informational problems that lead to market failures?

8. When should the government intervene in our economy?

PROBLEMS AND APPLICATIONS

1. Secondhand cigarette smoke is believed to have a negative effect on the health of those who inhale the smoke of cigarettes. These people have not chosen to smoke, but nevertheless are negatively affected by the choice by others to smoke. Draw the market for cigarettes showing the private marginal cost and social marginal cost of smoking cigarettes if this belief is correct.

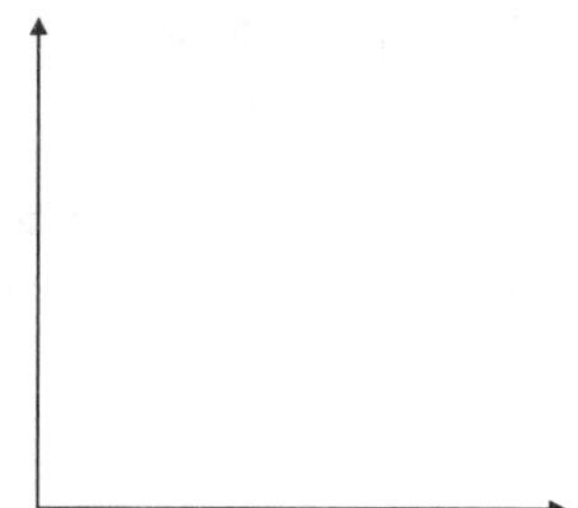

   a. Label the market price and quantity of cigarettes.

   b. Label the efficient level of cigarettes. Explain your answer.

   c. Demonstrate graphically the tax the government would have to impose on cigarettes to arrive at the efficient level and price of cigarettes.

d. Demonstrate graphically the tax revenue that government would collect from such a tax.

2. A small city located by a lake has been dumping its raw sewage into the lake. This has created a public outcry by those citizens who like to fish, swim and water-ski in the lake. The city council has surveyed the community and has estimated the social benefits associated with different levels of pollution control. These benefits, as well as the costs associated with pollution control efforts for the community, are shown in the table below. What is the optimal level of pollution control? Will there still be some pollution of the lake?

Pollution Control	Total Social Benefits	Total Social Costs
1	$200,000	$ 40,000
2	$275,000	$ 75,000
3	$330,000	$110,000
4	$375,000	$145,000
5	$410,000	$180,000
6	$435,000	$215,000

3. Assume a community has decided that there are some substantial social benefits associated with after-school organized recreational activities (such as basketball or soccer) provided to kids before many of their parents arrive home from work. The graph below shows the private demand (private marginal benefit) and society's demand (social marginal benefit) and the supply (private marginal plus social marginal cost) of these recreational activities.

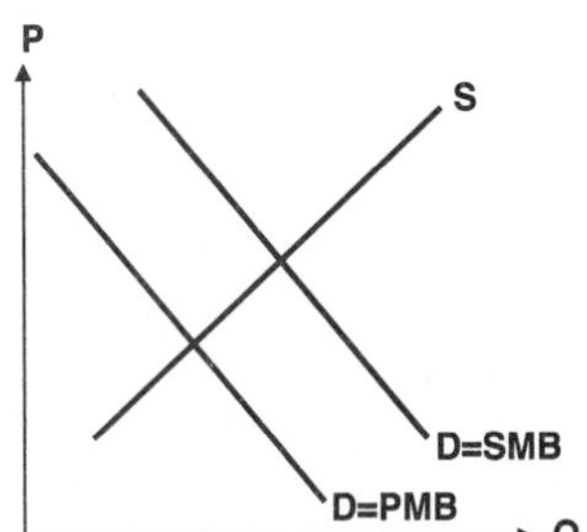

a. Indicate the efficient output level in the graph above. Why would this be an efficient output level?

b. Assume the government is interested in a policy to increase the number of children spending time at these facilities. What policy would you recommend?

4. a. If you are willing to pay $7,000 for a used car that is a "cherry" and $2,000 for a used car that is a "lemon," how much will you be willing to offer to purchase a car if there is a 50 percent chance of purchasing a lemon?

b. If owners of cherry cars want $5,000 for their cherries, and you are still willing to offer the same dollar amount for a used car as in part *a*, how will you estimate of the chance of getting a cherry change?

5. Suppose there are just two individuals, Bob and Susie, in a community. Bob and Susie are both interested in using a public park (a public good). Below are Bob and Susie's individual demand tables for the use of the public park per month.

Bob		Susie	
Price per month	**Qty Demanded in hours per month**	**Price per month**	**Qty Demanded in hours per month**
$13	4	$10	4
9	6	6	6
7	8	4	8

   a. Construct a market demand table for the public park in this community.

   b. Construct individual demand curves for Bob and Susie and place them on the same graph in the space below.

A BRAIN TEASER

1. Environmentalists are concerned about the deforestation of Canada. Some of these environmentalists have advocated government regulating the number of trees that can be cut down. As an economic adviser to the Department of the Environment, you are asked to evaluate this policy and provide any recommendations. What do you say?

POTENTIAL ESSAY QUESTIONS

You may also see essay questions similar to the "Problems & Applications" and "Brain Teasers" exercises.

1. Evaluate the benefits and costs of the regulatory versus the market approach to resolving informational problems that lead to market failure.

2. Discuss five reasons why government's solution to a market failure could worsen the market failure.

ANSWERS

MATCHING

1-k; 2-r; 3-z1; 4-z4; 5-z5; 6-d; 7-j; 8-f; 9-s; 10-z2; 11-c; 12-m; 13-l; 14-o; 15-a; 16-h; 17-z; 18-z3; 19-e; 20-t; 21-u; 22-p; 23-g; 24-v; 25-w; 26-x; 27-i; 28-y; 29-n; 30-b; 31-q.

ANSWERS

MULTIPLE CHOICE

1. d An outcome where individual buyers and sellers do not have any control over price (the invisible hand) is a desirable competitive market outcome. See pages 304-306.

2. a An externality occurs when there is an effect of a market transaction on a third party. See page 306.

3. d A negative externality of production makes the social marginal cost higher than the private marginal cost. See pages 306-307 and Figure 14-1.

4. a A positive externality of consumption makes the social marginal benefit higher than the private marginal benefit. See pages 307-308 and Figure 14-2.

5. b Subsidizing producers would increase the production of the product. Instead, we would want to restrict the production of a product that has a negative externality. See pages 308-311.

6. d The effluent fee should be set to equate social marginal cost with social marginal benefit (which, in absence of any information to the contrary, can be assumed to be represented by the demand curve). See pages 309-310 and Figure 14-3.

7. c The amount of reduction will be based on the marginal costs of reduction. Since the marginal costs of reduction are higher for Mr. A, economists would expect Mr. B to reduce his consumption by more. See pages 309-310.

8. b The socially efficient price is where the social marginal cost equals the social marginal benefit (which, in absence of any information to the contrary, can be assumed to be represented by the demand curve). See pages 306-307 and Figure 14-1.

9. c Economists prefer market incentive plans because they are more efficient. See pages 310-311.

10. b A public good is a good that is nonexcludable and whose consumption by one does not preclude its consumption by others. See page 314.

11. a Voluntary solutions lead people to supply less effort to contribute to the solution because they will have a tendency to rely on others to do it. Thus, "the free rider problem" is the best answer. See page 311.

12. b Whenever the marginal benefit exceeds the marginal cost then do more of that activity. Do less whenever the marginal benefit is less than the marginal cost. See page 312.

13. a To arrive at the market demand curve for a public good, we vertically add the price that each individual is willing to pay for each unit since each receives a benefit when the good is supplied. See pages 314-315 and Figure 14-4.

14. d With certainty, insurers would not offer to provide health insurance at a price low enough so that low-risk people would purchase insurance. The only people left looking for health insurance are high-risk people. The price will rise even further until very few will buy health insurance. This is known as adverse selection. See pages 316-318.

15. b Government failure occurs when government intervention does not improve the market failure. As with almost all economic issues, there is always an "on the other hand" so the "sometimes" is the right answer. See page 321.

ANSWERS

SHORT-ANSWER QUESTIONS

1. Three sources of market failures are: externalities, public goods, and asymmetric information. (305)

2. The pollution that you endure is an example of a negative externality. An externality is an effect of a decision on a third party that is not taken into account by the decision marker. In this case, the air pollution is the effect of steel production not taken into account by the firm. (306)

3. Ways to deal with externalities include (1) direct regulation (2) incentive policies (tax incentive policies and market incentive policies), and (3) voluntary solutions. In a program of direct regulation, the government directly limits the amount of a good people are allowed to use. A tax incentive program is a program using a tax to create incentives for individuals to structure their activities in a way that is consistent with the desired ends. A market incentive program is a plan requiring market participants to certify that they have reduced total consumption—not necessarily their own individual consumption—by a specified amount. Voluntary solutions leave individuals free to choose whether to follow what is socially optimal or what is privately optimal. (308-311)

4. Economists tend to like incentive policies to deal with externalities. Direct regulation tends to be more costly to society in achieving the desired end. Voluntary policies will tend to fail because even a small number of free riders can often undermine the social consciousness of many in society. (308-311)

5. An optimal policy is one in which the marginal cost of undertaking the policy equals the marginal benefit of that policy. (312)

6. A public good is a good that is nonexcluable (no one can be excluded from its benefits) and nonrival (consumption by one does not preclude consumption by others). It is difficult for government to decide the efficient quantity of a public good because of the free rider problem. If the public good is to be financed by a tax on citizens who benefit from it, individuals have an incentive to conceal their willingness to pay for it. Similarly, if citizens think they will not be the ones taxed to fund the public good, but will benefit from it, they have an incentive to exaggerate their willingness to pay. (314)

7. Two general policies to deal with informational problems include the regulatory approach and the market approach. The regulatory approach would have government regulate the market and see that individuals provide the right information, or the government could license individuals in the market, requiring those with licenses to reveal full information about the good being sold. The market approach suggests that allowing markets for information to develop may be the best approach. (319-320)

8. The government should intervene in the economy only if the benefits outweigh the costs or where markets fail to provide an efficient outcome in which the social marginal benefit equals the social marginal cost. One needs to weigh the benefits against the costs on a case-by-case basis and to remain as objective as possible. Government failure (government intervention only making matters worse) is always a real possibility. (321)

ANSWERS

PROBLEMS AND APPLICATIONS

1. **a.** When there is a negative externality, as with the case of secondhand cigarette smoke, the supply curve which represents the private marginal cost, *S*, is lower than the social marginal cost, *SMC*. The supply curve represents the private costs of smokers who chose to smoke. The cost for society is higher, and the social marginal cost is higher, because cigarette smoke hurts those who do not smoke. The demand curve represents social marginal benefits. These curves are drawn below. Because the market does not take into account the third-party effects, equilibrium quantity is Q_e and equilibrium price is P_e. (306-307 and Figure 14-3)

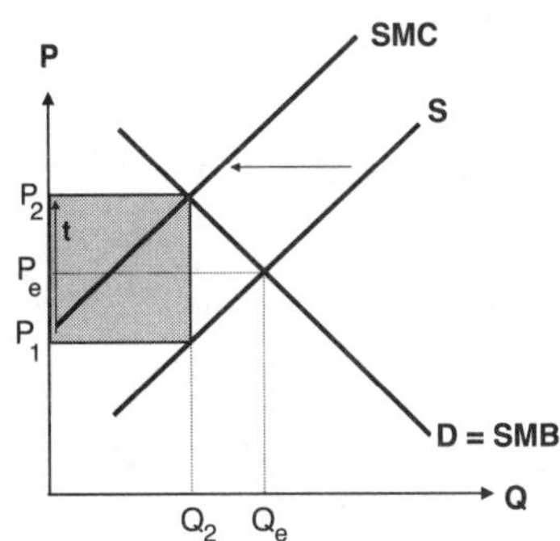

b. The efficient level of cigarettes is where social marginal costs equal social marginal benefits. This is at Q_2 and P_2. (306-307 and Figure 14-3)

c. The tax the government would have to impose on cigarettes to arrive at the efficient level of cigarettes is t equal to $P_2 - P_1$ sufficient to shift the supply curve back to the social marginal cost curve. (309-310 and Figure 14-3)

d. This is t times the quantity of cigarettes in the market after the tax. This is shown by the shaded boxed region in the graph above. (309-310 and Figure 14-3)

2. See the table below. The optimal level of pollution control is 5 units, because this is the quantity of pollution control in which the social marginal benefit of the control just equals its social marginal cost. There will still be some pollution of the lake as evidenced by the increased marginal benefits associated with the 6th unit of pollution control—but that amount of pollution control is not worth it to the community given its marginal cost. (312)

Pollution Control	Total Benefits	Total Costs	Marginal Benefit	Marginal Cost
1	$200,000	$40,000	$200,000	$40,000
2	$275,000	$75,000	$75,000	$35,000
3	$330,000	$110,000	$55,000	$35,000
4	$375,000	$145,000	$45,000	$35,000
5	$410,000	$180,000	**$35,000**	**$35,000**
6	$435,000	$215,000	$25,000	$35,000

Note: marginal benefits and costs are values between units of pollution control.

3. a. The efficient level of output (services provided in the community) is where the social marginal benefit equals the social marginal cost. This occurs at that output level where the SMB curve intersects the supply curve. (It is reasonable to assume there is no difference between the private and social costs. So, social marginal costs are given by the supply curve.) (306-307)

b. The private demand and/or the supply need to be increased. This could be accomplished by subsidizing parents (increasing demand) and/or subsidizing the facilities (increasing supply). Either one of these options would increase the output level toward the efficient level where SMB = SMC. It may be much easier to administer the subsidization of the facilities. (306-307)

4. a. Knowing that you have a 50 percent chance of buying a lemon, you will offer $4,500 (the average of $2,000 and $7,000). Given that offer price, individuals with cherries will be very hesitant to sell and will begin to exit the market, while individuals with lemons will be anxious to sell. (317)

b. If owners of cherries now want $5,000 and you are still willing to pay $4,500 for a used car, then there will be more owners of cherries left in the market, increasing the chance you willpurchase a cherry used car. (315)

5. a. The market demand table for the public park is shown below. Notice that to derive the market demand table for a public good, one needs to add the marginal benefit (the price) each individual receives from the public good at each quantity. (This is just the opposite from deriving a demand table for a private good where one would have to add the quantity demand at each price.) (315)

Price per month	Quantity Demanded in hours per month
$23	4
$15	6
$11	8

b.

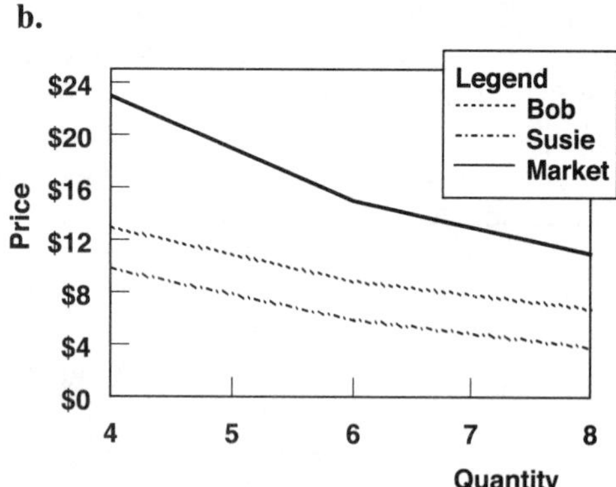

ANSWERS

A BRAIN TEASER

1. First, one must look carefully at the evidence to see if the social marginal benefit equals the social marginal cost at the current quantity of trees harvested in the timber industry. If so, then there is not a problem. After all, trees are a renewable resource. If they become scarcer, their price will rise and people will voluntarily conserve. Moreover, a higher price will increase the quantity supplied—more trees will be planted. However, if at the current market equilibrium quantity the social marginal cost exceeds the social marginal benefit, too many trees are being cut down. That is, an external cost exists. That external cost is often cited as the reduced ability of trees to clean the air—to absorb carbon dioxide. If we assume the external cost is sufficiently large to warrant government action then direct regulation by government often is not the most efficient approach.

   Instead, a typically more efficient proposal is to continue to impose a higher tax on the production of lumber until supply is restricted to that quantity in which the social marginal benefit just equals the social marginal cost. At the resulting higher market price for lumber, people will voluntarily conserve trees. Another possibility might be to subsidize people or communities to plant more trees to absorb carbon dioxide (and to continue to require the timber industry to plant a new tree to replace each one cut down). This course of action may preclude the necessity to tax the timber industry.

ANSWERS

POTENTIAL ESSAY QUESTIONS

The following are annotated answers. They indicate the general idea behind the answer.

1. The regulatory approach would have government regulate the market and see that individuals provide the right information, or the government could license individuals in the market, requiring those with licenses to reveal full information about the good being sold. Although regulatory solutions have their benefits, they may also create government failure. The market approach suggests that allowing markets for information to develop may be the best approach because it may at least avoid some government failure.

2. Government intervention may worsen the problems created by market failure. Government failure may occur because (1) governments don't have an incentive to correct the problem, (2) governments don't have enough information to deal with the problem, (3) intervention is more complicated that it initially seems, (4) the bureaucratic nature of government precludes fine-tuning, and (5) government intervention often leads to more government intervention.

COMPETITION POLICY

15

CHAPTER AT A GLANCE

Recently, we discussed the four market structures and how competition varied among them. Under monopoly, for example, we explored how government intervenes to regulate monopolies in order to ensure they operate efficiently and competitively and not to the detriment of society.

This chapter explores how government policy attempts to maintain and encourage competition in the private markets and to monitor monopolies and mergers.

One of the most important tools government has is a body of legislation called the Competition Act, which contains both a criminal and civil section dealing with a wide variety of potentially anti-competitive behaviours.

Part of the chapter deals with the concept of globalization and the competitive effects of globalization. Globalization encompasses many different trends in our economy – the integration of economies and financial markets, innovation and technological change, increased opportunities in international markets, tariff and trade policies worldwide, regulatory reform, privatization, etc. The competitive discipline imposed by global market forces on Canadian industries can lead to unanticipated, and sometimes undesirable changes in the domestic economy. In such a case, when the forces of globalization and Canadian competition policy lead to different outcomes, Canadians must decide which result they prefer. A classical example of this issue is the recent debate regarding the merits of Canadian banks wishing to merge in order to become more competitive globally.

The last part of the chapter explores how government can affect the competitive process by regulation, government ownership and industrial policy.

This review is based upon the learning objectives that open the chapter.

1. Competition policy is government action toward the competitive process. Competition generally has been a less effective means of controlling firm behavior and balancing market power than consumers would hope. When natural market forces fail to generate the desired competitive outcome, government intervention is required to set the rules for competitive behaviour and to level the playing field so that all firms may compete on an equal basis. (327-330)

The objectives of Canadian competition policy include:

1. economic efficiency
2. diffusing economic power
3. equalizing income distribution

2. There is a debate on whether markets should be judged on the basis of structure or on the basis of performance. Judgment by performance is the view that competitiveness of a market should be judged by the behavior of firms in that market; judgment by structure is the view that competitiveness of a market should be judged by the structure of the market. (328-330)

Both criteria have their problems. There are no definitive criteria for judging whether a firm has violated Competition Policy statutes. However, since 1945, most court decisions have relied on judgment by structure for the reason of practicality.

3. Competition policy is the regulatory framework that government uses to encourage or prohibit certain market practices. In 1923, the Combines Investigation Act was created with subsequent amendments made overtime until 1986 when the new Competition Act was introduced. (330-331)

Know what these Acts outlaw.

4. The Competition Act contains both a criminal and civil section dealing with a variety of anti-competitive behaviours. (331-336) They include:

1. Misleading advertising and deceptive marketing
2. Price maintenance – this relates to the undue influence of prices and the refusal to supply a product due to a firm's low pricing policy.
3. Predatory pricing – selling products at unreasonably low prices in order to lessen competition or eliminate a competitor.
4. Conspiracy – where parties enter into an agreement to unduly lessen competition.

5a. Horizontal mergers are companies in the same industry merging together. Vertical mergers are combinations of two companies, one of which supplied inputs to the other's production. Conglomerate mergers are combinations of relatively unrelated businesses. (336)

Know the differences. Also become familiar with the various terms associated with takeovers.

Most Canadian competition laws have concerned horizontal mergers.

5b. Five reasons why unrelated firms merge include: (337)

- To achieve economies of scope;
- To get a good buy;
- To diversify;
- To ward off a takeover bid; and
- To strengthen their political-economic influence.

When unrelated firms merge, this constitutes a conglomerate merger.

6. The proposals of four of the five big Canadian banks to merger were rejected on the grounds that they would lead to a substantial lessening or prevention of competition that would cause higher prices and lower levels of service for society. This decision tried to balance a number of goals – efficiency, innovation, and international competitiveness. (338-342)

7. Some countries' approaches toward anti-competitive behaviour parallel the Canadian approach, while other countries oppose competition laws because of economies of scale, lack of strong ideology supporting competition, and strong cultural ties between government and business. (342-344)

8. The government can also affect the competitive process by (1) regulation, (2) government ownership, and (3) industrial policy. (344-346)

Two types of regulation are price regulation and social regulation. Price regulation is regulation directed at industries that have natural monopoly elements. Social regulation is concerned with the condition under which goods and services are produced, the safety of those goods and the side effects of production on society.

Government-owned firms tend not to have an incentive to hold costs down.

An industrial policy is a formal policy that government takes toward business.

9. As Canada becomes more integrated into the global economy, big business faces significant international competition. Because of foreign competition, even highly-concentrated Canadian industries may be forced to behave competitively. This suggests that there is less need for strong anti-competition legislation. (346-347)

See Appendix A "Case Study: The Economics of the Microsoft Case

MATCHING THE TERMS

Match the terms to their definitions

All of these key terms are found at the end of the chapter.

___ **1.** acquisition
___ **2.** combine
___ **3.** competition policy
___ **4.** Competition Tribunal
___ **5.** conglomerate merger
___ **6.** conscious parrallelism
___ **7.** conspiracy
___ **8.** credible threat of entry
___ **9.** deacquisition
___ **10.** divestiture
___ **11.** efficiency defense
___ **12.** exclusive dealing
___ **13.** friendly takeover
___ **14.** globalization
___ **15.** horizontal merger
___ **16.** hostile takeover
___ **17.** industrial policy
___ **18.** judgment by performance
___ **19.** judgment by structure
___ **20.** market restriction.
___ **21.** merger
___ **22.** per se offence
___ **23.** prenotification
___ **24.** specialization agreement
___ **25.** tied selling
___ **26.** vertical merger
___ **27.** vertical restraint

a. A company buys another company; the buyer has direct control of the resulting venture, but does not necessarily exercise that right.
b. A merger of companies in the same industry.
c. A merger in which one company buys another that does not want to be bought.
d. A government's formal policy toward business.
e. The act of combining two firms.
f. If gains in efficiency offset the competition concerns, then the merger can be allowed.
g. Combination of relatively unrelated businesses.
h. Combination of two companies that are involved in different stages of producing a product.
i. Firms must make intention to merge known to the Competition Bureau ahead of time.
j. Judging the competitiveness of markets by the structure of the industry.
k. Judging the competitiveness of markets by the behavior of firms in that market.
l. When the supplier requires the buyer to restrict his operations to a particular geographic market.
m. One company's sale of parts of another company it has bought.
n. One corporation is willing to be acquired by the other.
o. Government's policy toward the competitive process.
p. Public court of record which is designed to deal with complex legal, economic, and business issues, informally and expeditiously.
q. Parties enter into an agreement where they know it would unduly lessen competition.
r. Any trust, merger, or monopoly that operates or is likely to operate to the detriment or against the interest of the public.
s. Requires a firm to sell off some portion of its assets so that its market power in some area is reduced.
t. When firms set similar prices and behave similarily with respect to other business practices without explicit agreement.
u. A violation of the Competition Act in which proof of undue lessening or prevention of competition is not required.
v. When a supplier requires the purchaser to deal with only the seller's particular product.
w. When a supplier requires the buyer to purchase another of the supplier's product as a condition of obtaining the desired product.
x. Integration of world markets.
y. Where firms believe others are likely to enter the market.
z. Linking the upstream and downstream segments of the market.
Z1. Agreements made by two or more Canadian firms to divide up production between them.

MULTIPLE CHOICE

Circle the one best answer for each of the following questions:

1. As discussed in the textbook, when judging the competitiveness of markets by the behavior of firms in that market, one is using the
   a. "judgment by performance" criteria.
   b. "judgment by structure" criteria.
   c. "judgment by merger" criteria.
   d. "judgment by antitrust" criteria.

2. An important law in the Canadian regulation of markets is
   a. the Standard Oil Antitrust Act of 1890.
   b. the Competition Act of 1986.
   c. the Alcoa Antitrust Act of 1890.
   d. the Lincoln Antitrust Act of 1890.

3. When two merging companies are in the same industry their merger is called a
   a. horizontal merger.
   b. vertical merger.
   c. conglomerate merger.
   d. takeover merger.

4. When one of two merging companies supplies one or more of the inputs to the other merging company, the merger is called a
   a. horizontal merger.
   b. vertical merger.
   c. conglomerate merger.
   d. takeover merger.

5. When two companies that are in unrelated industries merge, the merger is called a
   a. horizontal merger.
   b. vertical merger.
   c. conglomerate merger.
   d. takeover merger.

6. Reasons firms would want to enter into a conglomerate merger include all the following *except*
   a. to achieve economies of scope.
   b. to diversify.
   c. to strengthen their political and economic influence.
   d. to become a natural monopoly.

7. The proposed mergers of several Canadian banks in the late 1990s was not successful because
   a. the mergers would result in lower barriers to entry.
   b. the mergers would result in more competitors.
   c. lower costs of borrowing would have to be offered.
   d. the mergers were deemed to lead to a lessening of competition.

8. Antitrust laws in Japan
   a. tend to be weaker than in the United States.
   b. tend to be stronger than in the United States.
   c. tend to be approximately the same strength as antitrust laws in the United States.
   d. do not exist; there are no antitrust laws in Japan.

9. An important law in the U.S. regulation of markets is
   a. the Standard Oil Antitrust Act of 1890.
   b. the Competition Act of 1986.
   c. the Alcoa Antitrust Act of 1890.
   d. the Lincoln Antitrust Act of 1890.

10. The Clayton Antitrust Act made all of the following monopolistic practices illegal *except*:
    a. price discrimination.
    b. tie-in contracts
    c. interlocking directorships.
    d. creation of a natural monopoly.

11. A natural monopoly is a situation whereby
    a. there are few barriers to entry.
    b. there is little regulation.
    c. the firm is efficient.
    d. there are significant economies of scale making the existence of more than one firm inefficient.

12. Government can affect the competitive process by
    a. regulating the activities of firms.
    b. taking direct charge of firms and operating them.
    c. industrial policy
    d. any of the options listed here.

13. Industrial policy is
- **a.** a policy of government entering into competition with business.
- **b.** a policy of government industries entering into competition with business.
- **c.** a formal policy that government takes towards business.
- **d.** a laissez-faire policy of government towards business.

A1. The resolution of the IBM antitrust case was that
- **a.** IBM was broken up.
- **b.** IBM was combined with AT&T.
- **c.** the government dropped the IBM case.
- **d.** IBM was allowed to stay in the large-computer market but was kept out of the personal-computer market.

A2. The resolution of the Microsoft antitrust case of the late 1990s and early 2000s was
- **a.** the government ruled that Microsoft was a monopoly and involved in anti-competitive practices.
- **b.** the government dropped the Microsoft case.
- **c.** Microsoft agreed to government regulation of its prices.
- **d.** Microsoft was forced to get out of the Internet business.

SHORT-ANSWER QUESTIONS

1. How does judging competition by structure differ from judging competition by performance?

2. What is the purpose of the Competition Act (1986)? What year was it introduced?

3. What was the resolution of the bank merger issue in Canada?

4. What are horizontal, vertical, and conglomerate mergers?

5. What are five reasons why unrelated firms would want to merge?

6. What is the difference between U.S. antitrust policy and antitrust policy in other countries?

7. List three alternatives to antitrust policy that government can use to affect the competitive process.

A1. What was the resolution of the Microsoft antitrust case?

PROBLEMS AND APPLICATIONS

1. For each of the following situations determine what type of merger activity is being undertaken.

a. Pepsi-Cola Corporation buys Pizza Hut and Kentucky Fried Chicken.

b. A bakery corporation buys up a grocery store chain.

c. A steel manufacturer buys up all other steel producing factories.

2. Canadian auto manufacturers sell their models at a lower price on the West Coast in an effort to remain competitive with Japanese imports. This has upset many car dealers on the east coast who view this as price discrimination and therefore a violation of antitrust. Which antitrust law are these dealers referring to? What possible defense might the auto manufacturers claim?

3. Suppose a grocery store is interested in buying a particular brand name of canned tomato soup from a food processing vendor. However, before the vendor agrees to deliver any cans of tomato soup the grocer is required to sign a contract guaranteeing that the grocery store will buy all of its canned goods from the vendor. The grocery store objects because it argues that such a requirement is against the law. Which antitrust law would the grocer argue is being broken? What possible defense might the vendor claim?

4. You're an economist in the Antitrust Division of the Justice Department. In the personal computer market, suppose Compaq has petitioned to merge with AT&T. Compaq currently has 14% of the PC market and AT&T has 3%. The other three large firms in the market, Packard Bell, IBM, and Apple, have 11%, 9%, and 8% of the PC market respectively. In the Windows-based PC market, Compaq has 18% of the market and AT&T has 5%. The other three large firms in the Windows-based PC market, Packard Bell, IBM, and Hewlett Packard, have 14%, 12%, and 9% of the PC market respectively.

a. Calculate the approximate Herfindahl and 4-firm concentration ratios for these firms in each industry before the merger and after the merger.

b. If you were Compaq's economist, which industry definition would you suggest using when making your petition to the Justice Department?

c. Give an argument why the merger might decrease competition.

d. Give an argument why the merger might increase competition.

A BRAIN TEASER

1. Suppose you are advising a regulatory agency of the Federal government to regulate the prices of a monopolist depicted by the graph below.

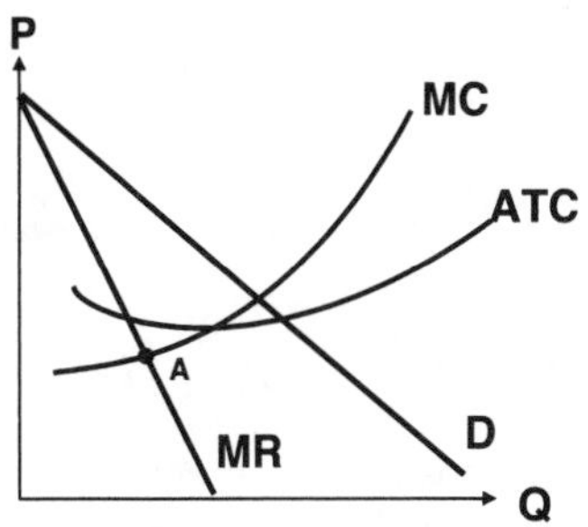

a. Would you recommend setting prices at point A where $MC = MR$? Why or why not?

b. What would be the minimum price you would recommend? Why?

c. Does the monopolist still enjoy economic profit at the minimum price you determined in *b*? If so, what are they?

d. What potential problem might be associated with your recommendation?

POTENTIAL ESSAY QUESTIONS

You may also see essay questions similar to the "Problems & Applications" and "Brain Teasers" exercises.

1. Why has there been a more lenient approach in the United States to the enforcement of antitrust laws in recent years?

2. What is the difference between horizontal, vertical and conglomerate mergers? Which merging activity has most U.S. antitrust policy been concerned with? What is the principle guideline used by the Department of Justice since 1982 with respect to mergers?

ANSWERS

MATCHING

1-a; 2-r; 3-d; 4-p; 5-g; 6-t; 7-q; 8-y; 9-m; 10-s; 11-f; 12-v; 13-n; 14-x; 15-b; 16-c; 17-d; 18-k; 19-j; 20-l; 21-e; 22-u; 23-i; 24-z1; 25-w; 26-h; 27-z.

ANSWERS

MULTIPLE CHOICE

1. a "Judgment by performance" is judging the competitiveness if markets by the performance (behavior) of firms in that market. See page 328.

2. b The Competition Act of 1986 was a major revision to the Combines Investigation Act of 1960 and 1923. See page 330-331.

3. a A horizontal merger is when two firms that produce the same product merge. See page 336.

4. b A vertical merger is when two firms each in different parts of the same production process merge. See page 336.

5. c A conglomerate merger is when two firms producing unrelated products merge. See page 336.

6. d Unrelated firms would want to merge to achieve economies of scope, to get a good buy, to diversify, to ward off a takeover bid, and to strengthen their political-economic influence. See pages 336-337.

7. d See pages 338-342.

8. a Most foreign countries have weaker antitrust laws compared to the United States. See page 343.

9. a The Sherman Antitrust Act passed in 1890 was an early law passed to regulate the competitive process. See pages 342-344.

10. d The Clayton Antitrust Act is a law that made four specific monopolistic practices illegal. They are price discrimination, tie-in contracts, interlocking directorships, and buying a competitor's stock to reduce competition. See page 344.

11. d See page 345.

12. d Government can regulate firms, take ownership and institute industrial policy. See page 344.

13. c Industrial policy is a formal policy government takes toward business. An example is the U.S. military-industrial complex. See page 346.

A1. c The antitrust suit was dropped since new competitors had changed the market structure. See pages 331-353.

A2. a The finding of the fact in 1999 was that Microsoft was a monopoly and that it had engaged in anti-competitive practices. At the same time this text was written no action had been taken. See pages 351-353.

ANSWERS

SHORT-ANSWER QUESTIONS

1. Judging competition by structure is the view that competitiveness of a market should be judged by the number or firms in the market and their market shares. Judging competition by performance is the view that competitiveness of a market should be judged by the behavior of firms in that market. (328-330)

2. The purpose of the Act is highlighted on page 345. In 1923, the Combines Investigation Act was created, and this Act (plus amendments to it in 1960) was the law until 1986, when the new Competition Act was brought in. (330-331)

3. The proposed mergers were considered likely to lead to a substantial lessening or prevention of competition that would cause higher prices and lower levels of service. Therefore, the

Competition Bureau declined to allow the mergers to take place. (338-342)

4. A horizontal merger is a merger between two companies in the same industry. A vertical merger is a firm merging with the supplier of one (or more) of its inputs. A conglomerate merger is a merger between unrelated businesses. (336)

5. Five reasons why unrelated firms would want to merge are (1) to achieve economies of scope, (2) to get a good buy, (3) to diversify, (4) to ward off a takeover bid, and (5) to strengthen political-economic influence. (337)

6. Other countries oppose antitrust laws because of economies of scale, lack of strong ideology supporting competition, and strong cultural ties between government and business. Although the enforcement of antitrust laws in the United States is much more ambitious than in other countries, enforcement in the U.S. is becoming more lax. (342-344)

7. The government can also affect the competitiveness process by (1) regulation, (2) government ownership, and (3) industrial policy. (344-346)

A1. The court found Microsoft guilty, but whether one sees Microsoft as a monopolist depends on whether one views it in a static or dynamic framework. (351-353)

ANSWERS

PROBLEMS AND APPLICATIONS

1. **a.** Conglomerate merger (designed to achieve economies of scope). (346)
   b. Vertical merger. (346)
   c. Horizontal merger. (346)

2. The Competition Act prohibits price discrimination if it has the effect of lessening competition. The auto manufacturers could claim that the lower prices on the West Coast do not result in less competition but are instead a consequence of the intense competition that exists on the West Coast. (331-343)

3. The Competition Act prohibits tie-in contracts in which the buyer must agree to deal exclusively with one seller and not to purchase goods from competing sellers. The vendor may claim that this is not reducing competition. (331-343)

4. **a.** The Herfindahl index is calculated by adding the squared value of the market shares of all the firms in the industry. The 4-firm concentration ratio is calculated by adding the market shares of the four firms with the largest market shares.
   PC Market: Before the merger, the Herfindahl index is greater than $14^2 + 11^2 + 9^2 + 8^2 + 3^2 = 196 + 121 + 81 + 64 + 9 = 471$. The exact Herfindahl index cannot be calculated since we do not know the market shares of all the firms in the market. The 4-firm concentration ratio before the merger is $14 + 11 + 9 + 8 = 42$. The Herfindahl index after the merger is at least $17^2 + 11^2 + 9^2 + 8^2 = 289 + 121 + 81 + 64 = 555$. The 4-firm concentration ratio after the merger is $17 + 11 + 9 + 8 = 45$.
   Windows-based PC market: Before the merger, the Herfindahl index is at least $18^2 + 14^2 + 12^2 + 9^2 + 5^2 = 324 + 196 + 121 + 81 + 25 = 747$. The 4-firm concentration ratio before the merger is $18 + 14 + 12 + 9 = 53$. The Herfindahl index after the merger is at least $23^2 + 14^2 + 12^2 + 9^2 = 529 + 196 + 144 + 81 = 950$. The 4-firm concentration ratio after the merger is $23 + 14 + 12 + 9 = 58$. (336-337)
   b. I would use the broader PC-based computer industry definition because the Herfindahl indexes and concentration ratios are lower in this market indicating more competition. (336-337)
   c. The merger might be expected to decrease competition because within the PC market the Herfindahl index rises from 471 to 555 and the 4-firm concentration ratio rises from 42 to 45. This suggests the merger would result in a less competitive market. The larger merged company may have more ability to set prices above marginal costs, resulting in a loss to society. (Welfare loss with a monopoly is shown graphically in the chapter on monopoly.) (336-337)
   d. This merger might be expected to increase competition if Compaq and AT&T cannot

compete separately against the other three firms in the market. A combined Compaq and AT&T might also be more competitive in a global market. Most likely, however, this merger will lower the level of domestic competition—especially if the merger would enable economies of scale and scope to be experienced. (336-337)

ANSWERS

A BRAIN TEASER

1. a. I would not recommend setting prices at point A where $MC = MR$ because at that point price is less than average total costs. The monopolist would be losing money and would eventually go out of business. This is shown in the graph below. (344-345; and the chapter on monopoly)

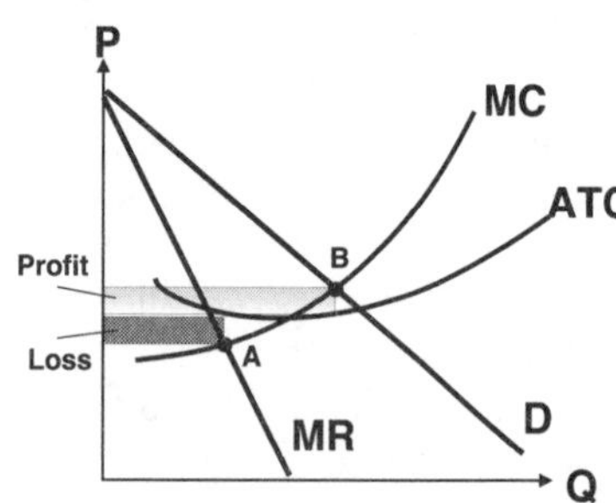

b. The minimum price I would recommend would be where the marginal cost curve intersects the demand curve at point B in the graph above. This eliminates all welfare loss to society associated with a monopoly and is the competitive price and quantity. (344-345; and the chapter on monopoly)

c. The monopolist still enjoys economic profit that is represented by the shaded area in the graph above. (344-345; and the chapter on monopoly)

d. There may be little incentive for the monopolist to hold down its costs. (344-345)

ANSWERS

POTENTIAL ESSAY QUESTIONS

The following are annotated answers. They indicate the general idea behind the answer.

1. In recent years antitrust law has worked mainly through its deterrent effect. First, because of a change in American ideology— "big business" is no longer viewed as necessarily being bad. Second, the market structure in the U.S. has become less relevant as the United States has become more integrated into the global economy where there is generally more competition. Third, as technologies have become more complicated, the issues in antitrust enforcement also have become more complicated for the courts to handle. Moreover, the IBM, AT&T and Microsoft cases have significantly influenced perceptions of antitrust creating a more lenient modern approach.

2. Two companies in the same industry merging is a horizontal merger. A firm merging with the supplier of one of its inputs is a vertical merger. Two firms in unrelated industries merging is a conglomerate merger. Horizontal mergers have attracted most U.S. antitrust policy attention. The principle guideline used by the Justice Department since 1982 is to carefully consider the approval or disapproval of a merger if, after the merger, the Herfindahl index would be above 1000.

SOCIAL ISSUES AND ECONOMIC POLICY

16

CHAPTER AT A GLANCE

One of the important jobs that economists have is giving advice to politicians and other policy makers on a variety of questions and issues relating to social policy. Social policy deals with issues such as how society can fairly distribute income as well as a wide variety of social programs such as employment insurance, minimum wages, health care, education, welfare, and retirement benefits such as the Canada Pension Plan.

Among economists, there are differing views and considerable debate regarding which policy should be implemented to achieve a specific goal. Many times, it centers around subjective value judgments, the interpretation of economic evidence and how political and social institutions work.

This chapter uses the demand and supply framework and extents it to a broader cost/benefit framework to consider the efficiencies of outcomes of various policies. The advantages and disadvantages of using this analysis to assist in the decision making process are also explored.

The last part of this chapter raises an interesting issue — that markets working efficiently may still lead to outcomes, which have undesirable characteristics. In many cases, society's goals may not be met. Again, this relates to the complex, dynamic nature of our economy. There are three separate types of failures of market outcomes which will be considered.

This review is based upon the learning objectives that open the chapter.

1a. Economists' views on social policy differ widely because

1. their objective economic analyses are influenced by their subjective value judgments;
2. their interpretations of economic evidence and of how political and social institutions work vary widely; and
3. their proposals are often based on various models that focus on different aspects of problems. (355)

Analysis should be as objective as possible. Unfortunately, in practice, social goals are seldom neat, they're generally vaguely understood and vaguely expressed.

1b. Liberal and conservative economists agree on many policy prescriptions because they use the same models. These models focus on incentives and individual choice. (357)

There is more agreement among economists than most lay people realize because <u>they all use cost/benefit analysis</u>. Disagreement among economists usually arises because they assess the qualitative benefits and costs (those benefits and costs that can not be easily measured) differently.

2. Cost/benefit analysis is analysis in which one assigns a cost and benefit to alternatives, and draws a conclusion on the basis of those costs and benefits. (357-358)

Economists argue that government should keep regulate until the marginal benefits of regulation just equal the marginal costs. Unfortunately, many costs and benefits (especially social and political) can not be easily quantified.

3. Three separate types of failure of market outcomes include:

1. failures due to distributional issues,
2. failures due to rationality problems of individuals, and
3. failures due to violations of inalienable, or at least partially inalienable, rights of individuals. (362)

Failure of market outcomes occurs when, even though it is functioning properly, the market is not achieving society's goals.

4a. Government failure is as pervasive as market failure. For the government to correct a problem, it must:

1. recognize the problem,
2. have the will to deal with it, and
3. have the ability to deal with it. (366)

Government can seldom do all three of these well. Often the result is that government action is directed at the wrong problem at the wrong time.

Sometimes the government fails to improve a situation (hence the term "government failure.")

4b. To the extent that the government's political decisions reflect the will of society, government is making a positive contribution. Unfortunately political decisions do not always reflect the will of society. (366-368)

Economics provides the tools, not the rules, for policy. Applying economics is much more than muttering "supply and demand." Economics involves the thoughtful use of economic insights and empirical evidence. An economist must carefully consider all views. Subjective moral value judgements can't be ignored.

MATCHING THE TERMS
Match the terms to their definitions

All of these key terms are found at the end of the chapter.

___ **1.** cost/benefit approach
___ **2.** economic efficiency
___ **3.** failure of market outcomes
___ **4.** inalienable rights
___ **5.** Marxian model
___ **6.** Pareto optimal policies
___ **7.** public choice model
___ **8.** quantifiable costs
___ **9.** rational
___ **10.** sin taxes

a. Approach in which one assigns costs and benefits and makes decisions on the basis of the relevant costs and benefits.
b. Policies that benefit some people and hurt no one.
c. A model that focuses on equitable distribution of power, rights, and income among social classes.
d. Taxes that discourage activities society believes are harmful.
e. A model that focuses on economic incentives as applied within a political framework.
f. What individuals do is in their own best interest.
g. Achieving a goal at the lowest possible cost.
h. Even though the market is functioning properly, it is not achieving society's goals.
i. We can put numbers to it.
j. Cannot be sold or given away.

MULTIPLE CHOICE

Circle the one best answer for each of the following questions:

1. Which statement follows from economic theory alone?
a. The minimum wage should be increased.
b. The minimum wage should be decreased.
c. There should be no minimum wage.
d. No policy prescription follows from economic theory alone.

2. It is important to be familiar with many economic models because:
a. the models are objective.
b. the models are subjective.
c. each model captures different aspects of reality.
d. the models are Pareto optimal.

3. When an economist states that whether baby seals should be killed depends upon the costs and benefits, according to the text they are being:
a. coldhearted.
b. subjective.
c. objective.
d. conjective.

4. In an automobile crash, people were killed because an automobile company saved $10 by placing the gas tank in the rear of the car. An economist would:
a. determine whether this made sense with cost/benefit analysis.
b. see this as reasonable.
c. see this as unreasonable.
d. argue that no amount of money should be spared to save a life.

5. Suppose that filtering your water at home reduces your chances from dying of giardia (an intestinal parasite) by 1/45,000. The filter costs you $400 to install. You have chosen to install the filter. Which dollar value best reflects the minimum value you implicitly place on your life?
a. $400.
b. $45,000.
c. $1,800,000.
d. $18,000,000.

6. If the equilibrium wage is below the wage necessary for survival:
a. there is no problem because the market is in equilibrium.
b. there is a market failure due to informational problems.
c. there is a market failure due to an externality.
d. there is a failure of market outcome.

7. Maximizing total producer and consumer surplus in a market means that:
   a. the economy is as well off as it can be.
   b. that total output is as large as it can be in that market.
   c. income is unfairly distributed.
   d. income is fairly distributed.

8. As economists generally use the term, in a society it is *inefficient* to supply medicine to those who do not have the income to pay for it. This statement is:
   a. correct because economists use the term efficiency as a shorthand to refer to total output.
   b. wrong because medicine is necessary for life.
   c. correct because economists do not care about the poor.
   d. wrong because economics does not take distribution into account.

9. If a person buys more of a good, that person is:
   a. better off.
   b. worse off.
   c. most likely better off.
   d. most likely worse off.

10. If society establishes a law preventing a person from selling themselves into slavery:
   a. consumer surplus will be lowered.
   b. consumer surplus will be increased.
   c. economic theory will find that law incorrect.
   d. economic theory will find that law correct.

11. A economist might *not favor* undertaking a policy to correct a failure of market outcome because economists:
   a. don't recognize failures in market outcomes.
   b. see the possibility of government failure.
   c. are trained to support the market no matter what.
   d. see the possibility of market failure offsetting the failure in market outcome.

SHORT-ANSWER QUESTIONS

1. List three reasons why the statement "If you laid all economists end to end, they still wouldn't reach a conclusion" is partly true with regard to social policy?

2. Although the quotation in Question #1 has some validity, nevertheless liberal and conservative economists often agree in their views on social policy. What is the basis for their agreement?

3. What is *cost/benefit analysis*?

4. When it comes to the actions of politicians regulating our economy, most economists are cynics. Why?

5. What are three types of failure of market outcomes?

6. Why are many economists doubtful that the government can correct failure of market outcomes?

7. List one positive and one negative political contribution to economic policy.

8. Your friend finds you tucked away in a cozy chair in the library studying for an economics exam on policy issues. Your friend says, "Why are you wasting your time? All you have to remember is *supply and demand* and you'll be able to answer any question in economics." How do you respond?

PROBLEMS AND APPLICATIONS

1. Which of the following regulations would you recommend government implement?

   a. A regulation requiring airline mechanics to check whether all bolts are tightened. This decreases the probability of having an accident by .001. The cost of the average crash is estimated at $200 million for the plane and $400 million in lives. The cost of implementing the program is $16 million.

   b. A regulation requiring all cars have driver-side airbags. This adds $500 to the cost of a car. Having an airbag in a car reduces the chance of dying in a car crash by 1/720. The average individual values his/her life at $500,000.

   c. A regulation stiffening government rules for workplace safety. The cost per worker is $5,000 and the regulations are expected to reduce workplace fatalities by .002. Workers value their lives at an average $2 million.

   d. What are the problems with using the cost/benefit approach to decide (a), (b), and (c)?

2. Why does it often appear to the lay public that economists never agree on social policy?

3. Assume economists have undertaken cost/benefit analysis of a problem and are unanimously in favor of a particular policy proposal over all other proposals. Why might this policy recommendation not be enacted as policy?

A BRAIN TEASER

1. Why did former President Harry S. Truman say in jest that he wished he could find a one-armed economist?

POTENTIAL ESSAY QUESTIONS

You may also see essay questions similar to the "Problems & Applications" and "Brain Teasers" exercises.

1. What is cost/benefit analysis? How is this related to why economists often find themselves united with one another but at odds with the general public?

2. How can the presence of the economic (market), social and political forces in all real world economies, and economists' use of benefit/cost analysis help explain the disagreement among economists concerning what is considered "appropriate" social policy? Even if economists all agreed upon what is "appropriate" policy, why might that policy never be enacted?

ANSWERS

MATCHING

1-a; 2-g; 3-h; 4-j; 5-c; 6-b; 7-e; 8-i; 9-f; 10-d.

ANSWERS

MULTIPLE CHOICE

1. d Economic theory must be combined with subjective value judgments and empirical evidence to arrive at policy recommendations. See pages 355-356.

2. c Models are neither objective, subjective, nor Pareto optimal. They simply are a framework for looking at reality. See pages 355-357.

3. c Economists are trained to look at every decision in reference to costs and benefits as a way of maintaining their objectivity and keeping their subjective views out of policy. Conjective is not a word. While that may seem cold-hearted, the text emphasizes that it seems so only in the short run. See pages 357-358.

4. a Economists approach all issues with cost/benefit analysis. See pages 357-359.

5. d You implicitly value your life at (45,000 X $400) = $18,000,000. See pages 357-359.

6. d The market is working as it is supposed to but almost all would agree that the result is undesirable; there is a failure of market outcome. See page 362.

7. b Consumer and producer surplus focus on total output regardless of how it is distributed. See pages 362-365.

8. a The statement is correct given the shorthand that economists use when referring to efficiency. What is efficient may not be desirable. See pages 362-365.

9. c While economists generally assume that people will do what is in their best interest, it is still possible that they will not do so. See pages 362-365.

10. a Since the law involves a restriction of trade, consumer surplus will be lowered. It still is a good law, however. Economic theory does not find laws correct or incorrect. See pages 362-365.

11. b Economists see government failure as important and sometimes government intervention can make a problem worse, not better. See page 366.

ANSWERS

SHORT-ANSWER QUESTIONS

1. The statement is true to the extent that economists sometimes differ in their views on social policy. Three reasons for their differing views are that (1) economists' suggestions are based upon subjective value judgments, (2) economists interpret data and the workings of institutions differently, and (3) economists use different models to explain the problem. (355)

2. Liberal and conservative economists often agree in their views on social policy because they use the same models, which focus on incentives and individual choice. (356-357)

3. *Cost/benefit analysis* is an analysis in which one assigns a cost and benefit to alternatives and draws a conclusion on the basis of those costs and benefits. (357-358)

4. The typical economist views regulations as the result of political expediency, not a reflection of cost/benefit considerations. Most economists believe that decisions should be made on a cost/benefit basis to society instead of on the pressure placed on politicians by special interest groups. (357-358)

5. Three separate type of failures of market outcomes include (1) failures due to distributional issues, (2) failures due to rationality problems of individuals, and (3) failures due to violations of inalienable or at least partially inalienable rights of individuals. (362-367)

6. For the government to correct a problem it must (1) recognize the problem, (2) have the will to deal with it, and (3) have the ability to deal with it. Government can seldom do all three of these well. (366-367)

7. To the extent that the government's political decisions reflect the will of society, government is making a positive contribution. The negative contribution is that political decisions do not always reflect the will of society. (367-368)

8. You tell a friend to remember the admonition in your textbook: "Teaching a parrot the phrase *supply and demand* does not make it an economist." Elaborating, you tell her that economics involves the thoughtful use of economic insights and empirical evidence. Real-world problems are complex and cannot be explained just with simple models. You are right in taking the time to learn the details. (367-368)

ANSWERS

PROBLEMS AND APPLICATIONS

1. For each of these, you calculate the costs and benefits of the regulation. If the cost is higher than the benefit, you would recommend not implementing the program. If the cost is lower than the benefit, you would recommend implementing the program. For each you are assuming you are given all relevant information.
   a. The benefit is saving a plane worth $200 million and saving lives worth $400 million. The regulation reduces the probability of a crash by .001. The marginal benefit is .001 times $600 million = $600,000. The marginal cost is $16 million. Don't implement the program. Marginal cost is more than marginal benefit. (357-360)
   b. The benefit is value of life saved of $500,000 times the increased probability of living, 1/720 = $694. This is greater than the marginal cost to consumers of $500. Implement the program. (357-360)
   c. The benefit is value of life saved of $2 million times the increased probability of not having a fatal accident, .002 = $4,000. The marginal cost is $5,000 per worker, which is greater than the marginal benefit. Don't implement the program. (357-360)
   d. The above examples include only quantifiable costs and benefits and involve a huge amount of ambiguity and subjectivity in the calculations. Economists' subjective estimates of the benefit of lives and costs of the program can vary enormously, thus affecting the recommendation enormously. (359)

2. Economists often disagree on social policy because of their different underlying subjective value judgements, because of imprecise empirical evidence and because they focus on different aspects of a policy or problem (because their underlying models differ). (355)

3. Because the policy-makers (e.g. politicians) may have weighed the non-quantifiable social and political costs and benefits of the policy recommendation differently than did the economists. Equally reasonable people disagree over non-quantifiable costs and benefits. Therefore, what makes sense from an economic perspective may not be deemed politically, or socially acceptable. (366-368)

ANSWERS

A BRAIN TEASER

1. Economists are trained to weigh both the benefits and the costs associated with any policy or course of action. On the one hand, there are the benefits. On the other hand, there are costs. Usually, like Harry Truman, politicians only want to hear the benefits. But, unfortunately, "there ain't no such thing as a free lunch." (358-359, and 366-368)

ANSWERS

POTENTIAL ESSAY QUESTIONS

The following are annotated answers. They indicate the general idea behind the answer.

1. Cost/benefit analysis is analysis in which one assigns costs and benefits to alternatives, and draws a conclusion on the basis of those costs and benefits. Note that it is marginal costs and marginal benefits that are relevant. Economists try to quantify those costs and benefits—to use empirical evidence to help reach a conclusion. The general public often does not.

2. Economists do take into consideration the economic, social and political consequences associated with a policy. However, not all the costs and benefits associated with a particular policy are quantifiable with respect to each of these three forces. This leaves some room for subjective value judgements with respect to what the benefits and costs of a policy are. Moreover, empirical evidence is not exact. There is also some room for focusing on different aspects of a problem. Finally, if the policy is undertaken in a political environment, as is usually the case, then political considerations by policymakers may take precedence over the social and economic considerations.

POLITICS AND ECONOMICS: THE CASE OF AGRICULTURAL MARKETS

CHAPTER AT A GLANCE

One of the most interesting industrial case studies within economics is the study of the agriculture sector, which is the closest example we have of a perfectly competitive market structure. The characteristics of this industry include the fact that there are many independent producers, none of which can individually influence the market price, all producing essentially the same product and where there are virtually no barriers to entry or exit of the industry.

However, the agriculture sector is far from being perfect as it is influenced by considerable government intervention taking many forms such as marketing boards, subsidy programs and a variety of price support programs.

This chapter explores some of the problems faced by the agriculture sector and some of the important government policies that are designed to deal with some of these problems.

Essentially, farmers are plagued with a paradox—when crops are good, prices for the output falls and farmer's incomes decline, and when crops are poor, the reduced supply leads to upward pressure on prices, and farmer's incomes rise. As a result, government intervenes to assist farmers. There are five different price support programs that governments consider to offset the downward price pressure. It will be important to know these five options and the effects each have on the costs to government and taxpayers and the benefits to farmers.

This review is based upon the learning objectives that open the chapter.

1. In many ways, agricultural markets fit the classic picture of perfect competition. In other ways, however, agricultural markets are far from perfectly competitive. The competitiveness of many agricultural markets is influenced by government programs. (372-373)

The study of agricultural markets shows us how powerful a tool supply and demand analysis is in helping us understand not only the workings of perfectly competitive markets, but also the effects of government intervention in a market.

2. The short-run farm problem is due to the slow growth in demand and the significant increase in supply as a result of technological advances in farming. This also puts downward pressure on prices. (373-374)

3. In the long run, demand for agricultural products is inelastic. Increases in productivity raises supply which leads downward pressure on prices and farmers income. (374-376)

Due to competition among farmers, most benefits of productivity increases in agriculture have gone to consumers in the form of lower prices.

4a. There are five unique problems associated with agriculture:

1. Farm incomes are low relative to other occupations.
2. Farming is a way of life.
3. Economic factors influence farming — poor weather, disease, infestation.
4. Farming is characterized by high fixed costs.
5. Agricultural products are produced under conditions approximating perfect competition, however, when bringing inputs are selling their output, farmers deals with markets that are far from perfectly competitive. (376-378)

4b. The general rule of political economy states that small groups that are significantly affected by a government policy will lobby more effectively than large groups that are equally affected by that same policy. (379)

The farm lobby has been successful in generating higher prices and incomes for farmers even though consumers and taxpayers are worse off. The benefits are concentrated while the costs are spread over a large group.

5a. In a price support system, the government maintains a higher-than-equilibrium price. (379)

Because the price support creates a surplus, which causes downward pressure on the price, government tries to offset this by various measures.

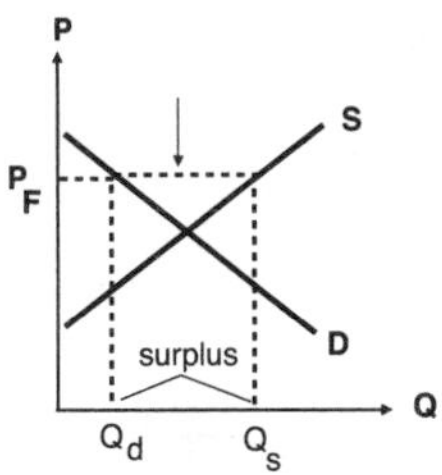

5b. Five methods of price support are: (379-385)

- Regulatory price floor.
- Economic incentives to reduce supply.
- Regulatory measures to reduce supply.
- Subsidizing the sale of goods to consumers.
- Buying up and storing, giving away, or destroying the good.

The distributional effects are shown in Figure 17-4 on page 381.

Know these! Study Figure 17-4! For each know who benefits the most and who is hurt the most–evaluate them.

5c. Politicians weigh the farm program options by attempting to balance their view of the general good with the power and preferences of the special interest groups that they represent or who contribute to their election campaigns. (387)

The special interest groups involved include consumers, taxpayers and farmers. They are not distinctly separate groups.

Always keep in mind the general law of political economy: When small groups are helped by a government action and large groups are hurt by that same action, the small group tends to lobby far more effectively than the large group. It will likely remain in force.

Another influence on the agriculture sector is government intervention. Market-distorting export and production subsidies, particularly by European and U.S. producers have depressed global prices for agricultural products.

MATCHING THE TERMS

Match the terms to their definitions

All of these key terms are found at the end of the chapter.

___ **1.** general rule of political economy	**a.** Small groups that are significantly affected by a government policy will lobby more effectively than large groups that are equally affected by that same policy.
___ **2.** grandfather	**b.** The individual farmer is permitted to produce and sell any quantity up to a maximum amount of product.
___ **3.** price stabilization programs	**c.** Programs designed to eliminate short-run fluctuations in prices but allow prices to follow their long-term trend line.
___ **4.** price support programs	**d.** Programs that maintain prices at a level higher than the market price.
___ **5.** quota	**e.** To pass a law affecting a specific group but providing that those in the group before the law was passed are not subject to the law.
___ **6.** subsidy	**f.** Holds down the price consumers pay but keeps the amount suppliers receive high.

MULTIPLE CHOICE

Circle the one best answer for each of the following questions:

1. The farm paradox exists because there is
- **a.** an inelastic demand for agricultural goods.
- **b.** an inelastic supply of agricultural goods.
- **c.** an elastic demand for agricultural goods.
- **d.** an elastic supply of agricultural goods.

2. Agriculture is a highly productive industry. This enormous productivity has
- **a.** caused agriculture to increase in relative importance as a percent of output.
- **b.** caused agriculture to decrease in relative importance as a percent of output.
- **c.** caused farmers to be rich and prosperous.
- **d.** increased the share of the labor force working in agriculture.

3. Say that most apple farmers are having a bad crop, but that in your particular area the weather was great so you are having a great crop. You would
- **a.** be unhappy because of the paradox.
- **b.** favor price controls.
- **c.** not be hurt by the paradox.
- **d.** receive a low price for your apple crop and not be able to sell much of it.

4. Refer to the graph below. What area represents the change in income going to farmers from an increase in supply from S_0 to S_1?
- **a.** A – C.
- **b.** A + C.
- **c.** A + B +C.
- **d.** C – A.

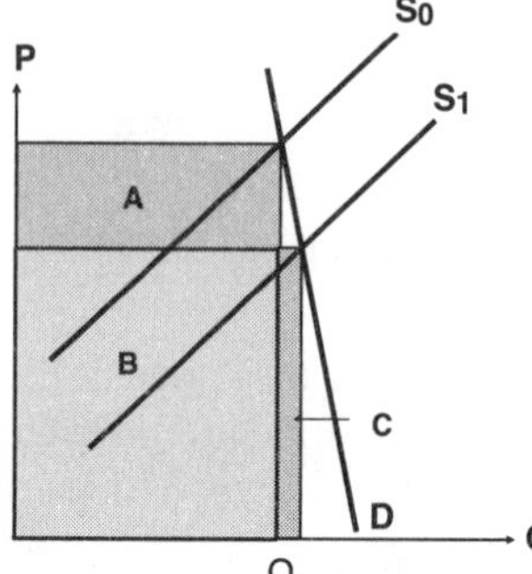

5. Refer to the graph above. What area represents the final income going to farmers after the supply shifts out from S_0 to S_1?
- **a.** A + B.
- **b.** B + C.
- **c.** A + C.
- **d.** A + B + C.

6. The general rule of political economy in a democracy states
- **a.** small groups that are significantly affected by a government policy will lobby more effectively than will large groups who are equally affected by that policy.
- **b.** large groups that are significantly affected by a government policy will lobby more effectively than small groups who are equally affected by that policy.
- **c.** large groups will always win in majority rule situations
- **d.** government will always be inefficient.

7. Refer to the graph below. If the government imposes a quantity restriction of Q_1 on suppliers, compared to the free market situation, suppliers' net income will
   a. fall by B.
   b. rise by A.
   c. rise by A − B.
   d. be unaffected.

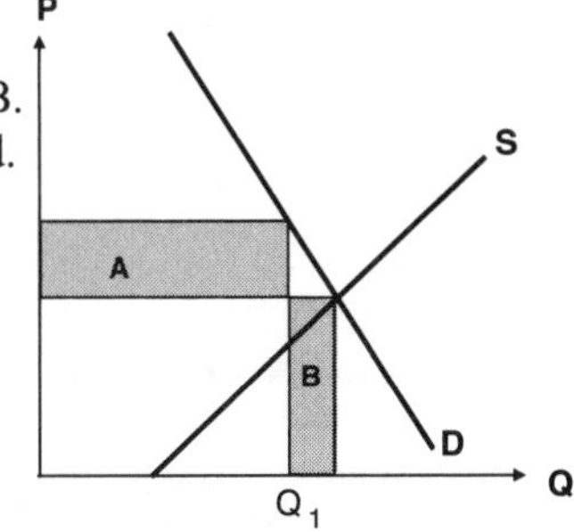

8. Refer to the graph below. The government gives enough economic incentives to suppliers to decrease output sufficiently so that the price rises to $5. The area *best* representing the amount that this program transfers from consumers to suppliers is
   a. A.
   b. B
   c. C
   d. A + B + C.

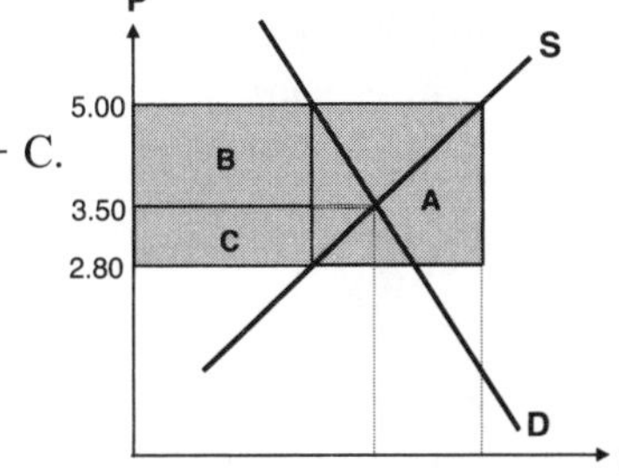

9. Refer to the graph below. If the government sets a price floor of $5 and buys up the surplus, the area *best* representing the cost to the government is
   a. A.
   b. A + B.
   c. B + C.
   d. A + C.

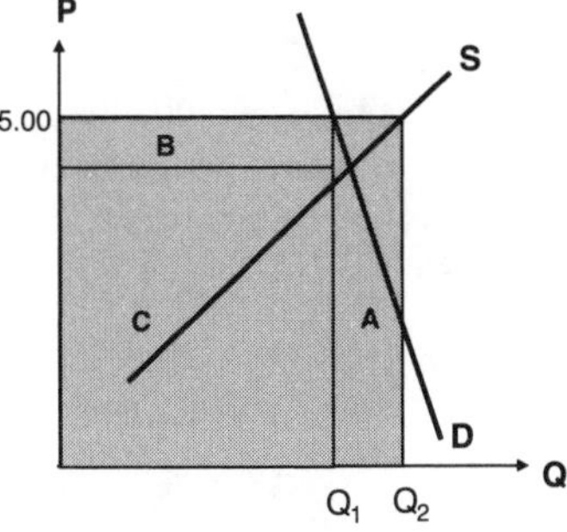

10. Refer to the graph below. If the government subsidizes the sale of wheat so that farmers get $5 but the price to consumers is brought down to $1.75, the cost to the government of doing so will be *best* represented by the area
   a. A.
   b. C.
   c. A +B.
   d. A + B + C.

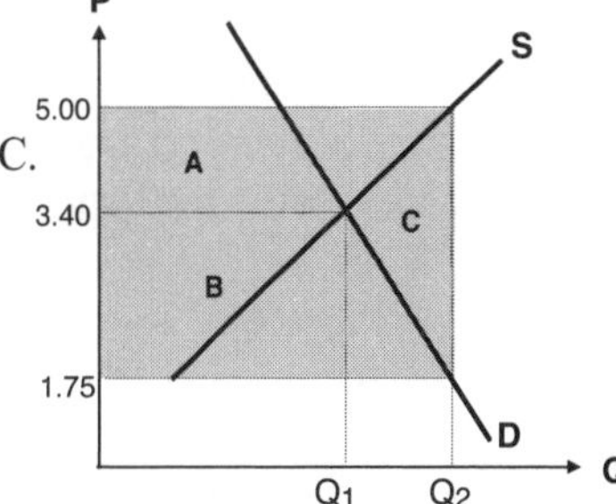

11. Which of the five methods of price supports would taxpayers favor *least*?
   a. Regulatory price floor.
   b. Economic incentives to reduce supply.
   c. Subsidizing the sale.
   d. Buying up and storing the good.
   e. Regulatory measures to reduce supply.

SHORT-ANSWER QUESTIONS

1. What is the paradox in farming?

2. What is the underlying cause of the paradox in farming?

3. What is the general rule of political economy in a democracy?

4. How does a price support system work?

5. What are the five price support options?

6. What are the distributional consequences of the five alternative methods of price support? Use supply and demand curves to support your answers.

7. What real-world influences affect the designing of agricultural policy?

PROBLEMS AND APPLICATIONS

1. Hog farming has become high tech. Companies now house thousands of genetically uniform pigs in large complexes and regulate their environment electronically. The effect of this technological change has been to increase the supply of pigs. The farm lobby is trying to convince government to regulate this industry.

   a. Why would the technological development be troublesome to pig farmers who have small operations? (Hint: use the paradox). Demonstrate this using supply and demand curves.

   b. Show the effect of regulation when it restricts the development of new agrifirms in order to get back to the original price. Who is hurt? Who is helped?

   c. Show the effect of a price support system in which government buys up all the supply that consumers don't buy at the support price (equal to the original price). Who is hurt? Who is helped?

   d. Show the effect of a price subsidy in which the government buys hogs at the original price, P_0, and then sells the hogs to consumers at P_2 so there is no surplus. Who is hurt? Who is helped?

   e. Which would the government favor if it wants to balance its budget without increasing taxes ? Why?

2. Consider the following market demand and supply schedules for peanuts in the U.S.

	Price per ton	Quantity Supplied	Quantity Demanded
A	$50	–1.0	4.25
B	100	–0.5	4.0
C	150	0.	3.75
D	200	0.5	3.5
E	250	1.0	3.25
F	300	1.5	3.0
G	350	2.0	2.75
H	400	2.5	2.5
I	450	3.0	2.25
J	500	3.5	2.0
K	550	4.0	1.75
L	600	4.5	1.5

a. Graph the corresponding demand and supply curves. What is equilibrium price and quantity?

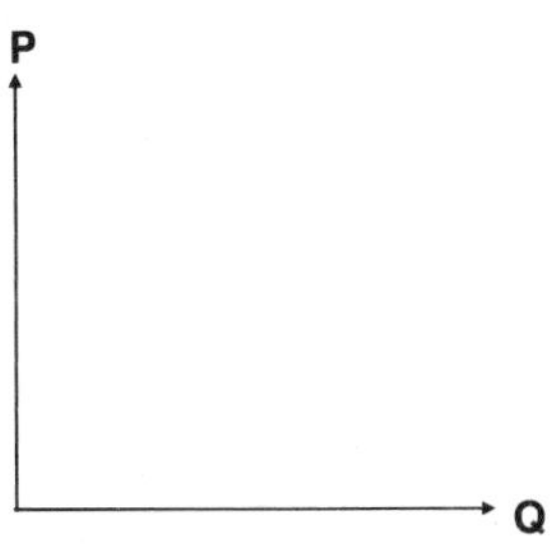

b. Calculate the elasticity of supply from H to G. Calculate the elasticity of demand from H to G. (Use the arc convention).

c. How would you characterize the elasticity of supply and demand calculated in (b)?

d. What would happen to revenue for peanut growers if price fell from H to G?

e. Suppose a technological innovation in peanut growing shifts supply to the following:

	Price per ton	Quantity Supplied
A	$50	–.25
B	100	.25
C	150	.75
D	200	1.25
E	250	1.75
F	300	2.25
G	350	2.75
H	400	3.25
I	450	3.75
J	500	4.25
K	550	4.75
L	600	5.25

Demonstrate the effect of this technological innovation on the graph in (a). What is equilibrium quantity and price?

f. As a result of the efforts by the peanut lobby, the government agrees to buy up all the supply that consumer's don't buy at the original equilibrium price. Show this program graphically.

g. Calculate how much consumers benefit or are hurt. Calculate the cost to taxpayers.

A BRAIN TEASER

1. Suppose government guarantees or supports the price of an agricultural commodity by using option #5 discussed in the textbook—buying up and storing, giving away, or destroying the good. Who is likely to benefit most: the large agrifirms, or the small family farms for which many people believe the program was designed to help? Why?

POTENTIAL ESSAY QUESTIONS

You may also see essay questions similar to the "Problems & Applications" and "Brain Teasers" exercises.

1. What are some of the benefits and the costs of government involvement in agricultural markets? That is, who benefits and who is hurt?

2. Explain using supply and demand curves the distributional consequences of five alternative methods of price supports.

ANSWERS

MATCHING

1-a; 2-e; 3-c; 4-d; 5-b; 6-f.

ANSWERS

MULTIPLE CHOICE

1. a The inelastic demand makes the total revenue vary inversely with shifts in supply. See page 373.

2. b The high level of productivity has led to falling food prices, and decreases agriculture in relative importance as a percent of the economy's output. This is an example of the long-run paradox. See pages 374-375.

3. c The paradox applies when you are part of a group of farmers that is having a bad year or a group of farmers that is having a good year. If you are an individual having a good year when most farmers are having a bad year, you are receiving a high price for your high level of output. See pages 373-374.

4. d The increased income from the higher quantity is the area *C* and the lost income from the lower price is the area *A*, so the net change in income going to farmers is the area $C - A$. It is a loss because the demand is inelastic. See page 374, especially Figure 17-1.

5. b The revenue or income going to farmers is represented by the rectangle determined by the price they receive and the quantity they sell. See page 374, especially Figure 17-1.

6. a Government may always be inefficient, but it is not the general rule of political economy. See page 379.

7. c Suppliers will lose the income *B* because of the quantity restriction, but will gain the area *A* due to the higher price. See Figure 17-4, and pages 380-381.

8. b Consumers lose the area under the demand curve at the higher price. Of that, producers gain area *B* in additional revenue. The triangles are welfare loss. See Figure 17-4, and pages 380-381.

9. a With a price floor of \$5, the surplus will be Q_2-Q_1, for which the government will have to pay \$5. See Figure 17-8, and page 385.

10. d If the price to consumers is held down at \$1.75, the quantity supplied will be Q_2 and the subsidy per unit supplied will have to be \$3.25. See Figure 17-7 and page 384.

11. c Taxpayers will likely *least* favor the price support method of subsidizing the sale of goods to consumers because this method costs taxpayers the most. The low price paid by consumers and the high price received by farmers necessitate large subsidies. See Figure 17-4 and pages 380-381.

ANSWERS

SHORT-ANSWER QUESTIONS

1. The paradox in farming is the phenomenon of doing poorly because you are doing well. That is, total revenue declines even though crop yield has risen. (373-374 and Figure 17-1)

2. The underlying cause of the paradox in farming is that demand for agricultural goods is inelastic so that if the supply of an agricultural good increases, and its price declines, total revenue to farmers also declines. (373-374 and Figure 17-1)

3. The general rule of political economy in a democracy is that small groups that are significantly affected by a government policy will lobby more effectively than large groups that are equally affected by that same policy. (379)

4. In a price support system, the government maintains a higher than equilibrium price. Referring to Figure 17-3 on page 380 of the text, at support price P_1, the quantity of goods demanded is only $Q_D{}^1$, while the quantity supplied is Q_S. This causes downward pressure on the price, shown by arrow A, which must be offset by government measures shown by arrow B. (379-380)

5. The five price support options are (1) regulatory price floor, (2) economic incentives to reduce supply, (3) regulatory measures to reduce supply, (4) subsidizing the sale of goods to consumers, and (5) buying up and storing, giving away, or destroying the good. (379)

6. The distributional consequences of the five alternative methods of price support are shown in the five graphs below. (379-385)

The following graph shows the effect of regulating price directly at P_2. Farmers are allowed to produce at Q_1. The farmers who can no longer sell their goods lose areas *B* and *C* but gain back *B* in their other pursuits. Revenue to remaining producers increases by area A. Consumers lose areas *A* and *D* in consumer surplus. Areas *C* and *D* are lost to society. (Figure 17-4 on p. 381)

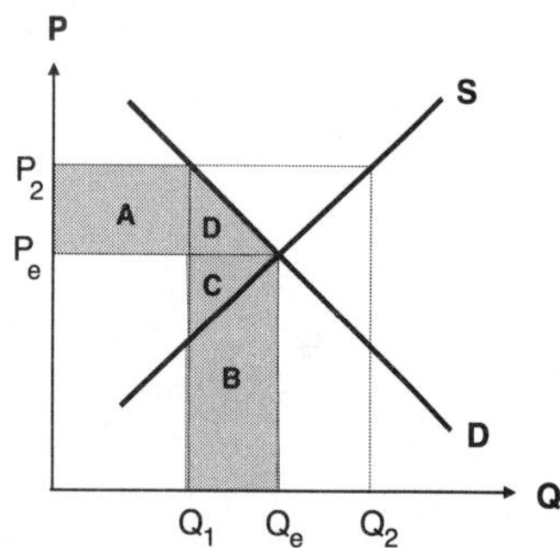

The graph below shows the effect of providing economic incentives to reduce supply by paying farmers not to produce. It must pay farmers the difference between market price P_e and the support price P_2. The government has to pay farmers area A to reduce the quantity supplied to Q_1. Existing farmers receive payment B from the government and get rectangle A from consumers in the form of higher prices. Consumers pay a higher price for fewer goods. (Figure 17-5 on p. 382)

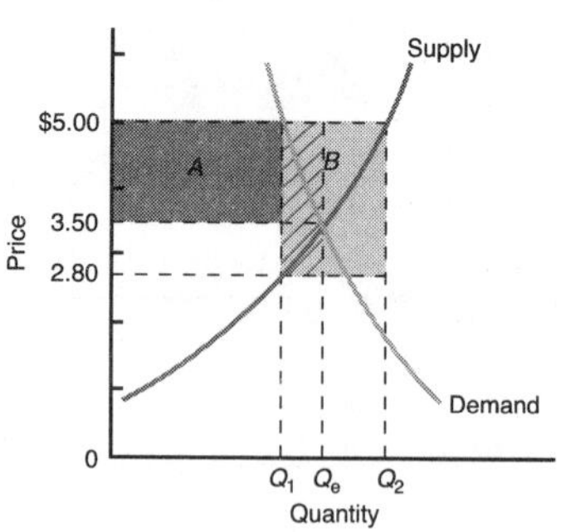

The graph below shows the effect of regulatory measures to reduce supply. A quota (Q_1) that restricts total supply is imposed. The inter-section of the demand curve and Q_1 results in quantity Q_1 sold at a higher market price P_2. Producers gain area *A*, however, lose areas *B* and *C* as output falls from Q_e to Q_1. Area *D* is the deadweight loss to society since this quantity ($Q_e - Q_1$) is no longer produced and consumed. (Figure 17-6 on p. 383)

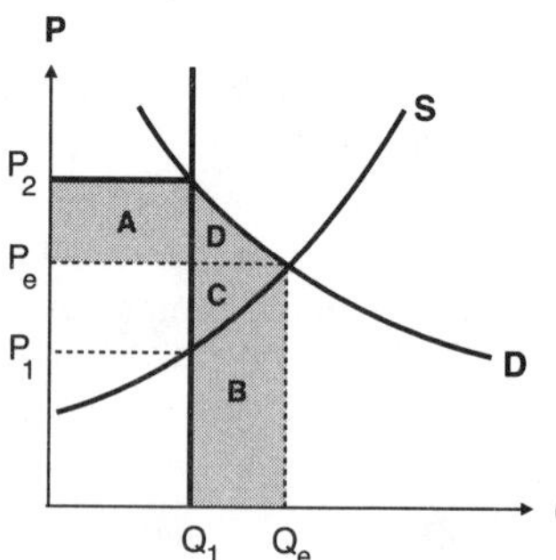

The graph below shows the effect of subsidizing the sale of the good. Suppliers supply quantity Q_2 to the government and are paid the price support P_2. Consumers purchase Q_2 at P_1 from the government. They are benefited by area *A*, getting more goods at a lower price. Suppliers are benefited by area *B*, getting a higher price. The taxpayers foot the bill which equals *A* + *B* + *C*. (Figure 17-7 on p. 384)

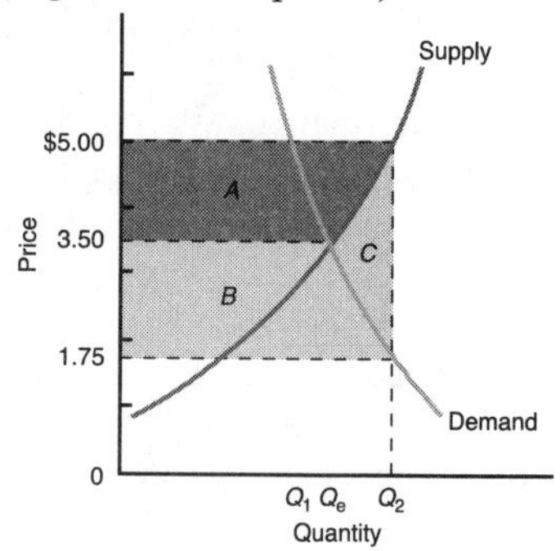

The graph below shows the effect of the government buying up the goods that consumers do not buy at the support price, P_2, and storing or otherwise disposing of the good. The government pays the farmers area *B*. Taxpayers foot the bill of *A* + *B*. To the extent that the government can get something for the goods it bought, its expenses are lower than area *B*. Area *A* is transferred from consumers to producers. (Figure 17-8 on p. 385)

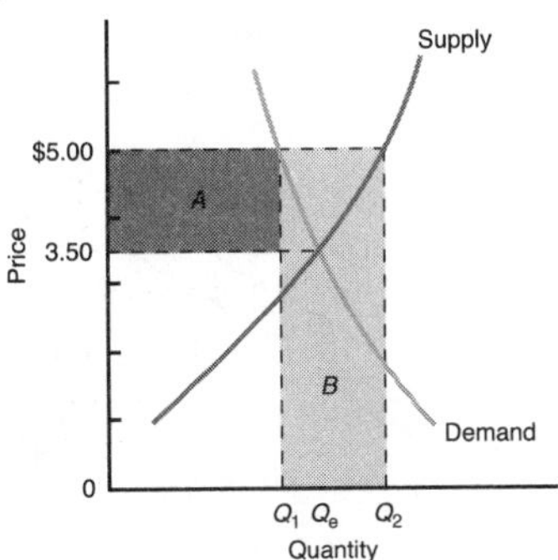

7. Politicians must weigh the agricultural policy options by attempting to balance their view of the general good with the power and preferences of the special interest groups that they represent (consumers, taxpayers, and farmers) or that contribute to their campaigns. (399-400) In addition, government intervention in the form of market distorting export and production subsidies have depressed global prices for agricultural products.

ANSWERS

PROBLEMS AND APPLICATIONS

1. a. Farmers are upset because demand for pork is relatively inelastic. This is shown in the graph below. Before the new technology, price and quantity are P_0 and Q_0. Total income is P_0Q_0. The supply of pigs, however, has shifted to S_1 with the development of agrifirms. Now, equilibrium price is P_1 and quantity is Q_1. Because demand is inelastic, farmers' income has fallen. The lost income, area *A*, is greater than the gain in income, area *C*. (375-376 and Figure 17-2)

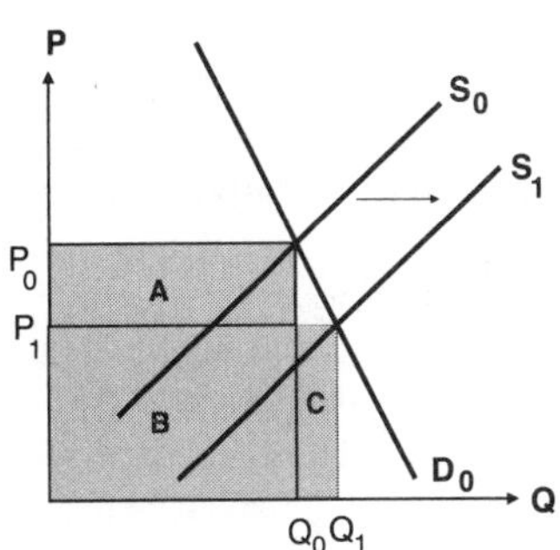

b. In this case, the government would restrict the supply of hogs to Q_0. Farmers' total revenue increases by area *A* and decreases by areas C and B. There is a net gain in revenue to suppliers. Some suppliers who want to supply Q1 – Q0 must be excluded from the market. Consumers must pay a higher price, P0 and get a lower quantity, Q0. The darkened triangle, areas D and C, represent deadweight loss. It represents a loss to society from the quantity restriction. (380-381 and Figure 17-4)

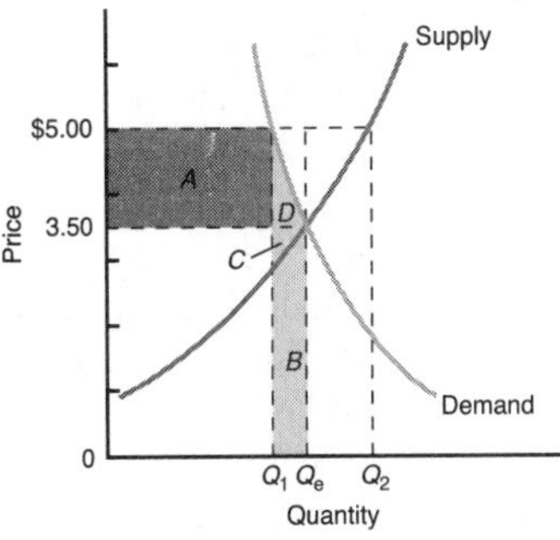

c. Consumers buy Q0 at P0. The government buys Q2 – Q0 at price P0, paying rectangle B in total. Consumer surplus equal to rectangle A is transferred to hog farmers. Taxpayers are hurt who have to pay rectangle B for goods that most likely cannot be sold elsewhere. Consumers are hurt by having to pay a higher price for fewer goods. (379-385 and Figure 17-8)

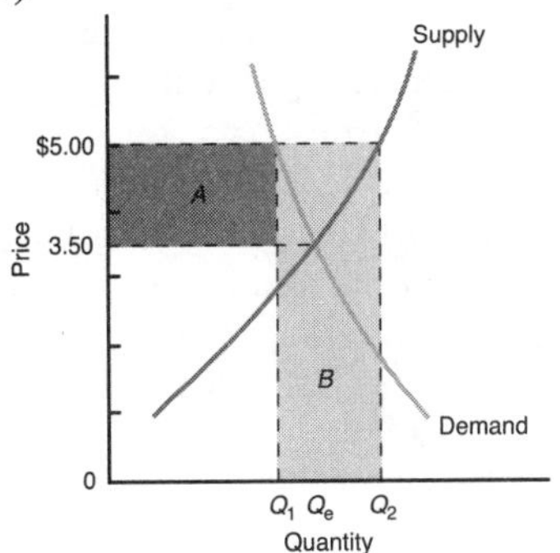

d. In this case, government spends P0Q2 to buy the hogs and sells them for P_2Q_2. Consumers benefit from enjoying the lower price P_2 and higher quantity represented by a net gain of area *B*. Suppliers benefit from a higher price, P_0, a and higher quantity, Q_2. Their net gain is represented by area *A*. The cost to taxpayers, however, is areas *A*, *B* and *C*, so the net welfare loss is area *C*. (384-385 and Figure 17-7)

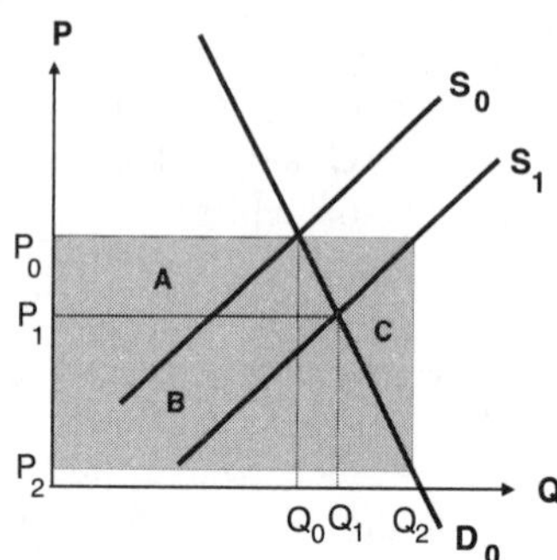

e. If government wanted to hold government expenditures down, it would favor (b) because the direct cost to government is zero, although there are enforcement and administrative costs. (379-385)

2. a. The corresponding demand and supply curves are shown below. Equilibrium quantity and price is where the two curves intersect: Quantity is 2.5 million tons at a price of $400 per ton. (379-385)

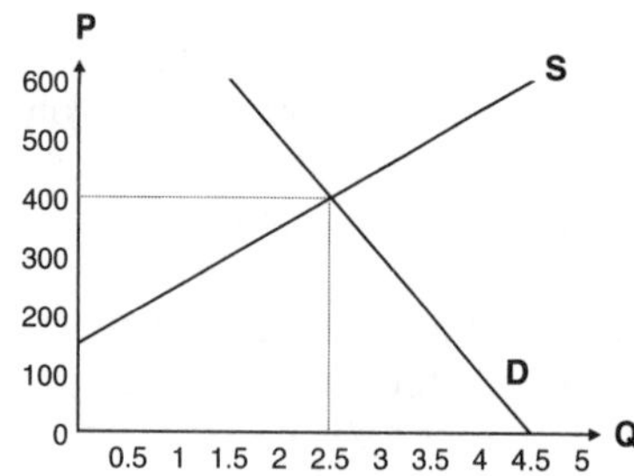

b. $E_s = 1.7$; $E_D = 0.7$. The elasticity of supply is percent change in quantity supplied divided by the percent change in price. From *H* to *G* this is [(2.5-2)/2.25]/[(400-350)/375] = 0.22/0.13 = 1.7. The elasticity of demand is percent change in quantity demanded divided by the percent change in price. From *H* to *G* this is |[(2.5-2.75)/2.675]/[(400-350)/375]| = 0.09/0.13 = 0.7. (See the chapter on elasticity.)

c. Supply is elastic since $E_s > 1$; Demand is inelastic since $E_D < 1$. (See the chapter on elasticity.)

d. Since demand is inelastic between *H* and *G*, total revenue would fall. (See the chapter on elasticity.)

e. The increase in supply will shift the curve to the right as shown in the graph below. Supply shifts from S_0 to S_1. Equilibrium quantity is now 2.75 million tons. Equilibrium price is now $350 per ton. (379-385)

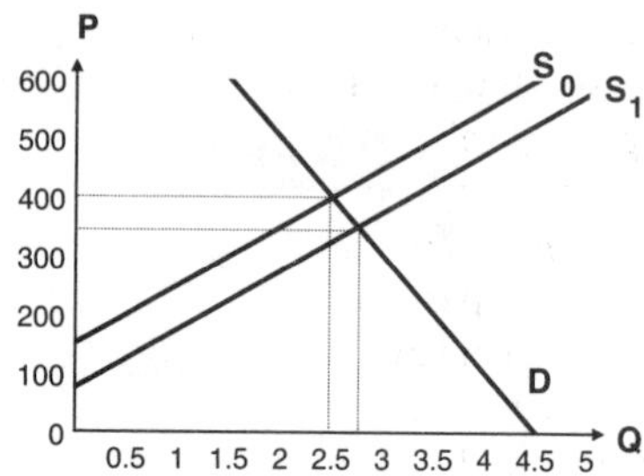

f. This program is shown in the graph below. Consumers buy 2.5 million tons at $400 per ton. Government buys 0.75 million tons at $400, spending a total of area B, or $300 million. (385 and Figure 17-8)

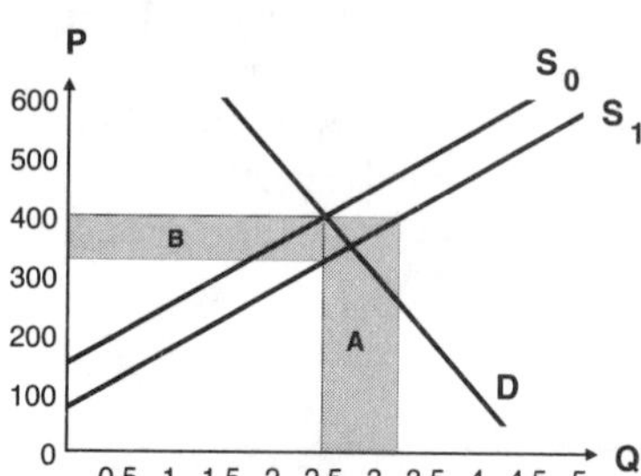

g. Consumers pay an extra $50 per ton over the $350 they would have paid if the new equilibrium were reached. This means they pay an additional $125 million (2.5 million × 50). This is represented by area *B*. The cost to taxpayers is area *A*, or $300 million. (379-385 and Figure 17-8)

ANSWERS

A BRAIN TEASER

1. The large agrifirms are likely to benefit most. These large corporate farms usually have lower average costs of production because of the economies of scale they are able to experience. Because the price received is the same for small and large farms alike, then much larger profits can be earned by the agrifirms. Moreover, the agrifirms may produce most of the output. Hence, most of the government tax revenues used to buy up the surplus production ends up in the hands of those large corporate farms which least need assistance. This has caused some critics to argue that this past prevalent form of government involvement in agricultural markets has resulted in an upside-down "welfare" program—it has benefited those most who need it least. Critics argue that it may be cheaper for taxpayers to simply make a cash payment to small family farms if it is their incomes which society wishes to support. (385)

ANSWERS

POTENTIAL ESSAY QUESTIONS

The following are annotated answers. They indicate the general idea behind the answer.

1. The benefit is more stable and higher prices and more stable and higher farm incomes. Farmers benefit. (However, it may benefit those "rich" farmers most—those who need it least. It may be an upside-down "welfare" program. See the "Brain Teaser" problem.) The costs to society are the higher prices consumers must pay for food and fiber. Taxpayers are also hurt by having to pay higher taxes to support farm prices and incomes. The government also may have to deal with the surplus production in some manner. This too can be costly.

2. Five methods of price support are:
   1. Regulatory price floor.
   2. Economic incentives to reduce supply.
   3. Economic incentives to reduce supply.
   3. Regulatory measures to reduce supply
   4. Subsidizing the sale of goods to consumers.
   5. Buying up and storing, giving away, or destroying the good.

   The distributional effects are shown in Figure 17-3, on page 380.

INTERNATIONAL TRADE POLICY

18

CHAPTER AT A GLANCE

Chapter 15 introduced the notion of the competitive effects of globalization—that economies now have to consider the impact of external influences when implementing independent domestic policies. This chapter expands on this theme by elaborating on the economics of international trade. There is now general consensus that promoting freer trade and entering into free trade arrangements leads to greater economic well being, higher standards of living and increased economic growth.

An in-depth discussion is presented on the different types of trade restrictions and why economists generally oppose these trade restrictions.

The principle of comparative advantage is introduced as the foundation of trade and specialization. It states that as long as the relative opportunity costs of producing goods differ among countries, then there are potential gains from trade.

The last part of the chapter reviews the different types of free trade associations designed to reduce barriers to trade among member countries.

This review is based upon the learning objectives that open the chapter.

1. Gains from trade deals with economic rationale that two countries can have access to more commodities without increasing their amount of resources utilized. It stems from the fact that rather than producing all commodities demanded, each specialize in the production of only one, thereby, increasing the output of that good. If all countries do this, there is more output available for export and all countries benefit with higher quantities of all commodities. (392-393)

2a. The principle of comparative advantage states that as long as the relative opportunity costs of producing goods differ among countries, there are potential gains from trade, even if one country has an absolute advantage in the other good. (396)

When countries specialize in the production of those goods for which each has a comparative advantage and then trade, all economies involved benefit.

2b. The principle of absolute advantage states that a country that can produce a good at a lower cost than another country is said to have an absolute advantage in the production of that good. (393)

2c. Three determinants of the gains of the terms of trade are: (398)

- The more competition, the less the trader gets.
- Smaller countries get a larger proportion of the gain than larger countries.
- Countries producing goods with economies of scale get a larger gain from trade.

Also: countries which specialize and trade along the lines of comparative advantage are able to consume more than if they did not undertake trade (they are able to escape the confines of their own production possibility curves).

3a. Countries can increase the gains from trade by specializing first, then trading. (401)

3b. Trade allows a country to produce on its PPC but consume at a point above its PPC. (401)

4a. Canada's reason for signing the original Free Trade Agreement (and the later North American Free Trade Agreement) was because the gains from trade outweighed the losses overall, and gainers potentially could compensate the losers.

Canada wanted to gain increased and more secure access to larger markers, especially the United States. (402)

4b. Trade agreements can cause trade creation which occurs when the volume of trade between the member countries increases, or it can result in trade diversion which occurs when trade increases between the member countries at the expense of trade with other countries. (403)

5. The emergence of globalization and trade generates several positive results which include access to technology and knowledge, fiscal and monetary responsibility attracting foreign direct investment, and increased influence of multinational corporations. (403-404)

6. Reasons for restricting trade include: (404)
- Unequal internal distribution of the gains from trade.
- Specialized production; learning by doing and economies of scale.
- Macroeconomic aspects of trade.
- National security.
- International politics.
- Increased revenue brought in by tariffs.

Understand these motives for trade barriers and be able to explain why they may be fallacious.

7. Economists generally favour free trade because: (408)
- from a global perspective, free trade increases total output;
- trade restrictions lead to retaliation; and
- international trade provides competition for domestic companies.

Economists generally argue that the benefits of free trade outweigh the costs—especially over time.

8. Three policies used to restrict trade are: (409-412)
- tariffs (taxes on internationally traded goods),
- quotas (quantity limits placed on imports), and
- regulatory trade restrictions (government-imposed procedures that limit imports).

Countries can also restrict trade through:
1. *voluntary restraint agreements*
2. *embargoes*
3. *nationalistic appeals.*

9. Free trade associations help trade by reducing barriers to trade among member nations. Free trade associations could hinder trade by building up barriers to trade with nations outside the association. (412-413)

A free trade association is a group of countries that allows free trade among its members and puts up common barriers against all other countries' goods.

MATCHING THE TERMS

Match the terms to their definitions

All key terms are found at the end of the chapter.

___ **1.** absolute advantage
___ **2.** autarky
___ **3.** comparative advantage
___ **4.** economies of scale
___ **5.** embargo
___ **6.** engine of growth
___ **7.** Free Trade Agreement (FTA)
___ **8.** free trade association
___ **9.** General agreement on Tariffs and Trade (GATT)
___ **10.** infant industry argument
___ **11.** learning by doing
___ **12.** most-favored nation
___ **13.** North American Free Trade Agreement
___ **14.** quotas
___ **15.** rationalization
___ **16.** regulatory trade restrictions
___ **17.** strategic bargaining
___ **18.** tariffs
___ **19.** terms of trade
___ **20.** trade adjustment assistance programs
___ **21.** trade creation
___ **22.** trade diversion.
___ **23.** World Trade Organization (WTO)

a. A tax governments place on internationally traded goods—generally imports.
b. Total restriction on the import or export of a good.
c. As long as the relative opportunity costs of producing goods differ among countries, there are potential gains from trade, even if one country has an absolute advantage in everything.
d. Costs per unit of output go down as output increases.
e. Country that will be charged the lowest tariff on its exports.
f. Demanding a larger share of the gains of trade than you can reasonably expect.
g. Government-imposed procedures that limit imports.
h. Group of countries that allows free trade among its members and put up common barriers against all other countries' goods.
i. A regular international conference to reduce trade barriers.
j. Programs designed to compensate losers for reductions in trade restrictions.
k. Quantity limit placed on imports.
l. An organization whose functions are generally the same as were those of GATT—to promote free and fair trade among countries.
m. With initial protection, an industry will be able to become competitive.
n. Becoming a better at a task by performing it repeatedly.
o. A country that can produce a good at a lower cost than another country.
p. A state in which a country produces everything it needs, and doesn't trade.
q. The exchange value of one good for the other.
r. Closing down inefficient high-cost plants and upgrading their more efficient lower-cost plants.
s. Occurs when the volume of trade between the member countries increases.
t. Occurs when trade increases between the member countries at the expense of trade with other countries.
u. A source of greater productivity that leads to rapid economic growth.
v. Free trade agreement between Canada and the United States.
w. Free trade agreement between Canada, the United States and Mexico.

MULTIPLE CHOICE

Circle the one best answer for each of the following questions:

1. Refer to the graph below. The graph demonstrates Saudi Arabia's and Canada's production possibility curves for widgets and wadgets. Given these production possibility curves, you would suggest that

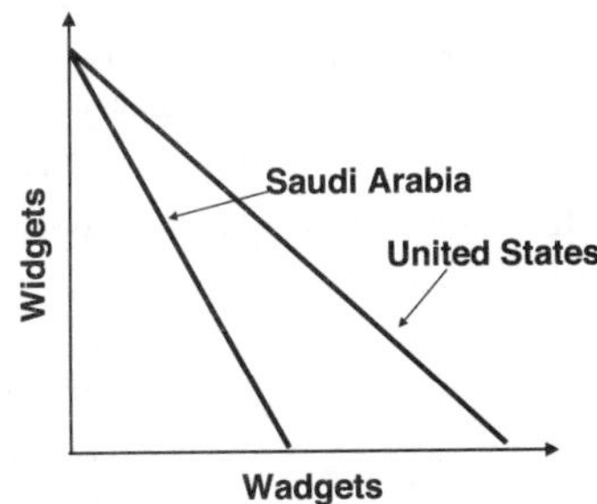

a. Saudi Arabia specialize in widgets and the United States in wadgets.
b. no trade should take place.
c. Saudi Arabia specialize in wadgets and the United States in widgets.
d. Both countries should produce an equal amount of each.

2. If a nation has a comparative advantage in the production of good X then:
a. it can produce good X at the lowest opportunity cost.
b. it will import good X.
c. it can produce more of good X than any other nation.
d. the opportunity cost of producing an additional unit of good X is greater than for any other nation.

3. A widget has an opportunity cost of 4 wadgets in Saudi Arabia and 2 wadgets in the United States. Given these opportunity costs, you would suggest that
a. Saudi Arabia specialize in widgets and the United States in wadgets.
b. no trade should take place.
c. Saudi Arabia specialize in wadgets and the United States in widgets.
d. both countries produce an equal amount of each.

4. Country A's cost of widgets is \$4.00 and cost of wadgets is \$8.00. Country B's cost of widgets is 8 francs and cost of wadgets is 16 francs. Which of the following would you suggest?
a. Country A should specialize in widgets and Country B in wadgets.
b. No trade should take place.
c. Country A should specialize in wadgets and Country B in widgets.
d. Both countries should produce an equal amount of each.

5. In considering the distribution of the gains from trade
a. smaller countries usually get a larger proportion of the gains from trade.
b. larger countries usually get a larger proportion of the gains from trade.
c. the gains are generally equally split equally between small and large countries.
d. no statement can be made about the general nature of the split.

6. Countries can increase the gains from trade by
a. practicing autarky.
b. considering their absolute advantage.
c. producing inside the PPC.
d. specializing first, then trading.

7. Canada signed the free trade agreements because
a. it felt that losers outweighed gainers.
b. everyone was signing them.
c. it wanted to gain more secure and increased access to U.S. markets.
d. it had several absolute advantages.

8. Trade restrictions
a. increase competition.
b. increase prices to consumers.
c. benefit consumers.
d. have economic benefits that outweigh the economic costs.

9. Reasons for restricting trade include all of the following *except*
a. the existence of learning by doing and economies of scale.
b. national security reasons.
c. the increased revenue brought in from tariffs.
d. the fact that trade decreases competitive pressures at home.

10. Economists generally favour free trade for all of the following reasons *except*
    a. from a global perspective, free trade increases total output.
    b. the infant industry argument.
    c. trade restrictions lead to retaliation.
    d. international politics.

11. A tariff is
    a. a tax government places on internationally-traded goods.
    b. a quantity limit placed on imports.
    c. a total restriction on imports.
    d. a government-imposed procedural rule that limits imports.

12. An embargo is
    a. a tax government places on imports.
    b. a quantity limit placed on imports.
    c. a total restriction on imports.
    d. a government-imposed procedural rule that limits imports.

SHORT-ANSWER QUESTIONS

1. What is the principle of comparative advantage?

2. Do smaller countries get a larger or smaller proportion of the gains from trade than larger countries? Why?

3. What are three determinants of the terms of trade?

4. In a talk to first-year students in economics, you reveal that you believe in free trade. Hands fly up from people just waiting to tell you why they want to restrict trade. What are some of their reasons?

5. After listening to their remarks, you gather your thoughts and offer them reasons why you generally favour free trade. What do you say?

6. The first-year students in economics disregard what you said and ask you what are the ways they can restrict trade. Although you are a proponent of free trade, you oblige.

7. The first year students in economics ask you how the nation joining a free trade association could help and hinder international trade. What do you say?

PROBLEMS AND APPLICATIONS

1. a. State whether there is a basis for trade in the following:

Case 1: In Country A, the opportunity cost of producing one widget is two wadgets. In Country B, the opportunity cost of producing two widgets is four wadgets.

Case 2: In Country C, the opportunity cost of producing one widget is two wadgets, In Country D, the opportunity cost of producing two widgets is one wadget.

Case 3: In Country E, the opportunity cost of producing one widget is two wadgets. In Country F, the opportunity cost of producing one widget is four wadgets.

b. On what general principle did you base your reasoning?

c. Assume that in Case 3, there are constant marginal returns and constant returns to scale. Country E is currently producing 10 widgets and 4 wadgets. Country F is currently producing 20 widgets and 20 wadgets. Can you make an offer involving trade that will make both countries better off?

d. How would your answer differ if each country experiences economies of scale?

2. Suppose Canada is considering trade restrictions against EU (European Union)-produced hams. Given the demand and supply curves drawn below, show a tariff and quota that would result in the same exports of ham to Canada

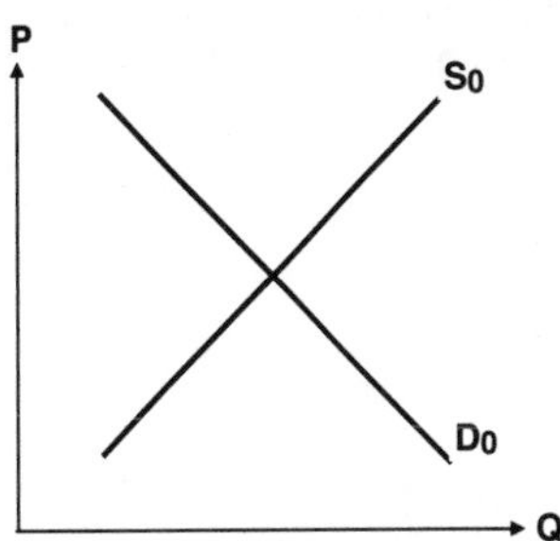

a. Which would result in higher government revenue?

b. Which would the EU prefer?

c. Which would Canadian ham producers prefer?

d. Which would Canadian consumers prefer?

3. Suppose Country A and Country B are potential trading partners. Each country produces two goods: fish and wine. If Country A devotes all of its resources to producing fish, it can produce 1000 fish, and if it devotes all of its resources to producing wine, it can produce 2000 bottles of wine. If Country B devotes all of its resources to producing fish, it can produce 3000 fish, and if it devotes all of its resources to producing wine it can produce 3000 bottles of wine. For simplicity, assume the production possibility curves of these countries are straight lines.

a. Draw the production possibility curve for Country A on the axes below. In Country A, what is the opportunity cost of one bottle of wine in terms of fish?

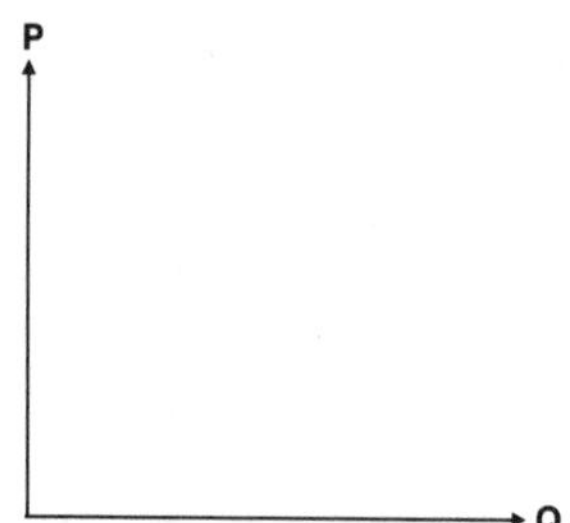

b. Draw the production possibility curve for Country B on the axes for (a). In Country B, what is the opportunity cost of one bottle of wine in terms of fish?

c. Does Country A have an absolute advantage in producing either wine or fish? Does Country B have an absolute advantage in producing either wine or fish?

d. Does Country A have a comparative advantage in producing either wine or fish? Does Country B have a comparative advantage in producing either wine or fish?

e. Suppose Country A specialized in that good for which it has a comparative advantage and Country B specialized in that good for which it has a comparative advantage. Each country would then trade the good it produced for the good the other country produced. What would be a fair exchange of goods?

A2. Suppose two countries A and B have the following production possibility tables:

	% Resources devoted to Machines	Country A Production Machines	Country A Production Food	Country B Production Machines	Country B Production Food
A	100	200	0	40	0
B	80	160	8	32	40
C	60	120	16	28	80
D	40	80	24	24	120
E	20	40	32	16	160
F	0	0	40	0	200

a. Draw the production possibility curves for Country A and Country B on the axes below.

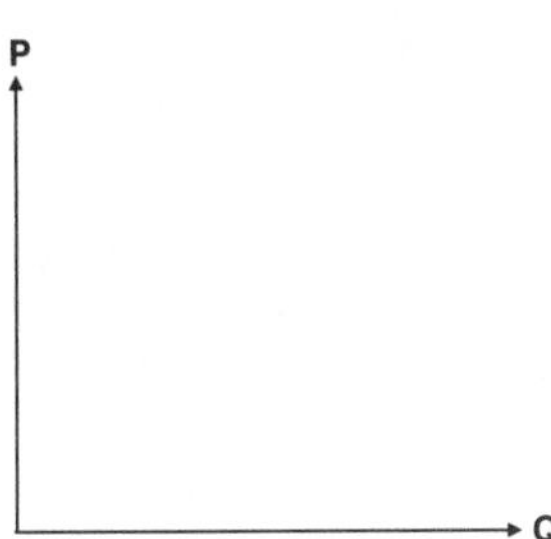

b. Which country has the absolute advantage in the production of food?

c. Which country has the comparative advantage in the production of food?

d. Suppose each country specializes in the production of one good. Explain how Country A can end up with 50 food units and 150 machines and Country B can end up with 150 food units and 50 machines. Both points are outside the production possibility curve for each country without trade.

A BRAIN TEASER

1. What are the benefits and the costs to a nation of lower trade barriers? Which are greater for the nation: the benefits or the costs of free trade?

POTENTIAL ESSAY QUESTIONS

You may also see essay questions similar to the "Problems & Applications" and "Brain Teasers" exercises.

1. What is the difference between a tariff and a quota? Why do governments prefer tariffs, while foreign producers prefer quotas? What is the result of tariffs and quotas on the price and equilibrium quantity of the imported good?

2. What are six ways in which a country may restrict trade? Why do most economists support free trade and oppose trade restrictions?

ANSWERS

MATCHING

1-o; 2-p; 3-c; 4-d; 5-b; 6-u; 7-v; 8-h; 9-i; 10-m; 11-n; 12-e; 13-w; 14-k; 15-r, 16-g; 17-f; 18-a; 19-q; 20-j; 21-s; 22-t; 23-l.

ANSWERS

MULTIPLE CHOICE

1. a The opportunity cost for Saudi Arabia of wadgets in terms of widgets is higher than the opportunity cost for Canada. So, Saudi Arabia should specialize in widgets and Canada in wadgets. See pages 395-397.

2. a A comparative advantage in the production of X means the nation can produce that good with a lower opportunity cost. Because the nation is relatively more efficient at producing X, it will specialize in its production and export that good. Answer c may be true, but it is also possible to have a comparative advantage in X without being able to produce more of X than any other nation. See pages 395-398.

3. c The opportunity cost for Canada of wadgets in terms of widgets is higher than the opportunity cost for Saudi Arabia. So, Canada should specialize in widgets and Saudi Arabia in wadgets. See pages 395-398.

4. b The opportunity cost of widgets and wadgets is equal in both countries so neither country has a comparative advantage in either good and there is no basis for trade. See pages 395-398.

5. a Smaller countries usually find that their production possibilities are changed more, and hence they benefit more. See page 398.

6. d Countries that concentrate on their comparative advantages, then specialize and trade, tend to experience gains from trade. See pages 399-402.

7. c See p. 402.

8. b Trade restrictions reduce competition and therefore increase prices to consumers. Thus, consumers are hurt. The benefits of trade restrictions go to the domestic producers that do not have to compete as aggressively. The economic costs of trade restrictions (in the form of higher prices consumers must pay) far outweigh their benefits (which go to the protected domestic industries in the form of higher profits and more secure jobs). See pages 405-408.

9. d Trade increases competitive pressures at home and increases competitiveness. See pages 405-408.

10. b The infant industry argument is an argument in favor of trade restrictions. Economists' response to the infant industry argument is that history shows that few infant industries have ever grown up. See pages 406-409.

11. a A tariff is a tax placed on imported goods. See page 409.

12. c An embargo is an all-out restriction on the trade of goods with another country. See pages 410-411.

ANSWERS

SHORT-ANSWER QUESTIONS

1. The principle of comparative advantage is that as long as the relative opportunity costs of producing goods differ among countries, there are potential gains from trade, even if one country has an absolute advantage in everything. (396-398)

2. Smaller countries tend to get a larger percentage of the gains from trade than do larger countries. There are more opportunities opened up for smaller countries leading to larger relative gains. (398)

3. Three determinants of the terms of trade are (1) the more competition, the less the trader gets and the more will go to the countries who are trading; (2) smaller countries get a larger proportion of the gain than larger countries; and (3) countries producing goods with economies of scale get a larger gain from trade. (398)

4. Their answers might include: (1) although foreign competition might make society better off, some people may lose their jobs because of foreign competition (unequal internal distribution of the gains from trade); (2) trade restrictions will protect new industries until they learn to be competitive (learning by doing and economies of scale); (3) imports hurt domestic income in the short run, and the economy needs to grow in the short run (trade can reduce domestic output in the short run); (4) some restrictions are needed to protect our national security; (5) we do not want to trade with countries who violate our human rights standards or whose ideology conflicts with our democratic ideals (international politics may dominate trade considerations); and (6) tariffs bring in revenue for the government. (405-408)

5. I would say that I generally favour free trade because (1) from a global perspective, free trade increases total output, (2) trade restrictions lead to retaliation, and (3) international trade provides competition for domestic companies. (408-409)

6. Three policies countries use to restrict trade are (1) tariffs, (2) quotas, and (3) regulatory trade restrictions. There are others. (409-412)

7. Free trade associations promote trade among members by reducing barriers to trade among the member nations. However, free trade associations could hinder trade by building up barriers to trade with nations outside the association. (412-413)

ANSWERS

PROBLEMS AND APPLICATIONS

1. a. There is a basis for trade in Cases 2 and 3 because opportunity costs differ. (395-402)

   b. The general principle is that there are gains from trade to be made when each country has a comparative advantage in one or the other good. (395-402)

   c. I would have country E specialize in widgets and country F specialize in wadgets. Since country E is currently producing 10 widgets and 4 wadgets, I would have it produce 12 widgets and no wadgets, promising that I will give it 5 wadgets for the extra two widgets it produced. I would have Country F produce 28 wadgets and 18 widgets, promising that I will give it 2 widgets in return for 7 of its wadgets. After I made this trade, both countries are one wadget better off. I am two wadgets better off. (These two wadgets are the return to me for organizing the trade.) (395-402)

   d. If there were economies of scale, there would be an even stronger argument for trade. (398)

2. A tariff would shift the supply curve to the left by the amount of the tariff. A quota with the same result would be at Q_1. Equilibrium quantity would fall from Q_0 to Q_1. Equilibrium price would rise from P_0 to P_1. This is shown on the graph below. (409-410)

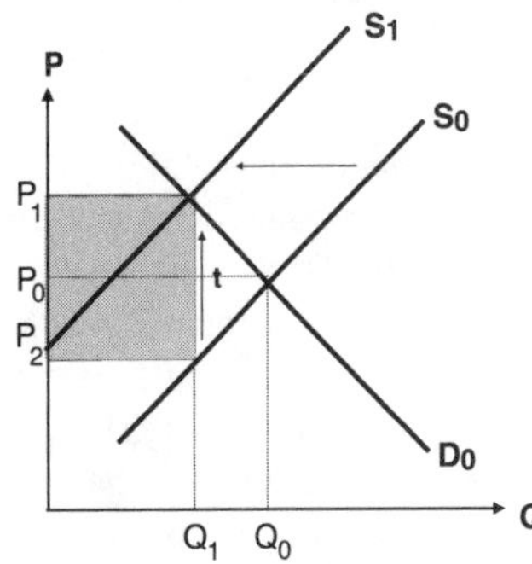

   a. The government receives no revenue from the quota, but receives the shaded region as revenue from the tariff as shown on the graph above. (409-410)

b. The EU would prefer the quota since it will receive a higher price, P_1, for the same quantity of goods, Q_1 as it would with a tariff. With a tariff, it would receive P_2, for Q_1. (409-410)

c. Canadian ham producers prefer the quota because any increase in domestic demand would be met by domestic supply. (409-410)

d. Canadian consumers do not prefer either since the resulting price and quantity is the same with both. If, however, the tariff revenue were to lead to lower taxes or higher government services, they might prefer the tariff over the quota. They also might prefer the tariff to the quota because any increase in domestic demand will be partially met with imports, keeping domestic producers more efficient than under a quota system. (409-410)

3. a. The production possibility curve for Country A is the curve labeled A in the graph below. In Country A, the opportunity cost of one bottle of wine is 1/2 fish. Each fish forgone frees up resources sufficient to make two bottles of wine. (395-402)

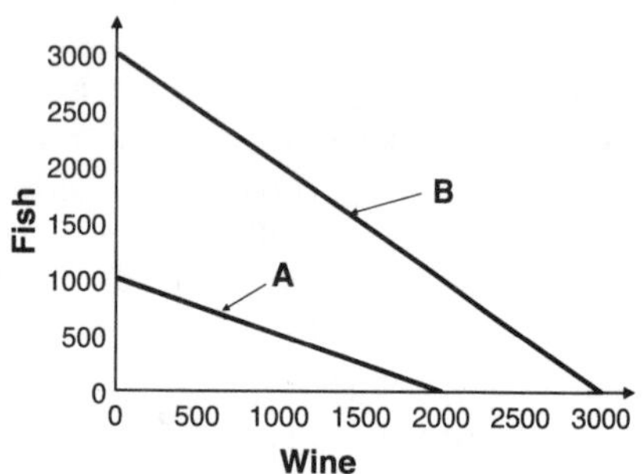

b. The production possibility curve for Country B is the curve labeled B in the graph above. In Country B, the opportunity cost of one bottle of wine is one fish. Each fish forgone frees up resources sufficient to make one bottle of wine. (395-402)

c. Country A does not have an absolute advantage in the production of either because if it devoted all of its resources to fish or wine, it would still produce less than if Country B devoted all of its resources to one or the other. Country B has an absolute advantage in producing both wine and fish. (395-402)

d. Country A has a comparative advantage in wine because it has to give up only 1/2 a fish for each bottle of wine, while Country B has to give up 1 fish for each bottle of wine. Country B must necessarily have a comparative advantage in fish. (395-402)

e. A fair exchange for B would be giving up one fish for one bottle of wine or better because that is its opportunity cost of producing one fish. A fair exchange for A would be giving up two bottles of wine for 1 fish or better since its opportunity cost of producing two bottles of wine is one fish. Any exchange between these two such as 2 fish for 3 bottles of wine, would be a fair exchange. (395-402)

4. a. The production possibility curves for Country A and Country B are drawn below. (395-402)

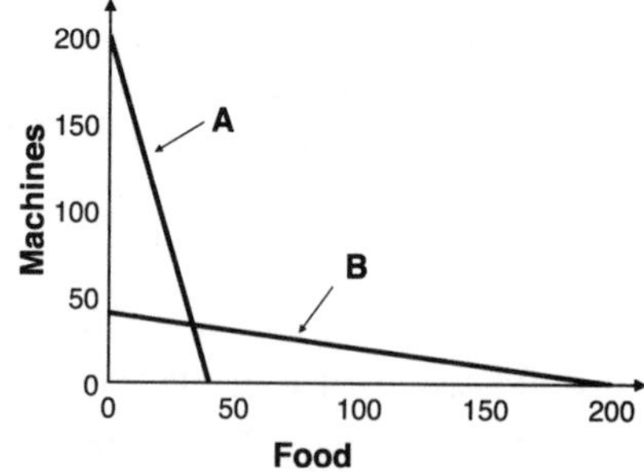

b. Country B has the absolute advantage in the production of food because it can produce more food if it devotes all its resources to the production of food than can Country A. (395-402)

c. Country B has the comparative advantage in the production of food since it has to give up only 1/5 machine to produce one unit of food while Country A has to give up 5 machines to produce one unit of food. (395-402)

d. Country A would be willing to supply 5 machines for 1 unit of food. Country A would be willing to supply 5 units of foods for one machine. Let's suppose they trade 1 for 1. Country A would produce 200 machines, selling 50 to Country B for 50 units of foods. Country B would produce 200 food units, and sell 50 to Country A for 50 machines. This way they each reach their desired level of consumption. (395-402)

ANSWERS

A BRAIN TEASER

1. The benefits of lower trade barriers are a wider variety of higher quality, lower-priced products made available to consumers. This translates into an increase in the average absolute standard of living for the nation. The costs of lower trade barriers to a nation are the loss of jobs in those industries that find it difficult to compete in the global economy. The economic benefits of free trade outweigh the costs; at least over time. This is why economists generally favor free trade. (408-409)

ANSWERS

POTENTIAL ESSAY QUESTIONS

The following are annotated answers. They indicate the general idea behind the answer.

1. A tariff is a tax on an imported item. A quota is a quantity limitation. Tariffs are preferred by governments because they raise revenues and are disliked by foreign producers because they require tax payments to government. However, notice that both tariffs and quotas raise prices and decrease the quantity of imported goods bought and sold.

2. Countries use a variety of policies to restrict trade. These include:
   - Tariffs.
   - Quotas.
   - Voluntary restraint agreements.
   - Embargoes.
   - Regulatory trade restrictions.
   - Nationalistic appeals.

   Economists generally oppose trade restrictions because: (1) from a global perspective, free trade increases total output—it raises standards of living; (2) trade restrictions lead to retaliation and possibly trade wars, which are mutually distressing; and (3) international trade provides competition for domestic companies. It forces domestic firms to be efficient—to provide higher quality goods at cheaper prices. Economists argue that trade restrictions may create some short-run benefits, but the costs (or harm done, which includes higher prices domestic consumers must pay) outweigh the benefits over time.

WHO GETS WHAT?
THE DISTRIBUTION OF INCOME

CHAPTER AT A GLANCE

One of the central issues in Canada is attempting to ensure an equitable distribution of income among its society's members. In order to achieve this goal, one has to first understand and be able to measure the amount of income inequality and poverty that currently exists.

The chapter begins by introducing the tools available to analyze the distribution of income – the Lorenz curve and the Gini coefficient. Before applying policies to redistribute incomes, one has to also be able to define and measure the poverty problem. There are essentially two different types of poverty—absolute and relative.

Despite Canada's economic prosperity, the distribution of income within Canada is unequal, particularly relative to other industrialized countries. The issue of why Canada's economic accomplishments are not being shared evenly by all of its citizens will also be explored. Many of the problems related to income inequality deal with socio-economic characteristics such as the different levels of education and training individuals possess, the amount of employment they have (fulltime versus parttime), age and gender.

The major debate facing economists centers around the tradeoff between equality and efficiency. Canadians tend to favour equality of income or fairness. This may, however, lead to several problems as people don't start from equivalent positions, people's needs differ and people's efforts differ. As well, efficiency within the market system may be compromised. There are side effects to redistributing income—it may reduce the incentive to work which reduces production, people may attempt to avoid or evade taxes, leading to a decrease in income, and redistributing money may cause people to make themselves look as if they are more needy than they really are.

The purpose of government policies is essentially to address these issues and the tradeoffs and to develop appropriate programs. The two types of programs considered are the expenditure and taxation programs for redistributing income.

This review is based upon the learning objectives that open the chapter.

1. There are several different ways to look at income distribution. (419)

- The share distribution of income is the relative division or allocation of total income amongst income groups.
- The socioeconomic distribution of income which is the relative allocation of total income amongst relevant socioeconomic groups.

2a. A Lorenz curve is a geometric representation of the share distribution of income among families in a given country at a given time. (419)

The curve shows the relative equality of the distribution of income. The farther below the diagonal line, which measures perfect equality, the more unequal the distribution of income.

2b. There are a number of reasons why the distribution of income in Canada is unequal: (420-423)
1. Economic restructuring
2. Household restructuring
3. Restructuring of government benefits

3. Although Canada has no official definition of poverty, the Low Income Cut Off (LICO) developed by Statistics Canada is used as Canada's working definition of poverty. An absolute measure of poverty measures the minimum income required to purchase basic necessities. The relative measure of poverty measure the income required to purchase basic necessities based on the average living standards of the community. (423-424)

4. The costs of poverty include lower expectations, health problems, social distress, and lost opportunities for the current as well as future generations. (424-427)

5. Among countries of the world, Canada has neither the most equal nor the most unequal distribution of income. Canada has less income inequality than most developing countries but more income inequality than many developed countries. (427-429)

There is more income inequality among countries than income inequality within a country. World-wide, income inequality is enormous. Therefore, the Lorenz curve of world income would show much more inequality than the Lorenz curve for a particular country.

6. Wealth is more unequally distributed in Canada than is income, mainly because the Canadian wealth distribution is unequal. (429)

7. Two alternative ways to describe income distribution is the size distribution of income inequality and income distribution according to socioeconomic characteristics. (430)

Most Canadians are in the middle class. However, income differs substantially by class and by other socioeconomic characteristics such as gender, education and type of job.

8. Three problems in determining whether an equal income distribution is fair are:
1. people don't start from equivalent positions;
2. people's needs differ; and
3. people's efforts differ. (433)

When most people talk about believing in equality of income, they usually mean an equality in opportunity to earn income.

Fairness is a philosophical question. People must judge a program's fairness for themselves.

9. Three side effects of redistribution of income include:
1. the labor/leisure incentive effect;
2. the avoidance and evasion incentive effect;
3. the incentive effect to look more needy than you are. (434)

Income is difficult to redistribute because of incentive effects of taxes, avoidance and evasion effects of taxes, and incentive effects of redistribution programs.

10. Expenditure programs have been more successful than taxation for redistributing income. (435-438)

On the whole, the Canadian tax system is roughly proportional, so it is not very effective as a means of redistributing income. Government spending programs are more effective than tax policy in reducing income inequality in Canada.

Federal government expenditures that contribute to redistribution include:
1. Welfare
2. Old Age Security
3. Guaranteed Income Supplement
4. Canada Pension Plan
5. Employment Insurance

MATCHING THE TERMS

Match the terms to their definitions

All of these key terms are found at the end of the chapter.

___ 1. Canada Pension Plan (CPP)
___ 2. Employment Insurance
___ 3. Guaranteed Income Supplement (GIS)
___ 4. income
___ 5. Lorenz curve
___ 6. Low Income Cut-Off Line (LICO)
___ 7. Old Age Security (OAS)
___ 8. poverty line
___ 9. progressive tax
___ 10. proportional tax
___ 11. quintile
___ 12. regressive tax
___ 13. share distribution of income
___ 14. socioeconomic distribution of income
___ 15. wealth

a. A geometric representation of the share distribution of income among families in a given country at a given time.
b. The minimum income required to purchase the basic necessities.
c. The relative division of total income among income groups.
d. The amount of money a person earns in a year.
e. The total amount of money a person has accumulated.
f. The relative division or allocation of total income among relevant socioeconomic groupings.
g. An average tax rate that increases with income.
h. A retirement income plan and a death and disability insurance plan.
i. A ranking of people's income into fifths.
j. An average tax rate that is constant regardless of income level.
k. Short-term financial assistance, regardless of need, to eligible individuals who are temporarily out of work.
l. Provides an additional monthly benefit for low-income pensioners.
m. An average tax rate that decreases as income increases.
n. Canada's largest public pension plan.
o. Used to identify individuals and families living in poverty in Canada.

MULTIPLE CHOICE

Circle the one best answer for each of the following questions:

1. The Lorenz curve is
   a. a type of supply curve.
   b. a type of demand curve.
   c. a geometric representation of the share distribution of income.
   d. a geometric representation of the socioeconomic distribution of income.

2. Refer to the graph below. Which of the four Lorenz curves demonstrates the most income inequality?
   a. A.
   b. B.
   c. C.
   d. D.

3. The official definition of poverty is:
   a. an absolute measure of poverty since it is based upon a minimum food budget determined in the 1960s.
   b. a relative measure of poverty since the poverty line is defined as the income level that exceeds the income of 15 percent of all households in Canada.
   c. not available in Canada, while the LICO is used as Canada's working definition of poverty.
   d. neither an absolute or relative measure of poverty since the poverty threshold changes each year.

4. A Lorenz curve for the entire world would show:
   a. more income inequality than in the United States.
   b. less income inequality than the United States.
   c. approximately the same level of income inequality as in the United States.
   d. no income inequality.

5. In a Lorenz curve for Canada, household wealth would:
   a. show the same amount of inequality as does family income.
   b. show more inequality than does family income.
   c. show less inequality than does family income.
   d. would show no wealth inequality at all.

6. Refer to the graph below. The gini coefficient is shown by which area?
   a. A/B
   b. A/(A + B).
   c. B/A.
   d. B/(A + B).

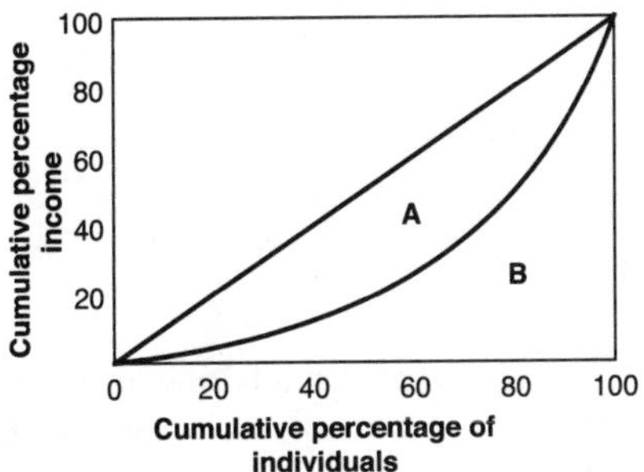

7. The Canadian class system is *best* represented by which shape?
   a. A diamond.
   b. A right-side-up pyramid with upper class on the top.
   c. An upside-down pyramid with upper class on the top.
   d. A square.

8. Imposing a tax of 40 percent on everyone's income may not be especially effective in redistributing income if the tax:
   a. has large incentive effects.
   b. has no incentive effects.
   c. is not progressive.
   d. is only proportional.

9. The largest government program to redistribute income to low income families is:
   a. Welfare.
   b. Old Age Security.
   c. Guaranteed Income Supplement.
   d. Canada Pension Plan.

SHORT-ANSWER QUESTIONS

1. What does a Lorenz curve show?

2. What is the official definition of *poverty*?

3. What are two measures to describe poverty?

4. List four costs of poverty.

5. How does income inequality in Canada compare with other countries?

6. How does the distribution of household wealth compare with distribution of family income in Canada?

7. What are two alternative ways to describe income distribution?

8. You and your friends are having a lunchtime discussion about fairness. A friend offers a statement that since income distribution has become more unequal in the past few decades, income in Canada has become less and less fair. Assume you are a contrarian. How do you respond?

9. "Nevertheless," your friend says, "I believe the current distribution is not fair. The government should do something to make the income distribution more equal." You agree to some extent, but warn that there are side effects of redistributing income. State your argument.

10. Which has been more successful in redistributing income: expenditure or taxation programs? Why?

11. What are five expenditure programs to redistribute income?

PROBLEMS AND APPLICATIONS

1. Use the Lorenz curve below to answer the following questions.

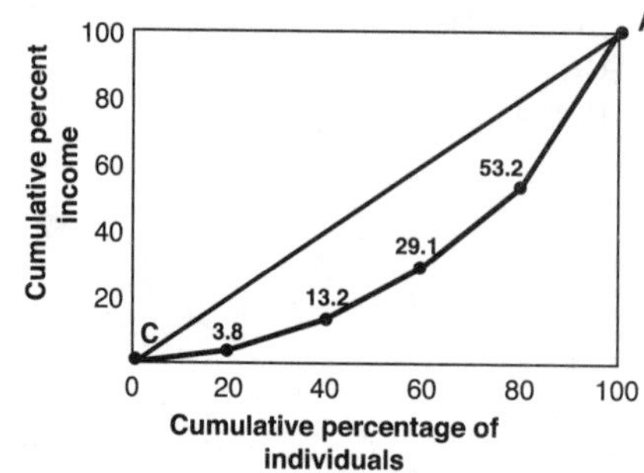

a. What percentage of total income do the top 20 percent of individuals in Ecoland receive?

b. What percentage of total income do the top 40 percent of individuals in Ecoland receive?

c. Which value, the one in (a) or the one (b), is greater? Why?

d. What does the straight line represent? Describe points A and C. Why is the Lorenz curve always anchored at those points?

2. Use the following table to answer the questions.

Income quintile	Eco-land	Fantasy-land	Text-land
Lowest 20%	5%	7%	2%
Second quintile	8	10	6
Third quintile	10	25	9
Fourth quintile	20	25	19
Highest 20%	57	33	64

a. Draw a Lorenz curve for each country.

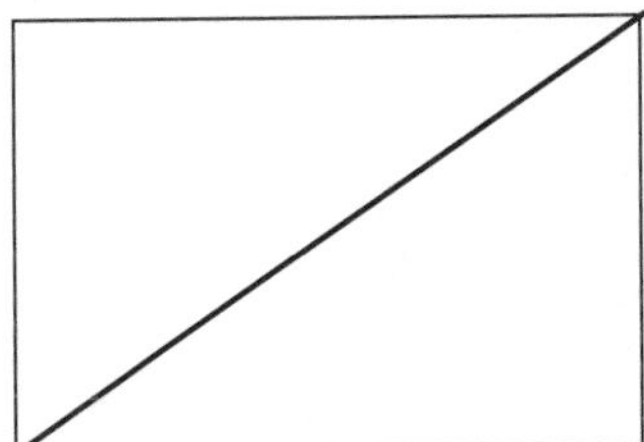

b. Rank the countries from most equal income distribution to least equal income distribution.

3. For each of the following state whether the tax is most likely proportional, regressive, or progressive with income.

a. 5 cent per gallon tax on gasoline.

b. School taxes based on assessed value of a home.

c. Sales tax of 6 percent.

d. Health care premiums of 1.45% on all income.

A BRAIN TEASER

1. You are completing your tax return. You are filing as a single taxpayer. Your income is $87,300. Deductions are $20,000. The rate is 15% for taxable income up to $22,750, 28% of income between $22,750 and $55,100, and 31% of income above $55,100.

   a. Calculate your tax liability.

   b. Calculate your average tax rate.

   c. Calculate your marginal tax rate.

   d. Is the tax schedule proportional, regressive, or progressive? Explain your answer.

POTENTIAL ESSAY QUESTIONS

You may also see essay questions similar to the "Problems & Applications" and "Brain Teasers" exercises.

1. Explain three problems in determining whether an equal income distribution is fair. When people talk about believing in the equality of income, what do they usually mean?

2. What are two direct methods through which government redistributes income? Which has generally been more successful and why?

ANSWERS

MATCHING

1-h; 2-k; 3-l; 4-d; 5-a; 6-o; 7-n; 8-b; 9-g; 10-j; 11-i; 12-m; 13-c; 14-f;15-e.

ANSWERS

MULTIPLE CHOICE

1. c A Lorenz curve describes how income is distributed in a country. It has proportion of the population on the horizontal axis and proportion of income on the vertical axis. See pages 419-420.

2. d A Lorenz curve describes how income is distributed in a country. It has proportion of the population on the horizontal axis and proportion of income on the vertical axis. The further the Lorenz curve is from the diagonal, the more unequally income is distributed. See pages 419-420.

3. c Although Canada has no official definition of poverty, the LICO is used as Canada's working definition of poverty. The LICO is calculated as the average family income spent on food, shelter, and clothing, plus 20 percent. Canada's definition of poverty is a relative definition. See pages 423-424.

4. a Since the world income is more unequally divided among countries, the world Lorenz curve would have to show more income inequality. See pages 427-429.

5. b Wealth is considerably less equally distributed than income in Canada. (429-430)

6. b The Gini coefficient describes the degree of income inequality. It is the area between the diagonal and the Lorenz curve divided by the total area below the diagonal. See page 426.

7. a The Canadian class system is best seen as a diamond. There is a small upper class and a small lower class, and a large middle class. See pages 430-432.

8. a Incentive effects can undermine attempts to redistribute income. See pages 434-435.

9. a As stated in the text, welfare is a provincially administered program of income assistance to support individuals and families which have no way of supporting themselves. See page 436.

ANSWERS

SHORT-ANSWER QUESTIONS

1. A Lorenz curve is a geometric representation of the share distribution of income among families in a given country at a given time. (419-420)

2. Although Canada has no official definition of poverty, the Low Income Cut-Off line developed by Statistics Canada is used as Canada's working definition of poverty. (423-424)

3. The absolute measure of poverty measures the minimum income required to purchase basic necessities. The relative measure of poverty measures the income required to purchase basic necessities based on the average living standards of the community. (423)

4. The costs of poverty include lower expectations, health problems, social distress, and lost opportunities for the current as well as future generations . (425-427)

5. Canada has less income inequality than most developing countries but more income inequality than many developed countries. (427-429)

6. Wealth is significantly more unequally distributed than income. (429-430)

7. Two alternative ways to describe income distribution are the size distribution of income inequality and income distribution according to socioeconomic characteristics. (430-432)

8. Determining whether an equal income distribution is fair is problematic. You tell your friend that, first of all, people do not start from equivalent positions and income depends upon those initial positions. Second, people's needs differ; some people are happy with less income, while others seem to need a higher income. Lastly, people's efforts differ; some people are willing to work harder than others. Shouldn't that effort be rewarded with higher income? Equality is not synonymous with fairness. (432-434)

9. Although some might agree that a more equal distribution is desirable, there are side effects of redistributing income. They are: (1) A tax to redistribute income may result in a switch from labour to leisure and, consequently, less production and less total income. (2) An increase in taxes to redistribute income might lead to attempts to avoid or evade taxes, leading to a decrease in measured income. (3) Government programs to redistribute money may cause people to make themselves look poorer than they really are. (434-435)

10. Expenditure programs have been more successful than taxation for redistributing income. This is because, on the whole, the Canadian tax system is roughly proportional, so it is not very effective as a means of redistributing income. (435-438)

11. Five expenditure programs to redistribute income are (1) welfare, (2) Old Age Security, (3) Guaranteed Income Supplement, (4) Canada Pension Plan, and (5) Employment Insurance. (436-437)

ANSWERS

PROBLEMS AND APPLICATIONS

1. a. 46.8%. The top 20 percent of individuals earn 46.8 percent of the income. Calculate this by starting at 80% on the horizontal axis. Draw a vertical line to the Lorenz curve. Look at the value on the vertical axis where this line intersects the Lorenz curve. This is the percent of income that the bottom 80% of individuals earn. To get the amount that the top 20% earn, subtract this number, 53.2, from 100. (419-420)

   b. 70.9%. Going through the same exercise as in 1(a) but starting at 60%, we find that the bottom 60% earn 29.1% of total income. Subtracting this from 100, we get 70.9%, the percent of total income earned by the top 40%. (419-420)

   c. (b) is greater than (a). This has to be true, because the vertical axis is the cumulative percentage of income. If the top 20% earn a certain percentage of the total, the top 40% includes that top 20% plus more. (419-420)

   d. The straight line represents the Lorenz curve if income were equally distributed. Point A says that 100% of individuals earn 100% of the income. This is true by definition. Point C says that 0% of individuals earn 0% of the income. The Lorenz curve is anchored at those points by definition. (419-420)

2. a. First we want to calculate the cumulative percentage of income for each country. We do this below by cumulatively adding together consecutive percentages.

Income quintile	Eco-land	Fantasy-land	Text-land
Lowest 20%	5%	7%	2%
Second quintile	8	10	6
Third quintile	10	25	9
Fourth quintile	20	25	19
Highest 20%	57	33	64

We then graph the values and connect the points. This is shown in the graph below. (419-420, 426)

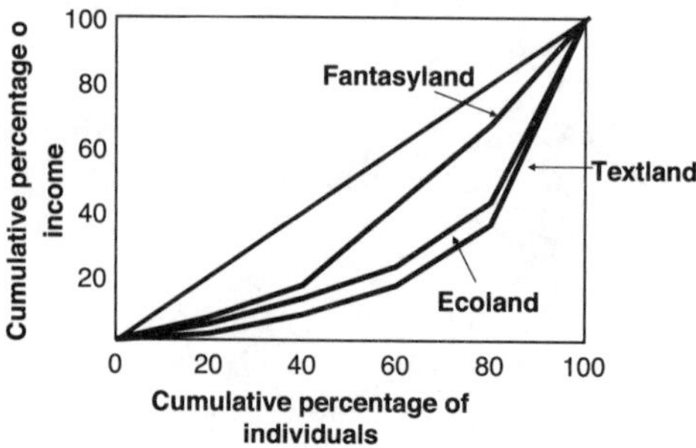

b. Fantasyland; Ecoland; Textland. The country bowed out to the right the most has the least equal income distribution. It is Textland. The country bowed out the least has the most equal income distribution. It is Fantasyland. Ecoland is in the middle. (419-420, 426)

3. a. 5 cent per gallon tax on gasoline is a sales tax and sales taxes tend to be slightly regressive since poor people often spend a higher percentage of their incomes on gasoline than do rich people. (435-436)
   b. School taxes based on assessed value of a home are considered to be roughly proportional since the value of a person's home is related to income. (435-436)
   c. A sales tax is regressive since poor people often consume a higher percentage of their incomes than do rich people. (435-436)
   d. Health care premiums are proportional since the rate is 1.45% on all income, no matter how high or low. (435-436)

ANSWERS

A BRAIN TEASER

1. a. $16,252.50. First deduct $20,000 from $87,300 to get taxable income of $67,300. You pay 15% on the first $22,750, 28% on income from $22,751 to $55,100, and 31% on the remaining $12,200. Your taxes are .15 $22,750 + .28 × 32,350 + .31 × $12,200 = $3,412.5 + $9,058 + $3,782 = $16,252.50. (435-436).
   b. 18.6%. Your average tax rate is total taxes divided by total income: $16,252.50/$87,300. (435-436).
   c. 31%. Your marginal tax rate is the rate at which your last dollar earned is taxed. This is 31%. (435-436).
   d. The tax schedule is progressive. A progressive tax is one in which the average tax rate increases with income. As can be seen by the tax schedule, the marginal tax rate is increasing. Since the marginal tax rate is increasing, and it is above the average tax rate (because of deductions), the average tax rate is increasing too. (435-436)

ANSWERS

POTENTIAL ESSAY QUESTIONS

The following are annotated answers. They indicate the general idea behind the answer.

1. Three problems in determining whether an equal income distribution is fair are (1) people don't start from equal positions, (2) people's needs differ, and (3) people's efforts differ.

   When people talk about believing in equality in income, they mean they believe in equality of opportunity for comparably endowed individuals to earn income. If equal opportunity of equals leads to inequality of income, that inequality in income is fair. Unfortunately, there's enormous latitude for debate on what constitutes equal opportunity of equals.

2. The two methods are: taxation (policies that tax the rich more than the poor) and expenditures (programs that help the poor more than the rich). Most government redistribution of income works through expenditures programs (public assistance; social programs), not through taxes. This is because on the whole, the Canadian tax system is roughly proportional, so it is not very effective as a means of redistributing income.

WORK AND THE LABOUR MARKET

20

CHAPTER AT A GLANCE

This textbook concludes with a discussion of the labour market—how wages are determined and some of the issues surrounding an economy's ability to supply and demand labour.

The decision of supply labour is typically based on wages—the higher the wage, the higher the quantity supplied. The level of income taxes also influences the labour supply as does the elasticity of market supply. Labour demand, on the other hand, follows the basic law of demand – the higher the wage, the lower the quantity of labour demanded. It is also determined by the elasticity of labour demand. You should understand the factors influencing the elasticities of labour demand and supply.

This chapter also discusses several different markets for labour. A monopsony occurs when there is only a single firm employing labour in the market. An example of this situation would be a one industry town. A monopsonist faces an upward sloping labour supply curve reflecting the fact that it can hire fewer units of labour and keep wages down, thereby holding wages below that of competitive firms.

When a union exists, there is an incentive to act as a monopsonist, restricting labour supply in order to increase its members' wages. Some markets are characterized by a bilateral monopoly in which a monopsonist faces a union with monopoly power. In this situation, it is difficult to predict where the resulting equilibrium market wage and labour quantity will end up as it depends on the power of the unions and the negotiating skills of the monopsonist.

The last part of the chapter looks at political and social forces on the labour market—pay equity, job discrimination, earnings differentials between men and women and collective bargaining.
This review is based upon the learning objectives that open the chapter.

1a. An increase in the marginal tax rate is likely to reduce the quantity of labour supplied because it reduces the net wage of individuals and hence, through individuals' incentive effect, causes them to work less. (445)

Higher marginal tax rates reduce the incentive to work.

1b. Elasticity of market supply depends on: (466)

- Individuals' opportunity cost of working.
- The elasticity of individuals' supply curves.
- Individuals entering and leaving the labour market.

An elastic supply of labour means workers are quite responsive to a change in the wage rate. For example, an increase in the wage will result in a relatively large increase in the quantity supplied of labour (number of people looking for work).

2. Derived demand is the demand for factors of production by firms, which depends on consumers' demands for the firm's product. (447)

For example, if the demand for automobiles increases, the demand for automotive workers increases. It simply takes more workers to produce more cars.

3. Three factors that influence the demand for labour are: (450)

- Changes in the firm's demand.
- Market structure and the demand for labour.
- Changes in other factors of production.

4. Technological developments in the last couple of decades has boosted labour productivity considerably, yet the overall demand for labour has not been reduced. Instead, there has been an increase in total output which has increased the demand for labour to produce that output. (454-455).

5. Efficiency wages are wages paid which are paid above the going market wage in order to keep workers happy and productive. (456)

6. A monopsony is a market in which a single firm is only one buyer. A bilateral monopoly is a market in which a single seller faces a single buyer. (457)

A monopsony will hire fewer workers and pay a lower wage compared to the competitive outcome.

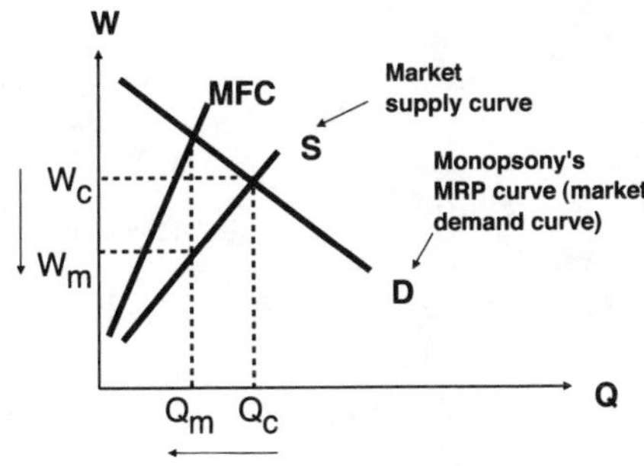

7a. To understand real-world labour markets, one must broaden the analysis. (459)

What we see in the real world is a consequence of the interaction of market, social and political forces.

7b. Three types of discrimination are: (460-461)

- Discrimination based on individual characteristics that will affect job performance.
- Discrimination based on group characteristics.
- Discrimination based on the structure of the job makes it difficult or impossible for certain groups or individuals to succeed.

One can think of discrimination as treating equals unequally, or treating unequals equally.

8. Labour laws and labour unions have improved working conditions. These laws include limiting the number of normal hours a person can work and the minimum ages that children can work. Labour unions protect the economic interests (wages and benefits) and working conditions (health, safety, and training) of its members. (462-463)

MATCHING THE TERMS

Match the terms to their definitions

All of these key terms are found at the end of the chapter.

___ 1. bilateral monopoly
___ 2. cost minimization condition
___ 3. derived demand
___ 4. derived demand curve for labour
___ 5. downsizing
___ 6. efficiency wages
___ 7. entrepreneurship
___ 8. focal-point phenomenon
___ 9. incentive effect
___ 10. labour market
___ 11. labour productivity
___ 12. labour union
___ 13. marginal factor cost
___ 14. marginal physical product (MPP)
___ 15. marginal revenue product (MRP)
___ 16. monopsony
___ 17. outsourcing
___ 18. pay equity laws
___ 19. value of marginal product (VMP)

a. A market in which only a single firm hires labour.
b. The average output per worker.
c. A market with only a single seller and a single buyer.
d. Laws mandating equal pay for equal work.
e. Wage paid above the going market wage to keep workers happy and productive.
f. Factor market in which individuals supply labour services for wages to other individuals and to firms that demand labour services.
g. Labour services that involve a high degree of organizational skill, responsibility, and creativity.
h. How much a person will change his or her hours worked in response to a change in the wage rate.
i. A firm shifting production from its own plants to other firms, often in the United States or abroad, where wages are lower.
j. The additional cost to a firm of hiring another worker.
k. A reduction in a firm's workforce.
l. The demand for factors of production by firms, which depends on consumer's demands for the firm's products.
m. Where the ratio of marginal product to the price of an input is equal for all inputs.
n. The maximum amount of labour, measured in labour hours, that a firm will hire.
o. The additional units of output that hiring an additional worker will bring about.
p. The marginal revenue product of a worker in the competitive firm.
q. MPP × MR.
r. A situation were a company chooses to move production to a particular country because other companies have already moved there.
s. An organization that protects the economic interests of its members.

MULTIPLE CHOICE

Circle the one best answer for each of the following questions:

1. Generally, economists believe the higher the wage
   a. the higher the quantity of labour supplied.
   b. the further to the right the supply of labour is.
   c. the further to the left the supply of labour is.
   d. the lower the quantity of labour supplied.

2. As the wage rate increases, the opportunity cost of *not working*
   a. increases.
   b. decreases.
   c. remains the same.
   d. cannot be determined given the information provided.

3. The irony of any need-based program is that
   a. it increases the number of needy.
   b. it decreases the number of needy.
   c. it creates other needs.
   d. it destroys needs.

4. Which of the following is *not* a reason why the labour supply for heads of household (primary income earners) is more inelastic than that for secondary income earners?
   a. Institutional factors, such as hours of work, are only slightly flexible.
   b. There are many more new secondary income earners who can enter the market than there are primary income earners.
   c. Heads of households have responsibility for seeing that there's food and shelter for the household family members.
   d. There are more secondary income earners than primary income earners.

5. The term "derived demand" refers to
   a. demand by consumers for advertised products.
   b. the demand for luxury goods that is derived from cultural phenomena such as fashion.
   c. the demand for factors of production by firms.
   d. the demand for derivatives.

6. The more elastic the demand for a firm's good,
   a. the more elastic the firm's derived demand for factors.
   b. the less elastic the firm's derived demand for factors.
   c. the elasticity of demand for a firm's good has nothing to do with the firm's derived demand.
   d. the elasticity of demand could cause the elasticity of the derived demand to be either higher or lower.

7. The more important the factor is in the production process
   a. the less elastic the firm's derived demand for the factor.
   b. the more elastic the firm's derived demand for the factor.
   c. the importance of a factor in the production process has nothing to do with the firm's derived demand.
   d. the importance of a factor in the production process could cause the elasticity of the derived demand to be either higher or lower.

8. Economists distinguish entrepreneurship from labour because
   a. entrepreneurship is more like capital.
   b. entrepreneurship has nothing to do with labour.
   c. entrepreneurship is such an important part of labour that it needs a specific discussion.
   d. entrepreneurs receive only profit.

9. A firm has just changed from being a competitive firm to being a monopolist. Its derived demand for labour
   a. will increase.
   b. will decrease.
   c. might increase or might decrease.
   d. is unaffected because whether the firm is a competitive firm or a monopolist has no effect on the firm's derived demand for labour.

10. A monopsony is a market with
    a. only a single seller and a single buyer of labour.
    b. only a single seller of labour.
    c. only a single buyer of labour.
    d. one seller and two buyers.

11. Compared to a competitive labour market, a monopsonist hires
    a. fewer workers and pays them a higher wage.
    b. fewer workers and pays them a lower wage.
    c. more workers and pays them a higher wage.
    d. more workers and pays them a lower wage.

12. Which of the following cases of discrimination is most easily eliminated with market forces?
    a. A warehousing firm turns down an applicant because she is physically unable to lift boxes of the weight required by the job.
    b. An Internet firm begins a younger worker at a lower pay because younger workers are more likely to leave the job shortly after being trained.
    c. A retail store decides against hiring an individual who is Catholic (even though the candidate is the most qualified) because the person doing the hiring is Protestant.
    d. A firm creates a special program to hire people with developmental disabilities.

13. A market in which there is a single seller and a single buyer is called a:
    a. monoposony.
    b. monopolist.
    c. competitive firm.
    d. bilateral monopoly.

14. For a perfectly competitive industry, the marginal revenue product of a worker (MRP) is equal to
    a. MPP × MR.
    b. MPP × P.
    c. hourly wage
    d. labour productivity.

SHORT-ANSWER QUESTIONS

1. Use the theory of rational choice and the concept of opportunity cost to explain why firms generally offer time-and-a-half for workers to work on Thanksgiving Day.

2. Suppose the federal government passes an increase in the marginal income tax rate. What is the likely effect on work effort?

3. List three factors that influence the elasticity of labour supply.

4. Explain how the demand for labour is a derived demand.

5. List the three factors affecting the demand for labour.

6. List four factors that influence the elasticity of labour demand.

7. Define the terms *monopsonist* and *bilateral monopoly*.

8. Define efficiency wages and discuss their impact.

9. In addition to wages, what are four other factors that firms must consider when deciding where to locate production?

10. On average, women earn about 75 cents for every $1 earned by men. Discuss this phenomenon in terms of political forces, social forces and market forces.

11. What are three types of discrimination?

PROBLEMS AND APPLICATIONS

1. Use the graph below to answer the following questions.

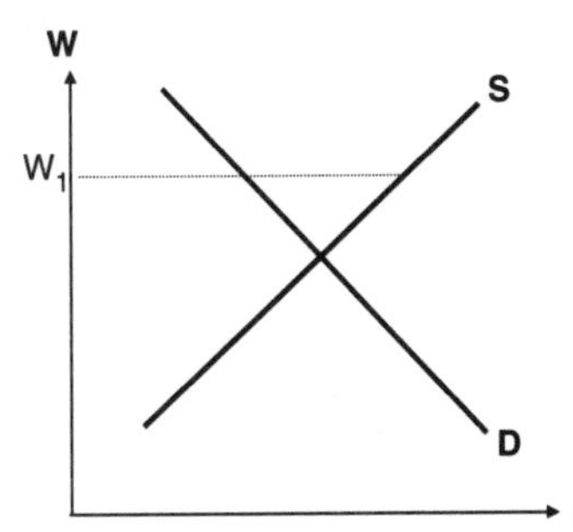

a. Label the equilibrium wage and number of workers.

b. If wages were set by the government at wage W_1 that is above the equilibrium wage, what happens to the quantity supplied and the quantity demanded for labour? How do they differ?

c. Show how a technological innovation that leads to a higher demand for labour affects equilibrium wage and quantity of labour.

2. Consider again demand and supply in a labour market. For each of the following situations, determine whether there would be an increase or a decrease in demand or supply of labour. Furthermore, determine the impact on the equilibrium wage rate (W) and the equilibrium quantity (Q) of labour. (You may want to use a graph of demand and supply curves for labour to help you correctly predict the impact on the wage and the equilibrium quantity of labour employed given a shift in the demand or the supply curve.)

a. The demand for the product workers are producing increases.

b. It is Christmas day, and workers value their leisure time more highly.

c. The other factory in town is now offering a higher wage rate.

d. The fringe (nonmonetary) benefits of this job have increased substantially. Now more lucrative health and dental coverage is provided, as well as a retirement program, paid vacations, a company car, etc.

e. The price of a machine, which is a substitute for this labour, is now less expensive and its productivity has increased substantially due to an increase in technology. Note: the new technology does not affect worker productivity.

f. The firms in this industry have successfully convinced government to impose stricter tariffs and import quotas on a foreign good which is a substitute for the good produced by these workers.

g. The government has just adopted an "open-door" immigration policy.

h. Workers are now more productive.

3. Answer the following questions using the graph below.

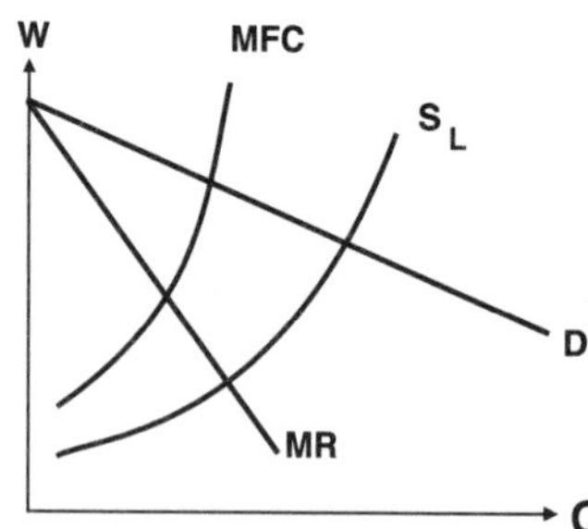

a. Label the equilibrium wage and number of workers on the graph if the market is competitive.

b. Label the equilibrium wage and number of workers on the graph under a monopsonist.

c. If there is a worker's union, what would be the equilibrium wage and level of employment?

4. Complete the table below for a perfectly competitive firm that produces halogen light bulbs. Each light bulb sells for $1. (Marginal values refers to the marginal change of increasing to that row, i.e., the marginal physical product of going from 23 to 24 workers is 9. The same goes for marginal revenue product.)

	No. of Workers	Total Product per hour	Marginal Physical Product per hour	Marginal Average Product per hour	Revenue Product per hour
	20	200		—	
A	21	—	—	—	15
B	22	228	—	—	—
C	23	—	—	10.39	—
D	24	—	8	—	—
E	25	—	—	10.16	—
F	26	259	—	—	—

a. Draw the corresponding labour demand curve, labeling the points on the graph that correspond to the lines of the table.

b. Suppose the price of halogen light bulbs falls to $.50 per bulb. How does your answer to (a) change?

c. If halogen light bulbs sold for $1 per bulb as in (a), how many workers would the firm hire if wages were $5 per hour? If the government set minimum wages at $9 per hour, how many workers would the firm hire?

A BRAIN TEASER

1. Your boss has given you three possible combinations of raw materials, labour and capital (machines) inputs which could be employed to produce the desired production target at the company's new production facility. Your job is to determine the least cost combination of inputs to employ. Suppose the price per unit of raw material usage per hour is $5, the wage rate per hour is $10, and the cost per hour for machines is $20. The marginal physical product (or productivity) of raw material, labour and capital usage associated with the three combinations of input usage is summarized in the table below. Which combination of input usage will minimize the firm's costs of production to produce the desired production target at the new facility?

	Mpp of Raw Material	MPP of Labour	MPP of Capital
Comb. A:	5	10	50
Comb. B:	10	20	40
Comb. C:	20	15	30

POTENTIAL ESSAY QUESTIONS

You may also see essay questions similar to the "Problems & Applications" and "Brain Teasers" exercises.

1. What is a monopsony and how does a monopsony determine the quantity of workers employed and the wage it pays? How does this compare with the competitive labour market outcome? What is a bilateral monopoly? Could a bilateral monopoly result in a competitive labour market outcome?

2. How do market, social, and political forces interact in determining the equilibrium wage and quantity of workers employed in any real-world labour market?

ANSWERS

MATCHING

1-c; 2-m; 3-l; 4-n; 5-k; 6-e; 7-g; 8-r; 9-h; 10-f; 11-b; 12-s; 13-j; 14-o; 15-q; 16-a; 17-i; 18-d; 19-p.

ANSWERS

MULTIPLE CHOICE

1. a The supply curve of labour is generally considered to be upward sloping. When there is a movement along the supply curve caused by an increase in the wage, the movement is called an increase in the quantity supplied, not an increase in supply. See pages 443-444.

2. a The opportunity cost of not working increases as the wage rate rises and that is why the labour supply curve slopes upward. See pages 444-445.

3. a A need-based program reduces people's incentives to prevent themselves from becoming needy, and thus a need-based program increases the number of needy. See pages 445-446.

4. d The number of primary income earners compared to the number of secondary income earners has nothing to do with elasticity. See pages 446-447.

5. c Derived demand refers to the fact that the demand for factors of production is derived from the demand for a firm's goods. Because consumers demand a firm's goods, the firm demands factors of production to produce those goods. See page 447.

6. b The firm should hire workers until the wage equals the marginal revenue product. See pages 448-453.

7. b The marginal revenue per dollar is higher for input B so it should hire more of B and less of A. The other answers do not meet the cost minimization condition. See pages 448-453.

8. a When a rise in price will cause significant loss of revenue (which it does when its demand is elastic), the firm takes that into account in its decision of what to pay workers and how many workers to hire. See page 453.

9. a As the importance of a factor to the production process rises, the less elastic is demand. This is because a more important factor has fewer substitutes. See pages 447-450.

10. c A monopsony is a market in which a single firm is the only buyer of labour. See page 457.

11. b A profit-maximizing monopsonist will pay a lower wage and hire fewer workers than if that labour market were competitive. See pages 457-458.

12. c Differential treatment based upon individual characteristics that does not affect job performance is costly to firms. Market forces will work toward eliminating this type of discrimination. The warehousing firm is turning down an applicant who cannot fulfill the duties of the job. The Internet firm is basing its decision on characteristics of group to which the individual belongs. Although the particular individual may not quit the job, such statistical discrimination, using such rules of thumb do have a basis in keeping costs of a firm down. See pages 460-461.

13. d A bilateral monopoly is a market in which there is a single seller and a single buyer. The wage and number of workers in a bilateral monopoly depends on the relative strength of the union and the monopsonist. See pages 457-458.

14. b The price of a competitive firm's output remains constant regardless of how many units it sells. Therefore, MRP = VMP which equals MPP × P. (448-451)

ANSWERS

SHORT-ANSWER QUESTIONS

1. Work involves opportunity cost. By working one more hour, you have one less hour to devote to nonmarket activities. The theory of rational choice in the case of work means that you will supply work as long as the opportunity cost of working is less than the wage received. Since the opportunity cost of working on a holiday is greater than on other days, firms must offer workers higher wages to work on Thanksgiving Day. This demonstrates that the supply curve for labour is upward sloping: the higher the wage, the higher the quantity of labour supplied. (443-445)

2. An increase in the marginal tax rate is likely to reduce the quantity of labour supplied because it reduces the net wage of individuals and hence lowers the opportunity cost of not working. (445-446)

3. Factors that affect the elasticity of labour supply include (1) the individuals' opportunity costs of working, (2) the elasticity of the individuals' supply curves, and (3) the individuals entering and leaving the labour market. (462)

4. Derived demand is the demand for factors of production by firms, which depends on consumers' demands for the firm's product. For example, if the demand for automobiles increases, the demand for automotive workers increases. It simply takes more workers to produce more cars. (447)

5. Factors that affect the demand for labour are (1) changes in the firm's demand, (2) market structure and the demand for labour, (3) changes in other factors of production. (450-452)

6. Factors that influence the elasticity of demand for labour are (1) the elasticity of demand for the firm's good, (2) the possibility of, and costs of, input substitution in production, and (3) the degree to which marginal productivity falls with an increase in labour. (453)

7. A monopsonist is a firm in a market where it is the only buyer of labour. A bilateral monopoly is a market in which a single seller faces a single buyer. (457)

8. Efficiency wages are wages paid to workers which are above the going market wage. Firms are willing to pay more for workers in order to obtain more qualified workers, to increase productivity and to make workers happy. (456)

9. Wages aren't the only consideration when a firm decides to locate production. Other factors include worker productivity, transportation costs, trade restrictions, and social institutions. (453-455)

10. Real-world labour markets are complicated and must be explained through the interaction of political, social and market forces. For example, the fact that women earn about 75 cents for every $1 earned by men must be explained by these forces. Here are some of the many ways in which these forces can explain this phenomenon: It is argued that employers discriminate against women, paying them less for the same job because they have a distaste for hiring women. This is an example of social forces at play. This would result in lower wages. Women's lower pay may also result from social forces that discourage mothers from working outside the home so that women will supply labour intermittently, lowering their wage. This is an example of social forces and market forces. Pay equity laws, anti-discrimination laws, and affirmative action laws have been passed in an effort to counteract this pay inequality. These are examples of political and legal forces at play in real-world labour markets. (459)

11. Three types of discrimination are (1) discrimination based on individual characteristics that affect job performance, (2) discrimination based on correctly perceived statistical characteristics of the group; and (3) discrimination in which the structure of the job makes it difficult or impossible for certain groups or individuals to succeed. (460)

ANSWERS

PROBLEMS AND APPLICATIONS

1. a. Equilibrium wage and number of workers with demand, D_0, and supply, S, is shown on the graph below as W_E and Q_E. At this point, the quantity of labour demanded equals the quantity of labour supplied. At a wage above W_E, there will be pressure for wages to fall as the quantity of labour supplied exceeds the quantity of labour demanded. At a wage below W_E, there will be pressure for wages to rise as the quantity of labour demanded exceeds the quantity of labour supplied. (Figure 20-4 on page 454)

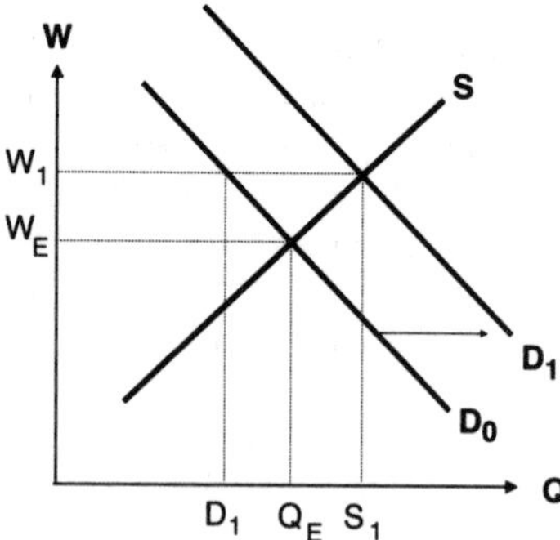

b. If wages were set by the government at W_1, the quantity of labour supplied would rise to S_1 and the quantity of labour demanded would fall to D_1. Quantity supplied would exceed quantity demanded. This is shown in the graph above. (Figure 20-5 on page 456)

c. A technological innovation that leads to a higher demand for labour will lead to a higher equilibrium wage and higher quantity of labour employed as the demand curve shifts to the right from D_0 to D_1. Equilibrium wage is now W_1 and equilibrium quantity of labour is S_1. (454-455 and Figure 20-5 on page 456)

2. a. The demand for labour would increase, increasing W and Q. The increase in the demand for the product increases the price of the product. The higher price for the product increases workers' marginal revenue product—MRP = MPP × P—which is the competitive firms' demand for labour.) (450-455)

b. The supply of labour would decrease on Christmas day, which would increase W and decrease Q on Christmas Day. (450-455)

c. Supply would decrease, increasing W and decreasing Q. (450-455)

d. Supply would increase, decreasing W and increasing Q. (450-455)

e. Demand would decrease, decreasing W and Q. (450-455)

f. Demand would increase, increasing W and Q. (450-455)

g. Supply would increase, decreasing W and increasing Q. (450-4552)

h. Demand would increase (according to the appendix: workers' MRP would be greater), increasing W and Q. (450-455)

3. a. If the market is competitive, the wage and employment level will be where the demand and supply curves for labour intersect. This is at W_c and Q_c respectively on the graph below. (454, and Figure 20-4)

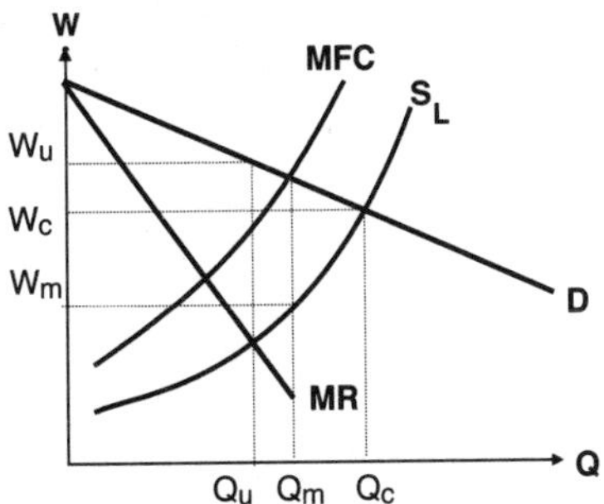

b. The monopsonist will hire workers where the marginal factor cost of labour intersects the demand for labour. A monopsonist would hire Q_m workers, less than the competitive level, and pay a wage W_m, lower than the competitive wage. (457-458, and Figure 20-6 on p. 457)

c. Unions would push for higher wages than a firm in a competitive market or a monopsonist would be willing to pay. Wage would be somewhere between W_u and W_m and would depend on negotiating skills and other noneconomic forces. The number of workers hired would then be somewhere between Q_u and Q_m depending upon the negotiated wage. (457-458, and Figure 20-6 on p. 457)

4. Below is the completed table for a perfectly competitive firm who produces halogen light bulbs. (Marginal values refers to the marginal change of increasing to that row, i.e., the marginal physical product of going from 23 to 24 workers is 8. The same goes for marginal revenue product.)

	No. of Workers	Total Product per hour	Marginal Physical Product per hour	Marginal Average Product per hour	Revenue Product per hour
	20	200		10	
A	21	215	15	10.24	15
B	22	228	13	10.36	13
C	23	239	11	10.39	11
D	24	248	9	10.33	9
E	25	255	7	10.2	7
F	26	260	5	10	5

We use the following relationships to fill in the table: Marginal physical product equals the change in the total product. Average product is the total product divided by the number of workers. Marginal revenue product equals marginal physical product times price of the product.

a. The corresponding labour demand curve is shown on the graph below. Labour demand is a derived demand. A firm is willing to pay the marginal revenue product of the additional worker to hire that additional worker. The wage at each level of workers is equal to the marginal revenue product. (450-452)

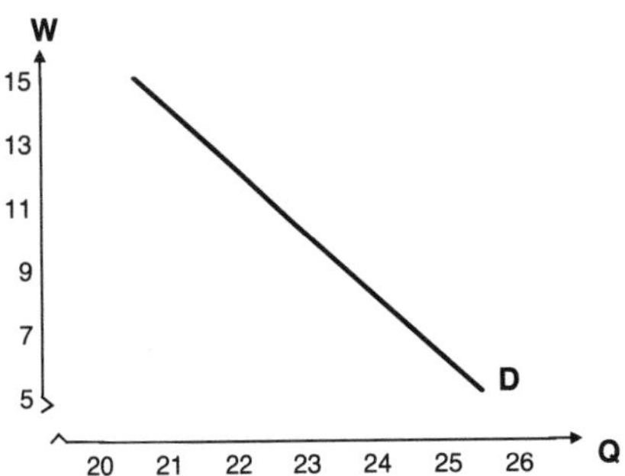

b. Suppose the demand for halogen light bulbs fell and their price fell to $.50 per bulb. The marginal revenue product would be halved and the demand curve for labour would shift in as shown on the graph below. The marginal revenue product is shown in the table7 below. (Marginal values refer to the marginal change of increasing to that row, i.e., the marginal physical product of going from 23 to 24 workers is 8. The same goes for marginal revenue product.) (450-452)

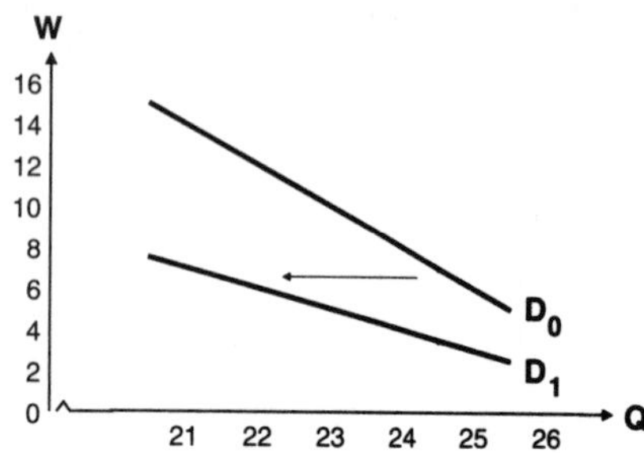

	No. of Workers	Total Product per hour	Marginal Physical Product per hour	Marginal Average Product per hour	($0.50) Revenue Product per hour
	20	200		10	
A	21	215	15	10.24	7.5
B	22	228	13	10.36	6.5
C	23	239	11	10.39	5.5
D	24	248	9	10.33	4.5
E	25	255	7	10.2	3.5
F	26	260	5	10	2.5

c. At $1 per bulb and wages of $5 per hour, the firm would hire between 25 and 26; At $1 per bulb and minimum wage of $9 per hour the firm would hire between 23 and 24. A firm in a competitive industry will hire up to the point where the wage equals *MPP* times *P*, or the fifth column of the table in (a). *MPP* times *P* is $5 between 25 and 26 workers. When wages are $5, it will hire between 25 and 26 workers. If the minimum wage was $9, the firm would hire workers to where *MPP* times *P* equals, $9, or between 23 and 24 workers. (450-452)

ANSWERS

A BRAIN TEASER

1. See the table below. The cost minimizing condition exists at that combination of inputs (factors) employed in which the MPP/P for each input is equal. Therefore, Combination B should be adopted. For Combination A, the productivity for the money spent (MPP/P) is greater for capital than for the other inputs. Therefore, more capital, and less labour and raw materials should be employed. By doing so, the firm will be able to produce the same amount at a lower cost. For Combination C, more raw materials should be employed in the production process while less labour and capital are employed (because MPP/P for raw materials is higher).

   Remember: if the cost minimization condition is not met, the firm could hire more of the input with the higher marginal product-to-price ratio and less of the other inputs, and produce the same amount of output at a lower cost.

	Mpp of Raw Material	**MPP of Labour**	**MPP of Capital**
Comb. A:	5	10	50
	(MPP/P=5/5=1)	(MPP/P=10/10=1)	(MPP/P=50/20=2.5)
Comb. B:	10	20	40
	(MPP/P=10/5=2)	(MPP/P=20/10=2)	(MPP/P=40/20=2)
Comb. C:	20	15	30
	(MPP/P=20/5=4)	(MPP/P=15/10=1.5)	(MPP/P=30/20=1.5)

ANSWERS

POTENTIAL ESSAY QUESTIONS

The following are annotated answers. They indicate the general idea behind the answer.

1. A monopsony is a market in which a single firm is the only buyer. The monopsonist's demand for labour is the market demand for labour. The monopsony also faces the market supply curve. The profit maximizing monopsony will hire fewer workers and pay a lower wage than the competitive outcome.

   A bilateral monopoly is a monopsony employing unionized workers. It's a bilateral monopoly because there is monopoly power on both sides of the labour market. It's possible that the monopoly power of the two sides will be cancelled out, giving rise to a competitive wage and quantity of labour employed.

2. The economic forces of demand and supply, social forces, and legal or government forces all interact in the labour market. Social forces of "fairness," seniority, and discrimination as well as the political forces of child labour laws, pay equity laws, equal opportunity laws, and laws governing unions etc., all affect the labour market along with the market forces of supply and demand.